The Cambridge Introduction to Applied Linguistics

The Cambridge Introduction to Applied Linguistics

Edited by

Susan Conrad

Portland State University

Alissa J. Hartig

Portland State University

Lynn Santelmann

Portland State University

CAMBRIDGE UNIVERSITY PRESS

CAMBRIDGE
UNIVERSITY PRESS

University Printing House, Cambridge CB2 8BS, United Kingdom

One Liberty Plaza, 20th Floor, New York, NY 10006, USA

477 Williamstown Road, Port Melbourne, VIC 3207, Australia

314–321, 3rd Floor, Plot 3, Splendor Forum, Jasola District Centre, New Delhi – 110025, India

79 Anson Road, #06-04/06, Singapore 079906

Cambridge University Press is part of the University of Cambridge.

It furthers the University's mission by disseminating knowledge in the pursuit of
education, learning, and research at the highest international levels of excellence.

www.cambridge.org
Information on this title: www.cambridge.org/conrad-hartig-santelmann
DOI: 10.1017/9781108658089

First published 2021

Printed in Singapore by Markono Print Media Pte Ltd

A catalogue record for this publication is available from the British Library.

Library of Congress Cataloging-in-Publication Data
Names: Conrad, Susan, editor. | Hartig, Alissa J., editor. | Santelmann, Lynn, editor.
Title: The Cambridge introduction to applied linguistics / edited by Susan Conrad, Alissa J. Hartig,
    Lynn Santelmann.
Description: 1. | New York : Cambridge University Press, 2021. | Includes bibliographical
    references and index.
Identifiers: LCCN 2020004498 (print) | LCCN 2020004499 (ebook) | ISBN 9781108470322
    (hardback) | ISBN 9781108455817 (paperback) | ISBN 9781108658089 (epub)
Subjects: LCSH: Applied linguistics.
Classification: LCC P129 .C358 2020 (print) | LCC P129 (ebook) | DDC 418–dc23
LC record available at https://lccn.loc.gov/2020004498
LC ebook record available at https://lccn.loc.gov/2020004499

ISBN 978-1-108-47032-2 Hardback
ISBN 978-1-108-45581-7 Paperback

Additional resources for this publication at www.cambridge.org/conrad-hartig-santelmann.

Contents

Figures

Tables

Acknowledgments

This book benefitted greatly from the input of an exceptional group of reviewers who commented on draft chapters from a student perspective. We thank Naila Bairamova, Karrie Brothers, Solomon Collins, Janice Deufel, Dana Divine, Melissa Hannen, Danielle Jochums, John Langland, Dustin Lanker, Jeana Menger, Batool Mohammad, Elsa Neal, Jillian Pettit, Erin Pryor, Sasha Reinwald Albrecht, Amber Sanchez, Sima Sokolov, Blake Stephens, and Andrew Utz. In addition, we would like to thank the anonymous reviewers who provided helpful comments on the proposal and draft chapters, and the editors and staff at Cambridge University Press, who encouraged us to undertake the project in the first place and assisted throughout its development. We also thank our colleagues in the Department of Applied Linguistics at Portland State University for helping us to think through the definition of applied linguistics and the many areas of work that are covered in our field.

Contributors

Nike Arnold, Department of Applied Linguistics, Portland State University, USA

Brody Bluemel, Department of Languages and Literatures, Delaware State University, USA

Kimberley Brown, Department of Applied Linguistics, Portland State University, USA

Lucien Brown, School of Languages, Literatures, Cultures, and Linguistics, Monash University, Australia

Luciana Cabrini Simões Calvo, Modern Languages Department, Universidade Estadual de Maringá, Brazil

Winnie Cheng, Department of English, The Hong Kong Polytechnic University, Hong Kong

G. Tucker Childs, Department of Applied Linguistics, Portland State University, USA

Susan Conrad, Department of Applied Linguistics, Portland State University, USA

Janet Cowal, Department of Applied Linguistics, Portland State University, USA

Rosa Dene David, Department of Foreign Languages and Culture, Universidad de La Sabana, Colombia

Boyd H. Davis, Department of English, University of North Carolina at Charlotte, USA

Michele Salles El Kadri, Foreign Language Department, Universidade Estadual de Londrina, Brazil

Telma Gimenez, Departamento de Letras Estrangeiras Modernas, Universidade Estadual de Londrina, Brazil

Kathy Harris, Department of Applied Linguistics, Portland State University, USA

Alissa J. Hartig, Department of Applied Linguistics, Portland State University, USA

John Hellermann, Department of Applied Linguistics, Portland State University, USA

Gloria Jacobs, Department of Applied Linguistics, Portland State University, USA

Keiko Koda, Department of Modern Languages, Carnegie Mellon University, USA

Phoenix Lam, Department of English, The Hong Kong Polytechnic University, Hong Kong

Genevieve Leung, Asian Pacific American Studies Program, University of San Francisco, USA

Xiaofei Lu, Department of Applied Linguistics, The Pennsylvania State University, USA

Michaela Mahlberg, Department of English Language and Applied Linguistics, University of Birmingham, UK

Ekaterina Moore, Rossier School of Education, University of Southern California, USA

Afaf Nash, Linguistics Program, Middlebury College and National Heritage Language Resource Center, University of California at Los Angeles, USA

Lucy Pickering, Department of Literature and Languages, Texas A&M University - Commerce, USA

Jeffrey Reaser, Department of English, North Carolina State University, USA

David Rose, Director, Reading to Learn and Linguistics Department, University of Sydney, Australia

Lynn Santelmann, Department of Applied Linguistics, Portland State University, USA

Tetyana Sydorenko, Department of Applied Linguistics, Portland State University, USA

Elin Thordardottir, School of Communication Sciences and Disorders, McGill University, Canada

Steven L. Thorne, Department of World Languages and Literatures, Portland State University, USA

Keith Walters, Department of Applied Linguistics, Portland State University, USA

Lionel Wee Hock Ann, Department of English Language & Literature, National University of Singapore, Singapore

Viola Wiegand, Department of English Language and Applied Linguistics, University of Birmingham, UK

PART A
Introduction

1 Introduction to the Field of Applied Linguistics

SUSAN CONRAD, ALISSA J. HARTIG, AND
LYNN SANTELMANN

What is Applied Linguistics?

Language teaching, dementia, personal identity, the training of law students – if you skim the contents of this book, you might wonder how a single field could cover such a diverse range of topics. But all the topics in this book have a common foundation: people's use of language. The way people use language can build relationships or cause interpersonal difficulties. Language can be used to exert power over others or to resist others' exertion of power. Language is used in different ways by different disciplines, increasing the challenge for novices in a field. And myriad social and psychological factors can affect success in learning a new language. All of these issues, and more, are covered in the field of applied linguistics.

In this book, we define applied linguistics this way:

> Applied linguistics is a field that investigates the development and use of language in real-world situations and institutions. It aims to understand how language choices reflect and create contexts, and to address communication-related problems. Applied linguists analyze language in context and examine social and psychological factors related to language use or development.

Unpacking this definition reveals many characteristics of applied linguistics that you will see in subsequent chapters of this book. First, this is a field that *investigates the development and use of language.* This means some investigations focus on the teaching and learning of language; in fact, this is the best-known area of work in applied linguistics. But applied linguists also investigate the use of language by proficient speakers in a range of contexts. An important aspect of the contexts is that they are *real-world situations and institutions.* They could be within organizations, such as schools or businesses, or casual settings, such as a visit to a grandparent or text messages with friends. The language can be spoken or written, in electronic form or on paper. The crucial point is that the language is not decontextualized examples of structures; instead, it is part of a real communication situation.

The second sentence in our definition identifies two purposes for applied linguistics. The first, *to understand how language choices reflect and create contexts*, might seem puzzling at first, especially if you haven't studied applied linguistics previously. You may never have thought of language as a set of choices, but every time you say or write something, you have numerous options, and the options you choose reflect your perspective on the circumstances and also create the circumstances. To take a simple example, suppose you meet one of the editors of this book, Alissa Hartig, as you are walking down the street. First, you could choose to greet her or not speak at all. If you decide to speak, you could say *bonjour, good morning*, or *hey, what's up?* You could address her as *Dr. Hartig, Alissa*, or *dude*. And these are just a few of your choices! No doubt you are thinking the appropriate choices depend on your relationship with her and your shared background (e.g., do you both speak French?). From this perspective, your choices will reflect the context. At the same time, the choices you make will help create your relationship with her. If you decide to call her *Alissa* rather than *Dr. Hartig*, you imply a closer or more equal relationship – and she may be pleased or displeased about that, depending how she views your relationship and how she views the social impact of first names rather than titles and last names.

Most studies that seek to understand language use are, of course, more complicated than this example. In Chapter 23 of this book, for instance, Winnie Cheng and Phoenix Lam investigate how Western and Chinese media portray Hong Kong. Typical of studies that seek to understand language use, there are important general implications for this study: if readers have a greater understanding of how news outlets use language to create different views of a country, they can become more sophisticated in their perceptions of biases in media. Other studies, however, focus more directly on the second purpose in our definition: *to address communication-related problems*. For example, in Chapter 24 Kathy Harris and Gloria Jacobs discuss a project to make digital health information services more accessible for a wider range of people, and in Chapter 3 Lynn Santelmann and Tanya Sydorenko discuss helping students learn to be more pragmatically appropriate when they use a new language. For both of these projects, the goal is to solve, or at least improve, a problematic situation where communication plays a central role.

The third sentence in our definition clarifies more about how work in applied linguistics is conducted. First, it emphasizes that applied linguists *analyze* data; in other words, **empirical** investigation is central. Empirical does not necessarily mean experimental. In fact, there are many different ways to gather and analyze data, as you will see in Chapter 2, but all studies are based on principled data collections, not on a single person's intuition about language. When the data are language samples, they are *language in context* because applied linguists realize their investigations must consider factors such as who is communicating with whom, under what circumstances, and in what form. An obvious example of context being important is in Lucy Pickering's Chapter 13 about augmentative and alternative communication (AAC) – technologies that enhance people's abilities to communicate when they have neurological conditions that interfere with speech production. As Pickering explains, to identify language needs and help improve AAC devices, data had to be collected from carefully chosen pairs of participants whose workplace contexts were similar but who differed in their AAC or non-AAC status.

Besides studying language itself, applied linguists also *examine social and psychological factors* related to language. A study might focus on people's attitudes and beliefs about language, as in Chapter 12, where Jeffrey Reaser examines attitudes toward non-standard dialects and the linguistic discrimination that decreases the effectiveness of education for many students. Like studies of language itself, studies of attitudes and beliefs about language also use principled data collection methods, not just anecdotes or impressions.

Our definition of applied linguistics is similar to those of other scholars over many years, but different definitions tend to emphasize slightly different areas. In the activities on the website accompanying this book, you will compare definitions from a few different authors and identify the consistencies and differences for yourself.

The Interdisciplinary Nature of Applied Linguistics

As you can tell from our definition of applied linguistics, the field requires understanding a great deal about humans and their interactions. Investigations often require data or perspectives that come from different fields. In training effective language teachers, for example, Grabe (2010) notes that, although language is an important factor, so are other considerations:

> How one trains effective language teachers may involve research that does not refer directly to aspects of language knowledge, but rather to aspects of learning psychology (cognitive processes), educational practice (task development and sequencing), and social interactions (autonomy, status, turn taking). (p. 43)

Besides aspects of language study, work in applied linguistics commonly uses knowledge from psychology, sociology, anthropology, public policy, information technology, health sciences, and other fields. Applied linguistics projects might have multiple collaborators with expertise in different fields, or a single applied linguist might gather knowledge from multiple fields. Applied linguists are often housed in different departments at different universities, reflecting the diversity of perspectives in the field. If there is not a department of applied linguistics, you might find applied linguists in education, communication, languages, anthropology, psychology, or elsewhere.

Given this **interdisciplinarity**, you might wonder how you will know when work fits within applied linguistics rather than some other field. In other words, what sets work in applied linguistics apart? A crucial characteristic is that systematic language analysis has a more central role than in other fields. As discussed in the next section, applied linguistics is not just an application of theories from theoretical linguistics; however, working in applied linguistics does require being able to analyze language. Thus, for example, you could read many articles about the diagnosis or progression of dementia from medical professionals, but in this book, Boyd Davis (Chapter 19) discusses the discourse structure of narratives and caregiver–patient interactions. Similarly, there are many literary studies that discuss author styles, but in this book, Michaela Mahlberg and Viola Wiegand (Chapter 15) use quantitative analysis of patterns in authors' language to investigate their styles.

Another characteristic typical of work in applied linguistics is that, although it uses theories from other fields, they are applied in new ways to language-related problems. As Kramsch (2015) explains, applied linguistics will often draw on theories from other fields, but the theories do not directly explain practices or ways to improve on problems. An applied linguist has to integrate theory and concepts from other fields with the analysis of language and the specific context of the language situation.

The Editors' Paths into Applied Linguistics

Because of the diversity within applied linguistics and the importance of language in so many types of human interactions, scholars follow many different paths on their way to becoming applied linguists. In each chapter of this book, the authors tell you how they got into their area of work. Here we share how the three editors got into applied linguistics as an illustrative case of diverse paths into the field.

Susan Conrad   In my bachelor's degree, I studied biology and English. I thought I would become a high school biology teacher, but I recognize now that I was actually fascinated by how people used language differently in these two fields and that's partly why I enjoyed studying them both. After I graduated, I served as a Peace Corps volunteer in Lesotho in southern Africa, teaching science and English, and through that experience I discovered the field of Teaching English as a Second Language (TESOL). While working on my M.A. in TESOL, I then realized how much I loved to analyze how people use language. I was motivated especially by seeing how I could apply what I learned to help improve students' preparation for studying specific disciplines. I worked as an ESL teacher in the United States and South Korea for a few years, but I soon entered a PhD program in applied linguistics because I wanted more training in researching language use and applying the findings.

Alissa Hartig   My path into applied linguistics started with a love for learning languages that unexpectedly became a love for teaching language as well. After graduating with a degree in French language and literature, I spent the next six years teaching English in various contexts: a rural high school in Guinea, a private language school in Mexico, and a university language center in South Korea. Toward the end of my time in Korea, I started thinking about graduate school and asked a friend who was doing a PhD in English for reading recommendations. She recommended that I check out some work by a scholar in multilingual writing, and after reading a couple of his books, I sent him an email to ask how someone like me could get involved in the kinds of work he was doing. He graciously responded to my email and suggested that I might want to consider a degree in applied linguistics. From then on, I knew I had found my niche.

Lynn Santelmann My journey into applied linguistics began when my college German teacher taught vocabulary by showing us the systematic sound changes between German and English. I was fascinated. At the time, I was an engineering/biology major contemplating a career in biomedical engineering. I excelled at chemistry, but was finding biology highly boring. My German teacher kept telling me that I should take linguistics. I finally did, and I was hooked. Finally, I'd found a field that combined my love of languages with the analysis and pattern finding that I loved from chemistry and math. I pursued a graduate degree in linguistics, focusing on child language acquisition. I wanted to know how children acquire language and why they show the patterns they do. Post-doctoral work in psychology/speech-language pathology expanded my interests to the link between language and cognition – how does language reflect what we know or influence how we learn? My subsequent employment in a department of applied linguistics has pushed me to consider context – how does previous experience with genres of language affect learning content and theories of a field?

Why Applied Linguistics is a Separate Field from Linguistics

We have said that projects in applied linguistics require being able to describe and analyze language. Sometimes this raises the question: Why is applied linguistics a field in itself and not just a matter of applying knowledge from theoretical linguistics?

Although both theoretical and applied linguistics describe and analyze language, they have different goals and typically approach the analysis of language very differently. The field of **theoretical linguistics** is focused on understanding people's internalized language knowledge rather than on understanding how people use language or on improving language-related problems. In most theoretical linguistics, the ultimate goal of the work is to describe the underlying rules of human language. For example, one of the best-known theoretical approaches to linguistics was developed by Noam Chomsky – **generative syntax**. It seeks to describe the rules that generate all the grammatical sentences in a language but none of the ungrammatical ones. Aspects of language variation, language choices, and social context that are important in applied linguistics are disregarded because they are not important for this theory. This theory, therefore, rarely appears in applied linguistics, although it may inform some fundamental language acquisition research. Some linguistic theories emphasize more of a functional perspective, and these tend to be more useful for applied linguistics. For example, systemic functional linguistics is used in David Rose's discussion of literacy education in Chapter 8.

Because applied linguistics has a different purpose and focus than linguistics, its methods and techniques are different from linguistics. Chapter 2 covers methods in detail. Right now, it is worth noting that applied linguistics differs by analyzing language in a specific social context and in using **empirical analysis** (not intuition-based arguments). Applied linguistics data also typically include discourse – that is, larger chunks of language in context – while theoretical linguistics more commonly uses decontextualized sentences.

In addition to theoretical linguistics and applied linguistics, you might also see the term "**descriptive linguistics**." This term is used for different meanings. It might be used in contrast to "**prescriptive linguistics**" – in other words, for describing what people do in language, as opposed to reciting prescriptive rules about what they *should* do. In addition, descriptive linguistics is used in reference to many sociolinguistic studies, such as those that describe how people of different social classes or from different regions pronounce words differently or use different grammatical structures (sometimes called **variationist studies**). Much of this work began with Labov's (1966) studies of speech in New York City. Such sociolinguistic work is focused on describing language variation, but it rarely grows out of the desire to address real-world problems. The **Association Internationale de Linguistique Appliquée** (International Association of Applied Linguistics, AILA), in fact, states, "Applied Linguistics differs from Linguistics in general mainly with respect to its explicit orientation toward practical, everyday problems related to language and communication" (Association Internationale de Linguistique Appliquée, n.d., para. 2).

A (Very) Short History of Applied Linguistics

Applied linguistics is a young field when compared to many other fields. The first journal to identify itself as publishing applied linguistics work was *Language Learning* in 1948, which then called itself "A quarterly journal of applied linguistics." (Its subtitle has since changed to "A journal of research in language studies," Wiley online library, n.d.) The Association Internationale de Linguistique Appliquée (AILA) was formed in 1964, and the journal *Applied Linguistics* published its first issue in spring 1980. In comparison, the world's largest professional organization of anthropologists, the American Anthropological Association, was founded in 1902 (American Anthropological Association, 2018). The Linguistic Society of America, which focuses more on theoretical and descriptive linguistics, was founded in 1925 and published its first issue of the journal *Language* that year (Linguistic Society of America, 2012).

Of course, people were writing about topics that fit within applied linguistics long before the name "applied linguistics" was used. Even thousands of years ago in ancient Greece, Plato and Aristotle wrote about effective designs for language instruction (Howatt, 1984). In fact, language teaching was the first impetus for identifying a field as applied linguistics. In the nineteenth century, anthropologists and linguists did a great deal of work describing languages, but in the twentieth century there was increased interest in how people learn languages and the most effective way to teach them. In the 1940s, 1950s, and 1960s, the term "applied linguistics" was used to refer to applying information from structural and functional linguistics to the practice of language teaching (Corder, 1973; Grabe, 2010). In the 1960s, interest grew in the process of how languages are acquired, and an area called "second language acquisition" emerged, in addition to other areas such as how to assess language development (Ortega, 2009). In the 1970s, work continued to expand in subfields such as second language literacy, multilingualism, language policies and planning, and language-minority rights (Kaplan, 1980; Widdowson 1979/1984). In this way, applied linguistics became the discipline it is today – focused on language-related problems in real-world contexts, including – but not limited to – language teaching.

Approaches to Language in Applied Linguistics

Throughout the history of the field described in the previous section, applied linguists have also looked at language in a wide range of ways. To get a sense of some of these perspectives, think about how you could analyze an interaction between two bilingual individuals. You might start by writing down, or transcribing, all of the words that were said in the conversation. But then you'd have some other choices. Would you include information about intonation or how these words were pronounced? Would you also make note of gestures, facial expressions, or pauses? When you started analyzing the transcript, what would you look for and how would you know what to focus on in your analysis? What aspects of the context would you need to know about, if any? Would the relationship between the speakers or the purpose of their interaction be relevant to the analysis?

Each of these choices represents a different way of looking at language. Approaching language in different ways allows applied linguists to see different things. Every approach highlights some parts of language while obscuring others. For this reason, applied linguists are often drawn to particular ways of understanding and looking at language because they allow them to examine aspects of language use that are important to them and that would otherwise be invisible, as you'll see in the descriptions in the next section. Each approach also allows applied linguists to answer different kinds of research questions or solve different kinds of problems. As a result, the choice among approaches is often motivated by the specific research questions being asked. And just because an applied linguist draws on one particular approach doesn't mean that they don't see the value of others. When considering which perspective is best suited to a particular project, an applied linguist needs to think about what this perspective offers: What can this perspective show me that I wouldn't be able to see through other lenses? What won't it allow me to see?

How Do Applied Linguists Look at Language?

To better understand the perspectives in the studies and projects described in Part B of this book, it is worth thinking about some of the major lenses that applied linguists use to study language. While some applied linguists may approach language through the lens of a specific, named theory, like systemic functional linguistics in Chapter 8, others may use a broader approach that doesn't have a specific name, like the more general functional approach used in Chapter 13. In the next several sections, we highlight typical characteristics of a few common approaches to studying language. In practice, applied linguists often combine aspects of multiple approaches, and you will also come across other perspectives that aren't covered here. As you read through the approaches below, though, think about which resonate most with you. Which align best with your own perspective? Can you think of any advantages of the other approaches for addressing certain kinds of questions or issues?

Structural approaches   If you've taken courses like syntax and phonetics, you are already familiar with this perspective. **Structural approaches** focus on the patterns in language forms – for example, how syllables, phrases, and clauses are formed and embedded in systematic, hierarchical ways. A focus on language structure means looking at the individual parts of language and how they are combined to form words, phrases, and clauses following regular rules or patterns. This focus on grammatically well-formed utterances looks at characteristics of language that are independent of the surrounding context or meaning. One famous Chomskyan example is the sentence "Colorless green ideas sleep furiously." Even though this sentence doesn't make any sense, it follows all of the structural grammar rules of English. Syntactically, it is indistinguishable from the sentences "Adorable little kittens play happily" and "Fundamental disciplinary concepts vary widely." All three sentences are structurally identical.

Structural approaches are often used in theoretical linguistics, such as in generative syntax, mentioned above. But patterns in structures can also be useful to applied linguists. In Chapter 6, by Xiaofei Lu and Brody Bluemel, for example, you'll learn more about automated language assessment. One of the tools that you'll read about in that chapter measures the syntactic complexity of a language sample by calculating a number of metrics, such as the number of complex noun phrases per clause. Looking at these patterns can allow applied linguists to see how individuals develop more complex and well-formed utterances over time, whether in a first language or in a language learned later in life. Structural approaches like this allow applied linguists to extract patterns in the structure of language irrespective of the immediate situation or the speaker's intended meaning, making the categorization of language features relatively transparent. This is particularly useful for work that uses computer programs to mark language categories. Structural approaches might also be a first step in a study that then moves to a functional approach.

Functional approaches **Functional approaches** to language emphasize the ways in which linguistic structures relate to context and meaning. One major difference between spoken conversational language and academic writing, for example, is that informal conversation uses a much higher proportion of pronouns than academic writing, which tends to use a much higher proportion of nouns. This difference relates largely to the contexts in which these two kinds of language are produced and the meanings that speakers and writers tend to convey in these contexts. Conversation is interactive and produced orally in real time, often with a great deal of shared information between the speakers. Academic writing, by contrast, is produced in a visible form over a longer time period, which allows for much more revision. While academic writers may use some features of dialogue, like asking questions to engage readers, an academic text is a monologue that can be read and re-read. Academic writing is also written for an audience who does not have direct access to the immediate context that the writer is referring to, so reference must be made much more specific so that readers will understand what is being referred to and how it relates to other information in the text.

A functional analysis, such as that used by David Rose or Lucy Pickering, allows researchers to understand not just which structures are present, but also why they are present in a given text or why they might seem strange in another context even when they are grammatically correct. Substituting nouns for pronouns in conversation, for example, sounds awkward and repetitive since speakers typically have enough mutual knowledge of the situation to understand the pronoun reference. Substituting pronouns for nouns in academic writing, on the other hand, often causes confusion for readers. A functional analysis can help uncover how combinations of structures like these create particular effects and reflect communicative needs.

Cognitive approaches   **Cognitive approaches** to language can refer to language as it is processed in the brain or language as a tool for conceptualization in the mind. If this distinction between brain and mind is unfamiliar, one way to think of the difference is that cognitive studies that focus on the brain are usually looking at biological processes while those that focus on the mind often relate more to the mental images or processes that language evokes or reflects. Chapter 7 provides some good examples of brain-based cognitive studies. Among other approaches, Elin Thordardottir describes studies that measure cognitive processing by producing images of electrical activity in the brain in response to linguistic stimuli or using tests that measure phonological working memory by having children repeat invented words. These kinds of studies, which look at language as a biological phenomenon, can provide insights into developmental language disorders as well as other questions involving how people process language.

In Chapter 23, Winnie Cheng and Phoenix Lam highlight an important area of **cognitive linguistics**, which is focused more on the mind than on the brain. The authors describe studies that examine the use of **conceptual metaphors**, which refer to the often subtle ways in which language is used to evoke particular mental associations. Unlike literary metaphors, which are used intentionally by authors in creative writing, conceptual metaphors are common throughout everyday language use, and speakers and listeners are often not consciously aware of them. One common conceptual metaphor in English, for example, is ARGUMENT IS WAR.[1] We might say that someone "shot down" all of our arguments or that two politicians "clashed" during a debate. We frequently refer to individuals as having to "defend" their arguments or "attack" the arguments of the other side. These expressions relate to an underlying image of an argument as a battle, which leads to other mental associations – such as the idea that there must be a winner and a loser. While these associations may seem natural within a given cultural context, imagine how our understanding of arguments would change if we talked about them instead as a kind of dance (Lakoff & Johnson, 1980). Instead of opponents, we might have partners, and the goal wouldn't be to defeat the other side but rather to work together to create a more sophisticated understanding of an issue. This kind of framing, which relates to the mental images we use to understand the world around us, is one area of cognitive linguistics. In this approach, language is seen as a tool for conceptualization.

Social approaches   **Social approaches** highlight how language manages interactions and signals relationships and identities, giving applied linguists tools for understanding how we perceive others and are perceived in turn by them. Focusing on the role of language in signaling identity in Chapter 12, Jeffrey Reaser

---

[1] In cognitive linguistics, small capital letters are used to distinguish underlying conceptual metaphors from specific instantiations of these metaphors.

discusses teaching materials created to help students understand and appreciate varieties of English associated with economically and socially marginalized communities. These materials show how language is used as a proxy for other identities, and that many of the prejudices people express about the ways that particular groups of people speak (e.g., that their language use reflects laziness or a lack of intelligence) have more to do with their own unconscious biases against these groups than with any actual linguistic characteristics.

One example of how such judgments can lead to real-world consequences comes from the trial of George Zimmerman, a man who killed an unarmed African American teenager named Trayvon Martin. In the Zimmerman trial, one of the most important witnesses for the prosecution was Rachel Jeantel, a close friend of Martin who was on the phone with him while the events in question were taking place. Throughout her testimony, Jeantel's language use was highly systematic and consistent with patterns of African American Vernacular English (AAVE) and other varieties from her community, including features such as use of preterit *ain't* for negation in the past tense (e.g., "They ain't call my number") (Rickford & King, 2016). Public attacks on her testimony, however, equated her language use with low intelligence and poor education, dismissing her testimony despite her unique knowledge of what had happened. Rather than focusing on the content of her testimony, many of those watching the trial questioned her character and competence based on the way in which she spoke. Reactions like this can reveal implicit biases that people carry against certain linguistically marked groups.

Multimodal approaches　Most of the approaches described so far relate to aspects of language that fit comfortably into what most people would classify as language. **Multimodal approaches** extend the scope of language to encompass not just the words and grammar that people use when speaking or writing, but also the ways in which speakers draw on other resources to create meaning. In Chapter 24, Kathy Harris and Gloria Jacobs demonstrate how limiting language to traditional linguistic forms and functions fails to account for the range of symbolic systems that adult literacy learners need in order to use digital platforms. In order to navigate the kinds of online health portals that are used by many medical providers in the United States, these learners need to be able to both read the words and sentences on the screen and understand how the layout of the site communicates meaning. They need to recognize how visual cues, like font color and underlining, or other symbols, like the three parallel horizontal bars frequently used to indicate a menu, encode information that will enable the user to interact with a site or app. These signals, which individuals with strong digital literacy skills may find highly intuitive, are communicated through conventions that are not necessarily obvious to new digital technology users. Multimodal approaches to language recognize these kinds of resources, as well as others, like gesture, music, and objects, as part of a larger set of semiotic resources that we use to communicate meaning. A multimodal approach to language considers all meaning-making resources, both verbal and non-verbal, as potentially relevant to a linguistic analysis.

Translingual approaches   **Translingual approaches** go a step beyond multimodal approaches. While multimodal approaches question the boundary between verbal and non-verbal resources for making meaning, translingual approaches go on to further question the idea that languages can be reliably separated into discrete units at all. In Chapter 11, for example, Lionel Wee highlights some of the problems with attempting to separate languages into clear and distinct named entities for the purpose of language policy and planning. In the studies described in that chapter, he shows how legislation designed to protect specific named languages does not adequately address the actual language practices that people use in everyday communication.

For many people, the idea that individually named languages like German and Swahili are separate and distinct systems seems like common sense. In practice, however, real-life language use in multilingual contexts is often much more fluid than this view suggests. Traditionally, when bilingual individuals would use elements of two different named languages, such as Spanish and English, in the same interaction, these codeswitches were seen as instances in which the individual was changing from one language system to another. Translingual approaches look at this kind of language use differently. Rather than seeing these as shifts between different systems, translingual approaches to language view these as instances in which the individual is highlighting different parts of a single communicative repertoire. Li (2018) offers an example from a fruit vendor in Taiwan (Figure 1.1).

A rendering of this sign's English meaning would be "Today's fruit is watermelon." The first and third lines use Chinese characters (今日, *jinri*, "today," and 水果, *shuiguo*, "fruit"), the second line uses a Japanese possessive marker (の, *no*), the fourth line uses the English copula "is," and the fifth line uses drawings of cut watermelon pieces.

The creator of this sign probably did not consciously consider the process of switching between linguistic or symbolic systems or spend a lot of time deliberating about which of them to use for which part of the advertisement. This person may or may not have extensive knowledge of English and Japanese, and it is unlikely that they expect all readers to have such an understanding – nor would such an understanding be necessary. In fact, if the goal is merely to signal a cosmopolitan image of some sort, this can be achieved even if the audience has no idea what the English or Japanese words on the sign mean. This kind of multilingual wordplay draws on the meaning potential of a range of symbolic tools in a way that does not rely on these tools being part of complete, separate, and independent systems. A translingual

Figure 1.1 Fruit vendor advertisement in Taiwan
(Li, 2018).
By permission of Li Wei.

approach allows applied linguists to account for multilingual language use that doesn't fit easily into traditional codeswitching accounts, such as in the sign above.

Critical approaches **Critical approaches** recognize that language is embedded in contexts in which power relations play a role, even when this influence may be hidden or obscured. In Chapter 21, for example, Janet Cowal and Genevieve Leung describe how activist applied linguists draw on theories of language that argue that language is never neutral. This approach shows that what we may take for granted as "normal" or "default" ways of speaking and writing are inherently linked to structures of power. Critical approaches consider which voices are heard and valued in society and which perspectives are marginalized.

Looking at political discourse through a critical lens can illuminate how language is used to shape public opinion. Kramsch (2014) offers the example of the phrase "enhanced interrogation techniques" as a euphemism for torture. While the two terms refer to the same procedures, few members of the public would view torture as an acceptable approach to interrogation. For an administration that is committed to using torture, however, representing it as merely a set of "enhanced interrogation techniques" downplays the extreme nature of such procedures, implying that they are simply a normal, acceptable tool for gathering information. A critical approach allows applied linguists to consider not just what is said, but also what else could be said and whose interests the current framing does and does not serve.

Choosing an Approach

After reading through these different approaches to language, you might be think-ing that it would be difficult to choose just one approach to looking at language. Isn't language all of these things? Most applied linguists would agree! At the same time, trying to account for all of these characteristics at once wouldn't be practical in a single study or project. Analysis requires us to focus in on a more limited set of features so that we can understand them in more detail. Trying to design studies or projects that account for every way of looking at language at the same time would not only be impractical, but also risk giving a very superficial view of the phenom-enon that the applied linguist is trying to understand. This is why most applied linguists choose a specific approach, and it is also why having multiple approaches to choose from is important.

As you'll see in the chapters in Part B of this book, applied linguists work in a broad range of areas. Even within a given area, like second language acquisition or language policy and planning, research and practice in applied linguistics can be informed by a number of different approaches to language. Some applied linguists work exclusively with one specific approach to language, often because it is particularly well suited to answering the kinds of questions they are most interested in. Other applied linguists may use different approaches for different projects. While some approaches are mutually exclusive, others can also be combined effectively to highlight different aspects of a question or issue. As you read the chapters in Part B, think about which approaches to language are involved in the studies in each chapter. How much variation is there in approaches in each area? How do authors' approaches fit with their experiences, interests, and research questions?

Using a given approach to looking at language allows us to focus our attention on language in a systematic way, offering insights that would be hard to achieve without these lenses. As you move forward in your studies of applied linguistics, keep this diversity of perspectives in mind. Over time, you will probably come to favor a few perspectives over others, and you will likely develop more expertise using these frameworks. When reading research in areas outside your main area of focus, though, think about what this perspective adds that your favored perspective doesn't. How do they complement or enrich each other?

Overview of the Book

This textbook is divided into three major parts: an introduction (Part A), chapters covering the major areas of focus in applied linguistics (Part B), and a conclusion (Part C). Part A includes this introductory chapter as well as Alissa

Table 1.1 Overview of chapter structure

Overview	• Key concepts and issues
Example work	• Brief author reflection/description of how authors got into the field
	• In-depth example from work by the authors
	• Activity (linked to data on the accompanying website)
Going further	• Steps students can take to continue in this area
	• Discussion questions
	• Suggested readings

Hartig's Chapter 2 which introduces students to the kinds of theories and data applied linguists use in their research, and how applied linguists approach analyzing the data they collect. These introductory chapters will provide helpful background if you are new to the field and provide a basis for understanding the research studies presented in Part B.

Part B is divided into five sections covering major areas of work within the field of applied linguistics: language acquisition; language socialization; language varieties and variation; language cognition and processing; and language rights, power, and ideology. Within each major area, three to five individual chapters cover topics related to that area. The goal of these chapters is to give you a sense of the range of topics that applied linguists study and to provide concrete examples of how applied linguists approach these language-related issues.

Each chapter in Part B follows the structure outlined in Table 1.1. The chapter begins with an overview that presents key concepts and issues in the area, illustrated with examples. The second component of the chapter has a brief reflection from the authors describing how they got into their area of applied linguistics and introducing an in-depth, concrete example from their own work. This concrete example is then described in detail and is connected to a data set or activity (available on the website accompanying this book) that gives you concrete practice with the material covered in the chapter. Each chapter concludes with a brief description of courses or experiences that will be helpful if you want to continue in the area, along with discussion questions and suggested readings.

Part C consists of two chapters which aim to give you some tools for your next steps as you continue your study of applied linguistics. The first chapter presents strategies for reading research articles and writing about your own investigations. The final chapter reviews themes in the book and discusses what you can do with a degree in applied linguistics.

Throughout the book, you will see four recurring themes: technology, interdisciplinarity, multilingualism, and personal stories. The first three areas can be studied as discrete topics themselves, but in applied linguistics today they are usually interwoven through many other areas. The fourth theme – personal stories – resulted from the personal reflections we asked each author to include in their chapter. As you read the text, note how and where these themes occur and consider the following issues:

- *Technology:* In many chapters, computers or other technologies are used as an integral part of the research. How many different ways do you see technology being used as you read chapters? If technology is not explicitly noted, ask yourself where and how it might be used. For example, how might technology be used when working with the language of aging patients with dementia? What role could (or should) technology play in the acquisition of literacy?
- *Interdisciplinarity:* Think about how and why issues discussed in a chapter interact with the content of other disciplines. As you read chapters, also consider what other disciplines you would need to study in order to work more in the area. For instance, what would you need to learn to study language policy? What about language documentation? In addition, consider the challenge that interdisciplinarity can present for communicating what we have learned as applied linguists. How could you explain important language-related information to someone who is interested in a chapter's topic but is trained in another field?
- *Multilingualism:* Note which chapters focus on English speakers (as first or additional languages) and which ones focus on other languages. What languages and language contexts are under- or unrepresented in this book or the research cited? What work has been done on the languages that you speak and how might the issues you're reading about apply to different languages, cultures, and regions of the world?
- *Personal stories:* Personal experiences have played an important role in shaping the work of all the authors in this book. As you read the chapters, think about how personal contexts may have shaped the research questions the authors are asking, the aspects of language the authors emphasize, and the methods with which they address their research questions. The fact that individual context so often influences research agendas should be encouraging to students of applied linguistics – everyone brings unique experiences and interests that can lead to contributions in the field. You do not need to be extraordinarily creative or come up with a brilliant new method of research. Often, reflecting on your own experiences, the languages you speak, and the contexts you know can lead to useful and interesting research. As you read each chapter, consider your own personal experiences and the kinds of questions that you would ask if you were to do research on this topic. Those questions just might be the beginning of an exciting career in applied linguistics!

Discussion Questions

1. Much work in applied linguistics is motivated by helping to solve language-related problems in the real world. Name three problems that you think could be better understood and improved on through applied linguistics research. The problems can be as big or small as you wish (e.g., global problems or problems in your own life).
2. In this chapter, we argued that each approach to language highlights some things while obscuring others. Take another look at the approaches to language described here. What trade-offs can you see for each approach? What aspects of language would each approach be useful for seeing more clearly? What aspects of language might each approach hide?
3. Where do you think technology could be most useful in applied linguistics research? Are there types of research where computer technology might not be useful or even harmful? What are these?
4. What areas of applied linguistics currently interest you the most? What experiences have drawn you to those interests? What other disciplines do these areas overlap with? What interdisciplinary studies would you need to undertake to become a researcher in this area?
5. What languages and cultures do you bring knowledge of to your study of applied linguistics? Use a library database or Google Scholar to see if there is a lot of research or only a little for your topics of interest in the languages or cultures you are familiar with. What do the results tell you about this topic and these languages/cultures?

REFERENCES

American Anthropological Association. (2018). About AAA. Retrieved from www .americananthro.org/ConnectWithAAA/Content.aspx?ItemNumber=1665&t navItemNumber=586

Association Internationale de Linguistique Appliquée. (n.d.). What is AILA. Retrieved from https://aila.info/

Corder, S. (1973). *Introducing applied linguistics*. Harmondsworth: Penguin.

Grabe, W. (2010). Applied linguistics: A twenty-first-century discipline. In R. B. Kaplan (Ed.), *Oxford handbook of applied linguistics* (2nd edn) (pp. 34–44). Oxford: Oxford University Press.

Howatt, A. (1984). *A history of English language teaching.* Oxford: Oxford University Press.

Kaplan, R. B. (Ed.). (1980). *On the scope of applied linguistics*. Rowley, MA: Newbury House.

Kramsch, C. (2014). Language and culture. *AILA Review*, *27*, 30–55. https://doi.org/10.1075/aila.27.02kra

    (2015). Applied linguistics: A theory of the practice. *Applied Linguistics*, *36*(4), 454–465. https://doi.org/10.1093/applin/amv039

Labov, W. (1966). *The social stratification of English in New York City.* Washington, DC: Center for Applied Linguistics.

Lakoff, G., & Johnson, M. (1980). *Metaphors we live by.* Chicago: University of Chicago Press.

Li, W. (2018, May 9). Translanguaging and code-switching: What's the difference? Retrieved from https://blog.oup.com/2018/05/translanguaging-code-switching-difference/

Linguistic Society of America. (2012). About LSA. Retrieved from www.linguisticsociety.org/about

Ortega, L. (2009). *Understanding second language acquisition.* London: Hodder Education.

Rickford, J. R., & King, S. (2016). Language and linguistics on trial: Hearing Rachel Jeantel (and other vernacular speakers) in the courtroom and beyond. *Language*, *92*(4), 948–988. https://doi.org/10.1353/lan.2016.0078

Widdowson, H. G. (1979/1984). *Explorations in applied linguistics* (2 vols.). Oxford: Oxford University Press.

Wiley online library. (n.d.) . Language learning. Retrieved from https://onlinelibrary.wiley.com/journal/14679922

2 Approaches to Research in Applied Linguistics

ALISSA J. HARTIG

When you hear the word "research," what do you think of? In the media, we often see examples of laboratory research that uses statistical analyses of measurements collected through experiments using high-tech equipment. While some applied linguists work in similar kinds of labs and many use statistical analyses, applied linguists are often interested in questions that require different kinds of data and analysis. If you're new to the field, it might be hard to imagine what kinds of data an applied linguist would collect. Throughout the chapters in Part B of this book, you'll see examples of many different kinds of data, and these examples can be understood in part in terms of their focus on features of spoken or written language, communication more broadly, or the context in which language is used.

What Count as Data in Applied Linguistics?

Applied linguists think about data[1] in a wide range of ways. Because applied linguists are interested in both language and the contexts in which it is used, one way to look at research in the field is as a continuum ranging from a focus on language as an object to a focus on the context of language use (Figure 2.1). At one end of the spectrum, research might focus on the smallest units of language, like individual sounds or components of words. At the other end of the spectrum, research can look at the broader social context in which language is used, where it can reveal attitudes or beliefs surrounding a particular social issue.

Most topics that are addressed in applied linguistics could be examined at a variety of points along this continuum. For example, at the "language as object"

---

[1] Throughout the book, you will likely notice that *data* can be used as a plural count noun (corresponding to the singular *datum*, based on its Latin origins), or as a non-count noun (treated as grammatically singular). Often, you will find authors using singular and plural forms interchangeably. In other instances, you may notice that an author exclusively uses one form or the other. While the plural form is often considered prescriptively correct, there is not a substantive difference in meaning between the two forms (though some researchers and editors have strong opinions on this issue!).

Figure 2.1 Language–context continuum

end of the continuum, someone interested in language and the law could analyze the language of jury instructions in order to identify aspects of the vocabulary and syntax used in these instructions that could be confusing for jurors (Levi, 1993). At the "context of language use" end of the continuum, an applied linguist could collect a corpus of newspaper articles related to a controversial referendum and analyze the use of metaphors that appear repeatedly throughout the corpus in order to better understand how those who support or oppose the referendum frame their arguments (Santa Ana, 1999). With respect to the topic of language and disability, an applied linguist working in the middle of the continuum could focus on how an individual with aphasia is able to use a highly restricted range of vocabulary together with gesture, intonation, and elements of the surrounding environment to communicate a wide range of meanings through interactions with family and caregivers (Goodwin, 2004). On the context of language use end of the continuum, the researcher could focus on how disability is represented in television series, sports coverage of the Paralympics, and Hollywood superhero movies (Grue, 2015).

Another way of thinking about the two ends of the continuum is this: Is the goal of the study to better understand particular aspects of language structure or use (language as object) or is the goal of the study to better understand some aspect of the context in which language is used? In the former case, researchers would focus on patterns in the use of specific linguistic features within a language sample, which could shed light on how language is used in particular contexts or how individuals' use of language changes over time, for example. In the latter case, researchers could use at least two different foci to understand the context of language use. One context-oriented focus involves analyzing patterns in the use of specific linguistic features in texts about a topic that is not directly related to language, such as a social or political issue. With this focus, patterns in the use of linguistic features are identified as a means of understanding some aspect of the broader social context rather than emphasizing how language or language acquisition works. The other context-oriented focus involves analyzing the content of what people say when they talk or write about linguistic issues, identifying key themes or topics, for example, rather than focusing on specific linguistic features.

How are Data Gathered in Applied Linguistics?

To get a better sense of what this language–context continuum looks like in practice, imagine an applied linguist who is interested in studying the learning of an additional language in a classroom setting. The researcher could ask a wide range of questions on this topic, and the questions they ask would play an important role in determining what kind of data they would collect and how they would gather it. In the scenarios that follow, we'll move progressively from one end of the continuum to the other. We'll begin by zooming in on studies that focus on some of the smallest components of language and then zoom out little by little to look at patterns across larger stretches of discourse and onward to a wide-angle view of contexts in which language is used. The examples that follow are based to varying degrees on a number of published studies (Crossley, Kyle, & McNamara, 2016; Hellerman, 2008; Kanno & Kangas, 2014; Nickels & Steinhauer, 2018; Yamaguchi & Pétursson, 2018; You & Dörnyei, 2016; Zhang & O'Halloran, 2012).

At the language as object end of the continuum, the researcher could look at language as electrical activity in the brain. For example, a researcher might be interested in whether there are differences in classroom learners' neurological processing of language as they move from lower proficiency levels to higher proficiency levels. To do this, a researcher might design a laboratory experiment using instruments that measure brain activity (such as ERPs, or event-related brain potentials) to see how a group of learners at a lower level of proficiency processes sentences differently from those who are at a much higher level of language proficiency. This could then allow the researcher to make recommendations for classroom instruction to better highlight the kinds of cues that more proficient learners pay attention to in order to understand sentences, such as rhythm and intonation.

Moving to language in an external form, the researcher could ask how learners' first language background might affect their pronunciation in their second language. This question could lead the researcher to look at the production of individual sounds by learners from two different first language backgrounds. Data for a study like this would consist of recordings of the learners' speech, which would likely be **elicited** using a script or a prompt that the researcher has designed, such as a picture description task. These recordings could be either evaluated by trained raters who listen to the samples and identify variations in learners' pronunciation or analyzed using a spectrogram that provides a fine-grained visual representation of the acoustic properties of the sounds that the learners produce.

Another researcher might be interested in patterns across larger stretches of language, investigating how learners' writing in their second language changes over time. At lower levels of proficiency, learners often focus on writing individual sentences and have difficulty showing connections between sentences and ideas within a paragraph or larger text. The researcher might be interested in seeing whether learners are able to acquire the language they need for writing more cohesive, or connected, texts as they advance in proficiency. To investigate this question, the researcher could collect samples of student writing from a number of individuals on a regular basis over the course of a semester or academic year. The researcher could then look at changes in each individual's use of specific linguistic features that create more cohesive texts, such as words that show relationships between ideas, like *however* and *because.* Another approach to the same question would be to collect writing samples from students enrolled in different levels of a writing program (e.g., beginner, intermediate, advanced) at a single time point and then compare how students in lower levels use these linguistic features compared to students in higher levels.

Yet another approach that the researcher could use for a question about cohesion in student writing would be to design an **experiment**. To do this, the researcher could recruit a group of students with similar proficiency levels to determine whether a particular teaching technique is effective for teaching students to write cohesive paragraphs. Before beginning the experiment, the researcher could ask students to complete a pre-test in which they are asked to write a paragraph on a given topic. Then, the students could be divided into a control group, who would not receive any special instruction about paragraph structure, and a treatment group, who would be taught using the technique that the researcher wants to evaluate. To see whether this teaching technique is effective, the researcher could then have the students write a paragraph on a new topic. This post-test would allow the researcher to compare what students in both groups were able to do at the beginning and end of the experiment, and to see whether there were any differences in the paragraphs written by the control group compared to the treatment group. If the researcher wanted to take this a step further, they could even create a delayed post-test a few weeks later to see whether the teaching technique had a long-term effect on students' writing or whether it was something they learned quickly and then promptly forgot.

Despite differences in how data are gathered, these three studies of cohesion in student writing all involve collecting similar kinds of data, namely written texts produced by students. In each case, the researcher would be interested not just in isolated words but also in the relationships between words and sentences within their immediate textual context. As a result, all three studies would fit in approximately the same segment of the language–context continuum.

In the middle of the continuum, the researcher might be interested in not just how learners use language individually, but also how they use language and their immediate environment to coordinate interactions with other individuals. For a study like this, the researcher would look not just at the sounds, words, grammar, and text structures that the learner uses in a given textual context, but also at other ways of communicating meaning. For example, a researcher might be interested in how language learners coordinate with one another when beginning small group activities in class. Rather than focusing only on what learners say, the researcher might collect video recordings of small groups of students so that they can also see how the learners use gesture, gaze, drawings, objects, or other aspects of the classroom context to coordinate these activities. Once the researcher has identified these types of interactions in the video recording, they could use **conversation analysis** techniques to transcribe what learners say, as well as how they say it, and add additional information from the video to the transcript to indicate other tools that learners use to interact with one another. The researcher could then use this highly detailed representation of students' interactions to analyze the structure of these interactions in order to better understand how they are organized.

Moving toward the context end of the continuum, a language education researcher might be less interested in the language that students produce than their motivations for studying a language in the first place. A researcher interested in these kinds of questions might prepare a questionnaire that students could complete online or on paper. This **questionnaire** could include questions that use a **Likert scale**, where respondents rate their answers to each question on a numerical scale. For example, one question might ask students to rate how strongly they agree or disagree with the statement "I believe that studying this language will be helpful for my future career goals," with *1* reflecting a response of "strongly agree" and *5* reflecting a response of "strongly disagree." If the researcher didn't have a clear idea about what kinds of prompts would be relevant to students, they might instead have them respond to open-ended questions in which students could write a few sentences to respond to a question like "What are your top three reasons for studying this language?" This difference in research design would lead to different kinds of data. For the Likert scale, the data would be the numerical ratings that students give for each question, while for the open-ended questionnaire, the data would consist of students' written responses.

A researcher might also be interested in how individuals who are learning the majority language in a public high school context are positioned with respect to their peers who grew up speaking this language from birth. Here, the focus would shift from the learners and their individual interactions to a broader view that examines the institutional context and includes both other individuals with whom learners interact and their learning environment. While this might at first sound similar to the example using conversation analysis above, the focus of the study here would be much broader. In a conversation analytic study, the focus would be to better understand how participants use language, but the focus of the study described here would be on how contextual factors shape students' experiences as language learners.

For this study, the researcher might decide to conduct an **ethnography**, spending several months at a high school. In ethnographic research, the goal of the study is to understand what is happening from the perspectives of the people involved and to provide what is called a "thick description" (Geertz, 1973), or a detailed account that offers an inside view of the research context. To achieve this kind of in-depth understanding of the high school context in this study, the researcher would need to spend a significant amount of time observing classes and other relevant activities; interviewing students, faculty, and administrators; analyzing written assignments from students' classes or policy documents from the high school administration; and writing notes to reflect on and synthesize what they are learning about the context on a regular basis. Ethnographic research relies on collecting many different kinds of data in order to understand the research context from different perspectives. Data for this kind of study can include audio or video recordings of interviews with participants or of other activities in which participants are engaged, photographs or sketches of the research context, relevant documents (whether formally published or produced by participants), and the researcher's own observation notes and reflections.

Even further along the context of language use end of the spectrum, other researchers would be interested in considering language learning in the broader context of views on language education at the level of multiple institutions, national education policy, or media representations. A question that a researcher might be interested in at this level could focus on identifying the ideologies associated with studying particular languages. For example, a researcher might analyze the websites of a number of university language departments to see how they describe the various languages that are taught and why students should study them. The researcher might perform a **multimodal analysis**, looking at how various elements of each website work together to create particular representations of each language and its speakers. The researcher's data set would be the websites them-selves, and it would encompass both the actual text that appears on each site and other design elements, such as text formatting, hyperlinks, color, font style, images, videos, and sound. The researcher might then consider how the representations created by these elements reflect geopolitical concerns at the national and inter-national levels.

As you can see, the contexts that are examined as we move away from a focus on language as an object toward the context of language use end of the continuum can include the surrounding linguistic context, the immediate physical context in which linguistic interaction occurs, the attitudes individuals have with respect to linguistic issues, institutional contexts that shape the experiences of language users, and ideologies that influence societal views about language use. The examples above focused on a single topic, classroom language learning, to illustrate the language–context continuum as a way of thinking about the various types of data that applied linguists collect and how these data are gathered. Throughout the book, you will encounter many other topics and examples of approaches to data collection as you read the chapters that follow.

It's also important to note that the various data sources that are offered as examples above aren't the only way of approaching these questions, and researchers may even combine approaches and data sources to get multiple perspectives on a given question. For example, a researcher might combine survey data and an analysis of students' written work to see if there is any relationship between students' reported motivation and their performance on assignments. As you read the chapters in Part B, pay attention to the range of different kinds of questions that researchers ask on each topic, and try to think of other questions that could be asked. Where would you situate each of these questions on the continuum? What kinds of data do researchers collect to answer the questions that are important to them? What other kinds of data could you collect to answer these questions or others?

How are Data Analyzed in Applied Linguistics?

In the examples above, we've focused primarily on how an applied linguist would select various kinds of data to answer their research questions and how they could go about collecting data. What we haven't really addressed yet, though, is how applied linguists analyze the data they've collected. While analysis happens after data have been collected and often during the data collection process, researchers think about how they will analyze their data before the study even begins. This approach to analysis shapes both what kinds of data they collect and how they collect it.

Distinguishing Quantitative and Qualitative Approaches

In a few of the examples in the previous section, we've hinted at different approaches to analyzing data, and some kinds of data lend themselves to being analyzed in specific ways. For example, most experiments will be analyzed using some kind of statistical test to see if there are significant differences between the control and the treatment groups. This approach, which uses statistics to make generalizable claims, would be very unusual in the context of analyzing ethnographic data, however. Most approaches to data analysis can be classified as either **quantitative** or **qualitative**, and some researchers combine the two to take a **mixed methods** approach. If you already have experience conducting research in another field, you may have a sense of some of the differences among these approaches. If you go on to conduct your own research in applied linguistics, you will likely learn much more about these approaches in greater depth later on. For now, though, it may be useful to start thinking about a few of the ways in which quantitative and qualitative studies typically differ in applied linguistics. As your instructor can tell you, the description here is a bit of an oversimplification, but it may be helpful for better understanding some of the choices that the authors of the chapters in Part B have made in the research they discuss throughout the book.

Quantitative research, as the name suggests, relies on measuring things that can be quantified. Studies that are situated closer to the language as object end of the continuum often lend themselves to quantitative analysis because clearly defined linguistic structures are relatively easy to count. For example, if you wanted to compare whether there are differences in how frequently expert or novice writers use the passive voice in writing in applied linguistics, you could count how many times the passive voice is used in a collection of published research articles versus a collection of student research papers. That said, things that we often think of as being difficult to quantify, like "motivation" or "willingness to communicate," can be made countable by using tools that help people translate their attitudes into numerical values, like the Likert scales described in the previous section. And it's also important to note that features that may at first seem easy to count can turn out to be very difficult in practice! For example, categories that work well for analyzing written grammar don't always work as well for analyzing conversational language.

Responses from a Likert scale questionnaire can be compiled directly into a spreadsheet, but many other kinds of data, like the written texts in the passive voice example, first need to be **coded**, or marked to identify the features or categories that the researcher is interested in, before they can be analyzed statistically. Depending on the features that are being analyzed and the size of the data set, coding can be done manually or using automated tools. While the process of designing the study and collecting and coding data can take a long time, once these features have been counted, a quantitative analysis can be conducted fairly quickly by using computer software to perform statistical tests. Because of the relatively shorter amount of time that such an analysis requires, quantitative research is especially useful for looking at large sets of data to provide insights into trends across a population. This approach typically emphasizes relationships between variables or differences between groups, allowing us to extrapolate from a smaller sample to make generalizable claims.

Qualitative research, on the other hand, offers insights into contexts of language use that can be difficult to get at using a quantitative approach. Rather than focusing on direct relationships between clearly defined variables, qualitative research investigates how something happens in a specific context from the per-spective of the participants. This perspective might differ for different participants, and uncovering some of these contradictions and where they come from can provide new insights into an issue. Coding qualitative data often starts by examining the data first and then making sense of it by identifying categories or themes based on what is in the data rather than a pre-determined coding scheme. In fact, coding and analysis are often inseparable in qualitative research, and this process requires looking at the same data set multiple times in order to examine what is happening and to identify evidence that either supports or challenges the researcher's develop-ing understanding. As a result, qualitative analysis tends to be time consuming, which can constrain the overall amount of data that can be analyzed.

For example, a researcher might decide to interview a group of unsuccessful learners in a course in order to better understand the learners' perspectives and the range of factors that contributed to this outcome. In the course of the study, the researcher might discover that while their instructor classifies them as unsuccessful, the students do not see themselves this way. It may turn out that the learners' goals don't align well with those of the instructor, and these learners may in fact be very successful at achieving their own goals for the course. This insight could in turn be relevant for students in other similar contexts and would have implications for curriculum design and assessment. While a qualitative approach like this would not allow the researcher to make broad claims about language learners in general, it would allow them to uncover unexpected findings that would have been difficult to identify otherwise. Had the researcher taken a quantitative approach to this kind of question, they may not have had an opportunity to question whether "unsuccessful learner" was a relevant category to learners in the first place.

After reading this description of quantitative and qualitative research, you may assume that any research that involves numbers will automatically be quantitative. This isn't the case, however. Qualitative approaches may also draw on statistics to describe a specific sample and provide further context for the phenomenon that the researcher is studying. Unlike the kind of statistics that are emphasized in quantitative studies, these types of statistics aren't intended to be used for making generalizable claims. Instead, statistics that are used in qualitative studies often provide an overview of the specific data set that was examined in the study. For example, a researcher might observe that 25 percent of the utterances in a particular sample were single clauses rather than complex sentences. While this statistic would give readers a clearer sense of patterns in this specific sample, it doesn't provide a strong basis for making predictions about what other similar texts will be like.

Likewise, the fact that a study uses a small number of texts or participants doesn't automatically make it qualitative. In general, quantitative studies tend to seek findings that can be generalized to a broader population while qualitative studies tend to focus on understanding particular instances of a phenomenon in depth. The descriptions provided here represent opposite ends of a spectrum, though, and many studies fall somewhere between these two extremes. Much like the distinction made earlier between studies that focus on language as an object versus the context of language use, the difference between quantitative and qualitative approaches is often more of a continuum than a clear categorical distinction.

In mixed methods research, researchers use quantitative and qualitative approaches together, often during different phases of the study. For example, to determine why students choose to learn specific languages, the researcher could begin by conducting interviews with a small group of carefully selected participants who are studying various languages at a given university and then perform a qualitative analysis to identify themes that are important to the participants. The researcher might find that, among the people they've interviewed, some languages seem to draw more learners who are motivated by a broader interest in the culture associated with that language, while other languages might draw more learners who are interested for religious reasons or to achieve professional goals. Some languages might tend to attract learners who are interested in being able to communicate more effectively with speakers of those languages in the community where they live or with members of their own family. Still other languages might be more often selected primarily as a way to fulfill a graduation requirement. Using these themes, the researcher could then develop an online questionnaire that uses closed-ended multiple choice questions to find out whether there are any trends in the main motivations of learners of various languages in universities more broadly. This questionnaire could be distributed to a very large number of respondents and their responses could be automatically tabulated and compiled, allowing the researcher to use quantitative techniques to see whether there are general statistical patterns in the motivations that learners have for studying specific languages.

Qualitative techniques can also offer insights into quantitative findings. For example, in a quantitative experiment to test a particular teaching technique, a researcher might find that there are no statistical differences in the results of the post-test scores between the control and treatment groups and that both groups scored poorly on the post-test overall. If the researcher had previously had success with this teaching technique, they would likely be surprised by this finding and wonder whether the teaching technique was actually ineffective or whether there was a problem with the design of the post-test. The researcher might ask a few participants from each group to participate in a focus group where they would look at the post-test together and talk about their interpretation of the test questions and experience taking the test. A qualitative analysis of their discussion might reveal that the problem wasn't related to the teaching technique itself but rather to the use of vocabulary items and cultural references that were unfamiliar to the participants.

Just as quantitative and qualitative approaches can sometimes be integrated in the same study, some analysis techniques can be used in both quantitative and qualitative ways. **Discourse analysis**, for example, refers to a wide range of approaches to looking at language use in context, some of which are more likely to be qualitative while others are quantitative. One approach to discourse analysis that can be used in both quantitative and qualitative ways is **genre analysis**. Genre analysis looks at patterns in spoken or written texts that make them recognizable as belonging to a particular spoken or written text type – for example, televised political campaign advertisements. A quantitative approach to genre analysis could be to code functional parts, or **moves** (e.g., mentioning the candidate's position on a political issue, indicating personal qualities of the candidate, making an attack on an opponent, indicating groups that have endorsed the candidate) in a large sample of ads from two political parties, count the frequency of occurrences of each move, and then use statistical methods to determine if some moves are used more often in ads produced by one political party or another. In a qualitative approach to genre analysis, a researcher might seek to identify the various tools that speakers in these kinds of ads use to position themselves with respect to their audience. For example, do they ask questions, make statements, or issue commands? What other linguistic techniques do they use to appeal to their target audience? How do they use images, movement, color, music, sound effects, or even font styles together with spoken or written language? Which elements could be removed without making the ad unrecognizable as a political campaign advertisement?

Other approaches to discourse analysis tend to strongly favor either a quantitative or a qualitative approach. For example, researchers in **corpus linguistics** use computer programs to mark and search for language features and patterns in collections of texts compiled for research purposes. One of the most important advantages of using corpus tools is that they allow researchers to systematically identify patterns in the use of particular words, combinations of words, or grammatical features across very large samples. Researchers can then conduct statistical analyses that allow them to make strong claims about the characteristics of the text types that have been included in the corpus and predict what other texts of these types will be like. Because the main advantages of this approach relate to the generalizability of the findings that they generate, corpus approaches to discourse analysis tend to emphasize quantitative analysis.

Conversation analysis (often referred to by the initials "CA") is much more likely to use a qualitative approach. Conversation analysis uses a highly detailed set of conventions for transcribing features of spoken language, including characteristics ranging from pauses and intonation to whispering and even the distinct sound of someone's voice when they're smiling. The finished transcript provides enough detail that a reader can almost hear the sounds of the original conversation, much like a musician reading sheet music. Because transcribing speech in this way is labor intensive and requires specialized training, it is difficult to use for large data sets. More importantly, though, conversation analysts are interested in the way in which spoken language is organized and how speakers build an interaction together. This means that conversation analysts are less likely to be interested in statistically measurable relationships between variables and more interested in understanding and interpreting how particular types of interactions unfold.

Evaluating Quantitative and Qualitative Studies

Understanding the different goals of analysis in quantitative and qualitative research has important implications for evaluating studies. As you read more and more research articles in applied linguistics, you'll need to examine studies critically in order to decide how to interpret their findings. How do you know when you can trust a study's findings? Because the goals and methods of quantitative and qualitative research are different, researchers using one or the other approach would answer this question differently. In a quantitative study, researchers typically take steps to ensure that their selection of participants or texts is done in a systematic and replicable way. Because quantitative researchers are interested in generalizability, or being able to apply the findings based on a study of a sample group to a broader population, they take steps to ensure that their data samples accurately reflect the broader population that they are interested in. They also use methods to avoid bias in selecting specific samples to include in their data set. In addition, quantitative researchers generally use large numbers of texts or participants in order to reduce the chance that their findings might be skewed by having an unusual sample. These steps, as well as other aspects of quantitative research design, help ensure that the study is measuring what it is designed to measure (referred to as the study's **validity**) and that it generates consistent results (**reliability**).

In qualitative research, however, an unusual case might be exactly what the researcher is interested in. Rather than using large sample sizes or a randomized selection of samples, qualitative researchers use other tools to ensure that their analysis is systematic, rigorous, and balanced. In a qualitative case study focusing on a single student, for example, the researcher could combine interviews with the student, an analysis of the student's writing, and classroom observations to develop a fuller picture of the student's experience. This approach uses multiple kinds of data or analysis to look at the same thing and is referred to as **triangulation**. Triangulation is one tool that qualitative researchers use to check their interpretation. Because qualitative research often examines smaller data sets or numbers of participants in greater detail, triangulation can help researchers balance their own perspective by checking whether looking at the same phenomenon from multiple angles offers a different picture of what's happening. In writing up their findings, qualitative researchers also often include any examples that don't fit the overall patterns in the data set. Rather than undermining the researcher's findings, this practice helps to show that the researcher has reviewed the data thoroughly and is honest about the limitations of their findings. Since data collected in real-life settings is messy, a study that doesn't explicitly address how difficult cases were dealt with should raise readers' suspicions about the author's findings. If all of the findings seem clear-cut and straightforward, the analysis may be not be taking important counterevidence into account.

Even if a qualitative researcher is only looking at one type of data source, as is often the case with discourse analysis, there are other tools for ensuring that the researcher's analysis provides an accurate picture of what's happening. Gee (2014), for example, offers four criteria for researchers to use in evaluating their own qualitative discourse analysis: convergence, agreement, coverage, and linguistic details. These criteria can be framed as a series of questions:

- *Convergence*: Does looking at the text through different lenses seem to offer the same overall representation?

- *Agreement*: Do participants or other researchers recognize this representation as valid?
- *Coverage*: Does this representation account for other similar texts and predict what they will be like?
- *Linguistic details*: Has this representation been connected to clear linguistic evidence in the text?

Likewise, when reading qualitative discourse analysis studies, it can be useful to keep these questions in mind. Does the author provide any evidence or make any statements that suggest that they have considered questions like these? If not, try applying these questions to the study yourself.

Making Choices in Research Design

The table below summarizes some of the choices that researchers think about when designing a study in applied linguistics. The researcher will need to start by thinking about whether their main focus is on language itself or the context of language use. From there, they will start to think about what kinds of data will answer the research questions they're interested in and how to gather and analyze these data. The examples in Table 2.1 offer some typical data types and orientations to analysis associated with different areas of the continuum, but it's important to note that these are tendencies rather than strict divisions. As you'll remember from the discussion of questionnaires using Likert scales above, for example, data collected through these kinds of questionnaires are typically analyzed using quantitative

Table 2.1 Connecting the language–context continuum to choices about research

Place on continuum	Examples of typical data gathered	Typical orientation to analysis
Language as object	Elicited speech	Quantitative
	Experimental measures (reading times, reaction times, measurement of brain activity)	
	Test scores	
Middle of continuum	Longer texts	Qualitative or Mixed Methods
	Video and audio recordings of interactions	
Context of language use	Questionnaires (Likert scale or open-ended)	Qualitative
	Interviews	
	Observation	
	Multimodal texts	

rather than qualitative means despite the fact that research that uses them tends to focus more on the context of language use.

In the topics addressed in each chapter in Part B of this book, you will see a range of different approaches to research. At the end of many chapters, you will also be presented with samples of data for both research and applied projects. On the website accompanying this book, you will find an activity that will help you become more aware of the choices that the authors of those chapters have made in their work. Becoming more aware of the choices that researchers make can help you better understand studies that you read about in research articles as well as guide your own decision-making process as you conduct your own research. If you go on to take further coursework in applied linguistics, and possibly even in the course you are taking now, you are likely to conduct small-scale studies of your own for course projects. In these course projects, the topic of your study may be pre-determined by the focus of the course itself, and other choices for your research design may also be constrained by the assignment instructions. In other course projects or if you go on to write a thesis, you will have a much greater degree of freedom in choosing what to investigate and how to investigate it. In this case, you may take additional coursework or do additional reading to learn more about different data types, data collection methods, and approaches to analysis, as well as research ethics and other important considerations for research design. You will also come across many concrete examples of research designs in the research articles that you read. In creating your own study, you will be faced with decisions that reflect not just the choices described in this chapter, but also a particular approach to language, as you saw in the previous chapter.

Discussion Questions

1. Take a look at the examples of possible studies of classroom language learning in the language–context continuum section of this chapter. What approaches to language from Chapter 1 does each of these studies reflect? How would you describe the relationship between the kinds of data collected in each of these studies and the approach to language that the researcher uses?
2. After reading the descriptions of quantitative and qualitative research above, what do you think the disadvantages of each approach might be?
3. Think of a topic that you are interested in. If you have trouble thinking of a topic, you can use the table of contents of this book to get some ideas. Using an academic database, identify three or four research articles that address this topic from an applied linguistics perspective. Linguistics and Language Behavior Abstracts (LLBA) is one popular database in applied linguistics,

and your professor will be able to recommend other similar databases. Read the abstract for each of these articles. Based on the descriptions in each abstract, answer the following questions. You may also need to skim the article to find some of this information.

a. What approach or approaches to language do the authors seem to be taking? (Review Chapter 1)

b. What kinds of data are being collected and where do they fit on the language–context continuum?

c. How were data gathered?

d. Do the authors seem to be using a quantitative, qualitative, or mixed methods approach to analysis? How can you tell?

FURTHER READING

Dörnyei, Z. (2007). *Research methods in applied linguistics: Quantitative, qualitative, and mixed methodologies.* Oxford: Oxford University Press.

Larson-Hall, J. (2016). *A guide to doing statistics in second language research using SPSS and R* (2nd edn). New York: Routledge.

Mackey, A., & Gass, S. M. (2016). *Second language research: Methodology and design* (2nd edn). New York: Routledge.

McKinley, J., & Rose, H. (2017). *Doing research in applied linguistics: Realities, dilemmas, and solutions.* London: Routledge.

Perry, F. L. (2017). *Research in applied linguistics: Becoming a discerning consumer* (3rd edn). New York: Routledge.

Richards, K. (2003). *Qualitative inquiry in TESOL.* Basingstoke, UK: Palgrave Macmillan.

REFERENCES

Crossley, S. A., Kyle, K., & McNamara, D. S. (2016). The development and use of cohesive devices in L2 writing and their relations to judgments of essay quality. *Journal of Second Language Writing, 32*, 1–16. https://doi.org/10.1016/j.jslw.2016.01.003

Gee, J. P. (2014). *How to do discourse analysis: A toolkit.* New York: Routledge.

Geertz, C. (1973). Thick description: Toward an interpretive theory of culture. In *The interpretation of cultures* (pp. 3–30). New York: Basic Books.

Goodwin, C. (2004). A competent speaker who can't speak: The social life of aphasia. *Journal of Linguistic Anthropology, 14*(2), 151–170. https://doi.org/10.1525/jlin.2004.14.2.151

Grue, J. (2015). *Disability and discourse analysis.* Farnham, UK: Ashgate.

Hellerman, J. (2008). *Social actions for classroom learning.* Bristol: Multilingual Matters.

Kanno, Y., & Kangas, S. E. N. (2014). "I'm not going to be, like, for the AP": English language learners' limited access to advanced college-preparatory courses in high school. *American Educational Research Journal, 51*(5), 848–878. https://doi.org/10.3102/0002831214544716

Levi, J. N. (1993). Evaluating jury comprehension of Illinois capital-sentencing instructions. *American Speech, 68*(1), 20–49. https://doi.org/10.2307/455834

Nickels, S., & Steinhauer, K. (2018). Prosody-syntax integration in a second language: Contrasting event-related potentials from German and Chinese learners of English using linear mixed effect models. *Second Language Research, 34*(1), 9–37. https://doi.org/10.1177/0267658316649998

Santa Ana, O. (1999). "Like an animal I was treated": Anti-immigrant metaphor in US public discourse. *Discourse & Society, 10*(2), 191–224. https://doi.org/10.1177/0957926599010002004

Yamaguchi, T., & Pétursson, M. (2018). Japanese English: Norm-dependency and emerging strategies. *English Today, 34*(2), 17–24. https://doi.org/10.1017/S0266078417000359

You, C. J., & Dörnyei, Z. (2016). Language learning motivation in China: Results of a large-scale stratified survey. *Applied Linguistics, 37*(4), 495–519. https://doi.org/10.1093/applin/amu046

Zhang, Y., & O'Halloran, K. L. (2012). The gate of the gateway: A hypermodal approach to university homepages. *Semiotica, 190*, 87–109. https://doi.org/10.1515/sem-2012-0041

PART B
Major Areas of Focus within the Field of Applied Linguistics

SECTION 1:
Language Acquisition

3 Second Language Acquisition and the Teaching of Pragmatics

LYNN SANTELMANN AND TETYANA SYDORENKO

Overview of Key Concepts and Issues in Second Language Acquisition

You step into a language classroom as the teacher. You have been teaching this class of adult students for six months. You greet the students and begin class. What kinds of activities do the students do in class: extensive reading, listening, and responding to the teacher, scripted conversations, or information exchange activities? When planning your lessons, do you plan specific, explicit instruction on grammar or vocabulary, or are the structures and vocabulary presented implicitly in context only? When the students make a mistake, as they inevitably will, did this error come from their first language or somewhere else? How do you motivate students or encourage quiet students to use the language? These are just some of the questions that language teachers face every day.

Research in **second language acquisition** (SLA) has examined both the kinds of questions that language teachers face and the basic issues about the nature of second language learning. The overview of key concepts in the first part of this chapter (written by Lynn Santelmann) will give a summary of how several major topics in SLA research have been addressed in recent years. This overview is intended to give you a sense of the important concepts in SLA and how researchers approach studying them, rather than being a comprehensive review of the field. Building on one of the approaches mentioned in the overview, the second half of the chapter (written by Tetyana Sydorenko) will discuss an example project that explores how second language learners ask for letters of recommendation.

What Do Learners Bring to the Task of Learning Language?
Prior Knowledge and Ability to Create Systematic Language from Input When someone learns another language (**second language** or L2), the task is different from learning a first language (L1) because the learner has already acquired at least one language that they can use to communicate. Every second language learner or teacher has experienced **transfer**, where structures or words from the L1 appear in the L2. For example, when Lynn taught German, her beginning German students

struggled to use the German pronunciations of the sound *r* and not the American English one.

However, learners bring more than knowledge of their L1 to language learning. Learners create structures, both target-like and non-target-like, based on the **input** (i.e., what learners see and hear in the L2). Some of these structures cannot be explained either by the structure of the L1 or the L2. To explain this phenomenon, Selinker (1972) posited that learners develop an **interlanguage**, or a grammar that is between the grammars of a learner's first language and the target language. This interlanguage, though not target-like, is systematic, and it changes over time. For example, beginning Spanish-speaking learners of English may consistently omit pronoun subjects, producing sentences like *came home yesterday* or *is raining*. This omission of subject pronouns is transferred from Spanish and is not grammatical in English. Later in their development these learners may learn that English requires personal pronouns and produce sentences such as *We came home yesterday*. However, they may still omit dummy pronouns as in *it is raining*, saying instead *is raining*. Including personal pronouns but omitting dummy pronouns is systematic, but this system is neither the Spanish nor the English system. Viewing learners' language as an interlanguage allows researchers and teachers to focus on more than just the errors learners make and to examine the system that learners construct as they learn language.

Research in SLA has examined the origins of learners' systems in several ways. One approach explores the idea that learners bring innate knowledge to the task of language learning. For example, **generative grammar** approaches to SLA have argued that learners create rules from the input and apply universal, innate principles to the task of SLA. For example, White and Juffs (1998) examined how Mandarin learners of English judged and produced wh-questions where the question word had been extracted from a subordinate clause, some of which were grammatical, and some of which were ungrammatical. In the first example below, the wh-word has been grammatically extracted from the subordinate clause. In the second, it has been ungrammatically extracted from the relative clause.

1. What did you believe [the children saw at the party __]?
2. *What did you believe [the claim the children saw __]?

Generative grammar accounts of these sentences argue that there are universal movement principles that specify when wh-word movement is possible. Since Mandarin does not have any wh-movement, Mandarin learners of English cannot have learned these rules through their L1. Additionally, because some of these test sentences are ungrammatical, it is unlikely learners would have encountered them in the input. Thus, White and Juffs argued, if Mandarin learners of English demonstrate that they can differentiate grammatical from ungrammatical wh-movement, this knowledge must come from universal, innate grammar principles. Their results indicated that Mandarin learners of English distinguished grammatical from ungrammatical wh-movement in both comprehension and production.

Other approaches to SLA reject the idea of innate language principles and focus instead on the information available in the input for the learner, and learners' general abilities to find patterns based on frequency and saliency. For example, **usage-based approaches** to SLA posit a central role for **constructions**, or form-meaning pairs, that are used for communicative purposes. Constructions range from concrete to abstract. Usage-based views of SLA argue that language development starts from use in a specific context, and generally progresses from concrete to abstract. Concrete constructions are formed and stored when the learner frequently receives tokens, or individual examples, of a construction in the input. For example, phrases such as *I don't know*, or *Can I help you?* might be stored as whole chunks. On the other hand, transitive verb constructions (e.g., *The dog ate a cookie*) appear with a variety of subjects, verbs, and objects, and thus might eventually be stored as abstract construction such as [Subject–Verb–Object].

An example of a study that took a usage-based approach can be found with Hall, Joyce, and Robson (2017). They examined the use of the constructions *Can you + verb* and *Could you + verb* in email requests produced by a highly proficient L2 speaker of English. This English user, Antonio, worked as a manager for a multinational corporation in South Africa, and his email correspondence included a wide variety of English users: some had English as their L1, others had English as an additional language. Hall et al. found that Antonio used *Can you + verb* significantly more frequently than would be expected for the genre, based on analysis of linguistic corpora (large collections of text/spoken language). They also found that the construction *Can you assist* was particularly common in the input he received, and was also used disproportionately in his output. They suggest that Antonio's frequent use of *Can you + verb* resulted from the frequency of this construction in his input, his individual learning context, including the semantics of his L1 (Italian), and his current context of use.

Individual Differences   In addition to the ability to use prior knowledge and learn from input, students of a second language bring other individual characteristics with them which will affect their language learning. These characteristics include individual abilities or skills such as intelligence, memory, language aptitude, and literacy; individual traits such as age, motivation, personality (risk-taking, willingness to communicate), identity, anxiety, and learning styles; and individual beliefs and strategies for learning language (e.g., Ellis, 2004).

Research in this area has suggested that many of these **individual differences** result from a combination of influences from the learners, teachers, and the larger society. For example, Lasagabaster (2017) examined students' **attitudes** and **motivations** to learn the Spanish regional minority languages Catalan, Galician or Basque, as well as the international language English. This study found that the majority of the population living in multilingual areas of Spain value bilingualism in Spanish and the regional minority language, as well as multilingualism that includes English. However, many immigrant students hold more favorable attitudes toward Spanish and English than to the regional languages. Nevertheless, when students (both immigrant and domestic) experience minority languages as positive (primarily through immersion programs and social interaction), they are more likely to view them favorably. Overall, Lasagabaster concluded that the regional multilingual language policies have had a positive effect on students' attitudes and motivations to learn multiple languages.

What Do Students Need to Learn a Second Language?

Input, Output, and Interaction   One obvious requirement for learning another language is experiencing the language. This experience, or input, can be anything from teacher's oral directions to reading texts to audio/visual media. For many years, SLA researchers and language teachers were concerned with input because teachers can control input and they believed that input in the L2 was a way to avoid **negative transfer** from the first language (i.e., applying rules from the first language to the L2, resulting in inaccuracies in the L2). Initially, some argued that comprehensible input was all that students needed to acquire a second language (Krashen, 1985).

Subsequent research revealed, however, that while input is clearly necessary for language learning, it is often not sufficient. For example, Swain (1985) noted that Canadian students in French immersion programs received considerable input, but had fewer opportunities for **output**, and they fell short in their acquisition of French. This result led Swain to hypothesize that output is necessary for language acquisition because it requires the learner to analyze the language and notice gaps between their own production and the input.

Long (1981) combined these ideas of input and output and argued that acquisition is driven by the combination of the two. Specifically, he proposed a strong role for **interaction**, especially at points when the conversation breaks down and the learner and their interlocutor must negotiate meaning in order to achieve understanding. These communication breakdowns drive language acquisition in two ways: first, they require the interlocutor to modify their input to make it more comprehensible to the learner; second, they require the learner to notice the gaps between their own language production and the input and to try out new ways of making themselves understood. Thus, this combination of modified input, noticing, and modified output leads to learning.

Instruction   **Instruction** is another important factor in SLA. Research has demonstrated that instructed learners develop faster than learners who acquire the language outside the classroom. Communicative language teaching (currently a very widely used approach) focuses on providing students with authentic situations in which to use the language and helping students acquire communicative functions in the new language. One question that arises, then, is how much explicit instruction or focus on forms should take place in the language classroom. Some language classrooms present structures only implicitly through context, while others present them explicitly, either in context or out of context. For example, in **implicit instruction**, learners might receive a variety of examples where *please* is used in context and would be asked to find rules or patterns for using *please*. In **explicit instruction**, these rules or patterns would be provided to the learners, followed by examples and then likely some practice. Research has shown that instruction on forms that is out of context is the least helpful in terms of acquisition. In context, both explicit and implicit instruction can help students become more target-like in their language use, but implicit instruction may not be as efficient as explicit instruction (Norris & Ortega, 2000).

Instruction most likely helps students in several different ways. First, it can focus learners' **attention** on forms that the learners might overlook when focusing on meaning in communication (Ellis, 2016). This focus can help learners link the form with the function or meaning in the language. For example, *I was wondering if you could...* is a polite way to make a request in English and can be used with someone who is your superior. The phrase *I want you to...*, on the other hand, is not a polite way of requesting, especially for someone who is a superior. However, learners of English sometimes make requests of professors using *I want you to ...* because they have not noticed that polite request forms often use an indirect question (*if you...*) with a modal verb (*could*). Formal instruction can focus learners' attention on the link between the form and its implications for pragmatics, as explained further below.

In addition to focusing attention, teachers can provide important **scaffolding**, or support, for students to help them move into independent understanding and use of the language. Van Compernolle and Kinginger (2013) demonstrate the importance of interaction, explicit instruction, and scaffolding by teachers. This case study used a sociocultural theory framework to examine metapragmatic awareness of the factors involved in choosing between the informal *tu* and the formal *vous* pronoun in French. Through prompts from the instructor and the use of materials designed to illustrate the factors involved in making the *tu/vous* distinction, the student came to recognize that multiple social factors must be taken into account when choosing a pronoun in French. She moved from thinking about the *tu/vous* distinction in purely self-representational terms (*do I wish to sound casual or formal?*) to understanding that the choice of pronoun could also indicate social distance and power relationships.

To summarize, SLA is a complex task that is affected by prior knowledge, learning abilities, individual characteristics, learning environment, opportunities for interaction, and instruction. Research in this area is conducted by scholars in many disciplines, including applied linguistics, psychology, and language. To provide an example, the second half of this chapter introduces a study by Tetyana Sydorenko looking at how learners of English make requests. As you read about this study, consider how individual learning abilities, individual background and characteristics, input and interaction, and type of instruction are exemplified in this study.

Our Work in Second Language Acquisition and the Teaching of Pragmatics

Personal Reflections

Lynn Santelmann   My interests in the field of SLA come from several aspects of my background. Since childhood, I have been fascinated by learning other languages. I can remember lying on the living room floor listening to "How to speak French" records that my French-teacher aunt had given me. My undergraduate major, after brief forays into engineering and biology, was in German, specifically focused on German linguistics. My subsequent graduate training focused on first language acquisition, linguistic theory, and cognitive science. While my interest in theory and language has remained, in recent years, my interests have broadened to the question of how people learn the language they need for the situations they find themselves in – that could be a new language in a new country or a new way to use the language they grew up speaking. This interest has developed because I work at a university with a large number of first-generation college students. These students often come to college with weak knowledge of how to use academic language and vocabulary, despite their obvious intelligence. The questions that inspire me are questions such as what is the link between learning content and language? How can we create a theory of language learning that includes first languages, second languages, and different registers?

Tetyana Sydorenko   Although I have several interests within the field of SLA, teaching and learning of L2 pragmatics has been my focus in the last several years. My own challenges with learning L2 pragmatics have prompted me to investigate how to best help learners acquire this aspect of linguistic competence. As a non-native speaker of English, I had to learn first-hand how to navigate cross-cultural communication appropriately. A personal story that I frequently tell in my pragmatics course is how I was offered food upon my arrival to the United States. I declined the first offer (because that is what a polite person does in Ukraine); to my surprise, I was not offered food immediately afterwards the second time, so I remained hungry (though not for a long time). The consequence of this cross-cultural misunderstanding was not grave, but it was unpleasant. This experience has influenced my current work where I give language learners a chance to practice actions with serious consequences before they are ready to implement those actions in the real world. Because I prefer to learn through multimodal input and I am especially interested in how learners notice language features, I wanted to use multimodal input to help learners become more aware of pragmatic features and practice actions with potentially serious consequences using computer-simulated conversations.

Tetyana Sydorenko's Work in Second Language Pragmatics: Learning Requests Through *SimCon*

Background on Teaching and Learning L2 Pragmatics   Before we go into the *SimCon* program itself, this section provides some useful background on what pragmatics is and what is known about its teaching and learning. Although **pragmatics** has an abundance of definitions, Crystal's (1997) definition of the term is most often cited:

> Pragmatics is the study of language from the point of view of users, especially of the choices they make, the constraints they encounter in using language in social interaction and the effects their use of language has on other participants in the act of communication. (p. 301)

For example, in many US academic contexts it may be **pragmatically appropriate** to address a classmate, but not an instructor, with "What's up, dude?" However, such generalities will be necessarily affected by relationships between individuals, among other things. Pragmatics encompasses various aspects of language in use, including literal versus intended meaning, level of formality, politeness, production, and comprehension of **speech acts**, and more (Timpe-Laughlin, Wain, & Schmidgall, 2015). In the project described in this chapter, the focus was on production of speech acts. Speech acts are actions like requests, apologies, greetings, compliments, and so on that are performed when one utters words that signify such actions (e.g., *I am sorry* signifies an apology).

While the knowledge of pragmatics in the L1, which most of us take for granted, is gained through socialization in a given community (Li, 2017), learning **L2 pragmatics** can be much more challenging. Some aspects of L2 pragmatics can be "figured out" by learners in various ways, including via **positive transfer** from their L1 (e.g., Kasper, 1997) and interactions with target language speakers (e.g., Sydorenko & Tuason, 2016). However, certain elements of L2 pragmatics benefit from instruction (e.g., Bardovi-Harlig, 2001; Jeon & Kaya, 2006; Kasper & Rose, 2002). For example, Bardovi-Harlig, Mossman, & Su's (2017) study, listed in the Further Reading section, illustrates how pragmatic routines – a type of formulaic expression – can be taught to improve **pragmatic competence** (i.e., the knowledge of how to use language in order to achieve a particular goal during interaction in a specific sociocultural context, cf. Kasper, 1997). There is overall agreement among scholars on the necessary components of **pragmatic instruction**: provision of authentic input, awareness-raising, communicative practice, and feedback (cf. Cohen, 2005; Martínez-Flor & Usó-Juan, 2006). There are likewise numerous exciting ideas for approaching these components of pragmatic instruction with technology, such as websites with interactive activities, games, or virtual environments (e.g., Sykes, 2018). However, from a technological point of view, communicative practice of pragmatics remains most challenging.

Without technology, communicative practice of pragmatics can be accomplished via learner–learner role plays or learner–target language speaker interactions. Such environments, while fruitful in many circumstances, can be unproductive in others – for example, learners do not always accurately represent pragmatic notions when acting out their parts during role plays (e.g., Sydorenko, 2015), and target language speakers may not be willing to offer crucial feedback (Kasper, 1997). Some learners may also be apprehensive of or lack access to expert speakers (e.g., Barron, 2003; Duff, 2007; Sykes, Oskoz, & Thorne, 2008). For this reason, recent efforts have concentrated on the development of simulated and gamified environments for learning **L2 pragmatics**. These branch out into (1) environments where users produce textual or "select option" output (e.g., Sykes, 2013) and (2) **simulations** that require users' oral output. The project described below focuses on the latter.

Spoken dialogue systems (SDS) are the most common example of technology that allows for simulated oral pragmatics practice. SDS include automated speech recognition and natural language processing, which makes it possible for learners to have a customized dialogue with a virtual conversational agent: a dialogue that changes based on the learner's output. For example, learners can practice buying a train ticket, ordering coffee, or talking to their boss (see Sydorenko, Daurio, & Thorne, 2018 for a more detailed review of existing SDS). However, the biggest challenge with SDS is speech recognition errors, which are especially high with non-native accents. To overcome this issue, a simulated conversation program called SimCon was developed by computer science students at Portland State University. The next section describes how this program works.

Description of *SimCon*   In this program, learners complete **simulated conversations** on a particular topic within a restricted domain, such as making a certain request to an instructor. Each simulation begins with a scenario description that includes details such as what the request is for, the surrounding contextual and situation factors, the instructor's name, etc. Next, learners watch a video that begins the simulation. This could be a video of an instructor greeting the student, an instructor working in their office, or other similar "conversation starters." After watching the video, participants audio-record their response to it. On the next screen, learners select one of the options

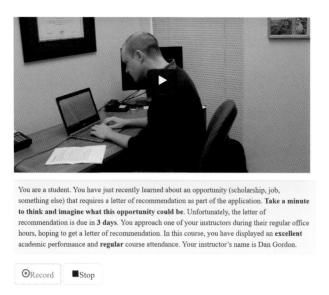

You are a student. You have just recently learned about an opportunity (scholarship, job, something else) that requires a letter of recommendation as part of the application. **Take a minute to think and imagine what this opportunity could be.** Unfortunately, the letter of recommendation is due in **3 days.** You approach one of your instructors during their regular office hours, hoping to get a letter of recommendation. In this course, you have displayed an **excellent** academic performance and **regular** course attendance. Your instructor's name is Dan Gordon.

⊙Record   ■Stop

Figure 3.1 Screenshot of video 1 in a specific *SimCon* simulation

in the list that best describes the action they completed via their spoken response, such as "I greeted my instructor." Each selection leads to a different subsequent video, which allows learners to experience different versions of the conversation based on their responses. Learners continue with the same sequencing of video watching – response recording – action selection until they reach the end of the conversation.

To better visualize what this process looks like for a particular simulation, examine Figure 3.1. The figure shows what the participants see when they begin the simulation involving a request for a letter of recommendation due in three days.

Once the learners read the scenario and watch the video, they record their spoken response. For example, after watching video 1 of this simulation, one of the participants said "Hi Dan. Can I come inside?" On the next screen (see Figure 3.2), the participant who made the aforementioned response should select "You greet the instructor and ask if you can come in."

If this selection is made, the participant would next see the video of the instructor who says "Yeah, definitely. What can I do for you?" Of particular pedagogical importance is the fact that the student receives implicit pragmatic feedback at each step because the response option the student chooses determines which video the student sees next. For example, the instructor indirectly declines to write a letter after the initial request; however, if a student chooses to reformulate their request, the instructor tentatively agrees to write the letter but warns that three days is generally not enough notice to write a thorough letter.

Research Study on Learning L2 Pragmatics via SimCon   Sydorenko et al. (2018) studied how much and what kind of learning took place via *SimCon*. After reading a

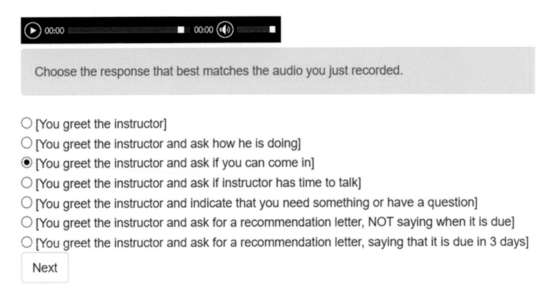

Figure 3.2 Screenshot of the response options after video 1 in a specific *SimCon* simulation

brief description of this study below, you will have an opportunity to practice analyzing such data.

Twelve learners of English, all Fulbright scholars in the United States from ten different countries and all with advanced levels of proficiency, completed six simulated conversations – as detailed below. All simulations focused on the request for a letter of recommendation from an instructor, but simulations 1 and 2 differed in the timing of the request (letter due in three days or one week, henceforth referred to as Three Days Simulation and One Week Simulation) and the student's course performance (average or excellent). The request scenarios in simulations 3 and 4 were the same as in 1 and 2; however, participants played instructor roles. By reversing the roles, we provided participants with model videos of native-speaking students responding to the same situations. Simulations 5 and 6 were identical to 1 and 2, allowing participants to respond as students again after having witnessed the models. Participants could thus theoretically incorporate information from model student responses from simulations 3 and 4 in their subsequent production in simulations 5 and 6.

In this study, learning was possible via the following mechanisms. First, participants could practice their responses as students to an instructor in a particular situation twice: such practice alone, without any feedback, can lead to improvements in fluency, accuracy, and complexity of oral production (see Ellis, 2009). Second, as described above, learners could then observe target-like input in models and incorporate such input into their own production. The benefits of such noticing are outlined in the Interaction Approach to SLA (see Gass & Mackey, 2015). Third, feedback in the form of consequences from videos linked to their responses and ideas for possible next actions could prompt learners to reformulate their second attempts at each simulation (i.e., simulations 5 and 6).

When analyzing the results, we compared learners' oral production data from simulations 1 and 2 (pre-test) with those from 5 and 6 (post-test) and looked for changes learners made. In doing so, we followed a microgenetic approach to data analysis (i.e., examination of changes over a short period of time).

A brief summary of the results is as follows:

- Most learners became more pragmatically appropriate.
- Learners made changes in content and language. Content changes were the use of different strategies, such as asking for the letter right away versus beginning with some small talk, or conceptually different explanations for the request. Linguistic changes were those where the initial content/idea expressed by the learner did not change, but the language used to convey that idea was different. For example, initially a learner may have made their request with "Could you write me a letter of recommendation?" while in the second attempt they may have used a more indirect expression from the model "I was wondering if you could write me a letter?" As shown by Taguchi (2011), both the content of the message and the language can have an effect on how individuals judge pragmatic appropriateness of speech acts).
- Learners made more content than linguistic changes.
- Most changes were based on the models; we called these "model changes." We further categorized these into model linguistic changes and model content changes. However, a portion of changes did not resemble input from the models; rather, they were based on learners' own repertoire of pragmatic strategies and linguistic expressions; these were called "personal content changes" and "personal linguistic changes." An example of a personal linguistic change is when one participant's initial explanation was "the scholarship unfortunately is really important for you – me," while on the second attempt this explanation was changed to "it's very crucial for me." We coded this as a personal linguistic change: the change did not resemble the specific language in the models and the content, or the gist, of the message did not change between the first and the second attempt.

The study's conclusion was that such simulations are useful for developing pragmatic competence because learners made a number of appropriate changes. However, several considerations and improvements are in order. You will be asked to entertain these considerations in the analysis task introduced below.

Data Analysis Activity

In the analysis task on the website accompanying this book, you will be asked to analyze the data from two learners for the changes that they made between the initial and the subsequent simulation. You will code the changes into linguistics vs. content and personal vs. model changes. Additionally, you will be asked to examine the data from a third participant and decide if this learner's data pattern is similar to or differently from the other learners. The website contains detailed instructions, several data files, a table for you to download, and transcripts and links to the model videos that the student participants saw.

Going Further

For students who want to become involved in second language acquisition, including second language pragmatics, we suggest taking the following courses: second language acquisition, pragmatics, discourse analysis, sociolinguistics. Spending time in a different language and culture is also helpful: in such an environment, you are likely to face some linguistic challenges and experience pragmatic mishaps that will shed light on difficulties L2 learners experience. Study abroad is one obvious way to spend time in a different language and culture. But, even if you are unable to travel abroad, you can spend time learning the language of an immigrant group in your area, and interacting with members of that community.

Discussion Questions

1. Think about your own second language learning experience(s). What kind of instruction did you receive? How did the courses or your experiences incorporate (or not incorporate) interaction into the learning experience? How did your own individual background and abilities affect your learning? How did your motivation or attitude affect your learning or willingness to learn?

2. In the study presented here, where do you see input, output, and interaction being used? Which of these three do you think *SimCon* uses the most? Which the least? Explain your answer.

3. What kind of instruction does the *SimCon* program use, implicit or explicit?

4. How does *SimCon* provide scaffolding (guide students to produce modified output) for learners of English?

5. The study was conducted with very advanced and motivated learners who were about to begin their master's and doctoral degrees in the United States. How effective were these simulations for this set of learners? How effective might such simulations be for less advanced learners? Would you suggest any

additional features or resources that can be added to supplement the existing simulations to maximize their benefits?

6. What other individual differences (skills, characteristics, beliefs) might learners bring to the task of making requests that could have affected their performance while using *SimCon*? List at least three and discuss how each difference might affect their language use.

7. With your classmates, have two people role play making a polite request in a different situation (e.g., asking a friend to come feed your cat while you're on vacation, or requesting time off from work). Do the role play once trying to be polite and once trying to be impolite. Have other students note what content was expressed and what linguistic forms were used in each situation. Then discuss which of those forms and which content you would choose to teach a language learner, and how you would go about teaching it.

FURTHER READING

Foundational Readings

Bardovi-Harlig, K. (2017). Acquisition of L2 pragmatics. In S. Loewen & M. Sato (Eds.) *The Routledge handbook of instructed second language acquisition* (pp. 224–245). New York: Routledge.

Taguchi, N., & Roever, C. (2017). *Second language pragmatics.* Oxford: Oxford University Press. (In particular, we suggest chapters 1 and 8 in this book.)

VanPatten, B., & Williams, J. (2015). *Theories in second language acquisition: An introduction.* Mahwah, NJ: Lawrence Erlbaum.

Recent Publications

Bardovi-Harlig, K., Mossman, S., & Su, Y. (2017). The effect of corpus-based instruction on pragmatic routines. *Language Learning & Technology*, *21*(3), 76–103.

Sykes, J. M. (2018). Interlanguage pragmatics, curricular innovation, and digital technologies. *CALICO Journal*, *35*(2), 120–141.

Taguchi, N. (2018). Contexts and pragmatics learning: Problems and opportunities of the study abroad research. *Language Teaching*, *51*, 124–137.

REFERENCES

Bardovi-Harlig, K. (2001). Evaluating the empirical evidence: Grounds for instruction in pragmatics? In K. Rose & G. Kasper (Eds.), *Pragmatics in language teaching* (pp. 13–32). Cambridge: Cambridge University Press.

Barron, A. (2003). *Acquisition in interlanguage pragmatics: Learning how to do things with words in a study abroad context.* Amsterdam: John Benjamins.

Cohen, A. (2005). Strategies for learning and performing L2 speech acts. *Intercultural Pragmatics, 2,* 275–301.

Crystal, D. (1997). *English as a global language.* Cambridge: Cambridge University Press.

Duff, P. A. (2007). Second language socialization as sociocultural theory: Insights and issues. *Language Teaching, 40*(4), 309–319.

Ellis, R. (2004). Individual differences in second language acquisition. In A. Davies & C. Elder (Eds.), *The handbook of applied linguistics* (pp. 525–551). Malden, MA: Blackwell.

(2009). The differential effects of three types of task planning on the fluency, complexity, and accuracy in L2 oral production. *Applied Linguistics, 30*(4), 474–509.

(2016). Focus on form: A critical review. *Language Teaching Research, 20*(3), 405–428.

Gass, S., & Mackey, A. (2015). Input, interaction, and output in SLA. In B. VanPatten & J. Williams (Eds.), *Theories in second language acquisition: An introduction* (2nd edn) (pp. 180–206). New York: Routledge.

Hall, C. J., Joyce, J., & Robson, C. (2017). Investigating the lexico-grammatical resources of a non-native user of English: The case of can and could in email requests. *Applied Linguistics Review, 8*(1), 35–59. https://doi.org/10.1515/applirev-2016-1001

Jeon, E. H., & Kaya, T. (2006). Effects of L2 instruction on interlanguage pragmatic development. In J. M. Norris & L. Ortega (Eds.), *Synthesizing research on language learning and teaching* (pp. 165–211). Amsterdam: John Benjamins.

Kasper, G. (1997). Can pragmatic competence be taught? NetWork, 6, 105–119. Retrieved from http://nflrc.hawaii.edu/NetWorks/NW06/

Kasper, G. & Rose, K. (2002). *Pragmatics in a Second Language.* Oxford: Blackwell.

Krashen, S. D. (1985). *The input hypothesis – issues and implications.* New York: Longman.

Lasagabaster, D. (2017). Language learning motivation and language attitudes in multilingual Spain from an international perspective. *The Modern Language Journal, 101*(3), 583–596.

Li, D. (2017). Pragmatic socialization. In P. A. Duff & S. May (Eds.), *Language socialization* (pp. 1–14). New York: Springer.

Long, M. H. (1981). Input, interaction, and second-language acquisition. *Annals of the New York Academy of Sciences, 379*(1), 259–278.

Martínez-Flor, A., & Usó-Juan, E. (2006). A comprehensive pedagogical framework to develop pragmatics in the foreign language classroom: The 6Rs approach. *Applied Language Learning, 16*(2), 39–64.

Norris, J. M., & Ortega, L. (2000). Effectiveness of L2 instruction: A research synthesis and quantitative meta-analysis. *Language Learning, 50*(3), 417–528.

Selinker, L. (1972). Interlanguage. *IRAL: International Review of Applied Linguistics in Language Teaching, 10,* 209–241.

Swain, M. (1985). Communicative competence: Some roles of comprehensible input and comprehensible output in its development. In S. Gass & C. Madden (Eds.), *Input in second language acquisition* (pp. 235–253). Rowley, MA: Newbury House.

Sydorenko, T. (2015). The use of computer-delivered structured tasks in pragmatic instruction: An exploratory study. *Intercultural Pragmatics, 12*(3), 333–362.

Sydorenko, T., Daurio, P., & Thorne, S. (2018). Refining pragmatically-appropriate oral communication via computer-simulated conversations. *Computer Assisted Language Learning, 31*, 157–180.

Sydorenko, T., & Tuason, G. H. (2016). Noticing of pragmatic features during spoken interaction. In K. Bardovi-Harlig and C. Félix-Brasdefer (Eds.), *Pragmatics & language learning, vol. 14* (pp. 233–264). Honolulu, HI: University of Hawai'i, National Foreign Language Resource Center.

Sykes, J. M. (2013). Multiuser virtual environments: Learner apologies in Spanish. In N. Taguchi & J. Sykes (Eds.), *Technology in interlanguage pragmatics research and teaching* (pp. 71–100). Amsterdam: John Benjamins.

Sykes, J. M., Oskoz, A., & Thorne, S. (2008). Web 2.0, synthetic immersive environments, and mobile resources for language education. *CALICO Journal, 25*, 528–546.

Taguchi, N. (2011). Rater variation in the assessment of speech acts. *Pragmatics, 21*(3), 453–471. https://doi.org/10.1075/prag.21.3.08tag

Timpe-Laughlin, V., Wain, J., & Schmidgall, J. (2015). Defining and operationalizing the construct of pragmatic competence: Review and recommendations. *ETS Research Reports*. Princeton, NJ: Educational Testing Service.

van Compernolle, R. A., & Kinginger, C. (2013). Promoting metapragmatic development through assessment in the zone of proximal development. *Language Teaching Research, 17*(3), 282–302.

White, L., & Juffs, A. (1998). Constraints on wh-movement in two different contexts of nonnative language acquisition: Competence and processing. In S. Flynn, G. Martohardjono, & W. O'Neil (Eds.), *The generative study of second language acquisition* (pp. 125–144). Mahwah, NJ: Erlbaum.

4 Heritage Language Education

EKATERINA MOORE AND AFAF NASH

After the tragic events of 9/11 in 2001, the lack of proficient bilinguals in the United States became evident. US security agencies "were so desperate for translators of Arabic and other languages of south Asia that they were forced to place want-ads in newspapers" (Crawford, 2004, p. 71). To meet the new challenges, many government programs were created to produce highly proficient bilinguals, especially in critical languages, to fulfill economic, military, and diplomatic needs. Strengthening languages of language-minority communities, known as heritage languages, is a potential resource to bridge the existing gap.

The September 11 events highlighted the need for proficient bilinguals for the sake of US national security, but the vicissitudes of world sociopolitics and geopolitics accelerated that need worldwide. The rapid population mobility due to political plights and unbalanced economic situations coupled with the omnipresence of social media have brought unprecedented contact among speakers of various languages. Classrooms throughout the world are increasingly filled with students from diverse backgrounds. In the United States alone, bilingualism and multilingualism is a fact of life for 12 million school-age children (Carreira & Kagan, 2018). Protecting the cultural and linguistic rights of these individuals is not only beneficial for national security and economy, but it is also an ethical stance.

This chapter discusses **heritage language** (HL) learning and research concentrating on a US context. We discuss definitions of HL learners (HLLs), HL linguistic development, and educational programs available for HLLs. We then provide examples from our own research on HLLs of Russian and Arabic. Finally, we suggest classroom activities for students interested in HL studies.

Overview of Key Concepts in Heritage Language Education

Heritage Language Learners

Although the term "**heritage language learners**" is new, the subject it represents is not. Other terms used include "HL speakers," "semi-speakers," "incomplete acquirers," and "unbalanced or pseudo-bilinguals." Some definitions highlight

HLLs' connection to their heritage culture and community (Fishman, 2014), while others concentrate on the proficiency in the HL (Valdés, 2001).

Viewed in a broad sense, an HLL is an individual who may have no proficiency in the HL, but has strong family connections with the language s/he is learning, and may be motivated to learn the language because of these connections. An example of this is a monolingual English-speaking university student enrolled in a Level 1 Greek class because her great-grandparents were from Greece. This learner may be motivated to learn Greek because of her family ancestry. In contrast to such a broad understanding of HLLs, a narrow view considers proficiency in the HL a determining factor in the definition. Viewed from the narrow perspective, in addition to the ancestral connections, an HLL would be an individual with exposure to the HL in the home and some ability to understand and speak the HL. An example is a child born in a Russian-speaking family in the United States who uses English in an American school and Russian at home and/or Russian Saturday school. This chapter adopts a narrow view of an HLL.

As reflected in the divergent views, HLLs have varied life experiences. In the United States, HLLs may come from immigrant, indigenous, or colonial backgrounds, and situations of adoption. Some are first-generation immigrants who moved to the United States as children with their families. They may remember the country they came from, maintain relationships with relatives in the home country, or make frequent trips to the home country. Other HLLs are second, third or fourth generations born and raised in the United States, who may have never visited their ancestral homeland. Some may speak their HL on a daily basis with their families, while others may only overhear the language spoken around them. What is common for all HLLs, however, is that they do not engage in one culture and language in isolation. The question of their linguistic competencies, therefore, becomes central in the discussion of HLLs.

Heritage Language Linguistic Proficiency   Research on HL proficiency works with the narrow definition of an HLL, the bilingual speaker with asymmetrical skills in home and dominant languages, with an aim to illuminate how language works and how it is acquired under various conditions (Benmamoun, Montrul, & Polinsky, 2013). Thus far, scholars have found a number of broad acquisition features among different HLLs. In the United States, most HLLs transfer from English and show signs of attrition and underdevelopment. Compared to **second language learners (L2Ls)**, HLLs demonstrate some advantages in pronunciation and phonemic perception even with limited exposure to the HL, but exhibit difficulties in inflectional morphology and complex syntax. HLLs tend to demonstrate higher accuracy with the lexical category of verbs than nouns and adjectives (Benmamoun et al., 2013). In terms of pragmatics, HLLs communicate familial and daily topics with ease, but have difficulties with abstract subjects due to gradual diminishing exposure and input in the HL (Carreira & Kagan, 2018). These acquisition patterns are influenced by characteristics in the HL environment, such as age, generational order, community support, and type and duration of input.

At the start of English-only formal instruction, HL grammatical structures may fail to develop to a mature stage due to diminishing access to the HL during the critical period for acquisition. Generally, the earlier and more English is used, the less HL attainment can be reached. Traditionally, cognitive studies celebrate early simultaneous bilingualism, but some research suggests that a context of sequential acquisition, in which a child is exposed to only HL before the age of 3, may offer advantages in terms of acquiring core-grammatical features (Montrul, 2012). Generational order is also consequential: foreign-born HL speakers (first generation) retain stronger language skills than their children (second generation) and grandchildren (third generation). In fact, in the third generation and beyond, most lack a functional knowledge of their HLs. Despite the prevalence of diminishing factors, reaching high proficiency in HL is not uncommon. Use of HLs at home, HL schooling, traveling, and community support correlate with better HL vitality.

Identity and Heritage Language Learning

A singular focus on describing HL from the perspective of what is missing can encourage a deficit view. Presenting HLs as incomplete systems undermines the rich linguistic practices HLLs perform in communal and familial contexts where issues of belonging are negotiated. In the sociocultural framework, language is action and a linguistic act is a performance of **identity**. Identity, then, is better placed at the center of HL development (He, 2006). This view allows for positioning learners within their bilingual/bicultural environment as well as for inclusion of lived experiences into a language classroom.

HLLs' identity, a common factor for studying HLs, is not a stable category, but is dynamic and socially constructed. Negotiated through discourse, identity is an individual's relationship with others, shaped and constrained by relevant socio-political and sociocultural contexts (Norton, 2010). HLLs relate to heritage and dominant languages and cultures in multiple ways that may be seen as a continuum with the two languages and cultures at the opposite ends (Valdés, 2001). In daily lives, individuals balance their identities according to the linguistic and cultural settings (Val & Vinogradova, 2010). HLLs' identities are also central to the types of learning opportunities and outcomes individuals are given in and out of a classroom.

Understanding identities of HLLs and the practices associated with these identities provides invaluable support for HL educators. One daily practice where HLLs engage in both the heritage and the dominant languages is **translation**. Immigrant children are often found to translate for their parents in educational, medical, commercial, and other daily real-life settings. As they mediate the two cultures on regular bases,

HLLs exercise agency, bilingual competency, problem-solving, and transcultural skills far more complex than those required in typical classroom exercises. They may also encounter different varieties and registers of their HL; an example of this research is provided later.

Heritage Language Instruction   HL education has a history of over 300 years in the United States. HL schools are established by ethnic groups to support the learning of HLs and culture of ethnic communities. Programs that serve HLLs, however, may be found not only in community schools, but also in public K–12 and higher education.

K–12 Schools   HLLs in American K–12 classrooms are recent immigrants, foreign-born children who have been in American schools for several years, and US-born children of immigrant or indigenous ancestry (Wang & Green, 2001). We can find these HLLs in K–12 **foreign language (FL)**, **dual language (DL) immersion**, as well as the more traditional monolingualism-oriented **transitional bilingual programs**.

Foreign language programs teach languages that are not normally used for communication in a given country or as a medium of instruction in that country's schools. French language classes taught in US schools where instruction is conducted in English is an example of FL education. In DL classrooms, where 50 percent of students speak English and 50 percent speak another language, HL is used to teach academic content. While DL and FL programs have bilingualism as their goal, the more commonly seen transitional programs often concentrate on learning English at the expense of the HL or where HL serves merely as a scaffold into the dominant language (Garcia & Kleifgen, 2018).

A variety of labels, including English Language Learners, Limited English Proficiency, and Long Term English Learners, are commonly used for HL speakers in such programs. In these labels, HLLs' identities as speakers of languages other than English are often ignored or treated as irrelevant. As a result of such monolingual orientation, HLLs spend a number of years in American schools concentrating solely on the development of English, losing proficiency in their HL. In high (and less frequently middle) school, these children may (re-)engage in formal study of their HL in the context of an FL classroom, where they are tasked with re-learning what did not have to get lost in the first place. Such an approach is problematic as it treats HLs (and often as an extension the learners themselves) as a problem, promoting the ideology of monolingualism as a norm. Additionally, this approach is inadequate as persistent gaps between language-minoritized and language-majority students' academic performance and graduation rates continue to exist.

While some HLs may be offered in K–12 classrooms as foreign languages, the selection of these languages is not representative of the variety of HLs spoken in the United States. Only Spanish is widely taught in US K–12 public schools, leaving almost 9 million 5 to 18-year-old speakers of other languages with little chance of studying their HLs (Fee, Rhodes, & Wiley, 2014). Even Spanish, a language that is commonly offered as an FL and is the number one spoken HL in the United States, is rarely offered as a course designed for HLLs. One avenue that allows HLLs of various languages to further their proficiency in the HL is through community schools.

Community Education   Community HL schools offer HL education outside of formal schooling. Three types of HL schools are identified based on frequency and number of instructional hours per week: all-day schools, weekday afternoon schools, and weekend schools. Other types of schools (models) are summer programs, evening classes, and special classes in community centers.

Community schools usually target school-age children, but adult HL classes also exist (see Avineri & Verschik, 2017). Typically, enrollment in community HL schools follows the pyramid model, where the number of students decreases as their grade levels increase. This can be explained by the increasing demands on the children as they progress in school, leaving little time for non-compulsory education. In terms of adult HL community-based education, we currently lack knowledge on the motivations that bring adult students back to community schools and their plans to leverage the accumulated knowledge. These schools, however, are vital for language revitalization, preservation, and maintenance efforts.

Community schools are normally associated with community organizations, such as cultural centers and churches, and often lack state, federal, and school district funding. Because of this, community schools may need to rely on a curriculum that is less formalized and teachers who lack formal teacher training. While little monetary support from state and federal agencies is provided for community schools, some recognition of the importance of these institutions by formal educational agencies is observed. Students attending community HL schools may receive high-school foreign language credits and be examined in their HL on College Entrance Examination Board tests for college admission (Fishman, 2014).

Higher Education   A continuous debate in Higher Education is whether or not to offer separate tracks for heritage and non-heritage language learners. In support of HL research and teaching, the National Heritage Language Resource Center (NHLRC) conducted a national survey to study practices and profiles of college language programs in the United States (Carreira & Kagan, 2011). Responses from 302 institutes show only a slight difference between the number of HL and mixed classrooms; the programs that offer separate HL tracks often have no more than one or two levels of HL classes. Unbalanced representations of HLs is also a fact in US language programs: Spanish, Korean, Russian, and Chinese are highly common, while Farsi, Arabic, and Hindi are less represented. To compensate for the gap, programs without separate HL tracks (about 48 percent of participating institutions) provide alternatives, such as independent studies, tutoring, internships, and professional preparation courses.

Advocates for separate tracks are motivated by studies that show diverse grammatical systems and learning processes for each group. HLLs come with wide-range proficiency levels and language varieties. Second/foreign language learners (L2Ls) also have different objectives and study skills. The result is mixed classrooms with double layers of diversity, one among HLLs and another between HLLs and L2Ls (Carreira & Chik, 2018). Although separate tracks may seem an ideal solution, it is one that comes with challenges, such as financial support, trained teachers, specialized curriculum, and body of students to sustain two tracks. Instead, instructors often rely on differentiated instruction (DI) to attenuate differences and offer customized support for HLLs and L2Ls.

Heritage Language Education: Looking Ahead   Current scholarship calls for programs to include critical pedagogies in HL education. A critical stance to HL teaching recognizes the dynamic relationship between language, culture, activism, ideologies, and identity (Leeman, Rabin, & Román-Mendoza, 2011). Service learning is one model of learning that connects language instruction with learners' identities and goals. It integrates meaningful community service with academic instruction to enrich the learning experience, teach civic responsibilities, and strengthen communities.

In terms of HLLs' linguistic development, more research is needed on adolescent HLLs. Children and adults in university language programs are the focus of most current HL research. However, individuals often stop attending HL schools and submerge in English-dominant spheres through schools, sports etc. during middle and high school. Research that investigates HL development during adolescence, however, is largely missing. HLLs born in multilingual contexts, where the child, in addition to English, is exposed to two or more languages, is another population absent in research and deserves in-depth attention.

Our Work in Heritage Language Learning

Personal Reflections

Ekaterina Moore   My interest in language started when I was a student, taking EFL classes from an excellent teacher who was passionate about her profession. Fast-forward many years, and I found myself studying to become an English teacher, teaching language, and currently working with aspiring language teachers as a college professor. I am fascinated with the central role that language plays in how people learn to become members of communities of various sorts, including those that immigrants join or create when they arrive in a new country. My research on language socialization practices of native Russian-speaking preschoolers and learners of Russian as an HL allows me to better understand how we become the people we are. While family upbringing plays an important part in the socialization process, schooling is equally crucial in shaping our life trajectories. Through language, embodied practices, and material resources around us, we as teachers and learners participate in an intricate process of shaping each other's identities as members of a community, individuals with values, emotions, likes and dislikes, passions, and aspirations.

Afaf Nash   I immigrated to the United States from Iraq during a critical time fraught with political crises and wars and have witnessed the rising interest in the Arabic language and its speakers. Meanwhile, I raised children with whom I used Arabic as the main home language and had enrolled them in mosque classes to learn formal Arabic and the Islamic religion and culture. I documented my children's shift from Arabic to English that started gradually from occasional lexical and grammar codeswitching to a dominant English that matured by entering high school. I also helped my parents and siblings to settle in the United States and have served as a language and cultural interpreter for many years. My life experiences inspire and inform my teaching and research. I examine the construction of identity and meaning-making in the bilingual practices of Arabic heritage speakers mainly to understand the sociocultural and sociopolitical contexts in sustaining US bilingual communities.

Ekaterina Moore's Work with a Russian Heritage Language School

Moore's research on HLLs is situated in a Russian community HL school in the United States. The research examines how through instructional practices, the children attending the HL school on Saturdays are not only taught the Russian language, but also socialized into identities and stances appropriate for the Russian diaspora toward the language, culture, and Orthodox Christianity. Combining ethnographic observations and detailed analysis of talk allowed Moore to identify central themes of **cultural affiliation** and to evaluate how beliefs are practiced, constructed, and reinforced in everyday classroom interactions.

In the context of the HL school, being respectful, humble, and obedient toward parents (Moore, 2014) and considerate toward classmates (Moore, 2017) is important. With the explicit goal of moral upbringing, the schoolteachers make complex moral concepts such as respect tangible through the use of various linguistic and embodied practices. Hypothetical reported speech produced by teachers, for example, allows the children to receive not only the model of what should and should not be said to the parents, but also the manner in which children are to speak to their parents even in disagreements. Directives, that is, utterances that attempt to make someone do something, issued during disciplining acts, position the children as moral actors who influence the well-being of peers and their ability to complete educational tasks (Moore, 2017). In Excerpt 1, a boy stops his reading out-loud when two girls start whispering. In her directive to get the girls to stop talking, the teacher produces an account for why their behavior is not acceptable. In this explanation, the whispering is presented as negatively affecting (unpleasant and interruptive) and disrespectful to the boy:

Excerpt 1: "Reading" (Moore, 2017)

```
(TEA = female teacher)
01              ((Two girls whisper as a boy is reading a text out loud))
02              ((Boy stops reading for 4 seconds))
03    TEA:    Devočki. (1.5) vy kogda čitaete vam prijatno<
              Girls, do you like it when you read,
04              <Čto (.) vas perebivajut. (.) A?
              And you get interrupted. Hm?
05    (0.8)
06    TEA:    Ili kto-to tam šuršit v klasse i šepčetsja.
              Or someone whispers or rustles in class.
07    (1.0)
08    TEA:    Davajte uvažat'drugix tože. (4.5)
              Let's also respect others.
```

Another prominent theme of cultural affiliation and identity of a Russian Orthodox Christian is a need to have positive feelings toward religious practices (Moore, 2020). The use of hypothetical stories, and assessments within these stories, serves as a vehicle for the socialization of positive affective stances or "mood, attitude, feeling and disposition" (Ochs, 1996, p. 410) toward religious practices. As the children learn vocabulary associated with the church, they are introduced to hypothetical stories and "participant examples" (Wortham, 1994) where they become characters.

The stories are not neutral in either the content or the way they are told, but are filled with positively laden assessments of the church objects and practices. Teachers use affect specifiers, or features that specify "affective orientations of utterances" and affect intensifiers, or features that modulate "affective intensity of utterances" (Ochs & Schieffelin, 1989). Such positive lexical items as "beautifully dressed" used to describe priests' clothing are combined with a whispering voice, in-awe-like inhaling, and vowel-lengthening to intensify the expression of the positive affective stance.

As the children are exposed to such stories, they become active participants in the telling of the stories, usually aligning with the positive **affect** projected by the teachers. This can be seen when children co-tell the stories with the teacher, positioning themselves and their classmates as participants in the hypothetical scenarios, and using positive assessments. In Excerpt 2, a girl (Ženja) demonstrates such an alignment by co-producing the teacher's utterance. The excerpt is part of the hypothetical story where the teacher describes clothes worn by a priest on his arms, expressing a positive affective stance. Ženja completes the teacher's utterance producing a congruent assessment through the use of positive vocabulary, prosody, and facial expression.

Excerpt 2: "Armlets" (Moore, 2020)

(TEA = male teacher, ŽEN = female student)
01   TEA: *A na rukax u nix u vsex vidite kakie krasivye (.)*
                 And on their arms they all you see have these beautiful

02   ⎡ *Vešči s krestom.*
                 ⎢ Things with a cross.
03   ŽEN: ⎣ *Uzo::ry*   ⎡ *Uzory ((smiles slightly))*
                    Patterns'   ⎢ Patterns
04   TEA: *Uzory.*   ⎣ *Oni nazyvajutsja poručni.*
                         Patterns. They are called armlets.

In this interaction, the teacher and the student co-construct the meaning of a new word "armlets" as they engage in the expression of affective stance. The display of positive affect starts with the teacher's use of the word "beautiful" (line 01). Aligning with this positive stance, Ženja completes the teacher's utterance not only with an appropriate part of speech (*uzory* "patterns," a plural noun), but also with a congruent positive stance using this highly positive word.[1] In addition, Ženja smiles slightly as she produces a vowel stretch (line 03: *uzo::ry*). In response, the teacher aligns with Ženja's stance through his repetition of this word (line 04).

Along with opportunities to learn new vocabulary, opportunities for stance displays and socialization are created and utilized through the use of language as the teacher and the student "co-participate in the experience offered by the assessment through an exchange of affective displays" (Goodwin & Goodwin, 1992, p. 159). The teachers' use of hypothetical stories allows for the presentation of desired realities, where children experience the positive affect associated with church practices, as well as receive the correction for displays of stances that do not align with such a view.

Through exposure to these stories, a child attending the school does not simply learn how to be a speaker of Russian; he or she learns how to be an individual who has proper feelings toward cultural religious practices and displays appropriate behaviors in and outside of school. While the children are provided with models for linguistic production, they are not told that they are to feel a certain way. Rather, through the use of hypothetical scenarios, children are put in a position of experiencing proper feelings. They learn the meaning of being a member of a Russian Orthodox Christian diaspora through concrete experiences, real or imagined, and the interpretations of these experiences by teachers.

---

[1] In Russian, the word *uzor* is positively connotated and is usually used to refer to an elaborate design (Ožegov's e-dictionary of the Russian language www.ozhegov.org/index.shtml).

Afaf Nash's Work with Arabic Heritage Language Learners

Studies that go beyond classroom interaction can inform HL curriculum, as found in Nash's research. Nash (2014, 2017) examines a linguistic practice common among immigrant families, known as **language brokering** (LB). LB is the act of non-professional interpretation that facilitates interactions among monolinguals. It can be found in any context of language barrier – for example, a Spanish-speaking nurse translating between an English-speaking physician and a Spanish-speaking patient. More commonly, however, these triadic interactions are constituted among immigrant families by a language broker (e.g., a bilingual child), a language brokeree (Nash, 2014) (e.g., a non-English speaking parent), and a dominant-culture representative (e.g., a shop owner, a doctor). The experience of LB is an integral part of the acculturation process for the family and can be influenced by specific linguistic, sociocultural, and sociopolitical contexts associated with each immigrant community (Guan, Nash, & Orellana, 2016). Huda, for example, an Iraqi language broker, who was participating in an Arabic summer program during the LB study, discusses in the excerpt below how she protects her mother from prejudice while brokering in medical visits:

> Sometimes, when they measure her blood pressure, they just remove her sleeves and order her without being nice to her, and I'm like, "be nice to her." And when they see me understand English, they say, "sorry, we're in a hurry," and then they become nice. When I translate to my mom, she's like, "no no, no it's OK," and I'm like, "No, it's not OK." My mom thinks it's her work, and she needs to do it, but I think it is because my mom is wearing a head covering and she doesn't speak English. I can be aggressive because I want them to be nice to my parents. I want things to be right for my parents. (Nash, 2017, pp. 137–138)

Participating in LB develops transcultural skills that position language brokers as knowledgeable in two world views (Orellana, 2009). Huda believes that her mother should be addressed directly before administering any medical exams. She also considers that excusing nurses' action as doing their job is part of the mother's cultural values. For Huda, however, her mother's cultural appearances and/or English proficiency put her mother in a vulnerable position, therefore she 'aggressively' calls for a better treatment. Huda plays a number of roles in this incident: an interpreter, a protector, and a socializer. In the latter, she socializes her mother into her civil rights, while the mother socializes Huda into cultural values of respecting professional authorities and moving the doing-of-business act forward.

In describing LB experiences, language brokers often talk about it as both troublesome and beneficial. It is a responsibility that takes from schoolwork and leisure time and burdens with worries about parents' well-being; but it also provides opportunities for bonding. In the example below, Leila, a Palestinian-American, talks about a bond with her mother formed around brokering the news. Leila translates English news to her mother, while her mother shares Arabic news reporting with her daughter:

The best part [of translating news] is that when we listen to the Al-Jazeera, I don't understand what they are saying. Sometimes, I pick up some words but mostly my mother translates for me. (Nash, 2017, p. 144)

The Arabic language is marked by **diglossia**, the daily existence of two or more linguistic forms. Arabic has a standard form known as Modern Standard Arabic (MSA), used in formal settings and learned at school, and many regional dialects acquired at home and used in everyday interactions. Arabic heritage speakers usually are familiar with home dialects and lack proficiency in MSA due to no or insufficient schooling. In the above example, the nature of the Arabic language affords the mother with an opportunity to introduce MSA to her daughter. Leila, who is proficient in the family Palestinian dialect and lacks equal ability in MSA, describes the news-translating act as "the best part," as she learns more about her HL. A mutual interest in the political climate of their homeland and in preserving the HL provides a space for reciprocal brokering. This specific context helps Leila develop sophisticated literacy skills, and as such, creates an opportunity to sustain Arabic among second-generation Arab Americans.

Sometimes, however, the hyper-visibility of Arab Americans at the present time may burden brokers in public space (Guan et al., 2016). Selma, for example, was shopping with her grandmother, who was wearing a traditional Palestinian dress, in an up-scale department store. The saleswoman asked if they were *lost* and needed help to locate another department. Selma responded simply: "No thanks, we're not lost." The grandmother became uncomfortable with the woman's tone and gaze and asked "What does this crazy woman want?" to which Selma replied that she was offering help. This engagement exhibits distrust between the two groups' representatives, Middle Eastern by the grandmother and American by the saleswoman, which Selma skillfully mediates to ensure civil exchange in a public space. The experience, however, left Selma with stressful feelings communicated as saying: "It's every time, why me?" (Guan et al., 2016).

Most LB literature centers on the language broker, but recent work presents LB as a triadic interaction in which all participants are involved equally in moving it forward. Moreover, Nash (2014) draws attention to the language brokeree's actions that have been somewhat invisible in the literature. Below, Hamid (HAM) interprets during his mother's (MOD) visit to an otolaryngologist to discuss her hearing aids (see Nash, 2014):

03	HAM:	the sound, it's not (0.3) very	well.
04	MOD:		*abad*
			never
05	HAM:	even- even she adjust	it. aah-
06	MOD:		*wrāsi [yūjˈnī min ahh- aḥuṭha*
			And my head hurts when I put it

Hamid above starts the medical complaint phase from the point of reporting on the device quality; it is not good even if adjusted. The mother, in an overlap with her son, reports that indeed, she never hears (line 04) and her head hurts (line 06). Her input, despite limited English knowledge, achieves many interactional goals: she 1) moves the interaction forward by focusing on her not the device, 2) presents the second condition, headaches, as consequential of the first, not hearing well, 3) sets back the speakers' roles to an expected convention with her being the reporting agent on her medical experience and her son as the interpreter.

These examples, taken from Nash's published research, highlight LB among Arab Americans as shaped by the linguistic and sociopolitical contexts of the community. It is associated with positive outcomes (e.g., developing MSA skills) and negative ones (e.g., exposure to stereotypes). Despite some formal calls for strict dependency on professional translators, immigrant families of all languages continue to depend on bilingual family members regardless of age, date of arrival, or language skills. Noting that, policy makers can instead augment this cognitive, cultural, and linguistic practice by supporting families and institutions where LB happens.

Application Activities

The activities on the website accompanying this book provide you with an opportunity to investigate a subfield of interest within HL studies: linguistic, pedagogical, or sociocultural. Those interested in the linguistic subfield will engage in analysis of a transcript of speech produced by an HLL. If you are interested in pedagogy, you will evaluate an HL program in your local community. If your interest is in the sociocultural aspects of HL learning, you will conduct a survey of HLLs in your school.

Going Further

For students interested in HL issues, we recommend taking courses in HL linguistics and pedagogy. The National Heritage Language Center (www.nhlrc.ucla) and Center for Applied Linguistics (www.cal.org/heritage/) provide excellent resources for students, teachers, and researchers. You can learn more about the field by attending a variety of conferences and workshops as well as through journals dedicated to HL issues.

Discussion Questions

1. What factors do you consider important in defining a heritage language learner?

2. What environmental influences do you consider the most consequential for heritage language development?
3. What are some benefits and issues associated with providing support for heritage language development in K–12 and higher education?
4. What are the benefits and issues associated with mixed/separate heritage language-foreign language-learner classrooms?
5. What do heritage language learners learn in heritage language schools? How does that compare with foreign language programs?
6. What advantages and disadvantages are associated with language brokering and what are possible ways to support language brokering among immigrant communities?

FURTHER READING

Foundational Readings

Fishman, J. A. (1966). *Language loyalty in the United States: The maintenance and perpetuation of non-English mother tongues by American ethnic and religious groups.* The Hague: Moon & Co.

Valdés, G. (1989). Teaching Spanish to Hispanic bilinguals: A look at oral proficiency testing and the proficiency movement. *Hispania, 72,* 392–401.

Recent Publications

Kagan, O., Carreira, M., & Chik, C. (Eds.). (2017). *The Routledge handbook of heritage language education: From innovation to program building.* New York: Taylor & Francis.

Polinsky, M. (2018) *Heritage languages and their speakers.* Cambridge: Cambridge University Press.

REFERENCES

Avineri, N., & Verschik, A. (2017). Innovation and tradition in Yiddish educational programs. In O. Kagan, M. Carreira, & C. Chik (Eds.), *The Routledge handbook of heritage language education: From innovation to program building* (pp. 451–468). New York: Routledge.

Benmamoun, E., Montrul, S., & Polinsky, M. (2013). Heritage languages and their speakers: Opportunities and challenges for linguistics. *Theoretical Linguistics, 39*(3–4), 129–181.

Carreira, M., & Chik, C. H. (2018). Differentiated teaching: A primer for heritage and mixed classes. In K. Potowski (Ed.), *The Routledge handbook of Spanish as a heritage language* (pp. 359–374). London: Routledge.

Carreira, M., & Kagan, O. (2011). The results of the National Heritage Language Survey: Implications for teaching, curriculum design, and professional development. *Foreign Language Annals, 44*(1), 40–64.

(2018). Heritage language education: A proposal for the next 50 years. *Foreign Language Annals*, *51*, 152–168.

Crawford, J. (2004). *Educating English learners: Language diversity in the classroom* (5th edn). Los Angeles: Bilingual Education Services.

Fee, M., Rhodes, N. C., & Wiley, T. G. (2014). Demographic realities, challenges, and opportunities. In T. G. Wiley, J. K. Peyton, D. Christian, S. C. K Moore, & N. Liu (Eds.), *Handbook of heritage, community, and Native American languages in the United States: Research, policy, and educational practice* (pp. 6–18). New York: Routledge.

Fishman, J. A. (2014). Three hundred-plus years of heritage language education in the United States. In T. G. Wiley, J. K. Peyton, D. Christian, S. C. K Moore, & N. Liu (Eds.), *Handbook of heritage, community, and Native American languages in the United States: Research, policy, and educational practice* (pp. 36–44). New York: Routledge.

García, O., & Kleifgen, J. A. (2018). *Educating emergent bilinguals: Policies, programs, and practices for English learners*. New York: Teachers College Press.

Goodwin, C., & Goodwin, M. H. (1992). Assessments and the construction of context. In A. Duranti & C. Goodwin (Eds.), *Rethinking context* (pp. 147–190). Cambridge: Cambridge University Press.

Guan, S. S. A., Nash, A., & Orellana, M. F. (2016). Cultural and social processes of language brokering among Arab, Asian, and Latino immigrants. *Journal of Multilingual and Multicultural Development*, *37*(2), 150–166.

He, A. W. (2006). Toward an identity theory of the development of Chinese as a heritage language. *Heritage Language Journal*, *4*(1), 1–28.

Leeman, J., Rabin, L., & Román-Mendoza, E. (2011). Critical pedagogy beyond the classroom walls: Community service-learning and Spanish heritage language education. *Heritage Language Journal*, *8*(3), 1–22.

Montrul, S. A. (2012). Is the heritage language like a second language? *Eurosla Yearbook*, *12*(1), 1–29.

Moore, E. (2014). "You are children, but you can always say…": Use of hypothetical direct reported speech in a heritage language classroom. *Text and Talk*, *34*(5), 591–621.

(2017). Managing classroom transgressions: Use of directives in a reading practice. *Linguistics and Education, 41*, 35–46.

(2020). Affective stance and socialization to values in a Russian heritage language classroom. In M. Burdelski & K. Howard (Eds.), *Language socialization in classrooms* (pp. 71-89). Cambridge: Cambridge University Press.

Nash, A. (2014). Participation and conversational involvement in brokered medical interviews: A case of Iraqi patients in Southern California (doctoral dissertation). UCLA.

(2017). Arab Americans' brokering in a context of tension and stereotypes: "It's just a head-cover. Get over it!" In R. Weisskirch (Ed.), *Language brokering in immigrant families* (pp. 132–152). New York: Routledge.

Norton, B. (2010). Language and identity. In N. H. Hornberger & S. L. McKay (Eds.), *Sociolinguistics and language education* (pp. 349–369). Bristol: Multilingual Matters.

Ochs, E. (1996). Linguistic resources for socializing humanity. In J. J. Gumperz & S. C. Levinson (Eds.), *Rethinking linguistic relativity* (pp. 407–437). Cambridge: Cambridge University Press.

Ochs, E., & Schieffelin, B. (1989). Language has a heart. *Text*, *9*(1), 7–25.

Orellana, M. F. (2009). *Translating childhoods: Immigrant youth, language, and culture.* New Brunswick, NJ: Rutgers University Press.

Val, A., & Vinogradova, P. (2010). Heritage briefs. *Center for Applied Linguistics.* www.cal .org/heritage/research/briefs.html

Valdés, G. (2001). Heritage language students: Profiles and possibilities. In J. Peyton, D. Ranard, & S. McGinnis (Eds.), *Heritage languages in America: Preserving a national resource* (pp. 37–77). Washington, DC: Center for Applied Linguistics; and McHenry, IL: Delta Systems.

Wang, S. C., & Green, N. (2001). Heritage language students in the K–12 education system. In J. Peyton, D. Ranard, & S. McGinnis (Eds.) *Heritage languages in America: Preserving a national resource* (pp. 167–196). Washington, DC: Center for Applied Linguistics; and McHenry, IL: Delta Systems.

Wortham, S. E. F. (1994). *Acting out participant examples in the classroom.* Amsterdam: John Benjamins.

5 Community, Group Dynamics, Identity, and Anxiety in Learning an Additional Language

NIKE ARNOLD

While learning is by definition a cognitive process, the *experience* of learning involves additional dimensions. As pointed out by Kramsch (2009), this is especially true for learning an additional language (Lx[1]): "The language-learning experience is likely to engage learners cognitively, emotionally, morally, and aesthetically" (p. 43). This chapter focuses on the emotional dimension of Lx learning in a classroom setting. Like others in the field of Second Language Acquisition (SLA), I will use the term **"affect"** to refer to this emotional dimension; in other words, "aspects of emotion, feeling, mood or attitude which condition behaviour" (Arnold & Brown, 1999, p. 1). Because of its potential impact on cognition, engagement, and other learner behaviors, affect plays a key role in Lx learning success. Moreover, it makes the difference between a positive and a negative learning experience and that alone warrants the attention of researchers and educators alike.

Overview of Key Concepts and Issues in Community, Group Dynamics, Identity, and Anxiety

From the literature on affect in classroom-based Lx learning, I have chosen four interconnected variables to highlight. By definition, community and group dynamics are social variables while identity and anxiety focus on individuals.

Community

As a student, you have undoubtedly been part of classes that did not feel like a community, not surprising since classes tend to be rather random collections of learners that often dissolve after a short time. Hopefully, you have also been part of classes where you did experience a sense of community; in other words, "a feeling that members have of belonging, a feeling that members matter to one another and to the group, that they have duties and obligations to each other . . . and that they

---

[1] Unlike the more widely used abbreviation "L2," "Lx" doesn't imply that it's the person's second language (e.g., not the third or fourth).

possess shared expectations that members' educational needs will be met through their commitment to shared goals" (Rovai & Lucking, 2000, as cited in Rovai, 2001, p. 34).

Classroom communities are a specific type of community whose primary goal is learning. Based on a synthesis of the general literature on community followed by statistical analysis, Rovai (2001, 2002) identified the following dimensions of classroom community: 1) spirit (group identity and cohesion, feelings of belonging and acceptance), 2) trust, 3) task-driven and socioemotional interaction that results in closeness and mutual benefits, and 4) learning. Building such a community takes not only time but also special processes and practices (Kling & Courtright, 2004, cited in Darhower, 2007). In fact, communities develop a unique culture that supports their activity and cohesion (Riel & Polin, 1994, cited in Darhower, 2007).

A sense of community plays a central role in classroom learning: it promotes the flow of information, the availability of support, a willingness to expose gaps in understanding, and ultimately task completion (Rovai, 2002). The advent of **online education** raised an important question: Can a class develop a sense of community when students and instructor never meet face-to-face (F2F)? This sparked research on online courses, including the development of the Classroom Community Scale (Rovai, 2002).

Although classroom community is believed to be especially important for Lx learning (Petersen, Divitini & Chabert, 2008), there has been a paucity of research, especially on F2F classrooms. Lately, computer-mediated settings have received some attention but researchers have favored the analysis of communication patterns over surveys. Miceli, Murray, and Kennedy (2010) and Petersen et al. (2008), for example, both investigated the implementation of blogs in F2F Lx classes. Miceli et al. analyzed blog posts for connected voice, that is, contributions that nurture community building (e.g., supporting statements, self-disclosure). Over 60 percent of contributions manifested connected voice and students reported that their feelings of belonging had increased. In contrast, Petersen et al. concluded that their class blog failed to foster a community.

Instead of the "if," Darhower (2007) focused on how communities develop by comparing two chat groups. While Group 1 developed a sense of community early on and established **roles**, group **norms** and social relationships, Group 2's unstable membership made it difficult to move beyond the acquaintance level.

Group Dynamics

If and how a classroom community develops is related to another "between people" factor (Dörnyei & Malderez, 1999, p. 155): **group dynamics**. The study of groups recognizes that individuals behave differently in a group than outside of it. Groups even develop a life of their own (Dörnyei & Malderez, 1997), including social structures (such as roles and a status system), norms and intermember relations that change and adapt continuously. During this process, successful groups become cohesive, that is, there are strong connections among members (Dörnyei & Malderez, 1999).

In the social sciences, there has been considerable research on group dynamics focusing on such topics as group formation, group development, group characteristics and the role of the group leader. Just like for community, however, there is little research on group dynamics in Lx classrooms, especially F2F ones. One exception is Gascoigne (2012), which administered a survey to beginning through advanced Lx learners of French and found a relationship between group dynamics and final course grades: the higher the students' grade, the more likely they were to report feelings of connectedness and cooperation. It is important to remember that this correlation does not establish cause and effect.

Recently, some research in the area of **computer-assisted language learning** (CALL) has looked at group dynamics, particularly among Lx learners writing collaboratively on wikis (i.e., websites like Wikipedia that are easily edited by any user). Li and Kim (2016), for example, found that group dynamics are not stable, even if group composition remains the same. For one task, one group exhibited individual accountability, balanced participation, and constructive interactions while all members showed reduced engagement with each other and the task when working on the next wiki task. Like Li and Kim, Elabdali (2016) described several types of group dynamics but noticed that they seemed related to the quality of the collaboratively written text: those groups where a leader emerged produced coherent stories while groups without a leader had incomplete or disjointed stories. Elabdali (2016) reported some conflict in the groups with leaders, which probably made the experience uncomfortable for some group members but, ultimately, the product benefited.

By evoking uniformity and collective identity, concepts like community and group dynamics have the potential to promote a reductive perspective (Thorne, 2009) in which the individual gets lost. Therefore, it is important to recognize that the social activity of groups is inherently tied to the identities of their individual members. In physical as well as virtual classrooms, learners have roles and occupy certain positions. These, in turn, are parts of their identity.

Identity

Identity is the first of two individual affective variables selected for this chapter. While the discussion of identity and anxiety will focus on the experience of Lx learners in formal learning contexts, both are also highly relevant outside of classrooms as well as to language educators.

In applied linguistics, early views of **identity** were "relatively simplistic" (Crookes, 2013, p. 104) because they focused on fixed features related to gender, class, and national/cultural identity. Starting in the mid-1990s, researchers began advocating a more fluid view, acknowledging the multiple shifting and interacting identities individuals negotiate with others in specific contexts (Norton, 2000). In other words, identity is "constructed across time and space" (Norton, 2014, p. 6) and therefore highly context-dependent. Contextual factors include the physical setting, an individual's relationships and interactions with others, as well as the ideological and **power** structures that are inherent in or emerge in this particular context (Norton, 2014). With inequitable power relations, identity often becomes "a site of struggle" (Norton, 2014, p. 61).

Defining identity as a social phenomenon foregrounds the central role language plays in identity construction and negotiation. In combination with other semiotic resources (e.g., body language, physical appearance), several linguistic practices contribute to identity construction, such as: 1) explicit mention of identity categories or labels (e.g., *nerd, non-native speaker*); 2) the use of the language associated with specific groups and personas; and 3) interactional moves through which individuals position themselves or others in certain roles (Bucholtz & Hall, 2005). For example, an instructor asking after the lecture "Any questions? Lorelei, what question do you have?" can position her as a struggling student or a curious questioner. All these practices can be deliberate, habitual, or otherwise subconscious.

In many online spaces, textual meaning plays a particularly critical role. Without visual (e.g., age, race, gender, facial expressions) and aural cues (e.g., accent, tone of voice), this information needs to be encoded differently (e.g., language, emojis, profile pictures), if one chooses to communicate it at all. If not, the resulting anonymity can allow individuals to enhance their identity or appropriate a more desirable one.

Identity construction is particularly complex in an Lx. In fact, "learning an additional language might be intimately involved with identity" (Crookes, 2013, p. 104). Instead of losing or disguising their first language identities, multilinguals often develop multiple identities rooted in the cultural and linguistic differences between their languages (Hemmi, 2014). Due to the discursive nature of identity, however, this process is not without challenges. Especially at lower proficiency levels, Lx learners typically feel that their proficiency offers them only a limited repertoire for identity work. They might also feel limited in their ability to resist any undesirable **positioning** by others (e.g., othering). This, in turn, can restrict their access to opportunities to learn or use the language (Norton, 2000).

Identity negotiations occur in mundane, everyday conversations: with family over a meal, on the phone with the customer support representative, or in an online chat with a friend. Of course, they also occur in classrooms, where the **situational identities** (Zimmerman, 1998) of instructor and student come into play in powerful ways. The instructor is usually expected to be the content expert who manages all aspects of the course and lesson. The students, in turn, typically play a reactive, less knowledgeable role. Clearly, these roles reflect an unequal power distribution that can affect identity negotiation.

Transportable identities, in contrast, are not situation-specific – "they are latent identities that 'tag along' with individuals as they move through their daily lives (Zimmerman, 1998, p. 90). It is often not relevant, for example, if a student is a passionate mountain biker or night owl. However, these transportable identities can become relevant to the subject matter at hand or an individual might choose to evoke them for community building or other purposes.

From the considerable body of research on Lx learner identity, two studies will be highlighted here. Harklau (2000) followed three immigrants from high school to community college. In high school, they were regarded as hardworking and motivated students; they even "collaborated in their teachers' construction of them as persevering, model students" (p. 49) by sharing personal stories of adversity. Apparently, they were very aware of the stories' power to evoke admiration. But their transition to community college marked a significant shift in their ascribed identities. There, the curriculum of their required classes in English as a second language (ESL) was geared toward newcomers in need of acculturation. It was therefore "diametrically opposed to the . . . students' self perceptions . . . as seasoned school-goers and residents of the United States" (p. 53) and positioned them as unable to function autonomously.

Like Harkau, Chang and Sperling (2014) illustrated how learner identities can shift across contexts, in this case the online and offline components of an ESL class. In the F2F lessons, the instructor's inherent power (situational identity) allowed her to repeatedly deny students' attempt to enact transportable identities: "When [they] strayed from the academic topic . . . attempting to fold knowledge from their own-life worlds into the discussion, their voices tended to be pushed aside, if not bluntly rejected" (p. 40). For the online discussions, the instructor also emphasized the need for academic content and language but due to her lack of participation, students were able to ignore these instructions and bring in non-academic experiences and knowledge, "[reflecting] a conglomeration of identities" (p. 43).

Anxiety

As mentioned above, Lx learners often feel limited by their proficiency, which "threatens [their] self-concept and worldview" (Horwitz, Horwitz & Cope, 1986, p. 125). As a result of feeling "like a babbling baby" (Price, 1991, p. 105), some Lx learners experience **anxiety**, "the subjective feeling of tension, apprehension, nervousness and worry associated with an arousal of the autonomic nervous system" (Horwitz et al., 1986, p. 125). As "conceptually distinct" (Horwitz et al., 1986, p. 125) from other anxieties, foreign language classroom anxiety is defined as situation specific but stable, often manifesting itself in a fear of negative evaluation, test anxiety, and communication apprehension (Horwitz et al., 1986).

Beyond a certain level of arousal, the negative thoughts associated with anxiety (e.g., expectations of failure, self-deprecation) consume cognitive resources, thereby reducing the cognitive capacity available for task-related processing (e.g., decoding oral messages, retrieving vocabulary to formulate a response) (Tobias, 1986). This, in turn, negatively impacts performance (e.g., Onwuegbuzie, Bailey & Daley, 2000; Phillips, 1992) and can ultimately lead to avoidance behaviors such as missing class or even dropping the course (Horwitz et al., 1986).

The field of language anxiety research was particularly active in the 1990s and 2000s and, similar to community, has relied on surveys (especially the Foreign Language Classroom Anxiety Scale; Horwitz et al., 1986) to measure anxiety levels. These studies have investigated topics such as: 1) the anxiety associated with Lx skills such as speaking, listening, and writing (e.g., Price, 1991; Vogely, 1999; Xiao & Wong, 2014), 2) triggers of anxiety (e.g., Koch & Terrell, 1991; Oxford, 1999), and 3) relationships between anxiety and other variables, including motivation, gender and beliefs (e.g., Campbell, 1999; Yan & Horwitz, 2008).

In recent years, there has been renewed interest in anxiety, including calls for a reorientation. Benesch (2012) has criticized the cognitive approach described above as a "utilitarian notion" (p. 34) of anxiety that doesn't recognize its complex and dynamic nature. Gregersen, Meza, and Macintyre (2014), for example, have shown that during a 3-minute oral presentation, learners experienced considerable fluctuation in anxiety levels. Benesch's second criticism relates to treating learners as "self-contained [individuals] sitting in self-contained classrooms" (p. 35). Failing to see anxiety (and other emotions, for that matter) as context-dependent and socially constructed means denying it as a legitimate reaction to unfavorable conditions and dynamics in the classroom and beyond. Emotions do not occur in a vacuum and yet much foreign language anxiety research has failed to account for the social and larger context. As shown by de Costa (2015), for example, outside expectations for success can trigger anxiety to the extent of "crush[ing]" a learner (p. 527). To truly understand learner emotions, we need to investigate them in context.

Of all the affective variables, "anxiety has been in the limelight of L2 research for decades" (Dörnyei, 2005, p. 198). Given the emotionally complex nature of Lx learning (Oxford, 2016), however, other emotions deserve attention: not only "negative" emotions (e.g., resentment and disappointment; Benesch, 2012) but also "positive" ones like hope, pride and empathy (Benesch, 2012; Oxford, 2016), which have received very little attention so far.

As this brief introduction has shown, affect is inside and between people and can be a powerful influence on Lx learners' experience. In addition to the four introduced here, there are additional variables such as motivation, learner beliefs, and self-efficacy. All of them make classrooms a complex ecosystem of emotions where the social and individual intersect.

My Work in Community, Group Dynamics, Identity, and Anxiety

Personal Reflection

I knew I had found "my thing" when working on a presentation about affective variables in an undergraduate SLA course. Even though I had never really experienced anxiety myself, the psychology of learning intrigued me. Several years later, when pursuing my PhD in Germanic Studies, a personal experience not only confirmed their important role in classroom learning but also showed me the affective power of technology. I was taking a course where my classmates seemed to have a much better grasp of the material. In the F2F class meetings, I was outside my comfort zone, hesitant to participate. To my surprise, the online class discussions were different – I felt like my usual (student) self, asking questions, and engaging with my peers and the instructor. Since then, much of my work has focused on the psychology of learners in computer-mediated settings. What happens when learners engage with others online? What group dynamics develop? Do learners experience anxiety? What identities do they construct for themselves and for others?

My Investigations into Community, Group Dynamics, Identity, and Anxiety

Before I describe one of my more recent projects, let me point out that most of my research has been in collaboration with colleagues. While collaborative research is unusual in the humanities and the norm in the natural sciences, applied linguistics lies somewhere in between. Based on the premise that "two heads are better than one," I strongly believe in the value of collaborative research.

The example study focused on learner identity but it wasn't designed that way. Originally, our goal was to look very broadly at learner interactions and attitudes toward educational technology. But identity emerged from the data as a relevant theme. We performed an **inductive analysis**, that is, we didn't rely on an a priori framework to analyze the data and instead let the data speak to us, so to speak. This has potential disadvantages, but this study illustrates one of its major strengths: its flexibility to encourage divergent thinking.

The study was conducted in a hybrid ESL course in an intensive English program at a US university, which met F2F twice a week and had an asynchronous online discussion as the third class meeting. The twenty-one students were all graduate students from the Middle East and East and Southeast Asia representing a variety of academic disciplines. We collected the following data: transcripts of the online discussions, surveys, field notes and observations, and interviews. Here, I will focus mostly on the transcripts.

Once learner identity had been established as the broad focus, we narrowed it down to the following research questions:

- What identities do learners create in this hybrid course?
- How do their identities in its F2F and online components compare?

From the pool of participants, two focal students were chosen using **maximum variation sampling**. In other words, our goal was to compare two very different cases to gain an understanding of the breadth of experiences. Table 5.1 profiles the two students, Omar and Jim. All names are pseudonyms.

Let's start by looking at the quantitative (numeric) data, in this case frequency counts of Omar's and Jim's participation in the online discussions (see Table 5.2). As described above, language plays a central role in identity construction, particularly so in online environments. Students who make no or few posts in online discussions are extremely limited in their ability to enact an identity for themselves (given that other semiotic resources like body language or even one's mere physical presence are absent). Therefore, how much Omar and Jim posted is a first indication of their online identity.

To put the numbers in Table 5.2 in perspective, the instructor generally expected students to post at least twice for each discussion. Both students clearly had a considerable online presence. Particularly interesting is the large number of posts by

Table 5.1 Profiles of focal students

	Omar	Jim
Gender	Male	Male
Age	35	38
Discipline	Engineering	Applied linguistics
Home Country	Iraq	South Korea
Personality (self-assessment on questionnaire based on predetermined descriptors)	– Talkative – Active classroom participation – Leader	– Not very talkative – Limited classroom participation – Somewhat shy, cautious and nervous
English Proficiency	Strong oral and written abilities	Oral abilities considerably weaker than written ones

Table 5.2 Omar's and Jim's online participation in number of posts

	Omar	Jim
Online Discussion 1	6	5
Online Discussion 2	2	2
Online Discussion 3	2	6
Online Discussion 4	9	8
Online Discussion 5	39	22

Omar and Jim in the last discussion, which took place on a different platform. Omar made the most contributions of all students in this discussion, and Jim ranked 4th overall. Not only do these numbers stand out compared to the previous four discussions – in Jim's case, they are also in stark contrast with his limited F2F class participation. These data illustrate the context-dependent nature of participation (and arguably identity as well) across online platforms and tasks. Furthermore, they point to a difference between Jim's online and offline identities.

The interview and surveys shed some light on possible reasons for Jim's increased participation online. He stated:

> I'm a talkative person in my language but in [class], I clam up because of my poor language skills.[2]
>
> I am not a good speaker because of my poor speaking skills. For those like me, online discussions are useful because I can take the time to organize the idea and make up the sentences.

The first quote from the interview indicates that Jim experienced some anxiety in the F2F classroom. It implies a discrepancy between who he is in his first language and who he can be in English. His English proficiency seemed to limit Jim in his ability to claim his desired Lx identity. As discussed above, foreign language anxiety is inherently tied to identity and this quote speaks to this connection. The second quote from the end-of-term survey illustrates the affective power of technology. By providing additional processing time, the online discussions seemed to reduce the cognitive interference of anxiety. Ultimately, this allowed Jim to participate more and reduced linguistic barriers to his identity work. By drawing on multiple data sources (data **triangulation**), we can be more confident in our finding that Jim's online and F2F identities differed and did so, at least in part, as a function of modality. Additionally, data triangulation provided new insights into the reasons for this variation.

Let's now turn to the **qualitative analysis** of the content of Omar's and Jim's posts. Unlike quantitative analysis, qualitative analysis doesn't deal in numbers but words to discern patterns and themes. One of the identity-related coding categories that emerged was that of leader, which is reflected in the quotes in Table 5.3. Quotes 1 and 2 are typical of Omar's participation in the last discussion, where students discussed synonyms for select items in a reading passage. With his task-focused leadership, Omar assumed the role of an expert, who provides answers and evaluates his peers' suggestions. Jim, in contrast, evoked a very different kind of leader identity, one with a strong socioemotional orientation: he encouraged sharing and complimented others. For Omar and Jim, the role of leader was a significant part of their online identity. Based on the connection between leadership and group

---

[2] The participants' quotes have not been edited except for spelling.

Table 5.3 Identity-related quotes from Omar and Jim (Excerpts 1–5)

Omar	Jim
1 "Disrupt = disturb = annoy"	4 "I am looking forward to sharing a lot
2 "I believe you are very close to the meaning."	of stories with you in this class."
3 "I think there is more than one in this class who	5 "Your presentation is so impressive."
is stressed. I say, good job all of you!"	

dynamics discussed above, we can assume that their leadership roles and styles affected the dynamics and sense of community of their groups.

Quote 3 is interesting: while Omar responds to a peer's feelings, the use of the pronoun 'you' creates distance between him and his group mates. In contrast, Jim often used "we" to create a group identity and community, for example in this quote (deletions by the author are marked with . . .):

Excerpt 6 (Jim):

"I think we, teachers don't trust students ability. We think, 'students need someone who leads them . . . That is why we are'. Therefore, we hesitate to do pumpkin project in our class. If I come back Korea, I will do another pumpkin project. :D Let's try it! Even if they disappoint us, let's try it . . . because . . . we are born educators!!!!!"

Linguistic practices play a central role in identity construction. Jim's use of the term "educator" is an explicit mention of an identity category that he applies to himself as well as his group mates through the use of the plural pronoun. These quotes show divergent identities for Jim online and offline: while he didn't have a strong F2F presence, he not only participated considerably more online but also even took on a leadership position.

The last excerpt is from a much longer exchange between Jim and his classmate Alim:

Excerpt 7:

JIM: "My dear friend Alim,
        Before I post my comment, I want to say again congratulations on having a beautiful princess. In my country, we call a daughter a princess . . . I am a father like you. I have two kids . . ."

ALIM: "My dearest friend JIM,
        . . . In regard to calling a daughter 'princess', we call her that too. Thanks for your good feeling."

Here, Jim evokes his and Alim's transportable identities as fathers. In an academic ESL class, students' identity as parents is typically not relevant but here Jim made it relevant. Their transportable identities as fathers allowed Jim and Alim to connect, which might have contributed to a sense of community. In contrast, Omar was a father too but when a classmate evoked his being a father, he seemed uncomfortable. It is noteworthy that Jim and Alim are from different cultures. In ESL classrooms, students from the same country/region often form subcommunities and it can be difficult to connect with peers from different backgrounds.

To summarize, this study powerfully illustrates the context-dependent nature of Lx learner identity. Jim's identity in the online component of the class was in stark contrast to his identity in the F2F meetings, where he felt limited by his oral proficiency. This, in turn, triggered anxiety. Online, however, Jim experienced less anxiety, which allowed him to actively create an identity, including that of a leader. He did so with a marked people orientation, drawing on a variety of linguistic tools: plural pronouns, identity labels ("educator"), imperatives ("let's"), words with a positive valence ("impressive," beautiful princess," "looking forward") and comparisons ("I'm a father like you"). In contrast, Omar's leader identity was task-oriented and linguistic and other semiotic tools helped him establish authority (the equal sign) and create distance ("you").

The findings of this study have clear implications for curriculum design because they underscore the value of combining different modalities. Interacting online as well as F2F provides students with opportunities for expanding their identities or claiming more desirable ones, which can be especially beneficial for more reticent or marginalized students. Additionally, it can foster community and allow learners to connect who otherwise would not.

Data Analysis Activity

On the website accompanying this book, you will find some more excerpts of data from Omar, Jim, Alim, and their classmates. Using the data, you will analyze the identities that are invoked and the linguistic tools that the students use to invoke those identities. You will also compare some of your findings to those in this chapter.

Going Further

If this chapter sparked your interest, here are some recommendations for coursework or topics for independent study:

- Second language acquisition
- Qualitative research methods (especially for identity)

- Discourse analysis, including critical discourse analysis (especially if Benesch's call to consider issues of power and inequality resonated with you)
- Sociolinguistics, including interactional sociolinguistics
- Quantitative research methods, especially survey methods and descriptive and basic inferential statistics (i.e., tests of statistical significance)

If you need to complete a project in these classes, you could:

- Observe an Lx class: Which students do you notice and why? What identities are at play and how are they evoked by the students themselves or others?
- Interview an Lx learner about their experiences with anxiety, Lx learner identity, group dynamics and community.
- Visit an online community: What are its norms? If they are not explicitly stated, try to infer them. What roles do members have? Are there hierarchies? How do members create an identity for themselves and others? Be sure to consider language as well as other resources.

Discussion Questions

1. Since classes often bring very different people together and only for a short time, how realistic is it to develop a sense of community? Whose responsibility is it? (How) can we facilitate it? Is this process any different in Lx classes than other classes?
2. Describing her experience as an Lx learner, author Katherine Russell Rich writes:

> The limbic system ... doesn't get revved much in language class. *"Où se trouve la pharmacie?"* ('Where is the pharmacy?') the French teacher asks, but unless you've got a headache, who cares? Need and fear are what stamp words in the cortex. Heartache's an iron press. So's desire. (2009, p. 14)

Discuss this quote in light of the information in this chapter as well as your own experiences and views.

3. What are the potential advantages and drawbacks of quantitative (e.g., surveys) and qualitative analysis (e.g., interaction patterns) in general but also specifically for investigating community, group dynamics, anxiety, and identity? Besides surveys and transcripts of interactions, what other types of data could provide insights into these variables? What are their potential advantages and drawbacks?

4. Language plays a central role in identity creation. In online contexts, how might visuals (e.g., profile pictures, emojis, font type/color) contribute to this process?

FURTHER READING

Foundational Readings

Dörnyei, Z., & Malderez, A. (1997). Group dynamics in foreign language teaching. *System*, *25*(1), 65–81.

Horwitz, E. K., Horwitz, M. B., & Cope, J. (1986). Foreign language classroom anxiety. *The Modern Language Journal*, *70*(2), 125–132.

Norton, B., & Toohey, K. (2011). Identity, language learning, and social change. *Language Teaching*, *44*(4), 412–446.

Recent Publications

Benesch, S. (2012). *Considering emotions in critical English language teaching: Theories and praxis.* New York: Routledge.

Douglas Fir Group. (2016). A transdisciplinary framework for SLA in a multilingual world. *The Modern Language Journal*, *100*, 19–47.

MacIntryre, P. D., & Mercer, S. (2014). Introducing positive psychology to SLA. *Studies in Second Language Learning and Teaching*, *4*(2), 153–172.

REFERENCES

Arnold, J., & Brown, H. D. (1999). A map of the terrain. In J. Arnold (Ed.), *Affect in language learning* (pp. 1–24). Cambridge: Cambridge University Press.

Benesch, S. (2012). *Considering emotions in critical English language teaching: Theories and praxis.* New York: Routledge.

Bucholtz, M., & Hall, K. (2005). Identity and interaction: A sociocultural linguistic approach. *Discourse Studies*, *7*(4–5), 585–614.

Campbell, C. M. (1999). Language anxiety in men and women: Dealing with gender difference in the language classroom. In D. J. Young (Ed.), *Affect in foreign language and second language learning: A practical guide to creating a low-anxiety classroom atmosphere* (pp. 191–215). Boston: McGraw-Hill.

Chang, Y., & Sperling, M. (2014). Discourse and identity among ESL learners: A case study of a community ESL classroom. *Research in the Teaching of English*, *49*(1), 31–51.

Crookes, G. V. (2013). *Critical ELT in action: Foundations, promises, praxis.* New York: Routledge.

Darhower, M. (2007). A tale of two communities: Group dynamics and community building in a Spanish-English telecollaboration. *CALICO Journal, 24*(3), 561–589.

de Costa, P. I. (2015). Reenvisioning language anxiety in the globalized classroom through a social imaginary lense. *Language Learning, 65*(3), 504–532.

Dörnyei, Z. (2005). *The psychology of the language learner: Individual differences in second language acquisition.* Mahwah, NJ: Lawrence Erlbaum.

Dörnyei, Z., & Malderez, A. (1997). Group dynamics in foreign language teaching. *System, 25*(1), 65–81.

   (1999). The role of group dynamics in foreign language learning and teaching. In J. Arnold (Ed.), *Affective language learning* (pp. 155–169). Cambridge: Cambridge University Press.

Elabdali, R. (2016). *Wiki-based collaborative creative writing in the ESL classroom* (unpublished master's thesis). Portland State University, Portland, OR.

Gascoigne, C. (2012). Towards an understanding of the relationship between classroom climate and performance in postsecondary French: An application of the Classroom Climate Inventory. *Foreign Language Annals, 45*(2), 193–202.

Gregersen, T., Meza, M. D., & Macintyre, P. D. (2014). The motion of emotion: Idiodynamic case studies of learners' foreign language anxiety. *The Modern Language Journal, 98*(2), 574–588.

Harklau, L. (2000). From the "good kids" to the "worst": Representations of English language learners across educational settings. *TESOL Quarterly, 34*(1), 35–67.

Hemmi, C. (2014). Dual identities perceived by bilinguals. In S. Mercer & M. Williams (Eds.), *Multiple perspectives on the self in SLA* (pp. 75–91). Bristol: Multilingual Matters.

Horwitz, E. K., Horwitz, M. B., & Cope, J. (1986). Foreign language classroom anxiety. *The Modern Language Journal, 70*(2), 125–132.

Kling, R., & Courtright, C. (2004). Group behavior and learning in electronic forums. In S. Barab, R. Kling, & J. Gray (Eds.), *Designing for virtual communities in the service of learning* (pp. 91–119). New York: Cambridge University Press.

Koch, A. S., & Terrell, T. D. (1991). Affective reactions of foreign language students to Natural Approach activities and teaching techniques. In D. Y. Young (Ed.), *Language anxiety: From theory and research to classroom implications* (pp. 109–126). Englewood Cliffs, NJ: Prentice Hall.

Kramsch, C. (2009). *The multilingual subject. What language learners say about their experience and why it matters.* Oxford: Oxford University Press.

Li, M., & Kim, D. (2016). One wiki, two groups: Dynamic interactions across ESL collaborative writing tasks. *Journal of Second Language Writing, 31*, 25–42.

Miceli, T., Murray, S. V., & Kennedy, C. (2010). Using an L2 blog to enhance learners' participation and sense of community. *Computer Assisted Language Learning, 23*(4), 321–341.

Norton, B. (2000): *Identity and language learning: Gender, ethnicity and educational change.* Harlow, UK: Longman/Pearson Education.

   (2014). Identity and poststructuralist theory in SLA. In S. Mercer & M. Williams (Eds.), *Multiple perspectives on the self in SLA* (pp. 59–74). Bristol: Multilingual Matters.

Onwuegbuzie, A. J., Bailey, P., & Daley, C. E. (2000). Cognitive, affective, personality and demographic predictors of foreign-language achievement. *The Journal of Educational Research*, *94*(1), 3–15.

Oxford, R. L. (1999). "Style wars" as a source of anxiety in language classrooms. In D. Y. Young (Ed.), *Affect in foreign language and second language learning: A practical guide to creating a low-anxiety classroom atmosphere* (pp. 219–238). Boston: McGraw-Hill College.

(2016). Powerfully positive: Search for a model of language learner well-being. In D. Gabryś-Barker & D. Gałajda (Eds.), *Positive psychology perspectives on foreign language learning and teaching* (pp. 21–38). Cham, Switzerland: Springer.

Petersen, S. A., Divitini, M., & Chabert, G. (2008). Identity, sense of community and connectedness in a community of mobile language learners. *ReCALL*, *20*(3), 361–379.

Phillips, E. M. (1992). The effects of language anxiety on students' oral test performance and attitudes. *The Modern Language Journal*, *76*(1), 14–25.

Price, M. L. (1991). The subjective experience of foreign language anxiety: Interviews with highly anxious students. In D. Y. Young (Ed.), *Language anxiety: From theory and research to classroom implications* (pp. 101–108). Englewood Cliffs, NJ: Prentice Hall.

Rich, K. R. (2009). *Dreaming in Hindi*. Boston: Mariner Books.

Riel, M., & Polin, L. (1994). Online learning communities: Common ground and critical differences in designing technical environments. In S. Barab, R. Kling, & J. Gray (Eds.), *Designing for virtual communities in the service of learning* (pp. 16–50). New York: Cambridge University Press.

Rovai, A. P. (2001). Building classroom community at a distance: A case study. *Educational Technology Research and Development*, *49*(4), 33–48.

(2002). Development of an instrument to measure classroom community. *Internet and Higher Education*, *5*(3), 197–211.

Thorne, S. (2009). "Community," semiotic flows, and mediated contribution to activity. *Language Teaching*, *42*(1), 81–94.

Tobias, S. (1986). Anxiety and cognitive processing of instruction. In R. Schwarzer (Ed.), *Self-related cognition in anxiety and motivation* (pp. 35–53). Hillsdale, NJ: Erlbaum.

Vogely, A. (1999). Addressing listening comprehension anxiety. In D. J. Young (Ed.), *Affect in foreign language and second language learning: A practical guide to creating a low-anxiety classroom atmosphere* (pp. 106–123). Boston: McGraw-Hill.

Xiao, Y., & Wong, K. F. (2014). Exploring heritage language anxiety: A study of Chinese heritage language learners. *The Modern Language Journal*, *98*(2), 589–611.

Yan, J. X., & Horwitz, E. K. (2008). Learners' perceptions of how anxiety interacts with personal and instructional factors to influence their achievement in English: A qualitative analysis of EFL learners in China. *Language Learning*, *58*(1), 151–183.

Zimmerman, D. H. (1998). Identity, context and interaction. In C. Antaki & S. Widdicombe (Eds.), *Identities in talk* (pp. 87–106). London: Sage.

6 Automated Assessment of Language

XIAOFEI LU AND BRODY BLUEMEL

Overview of Key Concepts and Issues in Automated Language Assessment

There's an app for that. Both language learners and language educators are familiar with many digital resources for learning and teaching languages, but how do they work? Many testing agencies, such as the Educational Testing Service (ETS, www.ets.org), use technology to evaluate and score language proficiency, but how does the computer know what "good" language is? These, and other, questions are best understood by exploring the research and development of **automated language assessment (ALA)**. ALA is concerned with the development of computational systems that can automate the assessment of language samples. These language samples may include spoken or written excerpts that are produced by first or second language speakers or writers. ALA allows us to objectively and efficiently evaluate large numbers of language samples, and to provide feedback to the language learners. Consider your current class – you may have anywhere from 10 to 100 classmates. Now, consider evaluating a 5-minute speech sample and providing helpful feedback for each individual. If you are in a class of 100, it would take over 8 hours just to listen to the samples. Testing agencies such as ETS evaluate thousands of written and spoken samples. ALA provides a way for effectively evaluating such large sample numbers and providing objective general feedback directly to the individual on specified features of language.

The core tasks in ALA research involve the identification of a set of features that capture the different dimensions of the speaking or writing construct. This is accomplished by a) deriving features from speech or writing samples using existing or newly developed natural language processing (NLP) technology, b) evaluating the correlations of these features with quality ratings of speech or writing samples by human raters, c) developing scoring models that use an optimal subset of the features evaluated to assign scores to speaking or writing samples with a satisfactory level of agreement with human ratings, and d) providing useful feedback to language learners to help them understand their strengths and improve on their problem areas.

In addition, automatic speech assessment entails the use of a high-quality **automated speech recognition (ASR)** system that can convert speech samples to text, and both speech and writing assessment systems also often integrate the capability to detect and flag anomalous language samples that are inappropriate to be assessed automatically. As this explanation illustrates, a lot of work goes into building an ALA system, and a lot of computational analysis occurs behind the digital screen for an ALA system to function properly. However, the up-front effort in developing an ALA system creates an effective tool to assess large samples of set features of language. In this section, we discuss the key concepts and issues involved in the core tasks of ALA and illustrate how they are tackled in the existing research.

Within the field of applied linguistics in general and language testing in particular, ALA research has largely taken a **construct-driven** approach. This means that ALA systems seek to identify quantifiable features of language use that not only predict human ratings of speaking or writing quality, but also reliably use the different dimensions of the speaking or writing construct. The speaking or writing construct itself may be understood in different ways depending on the theoretical models of first or second language speaking or writing. For example, the **six-trait model** (Culham, 2003) that is commonly used to assess writing defines six key qualities of good writing: ideas, organization, voice, word choice, sentence fluency, and conventions. In language testing, the scoring rubric of the speaking or writing task often serves as the de facto speaking or writing construct (Knoch, 2011). This is the case with the TOEFL internet-based test (iBT) Speaking rubrics (ETS, 2014), which delineate the TOEFL iBT Speaking construct (Chen et al., 2018) and specify a number of delivery, language use, and topic development criteria for responses at different score levels. As an illustration, the criteria to score level 4 for the independent speaking task requires that, "[t]he response demonstrates effective use of grammar and vocabulary. It exhibits a fairly high degree of automaticity with good control of basic and complex structures (as appropriate). Some minor (or systematic) errors are noticeable but do not obscure meaning" (ETS, 2014, p. 1).

In searching for features that cover the different **dimensions** of the speaking or writing construct, ALA researchers may look for insights from various subfields of linguistics or applied linguistics, such as second language pronunciation and speaking, second language writing, corpus linguistics, computational linguistics, and language testing. E-rater, the automated scoring system developed at ETS for scoring responses to the TOEFL iBT independent and integrated writing prompts, employs a number of features mapped to the six-trait model discussed above, including grammar, usage, mechanics, style, organization, development, lexical complexity, positive attributes, and topic-specific vocabulary usage (Ramineni, Trapani, Williamson, Davey, & Bridgeman, 2012). Each feature consists of several subfeatures, some of which in turn have multiple layers of microfeatures. For example, the usage feature has seven subfeatures: 1) article errors, 2) confused words, 3) incorrect word forms, 4) faulty comparisons, 5) non-standard verbs or word forms, 6) preposition errors, and 7) double negation. The first subfeature, article errors, is then further broken down into two microfeatures: a) missing article and b) wrong article. As this example illustrates, ALA systems evaluate a wide range of narrowly defined language features specific to the types of language samples being analyzed.

SpeechRater is the automatic scoring system designed at ETS for scoring native speech, such as that produced for the TOEFL Practice Online (TPO). This tool includes various fluency, pronunciation, prosody, rhythm, vocabulary, grammar, content, and discourse coherence features mapped to the TOEFL iBT Speaking construct (Chen et al., 2018). Some of the fluency subfeatures include mean silence duration (the mean time of silent pauses between speech), speaking rate in words per second, number of repetitions, number of disfluencies, and number of interruption points per clause, among others.

ALA systems rely on a set of **natural language processing (NLP)** modules to derive features that have been determined to achieve good construct coverage. These modules provide the capability to automatically analyze the language samples in ways that identify the selected features with an acceptable level of accuracy. The specific type of linguistic analysis entailed by each feature varies. Some features may be derived directly from the raw, unannotated language sample, such as average word length (one of the two lexical complexity subfeatures in the e-rater) or speaking rate in words per second (a fluency feature in the SpeechRater). Other features may require comparison against external resources (e.g., word frequency lists or some large reference corpora), such as **word frequency index**, the second lexical complexity feature in the e-rater. This feature relies on word frequency information derived from a large reference corpus to assess the degree of sophistication of the words used in the language sample.

Other ALA features further require **annotation** of the language sample at one or more linguistic levels and subsequent analysis of the annotated sample. For example, sentence structure microfeatures in e-rater, such as fragments, subject–verb agreement, and missing article, require **syntactic parsing**. Syntactic parsing is the process of annotating each sentence in the writing sample with structural information and grammatical error detection. It is important to understand that grammar errors generally cannot be automatically derived completely accurately, and the specific level of accuracy for each feature depends on the accuracy of the relevant NLP technology used (e.g., Jurafsky & Martin, 2008; Lu, 2014).

After using the ALA tool to identify the features in language samples, their correlations with the human ratings of speaking or writing quality are usually computed, and those with significant correlations are further considered in building the final scoring model that can be used to automatically assign scores to language samples. To generate these correlations, the ALA tool is used to evaluate a set number of language samples that have also been scored manually by human raters. The outcomes of both computer and human raters are compared to identify the **reliability** of the tool, or whether its analysis is consistent across samples. In construct-driven ALA research, it is important to "balance good empirical perform-ance with the validity and interpretability of the scoring models" (Chen et al., 2018, p. 21). In particular, Chen et al. (2018) note that the features included in the final scoring model should adequately reflect the core dimensions of the speaking or writing construct being assessed, that their relative contributions to different dimensions should be transparent, and that the directionality of the correlation coefficients (i.e., positive or negative) of the features in the final model should be consistent with the way they were designed to work. Typically, the final scoring model is usually built using a **supervised machine learning**[1] method that identifies an optimal way to combine some or all of the features to achieve the "balance" mentioned above. Both **prompt-specific models** (i.e., models for scoring responses to specific prompts) and **generic models** (i.e., models for scoring responses to all prompts) may be built and implemented. The e-rater, for example, uses a multiple regression procedure to determine the weights of the candidate features (Ramineni et al., 2012).

As mentioned earlier, automatic speech assessment systems necessarily contain an automated speech recognition (ASR) system. The SpeechRater, for example, uses a third-party ASR system trained on both non-native and native speech data; this ASR system achieves a 38.5 percent word error rate (i.e., the proportion of errone-ously recognized words) on the TPO TOEFL Practice Test data (Chen et al., 2018). As you can imagine, the performance of the ASR system directly influences the accuracy of the ALA tool in which it is used. Thus, in SpeechRater, this level of error rate would likely have a cascading effect on the accuracy of the derived features and the final scoring model. A better developed and more accurate ASR system would directly enhance the performance of the automated speech scoring system and the ALA tool.

Many ALA systems are also designed to detect and filter speech or writing samples that are inappropriate to be scored automatically and that should best be handled by human raters. For example, the e-rater flags essays that are excessively long or brief, that have too many language problems, or that significantly under-develop the key concepts in comparison to other essays on the same topic (Ramineni et al., 2012). SpeechRater, for example, filters responses that copy the question, that

---

[1] Supervised machine learning is a process wherein a set of texts are tagged or annotated with specific examples that the machine should look for and information on how those examples should be interpreted. This set of texts is used to "train" the machine algorithm, which can then be used to evaluate texts that have not been tagged or annotated.

contain no speech, or that are non-English, off-topic, or generic, among other issues (Chen et al., 2018). While these anomalous responses usually account for a very small proportion (less than 1 percent for independent prompts and just about 1 percent for integrated prompts in the case of SpeechRater) such filtering procedures nevertheless help ensure the reliability of automated scoring systems.

Existing ALA systems also provide feedback to language learners to help them understand their strengths and improve on their problem areas. Feedback may include an overall score, scores for different construct dimensions, overall comments, comments for different construct dimensions, and comments and suggestions on specific problems or errors. Examples of ALA systems that offer feedback in all the ways above include the ETS Criterion Online Writing Evaluation Service (available at www.ets.org/criterion), the Jukuu online essay scoring system (available at www.pigai.org), and the iWrite online writing evaluation system (available at iwrite.unipus.cn). Automated diagnostic and feedback systems such as Grammarly (available at www.grammarly.com), on the other hand, focus primarily on detecting problems and errors and providing comments and suggestions for revision.

As the discussion of the various tasks involved in ALA has hopefully made clear, research in this area is highly interdisciplinary and depends heavily on the advancement of NLP technology. ASR modules incorporated in automated speech evaluation systems already have to consider the speech production features of multilingual speakers. However, as is the case with language testing research in general, future ALA research needs to find ways to not only recognize unique features of language produced by multilingual speakers and writers but also consider how they should be accounted for in scoring models and whether and how feedback should be provided on such features.

Our Work in the Automated Assessment of Language

Personal Reflections

Xiaofei Lu   Trained as a computational linguist with a theoretical linguistics background, I found myself working as a corpus linguist in a department of applied linguistics around colleagues with inspiring enthusiasm for and expertise in second language acquisition, second and foreign language teaching and learning, teacher education, discourse and conversation analysis, language learning and technology, language assessment, and multilingualism, among others. Immersed in such a community of scholars, my search for ways to connect my own interest and expertise in computational linguistics to research of interest to the applied linguistics field started naturally in the direction of identifying the types of linguistic analysis of learner language that have been pursued by applied linguists and that have not yet been but have the potential to be reliably automated. I soon realized that the concepts and measurement of lexical and syntactic complexity were of tremendous importance in language proficiency, development, and assessment research and that the limited availability of tools for automating lexical and syntactic complexity analysis posed an analytical scale bottleneck for studies in these areas and in some ways affected the generalizability of their findings. I thus started working on developing tools for automating the assessment of lexical and syntactic complexity in language production (e.g., Lu, 2009, 2010, 2012). This developmental work was then followed by a range of analytical projects that applied these tools to large-scale corpora of learner language to answer questions related to language proficiency, development, and assessment that would have been difficult to address with small-scale manual analyses (e.g., Lu, 2011; Lu & Ai, 2015; Yang, Lu & Weigle, 2015). In terms of the core tasks in ALA research discussed above, my work directly contributes to the first three, that is, identifying lexical and syntactic complexity features that align with the language use dimension of the speaking or writing construct, utilizing existing and developing new NLP technology to derive such features from speech or writing samples, and evaluating the relationship of such features to human ratings of speaking or writing quality.

Brody Bluemel   My work has focused more directly on the development and application of pedagogical language learning technology. In one such project, I developed a parallel-corpus-based reading tool to assist learners of Chinese in the development of reading and Chinese character recognition (Bluemel, 2014). This tool was created by implementing many of the same automated language assessment features that have been outlined above in order to create output texts that are more accessible to readers. I also regularly use ALA tools such as the Lexical Complexity Analyzer (LCA) (Lu, 2012) and L2 Syntactic Complexity Analyzer (L2SCA) (Lu, 2010) as pedagogical resources in assisting students in the development of their English writing. Similar to the data analysis activity outlined below, I either evaluate or assist students in evaluating their own writing samples in comparison to model writing samples. For example, upper-level undergraduate students or graduate students seeking to improve their writing will submit their sample in LCA or L2SCA along with one (or multiple) published sample(s) on the same topic. The output of the analysis helps students to recognize specific output features of their writing that contrast with professional samples in their field. Thus, a student can identify lexical or syntactic aspects of their writing that can be further developed to improve their personal output. While such small applications of these ALA tools do not produce outputs that can be statistically analyzed, they do provide students with concrete and unique evaluative feedback into the development of their writing.

Xiaofei Lu's Work in Automated Language Assessment

In the rest of this section, we first briefly discuss Xiaofei Lu's work on developing the Lexical Complexity Analyzer (LCA; Lu, 2012) and L2 Syntactic Complexity Analyzer (L2SCA; Lu, 2010) and on applying them to the examination of the relationship of lexical complexity to L2 English speaking quality (Lu, 2012) and of syntactic complexity to L2 English writing quality (Yang et al., 2015). Following this is a data analysis activity that can be used to gain a sense of how the automated lexical and syntactic complexity assessment enabled by LCA and L2SCA may be used to evaluate language samples in your own analysis and/or assessment of learner language.

Lu (2012) designed LCA to automate the measurement of lexical richness using twenty-five indices. This research was motivated by the consistent focus on the relationship of lexical richness to the quality of language learners' speaking or writing quality in the language assessment literature (e.g., Wolfe-Quintero, Inagaki, & Kim, 1998; Yu, 2010) and the lack of computational tools for comprehensive lexical richness analysis. The twenty-five indices were selected from the large repertoire of lexical richness measures investigated in previous language acquisition and assessment research to reflect three of the four lexical richness dimensions Read (2000) posited, namely, lexical density, sophistication, and variation – the fourth dimension, lexical errors, was not considered. To compute the twenty-five indices for a language sample, LCA first uses the Stanford **part-of-speech tagger** (Toutanova, Klein, Manning, & Singer, 2003) to automatically annotate every word in the sample with its part-of-speech category (e.g., noun, verb); it then uses MORPHA (Minnen, Carroll, & Pearce, 2001), an automatic **lemmatizer**, to determine the lemma (base form of the word) and inflection of each word in the sample; finally, it uses a Python script to identify and count various types of words (e.g., adjectives, adverbs, lexical words) and subsequently computes the value of each of the twenty-five indices (e.g., the lexical word variation measure is computed by dividing the number of lexical word types or unique lexical words by the total number of lexical word tokens). Explicit definitions are provided for all types of words involved in computing the indices. For example, lexical words are defined as "nouns, adjectives, verbs (excluding modal verbs, auxiliary verbs, 'be,' and 'have'), and adverbs with an adjectival base" (Lu, 2012, p. 192). Lu (2012) also evaluated the relationship of the twenty-five lexical richness measures to the quality of oral narratives produced by L2 English speakers, using transcriptions of 408 test takers' oral productions in the Test for English Majors Band 4 spoken test administered to second-year English majors in four-year colleges in China. Analysis revealed a subset of features that significantly correlated with speaking quality and that significantly differentiated oral narratives at different score levels.

Lu (2010) developed L2SCA, a computational system to automate syntactic complexity analysis of L2 English writing samples using fourteen measures. Similar to the rationale for developing LCA, this endeavor was motivated by the prominent attention to the relationship between syntactic complexity and L2 proficiency, L2 development, and L2 writing quality in the language acquisition and assessment literature and the absence of computational tools for automating syntactic complexity analysis (e.g., Wolfe-Quintero et al., 1998). Wolfe-Quintero et al.'s (1998) and Ortega's (2003) comprehensive reviews of L2 writing syntactic complexity research were referenced in selecting the measures for inclusion in L2SCA. The final set of fourteen measures selected were of five different categories, as summarized in Table 6.1, adapted from Lu (2010). To compute these measures for a writing sample, L2SCA first uses the Stanford syntactic parser (Klein & Manning, 2003) to automatically analyze the syntactic structure of each sentence in the sample, represented in the output as a syntactic tree. It then counts the number of words in the sample and queries the syntactic trees with a set of manually defined patterns using Tregex (Levy & Andrew, 2006), a tool designed specifically for matching patterns in syntactic trees. Each pattern retrieves and tallies defined structural units in the sample. Finally, L2SCA uses the word and structural unit counts to calculate the values of the fourteen indices for the sample. Lu (2010) manually analyzed a set of argumentative essays written by Chinese English as a Foreign Language (EFL)

Table 6.1 Measures in L2 Writing Syntactic Complexity Analyzer (Lu, 2010)

Measure	Code	Definition
Length of production unit		
Mean length of clause	MLC	# of words / # of clauses
Mean length of sentence	MLS	# of words / # of sentences
Mean length of T-unit	MLT	# of words / # of T-units
Amount of subordination		
Clauses per T-unit	C/T	# of clauses / # of T-unit
Complex T-units per T-unit	CT/T	# of complex T-units / # of T-units
Dependent clauses per clause	DC/C	# of dependent clauses / # of clauses
Dependent clauses per T-unit	DC/T	# of dependent clauses / # of T-units
Amount of coordination		
Coordinate phrases per clause	CP/C	# of coordinate phrases / # of clauses
Coordinate phrases per T-unit	CP/T	# of coordinate phrases / # of T-units
T-units per sentence	T/S	# of T-units / # of sentences
Degree of phrasal sophistication		
Complex nominals per clause	CN/C	# of complex nominals / # of clauses
Complex nominals per T-unit	CN/T	# of complex nominals / # of T-units
Verb phrases per T-unit	VP/T	# of verb phrases / # of T-units
Overall sentence complexity		
Clauses per sentence	C/S	# of clauses / # of sentences

learners and Yoon and Polio (2017) manually annotated thirty essays produced by adult English as a Second Language (ESL) learners for twelve indices. The results of both of these studies indicated a high degree of reliability with respect to the indices generated by L2SCA.

In Yang et al. (2015), we investigated the relationship of syntactic complexity to writing quality as judged by human raters and the role of topic in this relationship. Our data consisted of 380 argumentative essays written by 190 ESL graduate students on two different TOEFL iBT independent writing prompts (two essays per student; 30 minutes per essay). The first prompt asked students to discuss whether people place too much emphasis on personal appearance, and the second whether careful planning while young ensures a good future. Each essay was rated by two trained human raters on a five-point scale following the TOEFL iBT Independent Writing scoring guide (ETS, 2008). Syntactic complexity was assessed using eight non-overlapping measures, including six directly generated by L2SCA, namely, MLS, T/S, MLT, DC/T, MLC, CP/C, and two derived from an adapted version of L2SCA, namely, complex noun phrases per clause (CNP/C) and non-finite elements per clause (NFE/C). Topic was found to significantly affect the syntactic complexity features of the essays, with the two topics eliciting a greater degree of complexity in different measures. Regression analyses revealed global sentence and T-unit complexity (MLS and MLT) as consistently significant predictors of scores across the two topics, but more local-level features showed differential predicting power for scores for the two topics. The study thus illustrates "the importance of considering syntactic complexity measurement choices in view of potential influences from the topic of the discourse and the cognitive operations that may be invited by the topic" (Yang et al., 2015, p. 64).

LCA and L2SCA are freely accessible through a fairly self-explanatory web-based interface (available at aihaiyang.com/software). Users can either use the single mode to analyze one or two samples at a time or the batch mode to analyze multiple samples (up to 200 per batch for LCA and up to thirty per batch for L2SCA). They are also both available as downloadable packages (available at www.personal.psu.edu/xxl13/download.html) that can be run through the command-line interface in Unix-like operating systems (e.g., Unix, Linux, and Mac OS X). Detailed, step-by-step instructions on how to use the two tools through the command-line interface are provided in Lu (2014). Additionally, L2SCA can be accessed through TAASSC (Kyle, 2016; available at www.linguisticanalysistools.org/taassc.html, a graphic user interface tool for syntactic analysis).

Since their release, LCA and L2SCA have been widely used by second language researchers to automate lexical and syntactic complexity assessment and to examine the relationship of lexical and syntactic complexity to language proficiency, language development, and speaking or writing quality (e.g., Yoon & Polio, 2017). The lexical and syntactic complexity features integrated in these tools, the tools' capability to automatically derive these features from language samples, and the findings on the relationship of these features to speaking and writing quality have useful implications for the core tasks of ALA research discussed in the first section.

Data Analysis Activity

On the website accompanying this book, you will find two hands-on activities designed to illustrate the functionality of LCA and L2SCA for automating lexical and syntactic complexity assessment and the potential use of this functionality to answer questions of relevance to ALA research. The first activity is an introductory exercise that demonstrates how the tools function and the type of data that is produced. The additional expansion activity will allow you to delve deeper in applying this technology in answering research questions and conducting preliminary statistical analysis.

Going Further

Students interested in becoming involved in ALA research will certainly benefit from courses on language assessment, computational and corpus linguistics, quantitative research methods, second language pronunciation and speaking, and second language writing, among others. In particular, it will be essential to acquire knowledge of the theoretical models of the speaking and writing constructs and skills to perform multi-level linguistic analysis of speaking and writing assessment data, to use or develop NLP technology to automate speech or writing sample analysis, to use statistical procedures to evaluate the relationship of different linguistic features to speaking or writing quality, and to employ machine learning methods to build scoring models. Throughout ALA research, it is certainly also critical to be aware of the importance of issues of reliability and validity. Meanwhile, ALA research necessarily involves collaboration among scholars with overlapping and complementary expertise; therefore, in-depth knowledge of and rich research experience in any combination of these areas, coupled with genuine enthusiasm for ALA research and a solid understanding of its overall framework, goals, and components, will well prepare one for entry into this field.

Discussion Questions

1. How might features characteristic of multilingual speakers and writers be recognized and considered in ALA?

2. ALA systems typically focus on identifying the presence and frequency of positive linguistic features in isolation. Thinking back to the various approaches to language described in the first chapter of this textbook, what approach to language does this focus reflect? How would an ALA system need to be adapted to address other approaches to language? Choose one approach and describe what ALA might look like using this approach.

3. Take another look at the section of the chapter that describes specific features and microfeatures associated with the six-trait model of writing. Which of these features do you think would be easiest to assess using ALA? Which do you think would be more challenging? Why? Based on what you have read about how ALA works, what kinds of information would be needed to develop an ALA system to assess these more challenging features?

4. ALA systems can be designed to provide feedback to language learners in a variety of ways. Based on what you read in the chapter or your own experience with ALA, what are a few different ways that this automated feedback can be provided? Which of these feedback formats do you think would be the most effective for helping language learners? Why?

5. What kinds of digital literacy skills do you think would be important for creating ALA systems? What kinds of digital literacy skills would users need in order to get the most out of these systems?

FURTHER READING

Foundational Readings

Bernstein, J., Van Moere, A., & Cheng, J. (2010). Validating automated speaking tests. *Language Testing, 27*(3), 355–377.

Deane, P. (2013). On the relation between automated essay scoring and modern views of the writing construct. *Assessing Writing, 18*(1), 7–24.

Weigle, S. C. (2013). English language learners and automated scoring of essays: Critical considerations. *Assessing Writing, 18*(1), 85–99.

Recent Publications

Lu, X. (2017). Automated measurement of syntactic complexity in corpus-based L2 writing research and implications for writing assessment. *Language Testing, 34*(4), 493–511.

Wang, Z., Zechner, K., & Sun, Y. (2018). Monitoring the performance of human and automated scores for spoken response. *Language Testing, 35*(1), 101–120.

Yoon, S.-Y., & Bhat, S. (2018). A comparison of grammatical proficiency measures in the automated assessment of spontaneous speech. *Speech Communication, 99*, 221–230.

REFERENCES

Bluemel, B. (2014). Learning in parallel: Using parallel corpora to enhance written language acquisition at the beginning level. *Dimension*, *1*, 31–48.

Chen, L., Zechner, K., Yoon, S.-Y., Evanini, K., Wang, X., Loukina, A., . . . Gyawali, B. (2018). Automated scoring of nonnative speech using the SpeechRater v. 5.0 engine. ETS Research Report (ETS RR-18-10). Princeton, NJ: Educational Testing Service.

Culham, R. (2003). *6 + 1 traits of writing: The complete guide.* New York: Scholastic.

ETS (2008). iBT/Next generation TOEFL test independent writing rubrics (scoring standards). Retrieved from www.ets.org/Media/Tests/TOEFL/pdf/Writing_Rubrics.pdf

(2014). TOEFL iBT speaking section scoring guide. Retrieved from www.ets.org/s/toefl/pdf/toefl_speaking_rubrics.pdf

Jurafsky, D., & Martin, J. H. (2008). *Speech and language processing* (2nd edn). Upper Saddle River, NJ: Prentice Hall.

Klein, D., & Manning, C. D. (2003). Fast exact inference with a factored model for natural language parsing. In S. Becker, S. Thrun, & K. Obermayer (Eds.), *Advances in neural information processing systems 15* (pp. 3–10). Cambridge, MA: MIT Press.

Knoch, U. (2011). Rating scales for diagnostic assessment of writing: What should they look like and where should the criteria come from? *Assessing Writing*, *16*(2), 81–96.

Kyle, K. (2016). *Measuring syntactic development in L2 writing: Fine grained indices of syntactic complexity and usage-based indices of syntactic sophistication* (unpublished doctoral dissertation). Georgia State University, Atlanta.

Levy, R., & Andrew, G. (2006). Tregex and Tsurgeon: Tools for querying and manipulating tree data structures. In *Proceedings of the Fifth International Conference on Language Resources and Evaluation* (pp. 2231–2234). Genoa, Italy: ELRA.

Lu, X. (2009). Automatic measurement of syntactic complexity in child language acquisition. *International Journal of Corpus Linguistics*, *14*(1), 3–28.

(2010). Automatic analysis of syntactic complexity in second language writing. *International Journal of Corpus Linguistics*, *15*(4), 474–496.

(2011). A corpus-based evaluation of syntactic complexity measures as indices of college-level ESL writers' language development. *TESOL Quarterly*, *45*(1), 36–62.

(2012). The relationship of lexical richness to the quality of ESL learners' oral narratives. *The Modern Language Journal*, *96*(2), 190–208.

(2014). *Computational methods for corpus annotation and analysis.* Dordrecht: Springer.

Lu, X., & Ai, H. (2015). Syntactic complexity in college-level English writing: Differences among writers with diverse L1 backgrounds. *Journal of Second Language Writing*, *29*, 16–27.

Minnen, G., Carroll, J., & Pearce, D. (2001). Applied morphological processing of English. *Natural Language Engineering*, *7*(3), 207–223.

Ortega, L. (2003). Syntactic complexity measures and their relationship to L2 proficiency: A research synthesis of college-level L2 writing. *Applied Linguistics*, *24*(4), 492–518.

Ramineni, C., Trapani, C. S., Williamson, D. M., Davey, T., & Bridgeman, B. (2012). Evaluation of the e-rater scoring engine for the TOEFL independent and integrated prompts. ETS Research Report (ETS RR-12-06). Princeton, NJ: Educational Testing Service.

Read, J. (2000). *Assessing vocabulary.* Oxford: Oxford University Press.

Toutanova, K., Klein, D., Manning, C., & Singer, Y. (2003). Feature-rich part-of-speech tagging with a cyclic dependency network. In *Proceedings of the 2003 Human Language Technology Conference of the North American Chapter of the Association for Computational Linguistics* (pp. 252–259). Edmonton, Canada: Association for Computational Linguistics.

Wolfe-Quintero, K., Inagaki, S., & Kim, H.-Y. (1998). *Second language development in writing: Measures of fluency, accuracy and complexity.* Honolulu: University of Hawaii, Second Language Teaching and Curriculum Center.

Yang, W., Lu, X., & Weigle, S. C. (2015). Different topics, different discourse: Relationships among writing topic, measures of syntactic complexity, and judgments of writing quality. *Journal of Second Language Writing, 28,* 53–67.

Yoon, H.-J., & Polio, C. (2017). The linguistic development of students of English as a second language in two written genres. *TESOL Quarterly, 51*(2), 275–301.

Yu, G. (2010). Lexical diversity in writing and speaking task performances. *Applied Linguistics, 31*(2), 236–259.

7 | Developmental Language Disorder and Bilingualism

ELIN THORDARDOTTIR

Suppose you are the parent of a young child and you feel that your child's language is not developing as rapidly or as well as that of your friend's child of a similar age. What could be the reason? Is this a normal stage of development that your child is likely to outgrow, or is it a problem that will persist? Now suppose you are a parent in a similar situation, except your child is exposed to two languages on a regular basis. Is this a problem? Would it be better to limit the child to one language? These are the types of questions that **speech-language pathologists (SLPs)** working with children face almost every day. Distinguishing typical development from language impairment in young children is complicated enough – adding **bilingualism** to the mix brings a whole set of complicating factors.

Overview of Key Concepts and Issues in Developmental Language Disorder and Bilingualism in Childhood

Developmental Language Disorders

Children who are learning the same language follow a remarkably similar sequence of development. They learn words and grammatical structures in a very predictable sequence that is specific to their language. However, they vary widely in how fast they learn. As a result, a large difference in the language skills of two children of the same age can be perfectly normal. In the hypothetical case presented above, it might simply be that your friend's child is developing unusually rapidly, causing you to hold your child to an unrealistic expectation. Alternatively, if your child is performing less well than *most* children of the same age, a **Developmental Language Disorder** (DLD) might be identified. This is why information on the achievement of *most* children (or normative information) is crucial to decision-making in SLP.

 Language impairment can occur as part of, or secondary to, another condition, such as hearing impairment, or a syndrome, such as Down's syndrome, or it can occur without other developmental diagnoses, leaving the underlying cause unclear. The term "DLD" was adopted recently to encompass various previous terms such as "language impairment," "specific language impairment," and "primary language impairment" (Bishop, Snowling, Thompson, Greenhaigh, & Catalise consortium, 2016). DLD entails failure to meet age expectations in learning linguistic elements such as words, grammatical inflections, sentence structures, and pragmatics (how to use language in different contexts) and an estimated high probability that the problem will persist without intervention. The search for the possible cause(s) of DLD has been the subject of much research. The search for the cause is intricately intertwined with the search for ways to correctly identify or rule out DLD in children who are suspected of having it.

A major theoretical debate in the search for the cause of DLD has been whether **language development** is dependent on **cognitive development** or a totally separate system dedicated exclusively to language. One major camp in this debate emphasizes the apparent ability of language to break down independently of cognition, as seen in children who have significantly low language skills but normal intelligence scores on clinical tests (termed **Specific Language Impairment** (SLI) to underscore this dissociation between language and cognition, e.g. Rice & Wexler, 1996). In research following such linguistic deficit accounts, it is assumed that the error patterns observed reflect the nature of the underlying problem and, furthermore, it is often proposed that these error patterns are useful as **clinical markers** for the diagnostic identification of DLD. This research has focused heavily on grammatical morphology. A notable clinical marker of DLD in English is the observation of children age 5 years or older still omitting obligatory verb inflections, saying things such as *she run* and *she running*; a pattern that is perfectly normal in a 3 year old, but should correct itself before age 5 years (Rice & Wexler, 1996). Does this marker also accurately identify DLD in other languages? The majority of research on DLD has focused on English. However, a fairly large body of cross-linguistic research has tested the applicability of linguistic deficit accounts to various other languages. This research has, to some extent, replicated findings across languages, but also uncovered inconsistencies in whether useful linguistic clinical markers can be found at all, the types of linguistic structures that are vulnerable across languages, and the age range in which such vulnerabilities are most pronounced (see review in Elin Thordardottir, 2016a). There are many examples of children with DLD who make very few or no grammatical mistakes, in particular older school-age children but also young children speaking a variety of languages. Instead of their language being characterized by errors, they may use language that is correct, but less sophisticated than that of most children the same age who speak that same language. This fact calls into question whether **grammatical errors** are a central characteristic of DLD as has long been assumed based on work in English.

A different account of the underlying cause of DLD proposes that the problem may stem from a deficit in **processing** complex information of various types. This view became prominent following the accumulation of evidence that children with DLD do evidence weakness in certain areas of cogntion – for example, in mental rotation,

short-term and **working memory**, and **executive function** (Johnston & Ellis Weismer, 1983; Montgomery, Magimarai, & Finney, 2010). Short-term memory is the ability to hold information in active memory (consciousness) while working memory is the ability to hold information in active memory and also manipulate it in some way. Executive function encompasses various processes of controlling one's attention and ignoring distractors. Studies across a large number of languages have consistently shown that children with DLD have significant difficulty in these areas. This is tested, for example, by asking children to repeat non-words (words that sound like real words but have no meaning), or by asking them to repeat sentences of increasing length or complexity, or both (see review in Elin Thordardottir et al., 2011). Tests of this kind have been shown to have good diagnostic accuracy for the identification of DLD in many languages and to be correlated with other language skills. They are used routinely in clinical evaluations (e.g., Conti-Ramsden, Botting, & Faragher, 2001; Elin Thordardottir et al., 2011). These are only two examples of research into the potential causes of DLD. Many questions remain on the nature of DLD, such as why problems manifest principally in language in these children and what additional factors may be at work causing language difficulties in children.

Current research on the nature of DLD uses methods that address linguistic complexity, processing ability or both, such as experimental tasks using items that manipulate frequency, complexity, or processing load (e.g., Elin Thordardottir, 2008; Grela, 2003; Rispens & DeBree, 2014). Other studies examine production in spontaneous language in various contexts such as conversation or narration. A large variety of language domains can be studied through such samples (Nippold, Frantz-Kaspar, Cramond, Kirk, Hayward-Mayhew, & MacKinnon, 2014; Rice & Wexler, 1996). Studies may also use electrophysiological response methods to examine the integrity of linguistic representations and the real-time processing of linguistic stimuli (Royle & Courteau, 2014). Further, intervention studies can provide insights into the nature of DLD, by examining the children's learning processes – for example, whether they learn more efficiently from being presented with the same word or structure multiple times or a variety of related words or structures (Plante et al., 2014). As this brief review reveals, researchers from various domains, including **speech-language pathology** (SLP), linguistics, and psychology have contributed to our evolving understanding of DLD. The identification of DLD and subsequent intervention is carried out by SLPs. Depending on the needs of particular children, an interdisciplinary approach is favored, which can involve such professionals as teachers, occupational therapists, physical therapists, audiologists, psychologists, and physicians.

Bilingualism

Bilingualism in childhood is a term that is used broadly to refer to children who are exposed to two languages on a regular basis and to a significant degree. Bilingual children are a heterogeneous population. Some children are exposed to two languages in their home, others are exposed to one language at home and another one at daycare or school, some from when they were very young, some from an older age. This heterogeneity is why it is so hard to establish what to expect of *most* bilingual children – the type of information that is so crucial to our ability to identify or rule out DLD. Although many factors impact on **bilingual development**, the sheer amount of exposure received in each language emerges as the single most important one (Elin Thordardottir, 2011, 2015a; Hoff, Core, Place, Rumiche, Señor, & Parra, 2012). Children who are exposed to both languages for similar amounts of time tend to master both to a similar degree and may score within the normal range compared to monolinguals in both languages, although, as a group, not quite as high. Those who spend significantly more time using one language than the other will have a stronger and a weaker language (Elin Thordardottir, 2011, 2015a; see review of school-age findings in Elin Thordardottir, 2017a).

Bilingual Developmental Language Disorders

Bilingual children are considered to be neither more nor less likely than monolingual children to have DLD. However, depending on the experiences of particular bilingual children, their developmental level in at least one of their languages can easily look much like DLD.

Assessment of both languages is strongly recommended because each language represents only a part of the child's complete linguistic knowledge. However, formal assessment of both languages is often not possible because of lack of bilingual personnel and adequate language tests, or both. Further, even when both languages can be assessed, the appropriate interpretation of assessments that cover two languages is far from straightforward. Cross-linguistic differences in sequence and rate of development are maintained even when two languages are being learned by the same child (de Houwer, 2005; Elin Thordardottir, 2015a). Thus, children with unequal exposure to their two languages can have vastly different language levels in the two languages, in terms of both vocabulary and grammar (Elin Thordardottir, 2011, 2015a) and even children with equal exposure to both languages can present with very different grammatical profiles in the two languages. Add to this the findings, reviewed in a previous section, showing that languages differ in which structures are most vulnerable to DLD, and it becomes apparent that the interpretation of the test results of a bilingual child is by no means a simple task. A comparison of relative standing compared to monolinguals in each language appears to be a more viable procedure given that the principal indicator of DLD is significantly low language levels (Elin Thordardottir, Rothenberg, Rivard & Naves, 2006; Elin Thordardottir, 2015a).

These considerations underscore the urgent need for assessment tools in various languages and a more refined understanding of the many factors that impact bilingual development in addition to amount of exposure. As for monolingual children, non-word repetition tests have been shown to be useful for the identification of DLD in bilingual children as they are sensitive to DLD but relatively unaffected by bilingualism (Chiat & Polisenska, 2016; Elin Thordardottir & Brandeker, 2013). Perhaps the largest single effort to date to provide solutions to the clinical assessment of bilingual children speaking a variety of languages was carried out by a European research network of SLPs, linguists, psychologists, and educators across European countries (Cost Action IS1804; Armon-Lotem, de Jong & Meir, 2015). Much more work remains to be done.

Beyond assessment, children with DLD need to receive **clinical treatment**. Much more research is available to date on the efficacy of such treatment for monolingual than for bilingual children (see review in Elin Thordardottir, 2017b). In the clinical treatment of bilingual children, the main question of interest tends to be the choice of the language of intervention. Although **bilingual treatment** was at one point considered potentially harmful and likely to cause confusion, studies have consistently shown some type of inclusion of both languages to be helpful, either within the same therapy session, or used by different individuals in different sessions (Elin Thordardottir, Ménard, Cloutier, Pelland-Blais, & Rvachew, 2015). Thinking back to the example of the bilingual child presented at the beginning of this chapter, parents of bilingual children are no longer advised to discontinue bilingual exposure if their child appears to be behind in language development, but rather to ensure that both languages are well supported. Another prominent issue in clinical work with bilingual children is that languages differ not only in terms of linguistic structure, but also in terms of social and pragmatic conventions, such as how families typically communicate with children, what they see as their role in their children's language learning process versus the role of educators and SLPs. Findings in this area from related fields such as anthropology need to be incorporated into clinical SLP work (Heath, 1983; van Kleeck, 1994). Most **clinical interventions** for DLD have been developed in English-speaking countries and were made to suit the needs and traditions of middle-class English speakers. The need for more research in this area is made even more urgent by recent sharp increases in migrant populations (Grech & Cheng, 2010). For example, intervention methods for DLD that involve strategies that use positive feedback to encourage children to speak freely may be less likely to be accepted or efficacious in cultures that do not encourage children to speak freely in the presence of adults. Methods that use books as a vehicle for linguistic interaction are not viable in cultures that do not have a script; in such cultures, books can be replaced by other materials around which communicative interactions can be centered (Johnston & Wong, 2002). Effects of cultural differences also extend to service delivery and policy. A survey conducted by European research network Cost Action IS1406 in over sixty countries and thirty languages identified important inequalities in children's access to services (Law, McKean, Murphy, & Elin Thordardottir, 2019). This fact highlights another important purpose of clinical research, which is to contribute to the development of policies that best serve the public.

My Work in the Area of Assessment of Monolingual and Bilingual Children

Personal Reflection

My interest in cross-linguistic similarities and differences in language development and how they impact assessment measures arose out of need. At the time I did my clinical training as an SLP and later in my doctoral work, there was no SLP training program in my country, Iceland. I received my training at the University of Wisconsin–Madison. Studying speech-language pathology in a different language from that in which one intends to work comes with many complications. I remember being shown a video in one of my classes showing a typical mother–child interaction. I was perplexed. The interaction was not at all typical of those mother–child interactions with which I was familiar. To me, the mother looked a bit exaggerated in her style of communicating with and directing the child. To become a student clinician in my program of study, I had to spend hours of observation to learn this interaction style, because it is culturally appropriate in that context. When working in my country, I need to be careful to undo this style.

My Work in the Development of Assessment Tools in Icelandic and Quebec French

Development of Assessment Tools in Icelandic In my master's thesis, I took on the Icelandic adaptation of the MacArthur–Bates parent report measure (Fenson et al., 1993; Elin Thordardottir & Ellis Weismer, 1996) – a checklist of words and grammatical structures. As another measure against which to validate the parent report, I developed a coding system for morphological and syntactic complexity in **language sample analysis** in Icelandic (Elin Thordardottir & Ellis Weismer, 1998). It was very apparent that the English checklist could not be simply translated into Icelandic nor could the English coding conventions for language samples be applied directly to Icelandic samples. The early words of children are very similar across languages – children speak about their toys, their clothes, the foods they eat, etc. However, children in different countries wear different clothes and eat different foods. Also, the checklist contains a grammatical section, which cannot be the same for all languages. Language sample analysis is one of the most widely used yardsticks of language development, dating back to the work of Roger Brown (1973), including the coding of fourteen English grammatical morphemes (termed Brown's morphemes). Mastery of these morphemes develops gradually between birth and about 5 years of age and they tend to be either correctly used or omitted by children during this period. Icelandic is much more highly inflected than English – in addition to more complex verb inflections, it has grammatical gender and case marking applied to nouns, pronouns, and adjectives, meaning that those words change depending on their syntactic function such as subject or object. Although the English coding conventions were not directly applicable, a similar principle was used. I needed to develop a coding scheme for Icelandic that would be sufficiently simple to be able to be used reliably by different coders, and yet sufficiently complex to capture developmental changes in length of utterance and morphological development. This process required much trial and error, and decisions on a number of issues such as how to code homophonous forms (e.g., two noun cases having the same form) and how to code so-called portmanteau morphemes – grammatical morphemes that denote many grammatical functions at the same time, such as plural, the masculine gender, and the accusative case. Another issue was that of productivity. In Brown's coding, some grammatical distinctions are not coded because of evidence that small children do not consider them as different grammatical forms, but as separate words. An example of this is the irregular past tense of verbs, such as *run* and *ran*, which are considered two different words in Brown's system. The sheer number of Icelandic inflections makes such decisions overly complicated and unreliable; thus, a decision was made to disregard considerations of productivity and to instead take the child's production at face value. As another example, Icelandic uses two forms of adjective declension depending on whether the noun that the adjective modifies is definite or indefinite (e.g., *gula* húsið, "the *yellow* house", versus *gult* hús, "a *yellow* house"). The coding system does not make a distinction between these because children were found not to make errors with these forms. Assessment tools such as this coding system are necessary not only for clinical assessments, but also for research. The resulting language sample analysis procedure was used in a number of subsequent studies on Icelandic-speaking children with typical language development and with DLD, showing that Icelandic morphology, although much more complex than English morphology, is also far more robust (less prone to error), not only in typical development, but also in DLD, even in the face of increased processing demands, and in second language learning (Elin Thordardottir, 2008, 2016a; Elin Thordardottir & Ellis Weismer, 1998; Elin Thordardottir & Gudbjörg Kristin Eiríksdóttir, 2012).

Development of Assessment Tools in Quebec French In my work in Montreal, in Quebec, the French-speaking province of Canada, but where English is also prevalent, I ran into similar issues in terms of the lack of assessment procedures for French. Given my experience with Icelandic and English language sample analysis, I developed a similar system for Quebec French, the complexity of which falls in between English and Icelandic (Elin Thordardottir, 2005). This analysis system has since been used in studies on the typical development and DLD in monolingual French-speaking children (Elin Thordardottir & Namazi, 2007) and bilingual children with and without DLD (Elin Thordardottir, 2015a). In a recent study, results from multiple studies were used to develop a less time-consuming, clinical friendly procedure using shorter samples (Elin Thordardottir, 2016b). These studies revealed that French is more similar to Icelandic than English in that **morphological errors** are few in the spontaneous language of preschoolers with and without DLD (Elin Thordardottir & Namazi, 2007). Together, these studies on Icelandic, French, and bilingual children indicate that particular error patterns are less accurate as clinical markers than the finding of generally low language skills and poor linguistic processing (see discussions in Elin Thordardottir, 2008, 2016a; Elin Thordardottir & Namazi, 2007). Subsequently, I have in my work proposed methods of assessment of bilingual children that use non-word repetition and sentence imitation (Elin Thordardottir & Brandeker, 2013) and the use of monolingual norms with cut-off scores pro-rated based on the child's amount of exposure to the language being tested (Elin Thordardottir, 2015b). Detailed analyses of linguistic structures may or may not be useful for diagnostic purposes, but they remain crucial for the planning of treatment goals. For example, suppose that a child omits certain obligatory grammatical morphemes. In order to get a better sense of whether this reflects an age-appropriate learning stage or whether it is a persistent problem that needs to be targeted in intervention, a detailed analysis of a language sample might be undertaken, similar to that shown in the data exercise provided with this chapter.

Looking back at this work, it is fairly tedious and can appear less appealing than other types of projects because it is undertaken not so much to answer an immediate question, but rather to build the tools necessary to conduct further studies. It is a necessary first step, because without such tools, the language levels of research participants cannot be adequately described or used to accurately match participant groups on linguistic variables. In spite of this, this type of work is surprisingly rewarding, not only because of its utility in research and clinical practice, but also because it leads to unexpected findings, as the following examples illustrate. In my use of a number of types of lexical and grammatical measures in Icelandic, French and English, it was not an unexpected finding that morphological measures would yield higher raw scores for French and Icelandic children compared to their English-speaking counterparts. After all, the former two languages are more highly inflected than English. A less expected but consistent finding is that French- and Icelandic-speaking children also have lower results on lexical measures, found across various types of measures, such as word counts from language samples, as well as formal tests that have been adapted across languages and are often considered to be equivalent versions across languages (e.g., the MacArthur–Bates or the Peabody Picture Vocabulary Test (PPVT)). An implication of this is that raw scores of such tests cannot be used to compare two languages of an individual child or of groups of children: a bilingual child who receives the same raw score on lexical tests in French and in English is not equally proficient in both, but actually probably a bit French dominant. Another finding from the morphological domain, is that both Icelandic- and French-speaking children contrast with English speakers in that they make fewer errors overall, but also in that the errors they do make are more likely to be substitution errors rather than omission errors (Elin Thordardottir, 2008, 2016a; Elin Thordardottir & Namazi, 2007). Further, whereas the errors of English-speaking children involve primarily verb inflection, Icelandic-speaking children make somewhat more errors in case marking (Elin Thordardottir, 2008, 2016a). At the same time, case marking also emerges as an important structure early on. In Icelandic, the distinction between the meanings *into* and *in* is not made by distinct prepositions but by case marking used with the same preposition (into: *í + accusative*; in: *í + dative*). Icelandic children between 2 and 3 years of age were found to use the appropriate case marking but omit the preposition, thus preserving the structure with greater information value (Elin Thordardottir & Ellis Weismer, 1998). Yet another finding, mentioned previously, is that bilingual children follow very language specific morphological patterns of development and can have very unequal levels of grammatical development across their languages. A consequence of this is that at age 5 years, bilingual children with typical development but with low exposure to English exhibited Extended Optional Infinitive patterns of omitting verbal inflection (Elin Thordardottir, 2015a), typically viewed as a strong sign of DLD in that age range. This finding has implications for the underlying nature of DLD, raising important theoretical questions about the reasons why children with DLD make such errors for a longer time than their typically developing counterparts and suggesting this may be tied not to specific linguistic breakdown, but rather to inefficient learning from the available input.

Data Analysis Activity

The data exercise involves language sample analysis of a type that is frequently undertaken for clinical work, for purposes of assessment, and selection of therapy goals. Two English language samples are provided, each from a child age 57 months. One of the children has been exposed exclusively to English; the other child has been exposed to English for 45 percent of her waking hours since birth (her other language is French). The exercise consists in coding the samples for the correct and incorrect use of grammatical morphology, and counting the Mean Length of Utterance (MLU) in words and in morphemes. In performing this exercise, students are encouraged to reflect on whether they can detect which of the children is the bilingual, and whether they think either child shows signs of having DLD, based on the discussion of DLD and bilingualism covered in this chapter.

Going Further

Speech-language pathology is an eclectic, clinical field addressing varied types of communication difficulties across the lifespan, including, in addition to language development and DLD, language breakdown in aging or following traumatic brain injury, speech motor development and speech motor disorders, stuttering, voice disorders, pragmatic communication breakdowns, communication using sign language, and augmented and alternative communication. SLPs receive broad training in various disciplines, including linguistics, psychology, anatomy, neurology, and education for the purpose of applying this knowledge base to clinical work involving assessment, intervention and monitoring of intervention efficacy. In addition to a solid knowledge base, strong interpersonal skills and enjoyment of working with people are a must for those wishing to engage in clinical work. There is a continuing shortage of SLPs with bilingual or multilingual proficiency. Working with bilingual clients requires not only bilingual proficiency, but also an understanding of cross-linguistic differences in the manifestation of DLD and sensitivity to cultural differences in communication and child rearing.

Discussion Questions

1. A finding reported in this chapter is that children who speak highly inflected languages have higher scores on morphological measures and also lower scores on lexical tests than English-speaking children. What are your initial thoughts on possible reasons for the lower scores on lexical tasks? Does it seem that the difference is related to the language learners or to the structure of different languages?
2. When a child who is brought in for language assessment because of suspected DLD is bilingual, what additional consideration would the SLP have to take into account compared to when the child is monolingual? Why is DLD more difficult to identify reliably in a bilingual child?
3. What are the implications of the fact that the large majority of research studies on language development and DLD have focused on English? Can you imagine what the state of research findings would be if research had largely focused on a very different language or cultural context?

FURTHER READING

Foundational Readings

Elin Thordardottir (2014). The typical development of simultaneous bilinguals. In J. Paradis & T. Grüter (Eds.), *Input and experience in bilingual development* (pp. 141–160). Chichester, UK: John Benjamins.

Leonard, L. (1998/2014). *Children with specific language impairment* (1st and 2nd edns). Cambridge, MA: MIT Press.

Paul, R., Norbury, C., & Gosse, C. (2017). *Language disorders from infancy through adolescence: Listening, speaking, reading, writing and communicating* (5th edn). St. Louis, MO: Mosbys.

Recent Publications

Armon-Lotem, S., de Jong, J., & Meir, N. (Eds.). (2015). *Methods for assessing multilingual children: Disentangling bilingualism from language impairment.* Bristol: Multilingual Matters.

Bishop, D. V. M., Snowling, M., Thompson, P., Greenhaigh, T., & Catalise consortium. (2016). CATALISE: A multinational and multidisciplinary Delphi consensus study. Identifying language impairments in children. *PloS One, 11*(17), e0158753.

Law, J., McKean, C., Murphy, C.-A., & Elin Thordardottir (2019). *The theory and practice of managing the child with language impairment – across Europe and beyond.* Routledge.

REFERENCES

Armon-Lotem, S., de Jong, J., & Meir, N. (Eds.). (2015). *Methods for assessing multilingual children: Disentangling bilingualism from language impairment.* Bristol: Multilingual Matters.

Bishop, D. V. M., Snowling, M., Thompson, P., Greenhaigh, T., & Catalise consortium. (2016). CATALISE: A multinational and multidisciplinary Delphi consensus study. Identifying language impairments in children. *PloS One, 11*(17), e0158753.

Brown, R. (1973). *A first language: The early stages.* Cambridge, MA: Harvard University Press.

Chiat, S., & Polišenska, K. (2016). A framework for cross-linguistic nonword repetition tests: Effects of bilingualism and socio-economic status on children's performance. *Journal of Speech-Language and Hearing Research, 59,* 1179–1189.

Conti-Ramsden, G., Botting, N., & Faragher, B. (2001). Psycholinguistic markers for specific language impairment (SLI). *Journal of Child Psychology and Psychiatry, 42,* 741–748.

De Houwer, A. (2005). Early bilingual acquisition: Focus on morphosyntax and the Separate Development Hypothesis. In J. Kroll & A. de Groot (Eds.), *Handbook of bilingualism: Psycholinguistic approaches* (pp. 30–48). New York: Oxford University Press.

Elin Thordardottir (2005). Early lexical and syntactic development in Quebec French and English: Implications for cross-linguistic and bilingual assessment. *International Journal of Language and Communication Disorders, 40*, 243–278.

(2008). Language specific effects of task demands on the manifestation of specific language impairment: A comparison of English and Icelandic. *Journal of Speech, Language and Hearing Research, 51*, 922–937.

(2011). The relationship between bilingual exposure and vocabulary development. *International Journal of Bilingualism, 14*(5), 426–445.

(2015a). The relationship between bilingual exposure and morphological development. *International Journal of Speech Language Pathology, 17*, 97–114.

(2015b). Proposed diagnostic procedures for use with bilingual and cross-linguistic contexts. In S. Armon-Lotem, J. de Jong & N. Meir (Eds.). *Methods for assessing multilingual children: Disentangling bilingualism from language impairment* (pp. 331–358). Bristol: Multilingual Matters.

(2016a). Morphological errors are not a sensitive marker of language impairment in Icelandic children age 4 to 14 years. *Journal of Communicative Disorders, 62*, 82–100.

(2016b). Long versus short language samples: A clinical procedure for French language samples. *Canadian Journal of Speech Language Pathology and Audiology, 40*, 176–197.

(2017a). Are background variables good predictors of need for L2 assistance in school? Effects of age, L1 amount, and timing of exposure on Icelandic language and nonword repetition scores. *International Journal of Bilingual Education and Bilingualism.* https://doi.org/10.1080/13670050.2017.1358695

(2017b). Implementing evidence based practice with limited evidence: The case of language intervention with bilingual children. *Revista de Logopedía, Foniatría y Audiología, 34*(4), 164–171.

Elin Thordardottir & Brandeker, M. (2013). The effect of bilingual exposure versus language impairment on nonword repetition and sentence imitation scores. *Journal of Communication Disorders, 46*, 1–16.

Elin T. Thordardottir & Ellis Weismer, S. (1996). Language assessment via parent report: Development of a screening instrument for Icelandic children. *First Language, 16*, 265–285.

(1998). Mean length of utterance and other language sample measures in early Icelandic. *First Language, 18*, 1–32.

Elin Thordardottir & Gudbjörg Kristin Eiriksdottir (2012). Use of Icelandic morphology by school-age L2 speakers. Poster presented at the Bilingual and Multilingual Interaction conference, ESRC Research Centre on Bilingualism, Bangor, Wales, March–April.

Elin Thordardottir, Kehayia, E., Mazer, B., Lessard, N., Majnemer, A., Sutton, A., Trudeau, N., Chilingarian, G. (2011). Sensitivity and specificity of French language measures for the identification of Primary Language Impairment at age 5. *Journal of Speech, Language and Hearing Research, 54*, 580–597.

Elin Thordardottir, Ménard, S., Cloutier, G., Pelland-Blais, E., & Rvachew, S. (2015). Effectiveness of monolingual L2 and bilingual language intervention for children from minority language groups: A randomized control trial. *Journal of Speech, Language and Hearing Research, 58*(2), 287–300.

Elin Thordardottir & Namazi, M. (2007), Specific language impairment in French-speaking children: Beyond grammatical morphology. *Journal of Speech, Language and Hearing Research, 50,* 698–715.

Elin Thordardottir, Rothenberg, A., Rivard, M-E., & Naves, R. (2006). Bilingual assessment: Can overall proficiency be estimated from separate measurement of two languages? *Journal of Multilingual Communication Disorders, 4,* 1–21.

Fenson, L., Dale, P., Reznick, S., Thal. D., Bates, E., Hartung, J., Pethick, S., Reilly, J. (1993). *Technical manual for the MacArthur Communicative Development Inventories.* San Diego, CA: San Diego State University.

Grech, H., & Cheng, L. (2010). Communication in the migrant community in Malta. *Folia Phoniatrica et Logopaedica, 62,* 246–254.

Grela, B. (2003). The omission of subject arguments in children with specific language impairment. *Clinical Linguistics and Phonetics, 17,* 153–169.

Heath, S. B. (1983). *Ways with words: Language, life and work in communities and classrooms.* Cambridge: Cambridge University Press.

Hoff, E., Core, C., Place, S., Rumiche, R., Señor, M., & Parra, M. (2012). Dual language exposure and early bilingual development. *Journal of Child Language, 39,* 1–27.

Johnston, J., & Ellis Weismer, S. (1983). Mental rotation abilities in language-disordered children. *Journal of Speech and Hearing Research, 26,* 397–403.

Johnston, J., & Wong, A. (2002). Cultural differences in beliefs and practices concerning talk to children. *Journal of Speech, Language and Hearing Research, 45,* 916–926.

Law, J., McKean, C., Murphy, C.-A., & Thordardottir, E. (2019). *The theory and practice of managing the child with language impairment – across Europe and beyond.* Abingdon: Routledge.

Montgomery, J., Magimairaj, B., & Finney, M. (2010). Working memory and specific language impairment: An update on the relation and perspectives on assessment and treatment. *American Journal of Speech Language Pathology, 19,* 78–94.

Nippold, M., Frantz-Kaspar, M., Cramond, P., Kirk, C., Hayward-Mayhew, C., & MacKinnon, M. (2014). Conversational and narrative speaking in adolescents: Examining the use of complex syntax. *Journal of Speech, Language, and Hearing Research, 57,* 876–886.

Plante, E., Ogilvie, T., Vance, R., Aguilar, J., Dailey, N., Meyers, C., Lieser, A., Burton, R. (2014). Variability in the language input to children enhances learning in a treatment context. *American Journal of Speech Language Pathology, 23,* 530–545.

Rice, M., & Wexler, K. (1996). Toward tense as a clinical marker of Specific Language Impairment in English-speaking children. *Journal of Speech, Language and Hearing Research, 39,* 1239–1257.

Rispens, J., & De Bree, E. (2014). Past tense productivity in Dutch children with and without SLI: The role of morphophonology and frequency. *The Journal of Child Language, 41,* 200–225.

Royle, P., & Courteau, E. (2014). Language processing in children with specific language impairment: A review of event-related potential studies. In L. T. Klein & V. Amato (Eds.), *Language Processing: New Research* (pp. 33–64). Hauppauge, NY: Nova Science Publishers.

van Kleeck, A. (1994). Potential cultural bias in training parents as conversational partners with their children who have delays in language development. *American Journal of Speech-Language Pathology, 3,* 67–78.

SECTION 2:
Language Socialization

8 Literacy Education and Systemic Functional Linguistics

DAVID ROSE

This chapter is not about an individual project in applied linguistics, but an entire approach to teaching spoken and written language that has been developed over many decades in the research tradition of systemic functional linguistics (SFL). The approach is known as **genre-based literacy pedagogy**. The term "genre" refers to the ways in which texts vary according to their social purposes. Stories engage and entertain readers; explanations explain sequences of cause and effect; procedures direct activities; arguments evaluate issues and points of view. Genre-based literacy pedagogy (or simply genre pedagogy) guides learners to recognize and use the text structures and language patterns of different genres in their reading and writing. This chapter starts with the SFL model of text-in-context. It then introduces analyses of two sets of genres in education. One set is the genres of educational curricula, such as stories, explanations, procedures, arguments. These are known as knowledge genres. The other is the genres of classroom teaching and learning. These are known as curriculum genres. Genre pedagogy is then exemplified with extracts from a science literacy lesson.

Overview of Key Concepts in Systemic Functional Linguistics and Literacy Education

For six decades, **systemic functional linguistic** theory has developed in tandem with its applications in language and literacy teaching. Its founder, M. A. K. Halliday, describes SFL as an "appliable linguistics":

> Applied linguistics is not a separate domain; it is the principles and practice that come from an understanding of language. Adopting these principles and practices provides, in turn, a way in to understanding language. In this perspective, you look for models of language that neutralize the difference between theory and application; in the light of which, research and development in language education become one process rather than two. (in Martin, 2013, p. 65)

Halliday was himself a language teacher in the post-World War II years, of English and Chinese, and the roots of SFL lay in ideals of education as social justice that he shared with colleagues. Through the 1960s, he worked on literacy projects such as *Breakthrough to Literacy* with primary, secondary, and tertiary language educators in the UK (Martin, 2013). However, it is since the 1980s that the influence of SFL in language teaching has grown internationally, with **genre-based approaches** to teaching developed in what has become known as the Sydney School (hereafter **genre pedagogy**). This methodology has been designed through a series of large-scale action research projects with teachers in various educational contexts, informed by SFL, by the educational sociology of Basil Bernstein, and by Halliday's and colleagues' work on language development. This research program and its numerous publications are surveyed by Martin (2000), Rose (2011, 2015a) and Rose and Martin (2012). Alongside language, SFL-based research has also examined other modalities, such as images, gesture, music, movement, and built spaces (Dreyfus, Hood & Stenglin, 2011).

There have been three major phases in genre pedagogy's development: the initial design of the genre writing pedagogy in the 1980s with a handful of genres that students write in the primary school; the extension of the writing pedagogy in the 1990s to genres across the secondary school curriculum, further education, and workplaces; and the development of the genre reading pedagogy from the late 1990s, known as **Reading to Learn** (R2L), which integrates reading and writing with teaching practice across the curriculum at primary, secondary, and tertiary education levels (Rose, 2019). The strategies developed in the initial stage are now standard literacy teaching practice in primary schools across Australia and increasingly internationally, as well as in ESL and academic literacy programs. The R2L reading and writing strategies have been consistently shown to accelerate literacy development at twice to over four times expected rates, at the same time as they narrow the achievement gap between the most and least successful students in any class (Carusi-Lees, 2017; Rose, 2015b; Shum, Tai & Shi, 2016).

The Systemic Functional Linguistics Model of Text in Social Context

Genre pedagogy is informed by the SFL model of language as text in social context (Halliday & Matthiessen, 2014; Martin & Rose, 2007, 2008). One dimension of this model is its organization in levels or strata that are related by realization. Educational contexts include the knowledge and values of the school curriculum and the pedagogic activities through which these fields are taught and learnt, together with relations between teachers and learners, and the spoken, written, and visual modalities through which meanings are exchanged. This level of social context is known as **register**. On the one hand is the **curriculum register** of knowledge and values; on the other is the **pedagogic register** of activities, relations, and modalities in the classroom.

In the SFL model, these variable dimensions of register are woven together at a more abstract contextual level of **genre**. A genre is a configuration of variations in fields of activity, social relations, and modalities. Genres are staged, goal-oriented social processes: social because they are negotiated between speakers, writers, and readers; goal oriented because texts unfold toward their participants' goals; staged, because it usually takes more than one step to reach their goals.

Two general families of genres constitute the culture of schooling. One is the genres of school knowledge that students learn to read and write, or **knowledge genres**, including varieties of stories, chronicles, explanations, reports, procedures, arguments, and text responses (see Table 8.1). Genre and register are independently variable. For example, stories may be spoken or written about all manner of fields. Explanations are used to explain natural processes in science, social processes in history or geography, technical processes in technology, or mathematical processes. Procedures may be used to direct activities in each of these subject areas. Arguments are used to negotiate positions around social issues, while responses are written about literature, arts, music, film, and drama. Written genres such as these have evolved in institutions such as sciences, humanities, industries, and public administration.

The other educational genre family is the multimodal genres of classroom practice, in which knowledge is exchanged between teachers and learners, or **curriculum genres**. A key curriculum genre in genre pedagogy is known as joint construction, in which an example text is used to model writing. Key features of the model are pointed out and discussed, and the teacher guides the class to construct a new text using a similar structure and features of language. This guided practice provides a strong foundation for students to successfully write texts in this genre. Curriculum genres configure two registers together – a curriculum register of knowledge and values, and a pedagogic register of activities, modalities and teacher/learner relations. Curriculum genres have evolved in educational institutions to reproduce and change the knowledge and values encoded in knowledge genres. The research tradition in SFL genre pedagogy has focused on describing knowledge genres, including their social functions, structures and language features, and on designing curriculum genres for students to succeed with reading and writing knowledge genres. In genre pedagogy, a key element of curriculum register is knowledge about language.

This model is critical for integrating language learning with curriculum learning, as the social contexts of education are realized (manifested/symbolized/expressed) in the language of its texts. The curriculum is learnt through the language in which it is written in texts and discussed in the classroom. SFL describes the organization of language itself in three strata. Patterns of meaning in texts (discourse) are realized as patterns of wordings in sentences (grammar), which are realized as patterns of sounding (phonology) or lettering (graphology). The strata of language and context are represented as sets of nested circles in Figure 8.1.

Table 8.1 Major knowledge genres in the school curriculum

	genre	purpose	stages	phases
Stories	recount	recounting events	Orientation Events	*setting* *description*
	narrative	resolving a complication	Orientation Complication Resolution	*events* *problem* *solution*
	exemplum	judging character or behavior	Orientation Complication Evaluation	*reaction* *result* *comment*
	anecdote	sharing an emotional reaction	Orientation Complication Evaluation	*reflection* *episode (includes other* *phases)*
Chronicles	autobiographical recount	recounting life events	Orientation Life events	*birth, family, early life* *events*
	biographical recount	recounting life stages	Orientation Life stages	*birth, family, early life,* *fame stages*
	historical recount	recounting historical events	Background Historical stages	*topic, background stage* *l, 2. . . (para* *structure)*
	historical account	explaining historical events (causes & effects)	Background Historical stages	*topic, background stage* *1, 2. . . (para* *structure)*
Explanations	sequential explanation	explaining a sequence	Phenomenon Explanation	*step 1, 2. . .*
	conditional explanation	alternative causes & effects (*if a, then b*)	(Phenomenon) Explanation	*condition 1, 2. . .*
	factorial explanation	multiple causes for one effect	Phenomenon: outcome Explanation	*outcome (preview* *factors) factor 1,* *2. . . (para structure)*
	consequential explanation	multiple effects from one cause	Phenomenon: cause Explanation	*cause (preview)* *consequence 1, 2. . .* *(para struct)*
Reports	descriptive report	classifying & describing a thing	Classification Description	*phases depend on topic* *(e.g., appearance,* *behavior. . .)*
	classifying report	classifying & describing types of things	Classification Description	*type 1, 2. . ..*
	compositional report	describing parts of wholes	Classification Description	*part 1, 2. . .*
Procedures	procedure	how to do an activity	Purpose, Equipment Method	*(hypothesis,* *ingredients. . .) steps*
	protocol	what to do & not do	Purpose Rules/List	*rules, warnings. . .*

Table 8.1 (*cont.*)

	genre	purpose	stages	phases
	experiment/ observation report	recounting & evaluating experiment/ observation	Aim, Equipment Method Results, Discussion	*(hypothesis, preview) steps (review) evaluate results*
	case study	recounting & evaluating in stances	Issue, Background Description, Evaluation Recommendations	*phases depend on topic & length*
	strategic plan	planning strategies	Purpose, Background Strategies, Evaluation	*phases depend on topic & length*
Arguments	exposition	arguing for a point of view	Thesis Arguments Restatement	*position statement, preview arguments, para structure review, restate position*
	discussion	discussing two or more points of view	Issue Sides Resolution	*issue statement, preview sides, para structure review, resolve issue*
Responses	review	evaluating a literacy, visual or musical text	Context Description of text Judgment	*text, author (audience) steps/components of text evaluation of text*
	interpretation	interpreting themes or aesthetics of a text	Evaluation Synopsis of text Reevaluation	*text, preview of themes themes, techniques, para struct evaluate, synthesize themes*
	comparative interpretation	interpreting themes in multiple texts	Evaluation Synopsis Reevaluation	*texts, preview of themes by themes or by texts evaluate, synthesize*

Within each stratum, SFL describes language as systems of resources for making meaning. For example, at the level of graphology, the ALPHABET is a system of letters for expressing words in writing. At the level of grammar, MOOD is a system for distinguishing statements from questions or commands (*it does/does it?/ do it!*). At the level of discourse, CONJUNCTION is a system of resources for logically relating sentences as a text unfolds (*and/then/so*). Resources such as these are deployed to make meaning as a text unfolds. A text is a series of instances of these resources.

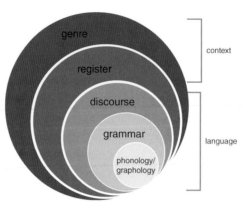

Figure 8.1 Strata of language in context

Systems of resources at each stratum of language and social context constitute the reservoir of potential meanings in a culture. From a culture's overall reservoir of meaning resources, groups and individuals in a community develop varying repertoires for making meaning. A central function of education is to expand the repertoires of learners by providing access to the meanings that are continually evolving in the institutions of modern culture. The model is rich enough to account for the complexity and diversity of teaching and learning in contemporary education. It is neither normative nor static, but allows us to systematically map processes of learning, and hence design effective strategies for teaching.

Describing Knowledge Genres

The stages of a genre are relatively stable components of its organization, but phases within each stage are more variable, and may be unique to the particular text. In written texts, each paragraph tends to express one or more phases of meaning. Table 8.1 maps the major families of knowledge genres that SFL research found students reading and writing in school, the social goals of these genres, and expected stages (described in depth in Martin & Rose, 2008). The first column groups genres in families, followed by genre names, their social goals or purpose, their typical stages, and common types of phases within genre stages.

An example is Text 1, a sequential explanation of the Water Cycle, from a junior secondary science textbook (Cash, Quinton & Tilley, 2012, p. 96). Stages are labeled with initial capitals, and phases in lower case.

The global structure of Text 1 is a sequence of causes and effects between and within steps. The Phenomenon stage presents a dual field, one common sense, *water … is constantly moving*, and the other technical, *it changes state in cycles*. The steps are named technically as *evaporation (transpiration)*, *condensation*, and *precipitation*.

Text 1 Sequential explanation

Phenomenon	Water is found in many different forms on Earth and is constantly moving from one place to another. As it moves it changes state in cycles, from liquid water, to water vapour, sometimes to ice, and back to liquid again.
Explanation step 1	The Sun evaporates water from the surface of rivers, lakes and streams, and from the soil. This change from liquid water to vapour is called evaporation. Other water vapour comes from trees and other plants through the process of transpiration.
step 2	Winds may carry this water vapour high into the atmosphere where it can become so cold that is forms clouds, which consist of tiny droplets of liquid water. The change from vapour to liquid is known as condensation.
step 3	When clouds become saturated, the water falls as rain, or even hail or snow. This is known as precipitation. Precipitation returns water to the land where it can seep into groundwater, or flow into streams and rivers.
step 4	Some water may have travelled thousands of kilometres, or some may have returned straight back to an ocean or lake where the Sun's heat once more causes evaporation. In this way the cycle starts again and the pattern can be repeated. These changes are known as the water cycle.

My Work in Literacy Education and SFL

Personal Reflection

My own involvement in genre pedagogy and R2L arose from many years working with Indigenous Australian communities, for whom literacy is a pressing matter of social justice (Rose, 2010). I worked as a community educator in remote central Australian communities from the 1980s, and learnt to speak the Pitjantjatjara language (Rose, 2001). However, the people's greatest wish was for their children and young people to become literate in English, for further education, to run the services in their communities, and to control their relations with mainstream Australia. This motivated my study of SFL and genre pedagogy, starting with master's degree courses in applied linguistics. Beginning in the late 1990s, I initiated action research projects with teachers of Indigenous students, applying genre pedagogy to reading and writing in school. These students were often up to eight years behind their non-Indigenous peers' literacy levels, but rapidly learnt to read and write at grade-appropriate levels, using the pedagogy we developed. This work has expanded over two decades as the *Reading to Learn* methodology, which now achieves similar results in educational contexts all over the world (Rose, 2017).

My Work Designing Curriculum Genres

In *Reading to Learn*, a large set of curriculum genres have been designed to guide reading and writing across the school (Martin & Rose, 2008; Rose, 2018). Within these curriculum genres, pedagogic activities are designed to prepare all students to succeed with learning tasks, pedagogic relations include all students equally in learning activities, and pedagogic modalities give students equal access to curriculum knowledge. Here we will review just four core curriculum genres in the R2L methodology. These four curriculum genres will then be illustrated with analyses of a lesson in junior secondary science that the reader may watch in online videos (NESA, 2018).

The first curriculum genre is known as **preparing for reading**, in which students are supported to read curriculum texts that may be beyond their independent reading skills. The task is to follow a text with general understanding as it is read. It is prepared with the background knowledge needed to access the text, and a preview of how the field unfolds through the text, step by step. This preview reduces the reading task, enabling students to follow the words of the text without struggling to recognize what is going on. With denser factual texts, the preview may be followed with reading paragraph by paragraph. Each paragraph is briefly previewed and read, and its key points reviewed. Students may also be guided to mark key information as it is reviewed. Preparing for reading enables teaching of curriculum content through reading, despite students' varying reading skills. It places curriculum texts at the center of classroom practice, supporting students to develop skills in independent learning through reading.

The next curriculum genre is **detailed reading**. Key passages from reading texts are selected and read sentence-by-sentence. The goal is to make the reading processes of proficient readers visible to learners, and simultaneously enable the teacher to monitor these otherwise hidden processes. The method is a carefully designed exchange between teachers and their classes. The teacher first previews a sentence and reads it aloud, as students follow the words. Each wording in the sentence is then previewed with a meaning cue. The students' task is to identify and mark the wording from the meaning cue. They are asked in turn to identify the words aloud, in order to engage and affirm all students equally, and the whole class marks the words in their copies. Once wordings are identified, their meanings may be elaborated with further discussion. Detailed reading is a powerful curriculum genre for supporting all students in a class to read passages of text in depth and detail, no matter what their level of independent reading skills and the level of difficulty of the text.

Writing begins with **joint rewriting**, in which the teacher guides students to use the language of a detailed reading passage to write a new passage of text. With factual texts, notes are made of the information highlighted during detailed reading, and new sentences are written using the same information. With a passage from a story, the same patterns of literary language are used but with new characters, events, and settings. With arguments and text responses, the same evaluative language patterns are borrowed from detailed reading passages, to evaluate a new issue or text.

The rewriting task is prepared by reviewing the language patterns in the detailed reading passage, or notes from a factual text. As in detailed reading, the new passage is constructed sentence-by-sentence, by reviewing each wording, proposing new wordings, and reviewing each proposal. Joint rewriting is a powerful method for learning how to appropriate the language resources of accomplished authors, to build students' repertoires. It makes explicit the otherwise intuitive process of learning to write from reading, as accomplished writers do themselves. Explicit teaching of this process has roots going back to the classical practice of *imitatio*. Joint rewriting may be followed by individual rewriting, in which students practice the same task with the teacher's guidance as needed.

The final genre in the sequence is **joint construction**, in which students are guided to construct whole texts in target genres. As in joint rewriting, the focus in R2L is on recognizing patterns in instances and appropriating them to create a new instance. To this end, texts are deconstructed into phases at the level of paragraphs, and the same patterns of phases are followed in joint construction. Again, joint construction may be followed by individual construction, in which students practice using the same generic structuring with the teacher's guidance, before writing independently for evaluation.

Independent writing follows the sequence of curriculum genres outlined here, in which learners apply their developing repertoires of genre, register, discourse, grammar, and spelling resources. The SFL model of language shows us the overwhelming complexity of the writing task, and why learners so often struggle with it. The R2L sequence of curriculum genres breaks this complexity into manageable tasks, supporting and handing control to learners to build their own repertoires in steps at each level, preparing every student to succeed at assessment tasks. The overall sequence in any curriculum unit starts and ends with whole texts, working on smaller units in more detail in the intervening activities.

This sequence of curriculum genres constitutes the core of the R2L genre methodology, but each genre is actually a resource in its own right. They are elements of teachers' repertoires that can be deployed flexibly depending on the teaching goals for each lesson and curriculum unit and student needs. In this respect they are no different from the range of standard curriculum genres that teachers deploy in their daily practice. A substantial difference is that these genres are explicitly designed, using the linguistic, pedagogic, and social principles of the methodology.

Analyzing and Designing Pedagogic Registers

Within each curriculum genre, pedagogic activities, relations and modalities are carefully designed. The aim is for all learners to participate successfully in learning interactions, and to get equal access to the knowledge of the curriculum, through spoken, written, and visual modalities. Fundamental to this design is an analysis of pedagogic activities that are always centered around learning tasks. Only the learner

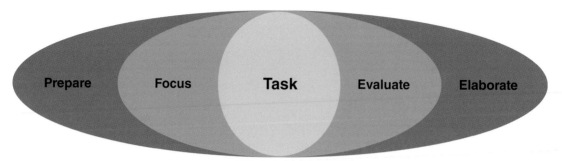

Figure 8.2 Orbital structuring of pedagogic activity

can do this task. A teacher cannot do it for them, but a teacher can guide the learner to succeed with a task, and then hand control to the learner to attempt it. This guidance is the essence of the pedagogic relation between teachers and learners. However, pedagogic relations are not static, they are structured in sequences of alternating teacher/learner roles.

Minimally, teacher guidance involves specifying a task, and usually evaluating the learner's performance. This gives a sequence of three core phases in a pedagogic activity, that we call Focus, Task, and Evaluate, in which the roles of teacher and learner alternate. However, more support can be provided by deliberately preparing the learner for the task. This is most apparent in manual tasks, which a teacher may demonstrate before handing control to the learner. If the learner is successful, it is also possible to elaborate by extending or reinforcing understanding. Prepare and Elaborate are optional outer phases in a pedagogic activity, modeled in Figure 8.2 as an orbital structure.

This analysis of pedagogic activity can be applied to the levels of curriculum units, lessons, and activities within each lesson. At the level of teacher/learner interactions, a series of micro-tasks are revealed, in which learners propose items from their knowledge or identify meanings in texts or images. These tasks are usually focused with a teacher question, evaluated by affirming or rejecting, and elaborated with further knowledge. They may also be prepared to ensure appropriate responses. We will use the term "**learning cycles**" for this level of pedagogic activities. (This pattern of classroom discourse is also widely known as initiation–response–feedback or IRF cycles.)

Exemplar Lesson Analysis

This analysis of teacher/learner interactions as learning cycles is applied to the following transcripts of a junior secondary science literacy lesson, using the Water Cycle explanation in Text 1. The lesson includes preparing for reading, detailed reading, notemaking, and joint construction. Videos of each stage can be viewed at

Table 8.2 Preparing for reading

1	T	*So what we're going to look at today is the Water Cycle. So we're going to look at how the water gets cycled around and can move through lots of different places.*	Prepare	topic1
		So what we're going to talk about first is summarized on our diagram here on the board [points to diagram].	Focus	diagram
		Where have we got water? Can we name some of the specific places?	Focus	topic1
	S1	*Ocean*	Identify	picture
	T	*OK. So we've got the ocean labelled [points to label]*	Affirm	
	S2	*River*	Identify	picture
	T	*Rivers. Shown on the diagram [points to rivers]*	Affirm	
	S3	*Lake*	Identify	picture
	T	*And the lake [points to lake]*	Affirm	
2	T	*What type of water is it there? Think back to our states of matter, solid, liquid, gas.*	Prepare	topic2
		What are we talking about in rivers, lakes and oceans?	Focus	topic2
	S4	*Liquid*	Propose	topic2
	T	*We're talking about liquid, thanks.*	Affirm	topic2
3	T	*What makes it go up into the sky?*	Focus	topic2
	S5	*Water vapour?*	Propose	topic2
	T	*OK, so it's becoming water vapour over here, excellent.*	Affirm	
		If we look at this label here, "water evaporates from forests, farms, rivers, lakes, swamps" [points to label].	Elaborate	technical term
		So we're talking about how it evaporates and I'll change that into a noun to change it into the process of evaporation. So I'm going to write that up here [writes label].		
	Ss	*[write label on own copies]*		
4	T	*Can you all say that for me?*	Focus	pronunciation
	Ss	*Evaporation*	Propose	pronunciation
	T	*OK*	Affirm	
		So we got evaporation. It's gone from liquid water, to water vapour, to water as a gas [points to diagram].	Elaborate	topic2

NESA (2018). These short videos should be viewed in tandem with reading these analyses, and applying the analyses in class and homework activities.

In preparing for reading, the teacher uses a projected diagram of the Water Cycle to orient learners to the technical field and the technical terms they will encounter in the text. There are four numbered learning cycles in this extract. Horizontal lines mark each learning cycle (Table 8.2).

In the first cycle, the teacher prepares the common-sense topic, *water moving* [topic1]. She then focuses on the diagram and asks students to identify places of water. Students identify three places which she affirms. In the second cycle, she reminds students about the technical topic, *states of matter* [topic2]. A student proposes *liquid* and she affirms. The third cycle is concerned with evaporation. A student proposes water vapour, which she affirms and elaborates by turning the process *evaporating* into a technical term *evaporation*, which is written on the diagram and in students' own copies. In the fourth cycle, students practice pronouncing this term.

Following the preparation for reading, the teacher guides students to read the text in detail. Table 8.3 is a transcript of reading the first paragraph. Cycles 1–3 concern the first sentence. The teacher first prepares the sentence, and then focuses on each wording in turn, preparing where necessary. Students identify the wordings, and she affirms and elaborates the technical topic [topic2] where appropriate. Cycles 4–7 concern the second sentence, following the same pattern, and culminate by elaborating on the two aspects of the topic [topic 1 and 2].

Following this detailed reading, students took turns to scribe the highlighted information as notes on the board, as other students dictated, and the teacher elaborated with more knowledge of the topic. She then guided them to label each stage and phase of the text, to make the structure of the topic explicit, as a sequence of Phenomenon and steps.

Table 8.4 illustrates Joint Construction using these notes. The teacher prepares the activity by pointing to the notes and the labels they have written to organize the information. She then asks a student to scribe on the board, as she guides the class to put the notes into new sentences. In response to her focus questions, various students propose wordings, which she accepts and adjusts as they are scribed on the board. Each learning cycle is concerned with one wording at a time. Cycles 1–3 negotiate *Water keeps on moving*; cycles 4–6 *It constantly changes state*; cycles 7–9 *from liquid water, to vapour, and back to liquid.*

In this exchange, teacher and students are negotiating, not just the wordings to write new sentences, but also the scientific concepts associated with the topic. The combination of explicit guidance, with increasing handover to the students, and the use of metadiscourse for elements of the text, ensures that all students will ultimately be able to successfully write their own texts in the same genre, using the kinds of scientific language they have negotiated in the joint construction. By embedding scientific literacy in science teaching, students who would otherwise be excluded from success in secondary science learn to control both the technical field, and the language that realizes the field.

Data Analysis Activity

Using the data on the website accompanying this book, you will practice analyzing knowledge and curriculum genres. Videos and resources for the lesson are available

Table 8.3 Detailed reading

#	Speaker	Text		
1	T	That first sentence is talking about what's going to be explained. It's talking about why it's called a Water Cycle overall. Alright, so I'll read you the sentence. "Water is found in many different forms on Earth and is constantly moving from one place to another. As it moves, it changes state in cycles, from liquid water to water vapour, sometimes to ice, and back to liquid again."	Prepare	sentence
		So Zac, can you tell me, What is this all about? What's the beginning there?	Focus	wording
	S1	Water	Identify	word
	T	Water. Fantastic, that's right.	Affirm	
		Can we all highlight the word water, please, the very first word in our text.	Direct	highlight
	Ss	[highlight word]		
2	T	OK, it goes on to say that water is found in many different forms.	Prepare	wording
		But what is the water doing? Have a look through our sentence. Rodney, what is the water doing?	Focus	wording
	S2	It's constantly moving	Identify	wording
	T	Excellent	Affirm	
3	T	Can you give me a little bit more information about that?	Focus	wording
	S2	from one place to another	Identify	wording
	T	OK, so let's highlight that whole section that it's constantly moving from one place to another.	Direct	highlight
	Ss	[highlight wording]		
4	T	OK, the next sentence gives us something else that the water is doing. Now, I've read it to you before.	Prepare	sentence
		As it moves it… Alex? As it moves it…?	Focus	wording
	S3	changes	Identify	word
	T	Changes. Changes what?	Focus	wording
	S	changes state	Identify	wording
	T	State	Affirm	
		Remember, state's the scientific word we use for whether it's a solid, a liquid or a gas, or what form it's in.	Elaborate	topic2
		So can we highlight "change of state".	Direct	highlight
	Ss	[highlight wording]		
	T	OK, can we highlight the "in cycles" as well. So we've actually got those four words highlighted together, "changes state in cycles'".	Direct	highlight
	Ss	[highlight wording]		
5	T	So what were those four states again? The end of the sentence names them.	Prepare	wording
		So, Amon, from…?	Focus	wording
	S4	from liquid water	Identify	wording
	T	Liquid to…?	Focus	wording
	S4	water	Identify	word

Table 8.3 (*cont.*)

	T	*Water vapour. OK.*	Affirm	
		That's the key that it's a gas, our word "vapour".	Elaborate	topic2
		So, if we can highlight "liquid water" and "water vapour".	Direct	highlight
6	T	*Peter, can you see sometimes there we might get a solid.*	Prepare	wording
		What's our name for solid water?	Focus	word
	S5	*ice*	Identify	word
	T	*Yep*	Affirm	
7	T	*And then back to... What's the end of the sentence there? The last one for us to highlight?*	Focus	wording
	S6	*liquid again*	Identify	wording
	T	*Back to liquid again.*	Affirm	
		So there are two sides to the Water Cycle. Water might have travelled a long way from the oceans to get to the mountains, or a long way through a long river system. But it's also changing state. It changes from liquid to gas to liquid, maybe to solid and then back again, all the way through the cycle.	Elaborate	topic1&2

in the public domain at the New South Wales Education Standards Authority website (NESA, 2018) and form the basis for the analysis activities.

Going Further

This chapter has very briefly outlined just a few of SFL's tools for describing and teaching spoken and written language. The model of language in context, as register and genre, and the analysis of knowledge genres and curriculum genres, facilitates design of highly effective pedagogic practice. However there is far more to both SFL and genre pedagogy. Courses in SFL will allow you to explore SFL as an appliable linguistics, and genre pedagogy as its outstanding application. You can get started with the further readings below, as well as the publications in the reference list, many of which are downloadable at www.readingtolearn.com.au.

Discussion Questions

Review the exemplar lesson and associated videos at NESA (2018) as you answer the following questions. Refer to specific examples to support your answers.

1. How do the activities and interactions in Preparing for Reading support students to comprehend and engage in the topic of the Water Cycle text?

Table 8.4 Joint construction

1	T	*So what we're going to do now is write our own explanation, making sure that we remember about the sequence of steps. So we're going to follow the same pattern in our writing as the text that we've just read. We need to have the same introduction, identify what it is we're going to talk about, move through the steps, and finish it with a conclusion [points to notes].*	Prepare	activity
		How about Peter? Can you come up and start the first sentence please? [student comes to board]	Direct	scribe
	T	*We're going to start with water.*	Focus	wording
	S	*moving*	Propose	word
	T	*It's moving. OK, good.*	Affirm	
2		*What does it do? I can't say "water moving", can I? We've got to change the word.*	Focus	wording
	S	*keeps on*	Propose	wording
	T	*We could say "keeps on moving". So yep, "keeps on".*	Affirm	
		So Peter, if you can write up, remember capital to start the sentence. "Water keeps on" [student scribes]	Direct	scribe
3	T	*What's it keeping on doing?*	Focus	wording
	S	*moving*	Propose	word
		"keeps on moving"	Affirm	
	T	*So it's moving. [student scribes].*	Direct	scribe
4	T	*What else is it doing? Jeremy, from our notes up here, what else is it doing?*	Focus	wording
	S	*changing*	Propose	word
	T	*Changing. Good.*	Affirm	
5	T	*What's it changing?*	Focus	word
	S	*state*	Propose	word
	T	*State*	Affirm	
		From solid, liquid, gas, OK.	Elaborate	topic
6	T	*So we're going to try to build that into the sentence.*	Focus	sentence
	S	*It constantly changes state*	Propose	wording
	T	*OK, great idea Trent.*	Affirm	
		"It constantly changes" [student scribes].	Direct	scribe
	S	*[spells out "constantly" "changes state"; student scribes]*	Direct	spelling
7	T	*What if we said, here in our notes, that it's going from. . .*	Focus	wording
	S	*liquid water*	Propose	wording
	T	*Liquid water, yep,*	Affirm	
8	T	*to. . .*	Focus	wording
	S	*to vapour, to ice, to liquid*	Propose	wording
	T	*OK, excellent.*	Affirm	
	S	*back to solid*	Propose	wording
	T	*Maybe to a solid.*	Elaborate	wording

Table 8.4 (*cont.*)

	S	*"maybe to a solid" [student scribes]*	Propose	wording
	S	*[spells out "solid"]*	Direct	spelling
	T	*You're doing well, that's alright.*	Affirm	
9	T	*And we want to get this idea of a cycle.*	Prepare	topic
		Where did it finish?	Focus	wording
	S	*back to liquid*	Propose	wording
	T	*OK.*	Affirm	
	S	*[student scribes]*		

2. How do the activities and interactions in detailed reading support students to read this technical text in depth and detail?
3. How do the activities and interactions in notemaking support students to participate actively and develop their knowledge and language skills?
4. How do the activities and interactions in joint construction support students to use language effectively for writing?

FURTHER READING

Foundational Readings

Martin, J. R., & Rose, D. (2007). *Working with discourse: Meaning beyond the clause* (2nd edn; 1st edn, 2003). London: Continuum.

    (2008). *Genre relations: Mapping culture.* London: Equinox.

Rose, D., & Martin, J. R. (2012). *Learning to write, reading to learn: Genre, knowledge and pedagogy in the Sydney School.* London: Equinox.

Recent Publications

Kartika-Ningsih, H., & Rose, D. (2018). Language shift: Analysing language use in multilingual classroom interactions. *Functional Linguistics*, *5*(1), 9. Retrieved from Springer Open Access, https://rdcu.be/be2d9

Rose, D. (2016). Engaging children in the pleasures of literature and verbal art. English in Australia (0155–2147), *51*(2), 52–62. Retrieved from https://search.informit.com.au/ documentSummary;dn=433103228151198;res=IELHSS,mwww.researchgate.net/ publication/310614907_Engaging_children_in_the_pleasures_of_literature_and_verbal_art

    (2017). Languages of schooling: Embedding literacy learning with genre-based pedagogy. *European Journal of Applied Linguistics (Special issue: Languages of schooling: Explorations into disciplinary literacies)*, *5*(2): 1–31. Retrieved from www.degruyter .com/view/j/eujal.ahead-of-print/eujal-2017-0008/eujal-2017-0008.xml

REFERENCES

Carusi-Lees, Z. (2017). Tackling literacy one classroom at a time: Teaching writing at a whole school level in a Secondary context. *Teachers as Practitioner Research Journal 1*(1), 1–30. Retrieved from www.researchgate.net/publication/314230604_Tackling_literacy_one_classroom_at_a_time_Teaching_writing_at_a_whole_school_level_in_a_Secondary_context

Cash, S., Quinton, G., & Tilley, C. (2012). *Oxford big ideas science 9 Australian curriculum.* Sydney: Oxford University Press.

Dreyfus, S., Hood, S., & Stenglin, M. (Eds.). (2011). *Semiotic margins: Meaning in multimodalities.* London: Continuum.

Halliday, M. A. K., & Matthiessen, C. (2014). *An Introduction to functional grammar.* London: Edward Arnold.

Martin, J. R. (2000). Grammar meets genre: Reflections on the "Sydney School". *Arts: The Journal of the Sydney University Arts Association, 22*: 47–95.

(Ed.). (2013). *Interviews with Michael Halliday: Language turned back on himself.* London: Bloomsbury.

Martin, J. R., & Rose, D. (2007). *Working with discourse: Meaning beyond the clause* (2nd edn). London: Continuum.

(2008). *Genre relations: Mapping culture.* London: Equinox.

NESA. (2018). *Learning through reading and writing.* Sydney: NSW Education & Standards Authority. Retrieved from http://educationstandards.nsw.edu.au/wps/portal/nesa/k-10/learning-areas/english-year-10/learning-through-reading-and-writing/stage-1-preparing-for-reading

Rose, D. (2001). Some variations in theme across languages. *Functions of Languages, 8*(1): 109–145.

(2010). Beating educational inequality with an integrated reading pedagogy. In F. Christie & A. Simpson (Eds.), *Literacy and social responsibility: Multiple perspectives* (pp. 101–115). London: Equinox.

(2011). Genre in the Sydney School. In J. Gee & M. Handford (Eds.), *The Routledge handbook of discourse analysis* (pp. 209–225). London: Routledge.

(2015a). Genre, knowledge and pedagogy in the "Sydney School." In N. Artemeva & A. Freedman (Eds.), *Genre studies around the globe: Beyond the three traditions* (pp. 299–338). Ottawa: Inkwell.

(2015b). New developments in genre-based literacy pedagogy. In C. A. MacArthur, S. Graham, & J. Fitzgerald (Eds.), *Handbook of writing research* (2nd edn) (pp. 227–242). New York: Guildford.

(2017). Languages of schooling: Embedding literacy learning with genre-based pedagogy. *European Journal of Applied Linguistics (Special issue: Languages of schooling: Explorations into disciplinary literacies), 5*(2): 1–31. Retrieved from

www.degruyter.com/view/j/eujal.ahead-of-print/eujal-2017-0008/eujal-2017-0008
.xml

(2018). *Reading to learn: Accelerating learning and closing the gap. Teacher
training books and DVDs.* Sydney: Reading to Learn. Retrieved from www.readingtolearn
.com.au

(2019). *Reading to learn: Accelerating learning and closing the gap.* Sydney: Reading to
Learn. Retrieved from www.readingtolearn.com.au

Rose, D., & Martin, J. R. (2012). *Learning to write, reading to learn: Genre, knowledge and
pedagogy in the Sydney School.* London: Equinox.

Shum, M. S-k., Shi, D., & Tai, C-p. (2016). The effectiveness of using 'reading to learn,
learning to write' pedagogy in teaching Chinese to non-Chinese speaking students in
Hong Kong. *International Journal of Language Studies, 10*(3): 43–60.

9 Disciplinary Education and Language for Specific Purposes

ALISSA J. HARTIG

Overview of Key Concepts and Issues in Language for Specific Purposes and Disciplinary Education

Have you ever been sitting in a language classroom and thought to yourself, "When am I ever going to use this in real life?" Having learned phrases like "Le singe est sur la branche" ("The monkey is on the branch") in his French classes in school, the British comedian Eddie Izzard joked that whenever he traveled to France, he always had to bring a monkey with him and walk around heavily wooded areas just so that he could fit this phrase into everyday conversation. If you've ever had to take a language class to fulfill a general education requirement, you've probably experienced what some teachers jokingly refer to as the "LNOP" approach, or "Language for No Obvious Purpose" (Trace, Hudson, & Brown, 2015, p. 3). This approach is often a response to the fact that, in many classes, it can be impossible to cater to all of the various interests and goals of a diverse group of learners. When a group of students is learning a language for a specific purpose, however, teachers have the opportunity to design much more tailored language instruction.

This tailored approach, referred to as **LSP (Language for Specific Purposes)**, is often contrasted with a "common core" approach (Bloor & Bloor, 1986, p. 2). In the common core approach, students are taught general language forms that are argued to be common across most contexts in which the language is used. In LSP, by contrast, teaching materials and activities are grounded in the analysis of the specific contexts, tasks, and text types that are most relevant to the situations for which learners plan to use the language they are studying and focus on the language forms that are especially frequent or important in these situations. For example, French mountain guides learning English for their work guiding climbers through the Alps would need to be able to give verbal instructions relevant to mountaineering as well as discuss safety procedures and weather conditions (Wozniak, 2010), while engineers learning English for their work at a semiconductor manufacturing company in Taiwan would need to be able to write project proposals and reports as well as deliver presentations (Spence & Liu, 2013). **English for Specific Purposes (ESP)** courses developed for each of these contexts would need to focus on very different kinds of vocabulary, grammatical features, genres, and tasks.

Context and Course Design in Language for Specific Purposes

One of the largest areas in which applied linguists develop LSP materials and curricula is in university settings. This area is referred to as **Language for Academic Purposes**, or LAP. While many LAP courses in these contexts enroll students from a range of fields at either the undergraduate or graduate level, others are situated within specific academic departments or programs. In designing an LAP course for students of veterinary medicine in Italy, for example, Cianflone (2012) interviewed faculty members to understand their perceptions of students' English language needs. The faculty in this study emphasized the importance of reading and writing skills over listening and speaking skills, and they also highlighted the need for students to be familiar with case reports. The case report genre is fairly uncommon outside of the medical community and explains the decision-making process in clinical practice in particularly interesting or challenging medical cases. Knowing this information would allow an LAP teacher to design a course that aligns well with the language skills and text types that students need for their coursework in the program.

English-speaking medical professionals learning Spanish for their work with patients, however, would need a very different kind of course. A course like this, which would focus more on workplace communication than academic language, falls under the second major area of LSP, referred to as **Language for Occupational Purposes**, or **LOP**. In gathering background information to design one such course, Lear (2005) observed and interviewed nurses and other health care professionals in a women's health clinic in the United States in order to learn when and how they most needed to use Spanish in their work. Lear also collected and analyzed the Spanish-language brochures that these professionals provided, and often needed to explain, to patients.

The health professionals in Lear's study highlighted the importance of being able to pronounce key medical terms, mentioning one patient's misunderstanding of a nurse's pronunciation of the word *estreñimiento* ("constipation") as *entendimiento* ("understanding") (p. 225). They also described communication challenges related to their difficulty with relevant grammatical features like verb conjugations, despite having access to ample study materials at home. One nutritionist, for example, exclusively conjugated verbs in the present tense, relying on context, gestures, and explicit time references (e.g., *anoche*, "last night") to attempt to make her meaning clear to the patient. This made it difficult for her to effectively communicate both descriptions of procedures that she was going to perform and questions about what had occurred before the patient's arrival. It also became clear that listening comprehension was a concern for these professionals and that they needed additional communicative strategies to ask patients effective follow-up and clarification questions. Lear argues that these health professionals needed contextualized language support that they could apply immediately in their work since it was difficult for them to connect the general-purpose study materials they had at home to their work in the clinic.

Despite the fact that the learners in both Cianflone's and Lear's studies were learning language for medical purposes of some kind, the types of language that each group needed were very different and went beyond more obvious areas like medical vocabulary. This process of identifying texts, tasks, and language features that are relevant to the needs of a specific group of learners is called a **needs analysis**, and it is a fundamental component of any LSP course. Needs analysis often begins by talking with various stakeholders, for example, faculty in students' disciplines, students' employers, and students themselves. Throughout this process, analysis typically focuses on identifying students' needs, wants, and lacks (Hutchinson & Waters, 1987), but mainly considers these from the perspective of conforming to institutional expectations. Sarah Benesch, a critical LSP scholar, has argued that another important component of course design should be a **rights analysis** (Benesch, 2001). A rights analysis considers how power relations shape institutional expectations about language use, as well as ways in which space can be created for learners to question and challenge these expectations.

Understanding Discipline-Specific Language Use

Understanding the perspectives of stakeholders is an important starting point and the next step for an applied linguist is to analyze relevant samples of language use. While a wide array of approaches to **discourse analysis** are possible in this kind of linguistic analysis, two of the most commonly used are **genre analysis** and **corpus linguistics**. Perhaps one of the most analyzed genres in LSP is the academic research article, and one common framework used in the analysis of this genre comes from John Swales, who examined patterns in the organization of introduction sections of research articles from a variety of fields. Swales (1990) presented a series of three **moves** that commonly appear in a predictable order in research article introductions in English:

Move 1: Establishing a research territory
Move 2: Establishing a niche
Move 3: Occupying the niche

Each of these moves is divided into more detailed subsections, called **steps**, to form what is known as the **"Create a Research Space," or CARS, model**. This model is commonly used as a teaching tool in **English for Academic Purposes (EAP)** courses, and move/step analyses like this are used widely in genre analysis for LSP across a range of languages today.

This approach is far from the only way to conduct a genre analysis in LSP, however. **Systemic functional linguistics (SFL)** offers another lens for looking at genre, which has been used, for example, to understand the different forms of discipline-specific language that English language learners need to make an effective argument in high school history classes. Making an effective argument in history requires different kinds of language than what students are likely to use in their everyday conversations. SFL analyses of the argument genre in history have shown that this genre often signals cause-and-effect relationships through subtle cues like time reference and verbs rather than using the kinds of conjunctions (like *because*) that students are more likely to be familiar with using for this purpose (Schleppegrell, Achugar, & Oteíza, 2004). An SFL analysis can help uncover how genres vary across disciplines to reflect discipline-specific communicative needs, values, and goals by connecting language form and meaning. This form of genre analysis can then be used in the classroom to help students better understand and produce the kinds of texts that are valued in the discipline.

Corpus linguistics, which uses specialized computer programs to identify patterns of language use in large collections of texts, is another important tool for discourse analysis in LSP. Friginal (2008), for example, created a corpus of 364 transcripts of phone calls between American callers and Filipino customer service agents based in call centers in the Philippines. The transcripts were segmented to indicate "agent" and "caller" sections and then **tagged,** or annotated, using an automatic program that labels the word classes and semantic categories of words in these texts. Friginal then analyzed this corpus using a method called **multi-dimensional analysis** (Biber, 1988), which uses statistical procedures to identify patterns in the way in which particular linguistic features appear together in texts. Friginal's (2008) study found that the use of language features associated with politeness and a focus on the addressee, such as second-person pronouns (*you, yours*), possibility modals (*can, could, might, may*), and words like *thanks* and *please*, were used by agents much more frequently in certain types of customer service interactions, such as when customers were purchasing mobile phone minutes, than they were in other types of service interactions. When agents were handling calls for an equipment order or inquiry, for example, these features were very infrequent. Understanding this kind of variation across different categories of service interactions can help call center trainees better understand when callers are likely to want more pared-down, efficient communication, and when they would expect a more polite and elaborated style.

Approaches to Teaching in the Language for Specific Purposes Classroom

In any LSP course, there needs to be some input from both content specialists and language specialists, and there are a range of models for these kinds of interdisciplinary partnerships. Dudley-Evans and St. John (1998) outline three levels of coordination between disciplinary specialists and language specialists: **cooperation**, **collaboration**, and **team-teaching**. The cooperation level is the minimum level necessary to conduct a needs analysis. At this level, disciplinary specialists provide syllabi, text samples, opportunities to observe the settings that the course is being designed for, or other information that will allow the language specialist to understand the specific language needs presented by this context. At the collaboration level, disciplinary specialists coordinate more closely with language specialists so that language specialists can design separate lessons that will directly support students in their content courses or specific tasks in the workplace. At the team-teaching level, disciplinary specialists and language specialists work together to design a curriculum that more fully integrates language and content instruction throughout the course, with both individuals playing an active role in most, if not all, class sessions.

A number of teaching approaches are used in LSP. Victoria University of Wellington's Language in the Workplace Project, for example, has designed a series of online instructional materials and simulated conversation videos to help new migrants understand the norms of workplace communication in New Zealand (https://worktalk.immigration.govt.nz/). Paltridge (2008) describes the use of **textographies**, a combination of text analysis and ethnography, as a tool for students to better understand both the linguistic features of discipline-specific academic texts and the underlying assumptions behind these genres. In this approach, students analyze texts in their field and interview faculty in their disciplines to better understand why these texts are written as they are. **Data-driven learning**, or **DDL**, is another teaching approach that is particularly well suited to the LSP classroom. In this approach, students learn to uncover patterns of language use themselves using some of the same corpus tools that applied linguists use for research purposes.

An example of DDL in an LAP context in Hong Kong illustrates what this approach looks like in practice. Chen and Flowerdew (2018) conducted a series of DDL workshops to familiarize graduate students in a variety of fields with free corpus tools like the AntConc corpus analysis toolkit, which includes a **concordancer** feature (Anthony, 2019). Among other functions, concordancers allow users to search a corpus and align the results so that the search term is centered and highlighted, making it easier to examine the contexts in which it occurs and what kinds of words typically appear before and after it. Figure 9.1 provides an example of concordance results for the word *word* in a sample corpus. In this example, the results are organized alphabetically by the word immediately following this search term. In Chen and Flowerdew's workshops, students engaged in hands-on, interactive activities using this tool with discipline-specific corpora to examine, for example, the ways in which researchers in different disciplines report the results

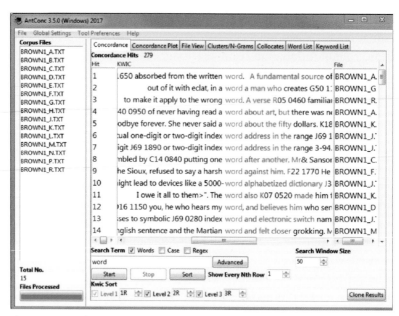

Figure 9.1 Sample AntConc concordance results for the word *word*
(Retrieved from www.laurenceanthony.net/software/antconc/)

of a research study. Once students were comfortable with conducting these kinds of searches, they learned how to compile their own discipline-specific corpora to help them with their academic writing.

Investigating Student Learning

There has been an increasing interest in understanding student learning in LSP classrooms as well, and some of the most widely cited studies in this area have focused on how students learn using genre-based approaches (see, e.g., Cheng, 2006; Tardy, 2009). Research on learning in LSP also examines ways that students negotiate their previous knowledge about writing, whether in negative or positive ways. Bangeni (2013), for example, shows how graduate students in marketing in South Africa transferred their understanding of the audience for their writing from their undergraduate studies in the social sciences, which led to problems in framing their writing in ways that aligned with discipline-specific norms. Mein (2012), by contrast, shows how students' prior knowledge of genre, even in other languages, can be helpful. In a case study of a graduate student who had completed her undergraduate education and a master's degree in education in Mexico and was now completing a PhD in the same field in Texas, Mein (2012) noted that the student's awareness of genre conventions from her academic studies and professional work in Spanish served as an important tool for facilitating her understanding of academic writing conventions in English. Depending on their prior experience, students in LSP classes may need help either moving away from familiar genre norms or making connections between their previous understanding of genre in their first language and their writing in their second language.

My Work in Disciplinary Education and Language for Specific Purposes

Personal Reflection

My first encounter with discipline-specific language and LSP came when I was teaching at a university language center in South Korea. One of my students in a general writing class was working on his PhD in nanophysics and asked me to help him revise a research article he was working on. As we met over the next few weeks, I began to get a better sense of just how different the kind of English that he needed for this task was. He was already an expert in the vocabulary of his field, and he didn't need much help with grammar errors. Most of our work together focused on managing how he would respond to the reviewer comments he had received. He had a good idea of who the reviewer might be, and he wanted to highlight why his lab's approach was better than others without inadvertently offending the reviewer. To do this, we looked at possible ways to rephrase key sentences and then considered whether these revisions would fit the style of language that other scientists in his field used to communicate similar ideas in published research articles. This allowed us to figure out strategies for communicating that his work was important and novel while still recognizing contributions made by others in the field.

When I started my own PhD in applied linguistics the following year, I knew that I wanted to study how people learn to do academic writing in a second language. When the law school on campus contacted our department looking for someone to work with international graduate students in their legal writing program, this seemed like the perfect opportunity to combine my interests in second language writing and discipline-specific language. Because I didn't have any background in law, I started reading as much as I could about legal writing, sat in on every session of the legal writing class, and spent a lot of time talking with the legal writing professor about her expectations for students. At the beginning, my role was mainly to serve as an individual writing tutor, helping students revise their legal writing assignments outside of class time. As the program expanded and I gained more experience, however, I collaborated with law faculty to develop courses where both language and content goals were combined, eventually even team-teaching with law faculty members.

My Research in Language for Specific Purposes

In my work with students at the law school, I kept coming across new questions that I wanted to answer. There seemed to be a mismatch, for example, between the plain English recommendations that were provided in students' textbooks and the main issues that I saw in their writing. These plain English recommendations included avoiding the use of the passive voice and nominalizations. I began to wonder: Do expert legal writers actually use these features less than students do? Do students who get better grades on their legal writing assignments use these features less than students who get lower grades? With my co-author, I collected and analyzed a set of legal memos from students and experts to answer these questions using techniques from corpus linguistics (Hartig & Lu, 2014). We found that, although experts used these features less frequently overall, there was no difference between the high- and low-rated student texts in how often they used these features. In fact, some of the highest rated student texts used these features much more frequently. These students seemed to be using these grammatical structures as a way to highlight their analysis more effectively – a finding that called into question the recommendations in students' textbooks.

I also started to notice some ways that the use of grammatical features like tense and articles in legal memos were used differently from what I would have expected in other forms of writing. Using a discourse analysis approach from cognitive linguistics, I looked at the Question Presented section of the legal memo genre, which seemed particularly unusual in its use of these features (Hartig, 2016). Since students often had difficulty with this section of the memo, I wanted to understand these features better so that I would be able to explain why they were being used in this way. After taking a closer look at a collection of sample texts and surveying legal writing faculty, it became clear that the unusual use of these grammatical features was a way of implicitly signaling the underlying parts of the legal analysis that would be addressed later on in the memo. The findings meant that in order for students to use these grammatical features effectively, they would have to know more than just general grammar rules. They would also need to understand the framework they needed to use for their legal analysis and know how these features signaled that framework to the reader.

To see what this looks like, consider the following Question Presented (QP), which comes from the data set analyzed for the study:

> Is a detached garage a "living quarters" in which the owners "actually reside" under Illinois' Residential Burglary Statute, when it has been converted into a retreat for the owners' college-age son, who uses it on a weekly basis as a get-a-way and sleeps there half the year, although the retreat does not have plumbing facilities? (Example from Wellford Slocum (2011), cited in Hartig (2016, p. 70))

The QP occurs at the very beginning of a legal memorandum, so the only context that the reader has comes from their prior understanding of the function of a legal memo and their knowledge of the law. The reader may or may not have much background knowledge of the client's situation. The first part of the QP above is framed as a general question that seems to apply to any hypothetical detached garage. The details in the second part of the question, though, make it clear that the author isn't really talking about just any hypothetical garage. These two parts of the QP work together to signal important aspects of the writer's legal analysis, which are addressed in detail throughout the rest of the memo.

The phrases in quotation marks in the first part of the sentence both relate to the same part of the relevant statute, which specifies that a theft must occur in a "dwelling place" in order to fit the legal definition of residential burglary. While the statute covers additional criteria that must be addressed to determine whether or not the situation fits this definition, these other parts of the statute aren't at issue in this particular case. By beginning the memo with a focus on whether the garage is a "living quarters" in which the owners "actually reside," the writer is signaling to the reader that this memo will focus on the question of whether or not the attached garage in this case fits the legal definition of a "dwelling place." This framing signals to readers that all of the other criteria from the statute for determining whether or not a burglary has occurred are clearly met.

The details in the second part of the QP also provide important information to a legal reader. By focusing on details that relate to the frequency of use, the type of use, and the facilities in the garage, the writer is not only introducing key client facts that will be addressed in their analysis, but also highlighting legal categories and criteria from relevant judicial decisions (also referred to as "cases") that will be explained and applied later in the memo. In this way, the QP integrates two key sources of law that are fundamental to legal analysis in the United States: statutes and case law. The QP also gives a preview of how these sources of law will be applied to the client's case.

Part of what makes the QP challenging for writers is that its use of language reflects its blended function in introducing both the general legal standards that apply to the client's case and the specific facts from the client's case that are relevant to these standards. For multilingual writers who have learned rules about article use that are based on determining whether a particular noun refers to something general or to something specific, for example, it would be difficult to know how to apply these rules effectively to reflect the blended function of the QP. For these students, general-purpose rules of thumb that are commonly used for teaching grammar aren't enough. They also need to understand how articles are used in discipline-specific ways.

The law students enrolled in this graduate program weren't just learning law in a second language, however. They were also learning law in a second legal system. Nearly all of the students in the program already held a law degree in their home country, and many had practiced law for years before starting their graduate program. Because the features of the texts that students encountered in the legal writing class were closely linked to culturally specific legal frameworks, I wondered how students managed the shift from one legal system to another and how this played out in their reading and writing for the course. From my experience in working with students, I noticed that the parts of the assignments that seemed to pose the most difficulty were those that were the most closely related to the US common law system, specifically those related to the use of cases as a primary source of law. Since most students came from legal systems where statutes or the civil code are the main sources of law, the importance of looking at the facts of a prior case or the judge's rationale in making a decision on it was not obvious. How did students navigate this shift in their reading and writing?

Data Analysis Activity

The data analysis activity for this chapter will help you answer this question of how students navigated the cultural shift in their legal writing. The data you'll be analyzing come from the study described in Hartig (2017) and are available on the website accompanying this textbook. The data include written assignments submitted by two students at the beginning of their graduate studies in law in the United States. In addition to the student writing samples, you'll find information on the move structure expected in two sections of the legal memorandum genre as well as some background on the client problem that students were asked to analyze for both assignments. Using this background information, you will analyze four short student writing samples in order to determine which paragraphs are more effective and why.

Going Further

If you're interested in learning more about LSP, taking a course in this area is a great place to start. Even if your department doesn't offer a course in LSP, you may be able to tailor course projects in other classes to make them relevant to an LSP context. One of the most important skills for anyone working in LSP is the ability to analyze discipline-specific texts, whether spoken or written, and coursework in discourse analysis and corpus linguistics can provide a good foundation for this. It can also be useful to take coursework in curriculum design and materials development since LSP practitioners often have to develop courses on their own rather than having readily available textbooks. Curriculum design courses often address needs analysis as well, making them a good fit for students with an interest in LSP.

Discussion Questions

1. Interdisciplinarity, multilingualism, and technology are important in applied linguistics today. Based on what you have read in this chapter, where do these themes appear in research and teaching in Language for Specific Purposes? How could these factors play a role in other ways in LSP?

2. Think of an academic program in which you have studied (including your current academic program) or a professional context in which you have worked. How would you conduct a needs analysis to design an LSP course for this setting? What kinds of information would you need to collect? What stakeholders would you speak with? What kinds of texts or tasks would be important for students in an LSP course to learn about in this context? Are there any language features you can think of that might be particularly important? What are they?

3. To conduct research or design materials for LSP contexts, some level of coordination with disciplinary specialists is needed. What challenges do you think this might pose? How could these challenges be overcome?

4. Thinking about rights analysis, what strategies could LSP teachers use to help students question or challenge institutional norms? What are some difficulties that using such strategies might pose? How would you address these?

FURTHER READING

Foundational Readings

Berkenkotter, C., & Huckin, T. N. (1995). *Genre knowledge in disciplinary communication: Cognition/culture/power.* Hillsdale, NJ: Lawrence Erlbaum.

Dudley-Evans, T., & St. John, M. J. (1998). *Developments in English for specific purposes: A multi-disciplinary approach.* Cambridge: Cambridge University Press.

Swales, J. (1990). *Genre analysis: English in academic and research settings.* Cambridge: Cambridge University Press.

Recent Publications

Anthony, L. (2018). *Introducing English for specific purposes.* Abingdon: Routledge.

Dreyfus, S. J., Humphrey, S., Mahboob, A., & Martin, J. R. (2016). *Genre pedagogy in higher education: The SLATE Project.* Basingstoke, UK: Palgrave Macmillan.

Trace, J., Hudson, T., & Brown, J. D. (Eds.). (2015). *Developing courses in languages for specific purposes.* Mānoa, Hawai'i: National Foreign Language Resource Center. Retreived from http://hdl.handle.net/10125/14573

REFERENCES

Anthony, L. (2019). AntConc (Version 3.5.8) [Computer Software]. Tokyo, Japan: Waseda University. Retrieved from www.laurenceanthony.net/software

Bangeni, B. (2013). An exploration of the impact of students' prior genre knowledge on their construction of "audience" in a marketing course at the postgraduate level. *English for Specific Purposes, 32*, 248–257. https://doi.org/10.1016/j.esp.2013.05.001

Benesch, S. (2001). *Critical English for academic purposes: Theory, politics, and practice.* Mahwah, NJ: Lawrence Erlbaum.

Biber, D. (1988). *Variation across speech and writing.* Cambridge: Cambridge University Press.

Bloor, M., & Bloor, T. (1986). Languages for specific purposes: Practice and theory. *CLCS Occasional Papers, 19*, 1–39.

Chen, M., & Flowerdew, J. (2018). Introducing data-driven learning to PhD students for research writing purposes: A territory-wide project in Hong Kong. *English for Specific Purposes, 50*, 97–112. https://doi.org/10.1016/j.esp.2017.11.004

Cheng, A. (2006). Understanding learners and learning in ESP genre-based writing instruction. *English for Specific Purposes, 25*, 76–89. https://doi.org/10.1016/j.esp.2005.07.002

Cianflone, E. (2012). What written academic genres do veterinary pathologists suggest for EAP students? *Ibérica: Revista de la Asociación Europea de Lenguas para Fines Específicos (AELFE), 23*, 173–182.

Dudley-Evans, T., & St. John, M. J. (1998). *Developments in English for specific purposes: A multi-disciplinary approach.* Cambridge: Cambridge University Press.

Friginal, E. (2008). Linguistic variation in the discourse of outsourced call centers. *Discourse Studies, 10*(6), 715–736. https://doi.org/10.1177/1461445608096570

Hartig, A. J. (2016). Conceptual blending in legal writing: Linking definitions to facts. *English for Specific Purposes, 42*, 66–75. https://doi.org/10.1016/j.esp.2015.12.002
(2017). *Connecting language and disciplinary knowledge in English for specific purposes: Case studies in law.* Clevedon: Multilingual Matters.

Hartig, A. J., & Lu, X. (2014). Plain English and legal writing: Comparing expert and novice writers. *English for Specific Purposes, 33*(2014), 87–96. https://doi.org/10.1016/j.esp.2013.09.001

Hutchinson, T., & Waters, A. (1987). *English for specific purposes: A learning-centred approach.* Cambridge: Cambridge University Press.

Lear, D. W. (2005). Spanish for working professionals: Linguistic needs. *Foreign Language Annals, 38*(2), 223–232.

Mein, E. (2012). Biliteracy in context: The use of L1/L2 genre knowledge in graduate studies. *International Journal of Bilingual Education and Bilingualism, 15*(6), 653–667.

Paltridge, B. (2008). Textographies and the researching and teaching of writing. *Ibérica: Revista de la Asociación Europea de Lenguas para Fines Específicos (AELFE), 15*, 9–24.

Schleppegrell, M. J., Achugar, M., & Oteíza, T. (2004). The grammar of history: Enhancing content-based instruction through a functional focus on language. *TESOL Quarterly*, *38*(1), 67–93.

Spence, P., & Liu, G.-Z. (2013). Engineering English and the high-tech industry: A case study of an English needs analysis of process integration engineers at a semiconductor manufacturing company in Taiwan. *English for Specific Purposes*, *32*, 97–109. http://dx .doi.org/10.1016/j.esp.2012.11.003

Swales, J. M. (1990). *Genre analysis: English in academic and research settings*. Cambridge: Cambridge University Press.

Tardy, C. M. (2009). *Building genre knowledge*. West Lafayette, IN: Parlor Press.

Trace, J., Hudson, T., & Brown, J. D. (Eds.). (2015). *Developing courses in languages for specific purposes*. Mānoa, Hawai'i: National Foreign Language Resource Center.

Wellford Slocum, R. (2011). *Legal reasoning, writing, and other lawyering skills* (3rd edn). Newark, NJ: LexisNexis.

Wozniak, S. (2010). Language needs analysis from a perspective of international professional mobility: The case of French mountain guides. *English for Specific Purposes*, *29*, 243–252. https://doi.org/10.1016/j.esp.2010.06.001

10 Language Socialization and Culture in Study Abroad Programs

LUCIEN BROWN

Overview of Key Concepts and Issues in Language Socialization and Culture in Study Abroad

In recent years **study abroad** has emerged as an important context in which the acquisition of second languages takes place. Language learners invest large sums of money to study the language in the country in which it is spoken. For university students, this often involves delaying their college graduation and living overseas for the first time in their lives. Universities and other language schools compete to set up the most innovative and enticing study abroad programs, which now often include the learning of other subject areas and skills (politics, management, fashion, art, winemaking, etc.) alongside state-of-the-art language programs.

This investment in study abroad belies an assumption that it represents the best environment not only for learners to perfect their second language grammar, learn new vocabulary, and so forth, but also for **language socialization** to occur. By language socialization, we refer to the process by which individuals acquire the knowledge and practices that enable them to use the language in a culturally appropriate manner (Longman, 2008). For instance, study abroad learners in the UK might be socialized into linguistic practices such as making indirect requests ("Could I possibly have a little more milk in my tea, if it's not too much trouble?") which are important in British culture, but which may not be shared by other cultures that prefer more direct forms of request ("More milk, please!"). Previous research shows that the preference for framing requests as questions in languages such as English and German is much weaker in Polish and Russian (Ogiermann, 2009) as well as Korean (Byon, 2006).

The concept of language socialization in actual fact has its origins in the study of how children learn their first language(s) from birth. It was pioneered by scholars such as Elinor Ochs and Bambi Schieffelin, who produced rich ethnographic and longitudinal accounts of how caregivers socialize children into social routines and, ultimately, into learning the language, culture, and values of the community (e.g., Ochs and Schieffelin, 2001). In second language contexts, language socialization works somewhat differently, since access and participation in the community where the language is spoken is typically limited. Even when second language learners are fully immersed in the second language culture, gaps in cultural and linguistic knowledge make socialization difficult. Patricia Duff's (2003) study of grade 10 classes in a Canadian high school found that ESL students (who were mostly from Asian backgrounds) struggled to participate in teacher–student discussions due to the way in which teachers frequently encouraged references to Western pop culture and use of slang. Although these teaching techniques were engaging for the Canada-born students, the techniques isolated the ESL students, whose silence was interpreted as evidence of stereotypes such as that Asian students were quiet, shy, and lacked English proficiency.

With the recognition that language learning is also social learning, applied linguists have thus turned their attention to investigating both the linguistic and the cultural gains made by students during study abroad. The research does indeed show that learners return from study abroad more fluent and more socialized than when they left. For example, Iwasaki (2010) compared performance on **Oral Proficiency Interviews (OPI)** administered to five American learners of Japanese before and after a one-year study abroad period in Japan. Four of the five learners improved their overall proficiency after study abroad, thus showing linguistic gains. In addition, qualitative analysis showed that all five of the learners made gains in their understandings of when to use polite and plain speech styles – different **registers** of Japanese that are used to mark differences in status, formality, and affect (i.e., emotion). In the post-study abroad OPIs, three of the learners in particular skillfully used the plain style to mark utterances that were close to their "selves," such as their self-directed thoughts, recollections, and emotions. This increased ability to use language in culturally appropriate ways to signal emotions can be taken as evidence of cultural gains and language socialization during study abroad.

However, the research has also shown that study abroad can have limitations as a context for language socialization. An underlying factor here is that study abroad students are only in the host country temporarily. In the terms of Fred Dervin (e.g., Dervin & Dirba, 2007), they are "liquid strangers" (people in the host country who are just passing through and who have a scheduled return home), rather than "solid strangers" (people who have moved to the host country permanently). At the universities they attend in the host countries, they are effectively temporary visitors and occupy positions on the peripheries of the university structure. In Siegal's (1994) study of four white women learning Japanese in Hiroshima, the author found that study abroad learners in Japan are distanced from the Japanese community in various ways, including being placed in dormitories that are specified for foreigners only. Isabelli-García (2006) looked at learners from the United States studying Spanish in Buenos Aires, Argentina, getting them to keep journals and logs of their social contacts. Comparison of this data with Oral Proficiency Interviews showed that learners who failed to establish social networks with Argentines and who spent more time speaking English with other exchange students made smaller linguistic gains than those who managed to establish such contacts.

In some study-abroad contexts the local **target language** community may not necessarily expect study abroad learners to gain socialization into local patterns of language interaction. Iino's (2006) study of American students in Japanese home-stays found that the Japanese hosts held low expectations as to how well the students could speak Japanese, adopt other Japanese practices such as eating Japanese food, and ultimately become members of Japanese society. The host families used a simplified and hyper-corrected register of Japanese when addressing the students, avoided using local dialect, and were accepting or even welcoming of their non-native language use, which they perceived as "cute" (p. 166). On the other hand, at times they negatively evaluated the use of native-like Japanese utterances. For example, when one student used the humble utterance *tsumaranai mono desu kedo douzo* "this is a useless thing but please accept" when giving a gift to her host family, the Japanese family perceived the utterance as insincere and forced since they assumed that there was "no such custom in Americans' mentality as *tsumaranai mono*" (pp. 166–167). Iino concludes that study abroad students are exposed to "modified norms of interaction" in contacts with the local community which do not – and indeed cannot – directly mirror native-like patterns of language socialization. Study abroad students from English-speaking countries may in fact find that they are frequently addressed in English, and that there is a low expectation that they can speak the target language at all (Brown, forthcoming). In short, the study abroad context often falls short of the image of an idealized "monolingual utopia" (Mori and Sanuth, 2018).

Some study abroad learners may take advantage of these lowered expectations and deliberately choose to flout the rules. Kumagai and Sato (2009) showed that study abroad learners in Japan may deliberately pretend not to speak Japanese in order, for example, to escape fines on the subway for having the wrong ticket. The authors refer to this as "using ignorance as a rhetorical strategy." Higgins (2011) found that Western female L2 Swahili speakers residing in Tanzania rejected "becoming Swahili" due to feelings that this was at odds with their self-images as "feminists, sojourners, and world citizens" and "intercultural adventurers without a firm concept of 'home'" (p. 189).

The Kumagai and Sato (2009) study also shows that the experiences of study abroad learners are variegated by issues of race. Whereas "using ignorance as a rhetorical strategy" was available to Caucasian learners in their study due to their visually obvious foreignness coupled with the prestige associated with whiteness in Japan, the strategy could not be so easily adopted by learners of Asian appearance. However, Asian learners enjoyed the language-learning advantage of being exposed to more authentic Japanese interactions, since Japanese interlocutors were more likely to assume that they could speak the language. Caucasian learners in Kumagai and Sato's study, on the other hand, complained that they would always be positioned as foreigners and that their ability or potential to use Japanese was constantly underestimated.

The study abroad literature also shows that issues related to **gender** and sexuality may influence the extent to which learners become socialized in the local community. First of all, female learners experience sexual harassment when studying abroad in a wide range of countries in Europe, Asia, and the Americas (see Kinginger, 2009, p. 7). In addition, female learners as well as homosexual learners may find that the subject positions (i.e., socially recognized identities) available to them are different than those in their home culture. Polanyi (1995) discovered that American female learners in Russia struggled to develop platonic relationships with Russian men, who seemed to presume that a heterosexual relationship must be sexual. This was inconsistent with the way in which these learners wanted to present themselves, and with the propensity for establishing platonic heterosexual relationships that had been available for them back in their native culture. Ultimately, it worked to limit their opportunities to integrate with Russians and to gain experience interacting in the language. In the Siegal (1994) study cited above, female learners of Japanese rejected subservient Japanese female identities and the language use that went with it to varying degrees. For these Western women, the available linguistic identity as a Japanese female and the humble demeanor and "squeaky voice" that went with it was considered demeaning. Diao's (2016) analysis of gendered language by Chinese learners in Shanghai found that both male and female participants were evaluated by their native-speaker roommates as sounding like the opposite gender. However, whereas for the female learner this was interpreted rather positively ("boyish," "cute," "sexy"), for the male learner it was perceived as "sounding gay." In my own recent paper (Brown, 2014), I looked at a case study of how a lesbian learner of Korean, Julie, negotiated her sexuality and language usage during study abroad in Seoul, in an environment which she perceived as hostile to homosexuality and in which visual markers that she saw as expressions of her sexuality (short hair, gender-neutral clothing, etc.) were not picked up on.

Since language socialization involves the acquisition of socially appropriate language, the ways in which learners are willing or able to become socialized into the target language culture is linguistically manifest. In the examples mentioned above, we saw that Japanese learners acquiring the ability to use speech styles to mark their emotions in culturally appropriate ways can be taken as evidence of social learning (Iwasaki, 2010). Likewise, Western women resisting the use of a squeaky voice when speaking Japanese (Siegal, 1994) also display learning of the way in which language usage is socially variegated. However, their rejection of such patterns may ultimately limit the degree to which they can socialize into the local community, and the types of local roles and identities they can take on.

My Work in Language Socialization and Culture in Study Abroad

Personal Reflection

After graduating from university in the United Kingdom with a BA in English Studies, I spent six years living and working in Seoul, South Korea. Learning Korean became an obsession for me, and I became particularly engrossed in the way in which politeness was encoded in the language. When addressing an elder or status superior, you need to use **honorific language**, which is known in Korean as *contaymal* "respect speech." This involves adding an honorific suffix such as –*yo* or –*supnita* to the end of each and every verb, and also addressing people with titles rather than their name or "you." When interacting with friends of similar or younger age, you can drop all the honorifics and use a register of language known as *panmal*, or "half speech."

On returning to the UK in 2003 to do graduate studies in Korean applied linguistics at SOAS (University of London), I wanted to explore how second language learners of Korean acquired and used this system of honorifics. However, I found at this point that linguistic studies of Korean honorifics focused mostly on describing their grammatical formation, and the acquisition of honorifics as well was seen as being a question of grammatical acquisition. Around this time, a lot of new work was appearing on social aspects of second language acquisition, led by researchers such as Bonny Norton (e.g., Norton, 2000), David Block (e.g., Block, 2009) and, in the study abroad context, Celeste Kinginger (e.g., Kinginger & Farrell, 2004) and Livia Polanyi (e.g., Polanyi, 1995). I saw an opportunity here to look at the acquisition of Korean honorifics from a new perspective. And by focusing on the acquisition of Korean honorifics, I hoped to see how language socialization could be manifested in the acquisition of this particularly salient part of the Korean language.

In 2005–2006, I spent a year at a university in Seoul doing fieldwork on how students studying abroad in South Korea learned and used honorifics. Out of the data that I collected, I wrote my PhD dissertation, which was subsequently published in revised form (Brown, 2011). I also published two papers from the same project (Brown, 2010, 2013), the latter of which will be discussed in more detail below. I was fortunate that my work coincided not only with what Block (2009) has called a "social turn" in applied linguistics, but also with a boom in global interest in the Korean language, boosted by the rising profile of Korean pop culture. After gaining my PhD, I have been fortunate enough to work both in the United States (at University of Oregon) and Australia (Monash University).

My Work in Language Socialization and Culture in Study Abroad

In Brown (2013), I examined how four male learners from the data collected in Seoul in 2005–2006 were socialized into the use of Korean honorifics while spending a

Table 10.1 Background of participants

	Age	Nationality	Country of Residence	Ethnicity	Other Languages
Richard	21	UK	UK	White-British	English (native)
Hiroki	23	Japan	UK	Japanese	Japanese (native)
					English (fluent)
Patrick	23	Austria	Australia	White-	German (native)
				Austrian	English (fluent)
					Japanese (adv.)
Daniel	25	Germany	UK	Korean	German (native)
					English (fluent)
					French (adv.)

year studying abroad at a large university in Seoul. I looked at how these advanced-level learners of Korean used honorifics as markers of their identities as second language learners, exchange students, foreigners in Korea, and also as males. An assumption here was that since honorifics mark the speaker's relationship vis-à-vis the hearer, that they play a crucial role in defining the social relations of the speaker and also in creating the speaker's social identity and image. By using honorifics appropriately according to social norms, the speaker can go some way to becoming socialized as a competent member of Korean society.

The four male learners were of different nationalities and ethnic backgrounds, but were all permanently based at universities in English-speaking countries (see Table 10.1). Japanese participant Hiroki had lived in Europe (Germany and the UK) from the age of 9. The one learner of Korean heritage, Daniel, had been raised speaking German as a first language and had only a rudimentary knowledge of Korean before taking Korean classes.

Three types of data were analyzed in this study. First, in order to assess the learners' underlying linguistic knowledge of Korean honorifics, I used a **Discourse Completion Task (DCT)**: a kind of language-use questionnaire where participants are presented with a situation and/or dialogue and asked to fill in what they would say in that situation. The learners' use of honorific language on the DCT was then judged in comparison to baseline data collected from forty native speakers. Second, to obtain examples of how the participants actually used honorifics in the "real world," I collected recordings of natural conversations from the learners. In order to reduce observer effects (i.e., participants altering their behavior due to the presence of the researcher), the data were collected remotely by supplying participants with a recording device. Third, I carried out retrospective interviews with the participants, during which I quizzed them on their application of honorifics in the recordings and their general use of and attitudes toward these forms. I also obtained learner stories or anecdotes regarding their use of honorifics.

Analysis of the DCT data showed that learners' underlying linguistic knowledge of when to use honorific language essentially matched that of native speakers. All four learners scored over 90 percent correct/appropriate. However, comparison of the DCT data with the natural conversations and interview data showed that this underlying knowledge of when honorifics should be used did not necessarily translate into appropriate use of honorifics in "real-world" interactions with Koreans.

In "real-world" interactions, British learner Richard tried to negotiate egalitarian use of non-honorific *panmal* in interactions with Koreans, even in situations where he understood that this was not the norm in Korean culture. Consider the following incident that Richard relayed during the interview:

(1) *There was this one girl who was four years older than me. We were conversing and it was obvious that we were getting quite close. So I asked her if it was okay to speak* panmal. *And she just said "yeah." It would probably be fairly bad manners to do that if I was a Korean. But she didn't have any complaints and we both just dropped down.*

Richard appears correct in his assessment that it would be "fairly bad manners to do that if I was a Korean." In Korean native speaker interaction, the younger party should invite the older party to use *panmal* to them, rather than suggesting that they use *panmal* themselves. Richard, however, was aware that his identity as a foreigner meant that he was not necessarily expected to be socialized into Korean norms, and that he was afforded the leeway to initiate patterns of language usage that he found more comfortable as someone who came from a culture that valued egalitarian and casual language usage.

Whereas Richard saw his identity as a foreigner as an advantage that he could manipulate in order to negotiate his own patterns of language, Austrian learner Patrick viewed things rather differently. He saw using honorifics correctly as an important tool that he could use to integrate into Korean society. He reacted extremely negatively to any suggestions that his non-Korean identity should exclude him from using or receiving non-native patterns of honorifics:

(2) *There was a situation when a girl who was three years younger than me, she always kept talking to me using* panmal, *almost from the start. But if the person thinks they don't need to use honorifics to me because I'm a foreigner, then that's rude.*

(3) *There was a conversation going on about whether people should use honorifics to foreigners between myself and three Koreans, two older and one younger than me. And one of them said that he thought you wouldn't need to use honorifics to a foreigner. At that time, I felt a bit offended.*

From these experiences, Patrick had developed a strong belief that it was rude, offensive, and discriminatory for Korean native speakers to apply anything less than native-like norms during language socialization. He thus made every attempt to adhere to native speaker norms of language use, including honorifics, and by doing so claim for himself an identity of equal status to Korean native speakers.

Daniel was an ethnic Korean born and raised in Germany. Due to his Korean heritage, we may expect that Daniel would enjoy an advantage when it came to being socialized into the usage of honorifics. Indeed, the data showed that Daniel was highly proficient in the use of honorifics and slipped comfortably and appropriately between honorific and non-honorific language. However, the socialization opportunities afforded to him had limitations. During the interviews, Daniel complained that Korean native speakers would cast him as someone "not familiar" with the norms of honorifics use and, in addition, that they would judge him harshly for any slips or intentional flouts of honorific norms. In one incident when Daniel used non-honorific language as a joke, a Korean native speaker corrected him, saying "I totally understand that you are not familiar with these issues." Daniel furthermore reported "culture problems" in adapting to a social structure in which there was no "equal basis." Although he accepted the norm of having to use honorifics toward his elders, he did not see the need for his juniors to use honorifics toward him. Indeed, he would "always tell them to use *panmal*" regardless of their age: "as long as I know them, that's ok." Although more nuanced than the case of Richard mentioned above, Daniel also knowingly negotiated patterns of honorifics usage that strayed from native norms. Even though he was of Korean heritage, he had not been fully socialized into Korean patterns of interaction.

Finally, the case of Japanese-born Hiroki is perhaps most illustrative of the limitations of study abroad as a context for language socialization. The recordings of natural interactions revealed that although Hiroki understood when to use honorifics, he actually only used a simplified form of it, which lacked some of the more advanced verb endings needed in this register when addressing social superiors. When asked about this during the interviews, Hiroki pointed to the impoverished socialization opportunities available to exchange students who mostly interacted only with "other foreigners." And even when he did encounter Koreans, they were normally peers of similar age and thus, in his own words, "I don't have so much opportunities to use these kinds of words [honorifics]." He explained that it was "difficult" for exchange students to "integrate into Korean society very much," blaming this on the temporal and sequestered identity of exchange students. As an exchange student, Hiroki occupied a subject position outside of the relational and hierarchical structure of the university. Significantly, he was aware that he lacked one crucial component of a Korean student identity: he had no *haknyen* ("university year," as in first year, second year, etc.). Without this, there was no clear indication of where he fitted into the university's hierarchical structure, and therefore which level of honorifics would be needed:

(4) *It's different, you know, as an exchange student [...] Things would be much more clear if I'm il-haknyen [a first year] or i-haknyen [a second year] here, then*

people would just- because it's- I think it's one of the ways which you can- it's like one measurement- like, "oh, you- which year are you in?", "I'm the second." Okay, I should use contaymal *[honorific language] to you.*

The case of Hiroki illustrates that exchange students occupy positions on the peripheries of Korean society, from where opportunities for cultural learning may be limited.

The findings from these four learners show that studying abroad in Korea may not afford learners with the necessary socialization opportunities needed to acquire native-like patterns of language use. On one side of the coin, native-like patterns of interaction might not be available to these learners in the subject positions they are able to negotiate as exchange students and foreigners. On the other side of the coin, it was shown that these learners were not always willing to adopt native-like patterns of use when these clashed with their identities as Westerners and the more egalitarian use of language that this entailed. Rather than passively being socialized into native-like patterns of honorifics usage, these learners found themselves involved in active struggles to establish what constituted appropriate honorifics usage for them in the identities that they were able to establish in Korean society.

Data Analysis Activity

On the website accompanying this book, I have uploaded a file containing stories and anecdotes regarding the usage of honorifics collected from study abroad learners in Seoul. I would like you to analyze this data for evidence of the following:

1. Learners being socialized into native-like patterns of honorifics usage (or a lack of this).
2. Local community expectations regarding how or whether language learners should be socialized into native-like patterns of honorifics usage.
3. Learners' identities interacting with (facilitating or hindering) the process of socialization into native-like patterns of honorifics usage.
4. Learners expressing their own identities in the ways they talk about their experiences.

Going Further

To get more closely involved in the themes and topics addressed in this chapter, there is of course no substitute for directly experiencing study abroad itself, and therefore creating for yourself the opportunities to think about study abroad critically. Most universities now offer a diverse range of study abroad experiences, which do not necessarily require a high level of language competence.

To pursue project work in this area, you could try collecting your own data from students going on study abroad. Ideally, you would want to collect a language sample and perform an interview before they study abroad and then once again when they return. To facilitate this, it might be preferable to find students who are studying abroad on short-term programs (e.g., a six-week summer program).

Discussion Questions

1. The data presented in this chapter in some ways shows that being white (as well as being male) is not necessarily an advantage for second language learners of Korean on study abroad. Being white (rather than Asian) leads to decreased expectations regarding Korean ability, and limitations about the extent to which learners need to be socialized into Korean interactions. Do you agree with this line of argument, or do you think that being white may also come with advantages for language learning?

2. From the viewpoint of language socialization, language learning is seen as being primarily cultural learning. Language acquisition occurs as learners are socialized into the linguistic and cultural practices of the local community. Although this conceptualization of language learning works for native speakers, do you see limitations in applying it to second language learners, even in study abroad contexts?

3. Think about your own experiences learning a language, whether that was through study abroad, living in another country, or just learning a language in class. What did native speakers (or other people more linguistically and culturally competent than you, including teachers) do (or not do) in order to socialize you (or not socialize you) into culturally appropriate language usage? How did you respond to this? How did these patterns of culturally appropriate language use "fit" with your own sense of self?

FURTHER READING

Foundational Readings

Block, D. (2009). *Second language identities*. London: Continuum.

DuFon, M. A., & Churchill, E. (Eds.). (2006). *Language learners in study abroad contexts*. Clevedon: Multilingual Matters.

Norton, B. (2000). *Identity and language learning: Gender, ethnicity and educational change*. Harlow: Pearson.

Recent Publications

Diao, W., & Trentman, E. (Eds.) (forthcoming). *Multilingual turn for study abroad*. Bristol: Multilingual Matters.

Kinginger, C. (2009). *Language learning and study abroad: A critical reading of research*. Basingstoke: Palgrave MacMillan.

Kinginger, C. (Ed.). (2013). *Social and cultural aspects of language learning in study abroad*. Amsterdam: John Benjamins.

REFERENCES

Block, D. (2009). *Second language identities*. London: Continuum.

Brown, L. (2010). Politeness and second language learning: The case of Korean speech styles. *Journal of Politeness Research*, 6(2), 243–270.

(2011). *Korean honorifics and politeness in second language learning*. Amsterdam: John Benjamins.

(2013). Identity and honorifics use in Korean study abroad. In C. Kinginger (Ed.), *Social and cultural aspects of language learning in study abroad* (pp. 269–298). Amsterdam: John Benjamins.

(2014). An activity-theoretic study of agency and identity in the study abroad experiences of a lesbian nontraditional learner of Korean. *Applied Linguistics*, 37(6), 808–827.

(forthcoming). "Sorry, I don't speak any English": An activity-theoretic account of language choice in study abroad in South Korea. In W. Diao & E. Trentman (Eds.), *Multilingual turn for study abroad*. Bristol: Multilingual Matters.

Byon, A. S. (2006). The role of linguistic indirectness and honorifics in achieving linguistic politeness in Korean requests. *Journal of Politeness Research*, 2(2), 247–276.

Dervin, F., & Dirba, M. (2007). Figures of strangeness: Blending perspectives from mobile academics. In M. Byram & F. Dervin (Eds.), *Students, staff and academic mobility in higher education* (pp. 237–260). Cambridge: Cambridge Scholars.

Diao, W. (2016). Peer socialization into gendered L2 Mandarin practices in a study abroad context: Talk in the dorm. *Applied Linguistics*, 37(5), 599–620.

Duff, P. A. (2003). Intertextuality and hybrid discourses: The infusion of pop culture in educational discourse. *Linguistics and Education*, 14(3–4), 231–276.

Higgins, C. (2011). "You're a real Swahili!": Western women's resistance to identity slippage in Tanzania. In C. Higgins (Ed.), *Identity formation in globalizing contexts* (pp. 167–192). New York: Walter de Gruyter.

Iino, M. (2006). Norms of interaction in a Japanese homestay setting: Toward a two-way flow of linguistic and cultural resources. In M. DuFon & E. Churchill (Eds.), *Language learners in study abroad contexts* (pp. 151–173). Clevedon: Multilingual Matters.

Isabelli-García, C. (2006). Study abroad social networks, motivation and attitudes: Implications for second language acquisition. In M. DuFon, & E. Churchill (Eds.), *Language learners in study abroad contexts* (pp. 231–258). Clevedon: Multilingual Matters.

Iwasaki, N. (2010). Style shifts among Japanese learners before and after study abroad in Japan: Becoming active social agents in Japanese. *Applied Linguistics*, *31*(1), 45–71.

Kinginger, C. (2009). *Language learning and study abroad: A critical reading of research*. Basingstoke: Palgrave MacMillan.

Kinginger, C., & Farrell, K. (2004). Assessing development of meta-pragmatic awareness in study abroad. *Frontiers: The interdisciplinary journal of study abroad*, *10*, 19–42.

Kumagai, Y., & Sato, S. (2009). "Ignorance" as a rhetorical strategy: How Japanese language learners living in Japan maneuver their subject positions to shift power dynamics. *Critical Studies in Education*, *50*(3), 309–321.

Longman, J. (2008). Language socialization. In J. González (Ed.), *Encyclopedia of bilingual education* (pp. 489–493). Thousand Oaks, CA: Sage.

Mori, J., & Sanuth, K. K. (2018). Navigating between a monolingual utopia and translingual realities: Experiences of American learners of Yorùbá as an additional language. *Applied Linguistics*, *39*(1), 78–98.

Norton, B. (2000). *Identity and language learning: Gender, ethnicity and educational change*. Harlow: Pearson.

Ochs, E., & Schieffelin, B. (2001). Language acquisition and socialization: Three developmental stories and their implications. In A. Duranti (Ed.), *Linguistic anthropology: A reader* (pp. 263–301). Oxford: Wiley.

Ogiermann, E. (2009). Politeness and in-directness across cultures: A comparison of English, German, Polish and Russian requests. *Journal of Politeness Research*, *5*, 189–216.

Polanyi, L. (1995). Language learning and living abroad: Stories from the field. In B. Freed (Ed.), *Second language acquisition in a study abroad context* (pp. 271–292). Amsterdam: John Benjamins.

Siegal, M. (1994). Looking East: Learning Japanese as a second language in Japan and the interaction of race, gender and social context (unpublished PhD dissertation). University of California-Berkeley.

11 Language Policy and Planning

LIONEL WEE HOCK ANN

Overview of Key Concepts and Issues in Language Planning and Policy

Language policy and planning (LPP) is broadly concerned with understanding the language practices of a group or community, the bases for these practices, and where relevant, the ways in which such practices might be sustained or modified. Scholars working in LPP in the 1960s and 1970s were primarily focused on adopting a highly technocratic approach. The goal of the discipline at the time was construed as one of helping to deal with language "problems," particularly the challenges faced by newly independent nation-states, by identifying "rational solutions." The field of LPP then revolved mainly around the processes of language selection, codification, and elaboration and how these could be implemented (Haugen, 1966). Consequently, from this **technocratic perspective**, "successful language planning, or degrees of it, can be understood in terms of the efficacy of planned policy measures as well as the target populations' propensity to comply with the public policies pertaining to language planning" (Das Gupta and Ferguson, 1977, p. 6). In other words, the main steps involved in LPP were 1) identify a language problem, 2) arrive rationally at a solution, and 3) get the target populations to comply with the prescribed solution.

But by the 1980s and 1990s, it had become quite clear that many of the state-level LPP projects were failures, since social and ethnic unrest continued despite the implementation of LPP programs (Blommaert, 1996, p. 203). Consider, for example, the dilemma faced by speakers of Northern SiNdebele in South Africa (Stroud, 2001). Though both Northern and Southern SiNdebele formed part of the Nguni group, only speakers of the latter had their language officially recognized under apartheid because they had accepted the offer of a homeland. This was the situation inherited in 1994 by the new South African government so that Northern SiNdebele speakers still found themselves without any official language of their own. These speakers lobbied for their own language to be recognized but were told instead that they spoke a dialectal variant of Southern SiNdebele unless they could prove otherwise (Stroud, 2001, p. 349).

In trying to understand the reasons for these failures, scholars started to realize that it was important to better appreciate the role of **ideology** in shaping LPP. Ideological assumptions about language – including its assumed relationship to ethnic and national identities, its presumed role in strengthening or weakening group solidarities, and its perceived influence in sustaining or challenging vested interests – had been largely ignored in the earlier decades when the field aimed to be as technically precise and scientific as possible (Lo Bianco, 2004, p. 739).

This increased appreciation of the role of ideology in LPP has resulted in three major implications. One, because language policies are inevitably formulated under the influence of particular ideological assumptions, however implicit these may be, this means that even in those cases where no explicit language policy is being formulated, ideology still "operates as 'default' policy" (Lo Bianco, 2004, p. 750). In short, LPP need not always be explicit or official. But it is always ideological.

Two, since LPP is always present even when no official policy exists, there is a need to go beyond the state and a narrow understanding of language to look at how communicative practices in general might be ideologically constrained. As a result, scholarly concerns have started to widen so that a number of domains other than the state – such as the family, religion, the workplace, the military, the media, schools, and various international organizations, including NGOs – are also acknowledged to come within the purview of LPP (Spolsky, 2009).

Three, while the field of LPP does have a history of being interventionist, as seen in the early well-intentioned (though ultimately unsuccessful) attempts at providing "solutions" for newly independent states, awareness of the critical influence of ideologies has caused LPP scholars to be particularly appreciative that what is characterized as a problem is very much a reflection of perspective and vested interest. This means that an applied linguist who is working on LPP cannot be blind to particular interests or political factionalism, including his/her own (Wee, 2011, p. 15). For example, the applied linguist has to be aware that, by acting as expert consultant to a group, community, institution, or state, he/she needs to be both clear about and comfortable with the goals of the client. At times, this may even require that the applied linguist engage the client in a critical discussion about the viability and appropriateness of the goals.

Having provided a broad sketch of the history of LPP, I now highlight some examples to provide a more concrete sense of the issues involved and lessons learnt. I noted that early LPP tended to focus on the "needs" of developing nation-states. Because of this, early LPP works sometimes carried an assumption that the developed nation-states represented "linguistically settled end-points" (Lo Bianco, 2004, p. 743). In other words, the linguistic situations found in developed nation-states were presumed to constitute aspirational models, and because of this, the greater the perceived divergence from these aspirational models in developing nation-states, the greater the need for some sort of solution that would, ideally, help move the latter toward the idealized end-points. This presumption was applied to considerations of **multilingualism**, for example, where the multilingual nature of developing nation-states was treated as a societal problem that stood in the way of their maturation into "proper" nation-states. As Blommaert (1996, p. 202) observes, there was "an abnormalization of the Other" so that recently decolonized states or emergent states such as Israel were seen to be in particular need of language problem-solving, whereas patterns of language distribution in Western countries were considered "normal" and "stable." Even when language policy turned its attention to Europe in the later 1970s, and attention focused on the national minorities in European countries, such as the Basques, the Bretons, and the Welsh, "the abnormalization was continued, even exacerbated ... multilingualism is a problem, not because it would be an unworkable situation for administrative and educational practice, but because it is politically denied" (Blommaert, 1996, p. 203).

There are two observations worth making here. The first is the problematic assumption that there is a linguistically settled end-point toward which less developed nations should aspire, with this end-point being exemplified by their supposedly more developed counterparts. The second is the equally problematic idea that multilingualism is a societal problem that needs to be reduced or eliminated, such that the more monolingual a society is, the more unified and stronger it becomes. Both these points smack of hubris, of course, with developed Western countries holding themselves up as the aspirational end-points that developing countries were expected to use as reference models. And they are belied by the fact that many Western countries today are dealing with increased multilingualism amidst increased social and cultural diversity, often as a result of inward and outward migration.

Another lesson learnt from the history of LPP concerns the appreciation that language names only imperfectly correspond to the diversities in actual language practices. Failure to recognize this point often leads policy makers to give too much political weight to **language names**, on the assumption that differences in language names necessarily refer to differences in language practices. This can even result in cases where language practices have had to be modified in order to retroactively help give credence to what was initially more linguistic imagination than reality.

These problems are illustrated in the dilemma faced by speakers of Northern SiNdebele in South Africa (Stroud, 2001). Although both Northern and Southern SiNdebele formed part of the Nguni group, only speakers of the latter had their language officially recognized under apartheid because they had accepted the offer of a homeland. This was the situation inherited by the new South African government in 1994, so that Northern SiNdebele speakers still found themselves excluded from any discussion of language rights. This then led the Northern AmaNdebele National Organization (NANO) to lobby the government and the Pan South African Language Board (PANSALB) to have their language officially recognized. The call was rejected, however, because, as one PANSALB executive explained (quoted in Stroud, 2001, p. 349, italics in original), "we could not promote their case until we had clarity on whether Northern SiNdebele was a *separate language* from Southern SiNdebele." Northern SiNdebele was considered a dialectal variant of Southern SiNdebele, and until proven otherwise, could not be considered sufficiently important to warrant the status of a right. As a result, Northern SiNdebele speakers have had to accommodate a rights discourse that "views language as an essentially unproblematic construct – an identifiable ontological entity" (Stroud, 2001, p. 348). As Stroud explains:

> NANO found itself in the position of having to argue that Northern SiNdebele was a language, which meant a grassroots investment in developing orthography, grammar and glossaries for school. The organization also developed grassroots strategies to demand the use of SiNdebele as a medium of instruction in primary education. (2001, p. 349)

The language practices of speakers of Northern SiNdebele therefore had to be changed in order to fit the expectations of a politicized demand, that the name "Northern SiNdebele" refer to a language as opposed to a dialect. The political debates were thus conducted at the level of the language name itself, along with concomitant arguments over whether this "thing" that the name denoted was really a language or a dialect. Missing from these debates and arguments was a more nuanced appreciation of the fact that there is a gap between the name being bandied about, on the one hand, and the speakers' language practices, on the other. Crucially, this gap between name and practice remains regardless of whether Northern SiNdebele is categorized as a language or a dialect – a point that seemed to have been lost on the South African policy makers. As a consequence, there was no appreciation of the irony that introducing orthography and standardizing grammar all meant changing the character of the "thing" that was being debated.[1]

Another example of LPP comes from more recent work in urban contexts, illustrating the need to appreciate that LPP can and does occur in many different domains, and not just in nation-states. Though cities have not been the focus of LPP in the early days of the field, they have become much more prominent of late because of their increased social, linguistic, and cultural diversity. As Hogan-Brun points out:

> Growing social mobility has led to greater urbanisation worldwide and includes many new speakers from different countries. The make-up of urban populations is becoming

---

[1] This is not a value judgment. That is, I hold no opinion on whether the introduction of orthography or the standardizing of grammar is a "good" or "bad" move vis-à-vis the linguistic integrity of Northern SiNdebele. My only concern here is to highlight how a preoccupation with the linguistic baptism (Park and Wee, 2013) can detract from the more complex issue of addressing the relationship between language practices and their names.

culturally more diverse and less permanent, creating what has come to be termed as superdiversity (Vertovec, 2007). (2012, p. 145)

Cities in particular can present spaces for innovative, forward-looking language planning practices to serve the best interests of the public. They are places where local authorities have significant capacity and instruments to provide equal opportunities for all residents. In this vein many city councils have started to address the shift to multilingual practices through multilingual services and signage. The challenge is (how) to effectively harness urban multilingual ecosystems for equitable social and economic development.

In this regard, McDermott's study of **urban planning** in Northern Ireland shows that even projects or activities "which have no initial linguistic objectives often have an impact on language issues" (2012, p. 203). McDermott gives the example of libraries, which have "also played an important role in supporting migrants to accessing information on social issues as well as providing opportunities for community networking" (2012, p. 203). McDermott thus calls for "unexpected outcomes" to be "effectively documented in a manner that can inform evolving policy" (2012, p. 203).

McDermott also points out that Northern Ireland's two largest cities, Belfast and Derry/Londonderry, have consciously tried to accommodate and recognize the presence of linguistic and cultural minorities by organizing community festivals and arts projects that celebrate their specific identities so that "higher levels of inclusion and accessibility to urban spaces" (2012, p. 187) are created for such communities. While acknowledging that such activities can be contentious because opponents do claim that they "contribute to the creation of division, rather than the promotion of cohesion" (2012, p. 193), McDermott (2012, pp. 194–195) nevertheless notes that they have had beneficial effects in both fostering a greater sense of belonging amongst minorities as well as promoting a general interest in and appreciation of a city's social and cultural diversity:

> One of the most prominent ways that migrant communities have established their visibility in city spaces is through open-air festival events and arts projects. These often celebrate a particular cultural or religious period of importance for migrant communities, or may simply be an attempt to showcase the community's culture, literature and language, music, or dance. Festivals, therefore, provide an important alternative to the narrative which sees migrants 'in terms of social problems – needing housing, education, language teaching, health provision and so on.' (Khan, 2007, p. 4, cited in McDermott, 2012, pp. 194–195).

One example of a festival that has been supported includes the Belfast Mela, which has attracted over 60,000 visitors in its first four years of operation and which is organized by members of the Indian community. The aim has been to celebrate South Asian identity and language and also to promote cross-cultural learning by "promoting a large number of cultures through the arts" (Belfast Mela, n.d.). Likewise, the Chinese community has benefitted from public funding for annual events like the dragon boat race held on the River Lagan in central Belfast and the Chinese New Year celebrations held in St. George's Market, a well-known cultural space in the city which was renovated in the early years of the peace process. As McDermott emphasizes:

> festivals such as those described above are so important for linguistic minorities for their ability to make individuals feel comfortable to converse in their heritage language in a public place, which is not always possible. This is an important role considering that in some locations migrants feel uneasy when speaking their first language publicly and therefore is totally in keeping with the theme of shared and neutral space. (2012, p. 195)

In conducting research in LPP, it is therefore important to keep in mind that the idea of a linguistic end-point is a chimera; that language names and language practices exist in imperfect correspondence to each; that activities that have no initial linguistic objectives may nonetheless still have linguistic outcomes or impacts.

My Work in Language Planning and Policy

Personal Reflection

I became interested in LPP because I was able to observe the direct effects of policy initiatives on friends and family. When the Singapore government made Mandarin the official mother tongue of Chinese Singaporeans in 1979, it banned all other Chinese dialects such as Hokkien, Teochew, and Cantonese. As a result, my grandmother, who spoke no Mandarin and very little English, found herself without access to news or entertainment because of the media ban on Chinese dialects. Likewise, my friends who were unable to pass the Mandarin language examination were in danger of not being able to enter university despite doing well in the other subjects.

My own work in LPP has tended to focus on how problematic assumptions about the nature of language are taken for granted, in particular, the assumption that language is a self-contained bounded system that is properly identified by using a conventionalized language name. So, when people talk about learning English or worry that speakers are speaking English instead of, say, Japanese, it is assumed that the language practices that are being referred to by the use of labels such as "English" or "Japanese" is clear and stable. That is, we all know what these labels refer to and we all agree on what they are supposed to refer to so that we are all referring to the same thing.

But this is not the case, and it is easy to see this once we look at labels like "bad English" or "standard English," where there are clearly disagreements about what counts as bad or standard. Even the distinction between Japanese and English is not that easy to make once we look at actual speech practices. Speakers have been observed to comfortably and fluently mix elements that are conventionally associated with the different labels to the point where we have to ask whether there are even separate linguistic systems in the first place, or whether we are being misled by the labels into thinking that separate systems exist (Otsuji & Pennycook, 2010).

Arguments for Language Rights

This concern about how ideological assumptions about the nature of language influence LPP drew me to critically examine arguments for language rights (Wee, 2010). The general motivation behind the concept of **language rights** "is to ensure that an identifiable group – usually an **ethnic minority** – is granted specific forms of protection and consideration on the basis of their associated language" (Wee, 2010, p. 4). But there are serious conceptual problems with the notion of language rights:

> Exactly what is meant by the concept of language rights, however, is not always clear, since it has been variously asserted that the holders of such rights need not be speakers of languages, but can include the languages themselves, usually on the grounds that languages are intrinsically valuable. If speakers have rights, then we need to further clarify whether such rights accrue to speakers as individuals or by virtue of their status as members of particular groups. And if languages also have rights, then we need to ask whether we are in danger of reifying a social practice that is inherently changeable and variable by dissociating it from the interests of speakers. (Wee, 2010, p. 1)

An appeal to language rights focuses on named varieties but fails to acknowledge that there are also language practices that have no conventionally recognized names. However, these language practices are just as important to their speakers despite not having any conventionally recognized names. And speakers of these unnamed practices may become penalized. This is because, as in the case of asylum seekers, for example, they may not be viewed as speaking proper languages and so their attempts at explaining why they need asylum risk being misunderstood or simply ignored because there is no institutional recognition of their ways of speaking (cf. Maryns and Blommaert, 2001). For example, Maryns (2005) describes the problems faced by a young female from Sierra Leone seeking asylum in Belgium. The asylum-seeking procedure only recognizes "monolingual standard varieties" and has no place for "pidgins and creoles" (2005, p. 300), forcing the asylum seeker to explain "her very complex and dense case" under conditions that "offer very little space for negotiating intended meanings" (2005, p. 312). Consequently, as I point out:

> And this brings us to what is perhaps the most serious problem with the notion of language rights: the ontological assumption that there is an identifiable linguistic variety that can be

coherently treated as the object of a rights discourse. . . . An approach that advocates language rights, however, is likely to find it extremely difficult to deal with such a situation, where sociolinguistic categories and practices are not only unstable, but so incipient that no clear named varieties can yet be said to exist. (Wee, 2010, pp. 45–46)

The kind of hybridity that is characteristic of contact situations and the problems it raises for language rights should in fact *not* be considered exceptional; rather, it should be treated as a characteristic of languages in general.

The Singlish Controversy

It was also this concern and, indeed, frustration with problematic assumptions about the nature of language that led me to write a book about the Singlish controversy in Singapore (Wee, 2018). Singlish has been described as the colloquial variety of English spoken in Singapore. But it has also been described as broken English. Its existence has sparked much public debate, but the complex question of what Singlish really is and what it means to its speakers remains obscured.

Singlish is influential in calibrating the linguistic practices of Singaporeans through which identities of various sorts are indexed, including meta-linguistic identities that index the speakers as being "for" or "against" Singlish, often on the grounds that this variety is something that Singaporeans should be either proud or ashamed of. In other words, Singlish represents a highly contested concept that has provoked very open and public disagreements amongst Singaporeans as to its legitimacy and desirability, particularly because it is seen to have very different implications for the national identity and, indeed, the national economy as well. Some Singaporeans, as well as the Singapore government, denounce Singlish as a problem on the grounds that it supposedly compromises the ability of Singaporeans to learn proper/good English (which is usually a synonym for Standard American English or Standard British English). In contrast, other Singaporeans defend Singlish as an important marker of national identity that is worth preserving, and they reject the idea that it adversely affects the learning of Standard English. Instead, these supporters of Singlish usually offer a defense loosely based on assumptions involving diglossia and situational codeswitching: Singaporeans, they claim, know when to use Singlish and when not to, restricting its use to informal situations involving fellow Singaporeans and adopting the more standard variety in formal situations, including situations where non-Singaporeans are present. My concern about the ways in which Singlish is being understood and debated in the public sphere has continued to grow. This is because each time Singlish is discussed in public, the same arguments tend to be thrown up and the same responses made. The result is that previously established views and attitudes (simplistically, either "for" or "against" Singlish because it is a "good" or "bad" thing) are further entrenched; there is no evidence of a better appreciation of different positions or a more nuanced understanding of the ideological assumptions involved. And most importantly, despite robust and vigorous debates about the desirability and legitimacy of Singlish, there has been very little attempt to address the fundamental question "What is Singlish?"

Concrete Example of Singlish Issues   Consider, for example, the use of the label "Singlish" for both colloquial (i.e., non-standard) as well as ungrammatical English. We see this when Goh Chok Tong, then Singapore's second prime minister, expressed the hope that, in time to come, Singaporeans will no longer speak Singlish:

> Singlish is broken, ungrammatical English sprinkled with words and phrases from local dialects and Malay which English speakers outside Singapore have difficulties in understanding . . . Let me emphasise that my message that we must speak Standard English is targeted primarily at the younger generation. (*The Straits Times*, August 29, 1999)

Thus, in 2000, the government launched the Speak Good English Movement (SGEM), whose goal was to promote Standard English and discourage the use of Singlish. As Gupta points out, the SGEM

> was promoting a narrow concept of Standard English, which did not allow for anything local, or informal, rejecting even words that had been unproblematically accepted since the 1980s . . . Once again, Singaporeans are being told to look overseas for correction of their English, and are being given advice that is often based on the strictest possible concept of correctness. (Gupta, 2010, p. 58)

The claim here is that Singlish can be unproblematically equated with ungrammatical English, even though this elides the distinction between the colloquial and the ungrammatical. However, it is important not to conflate colloquial language practices with ungrammatical ones. For example, Singlish (qua colloquial English) does appear quite widely in various Internet forums and Singapore Anglophone literature, whose contributors tend to have been educated at elite English-medium schools and universities (Goh, 2009). The categorization of particular linguistic constructions as "colloquial" or "ungrammatical" is admittedly fairly fluid and open to contestation and negotiation (Wee, 2010, p. 80). Nevertheless, it is important not to lose sight of the fact that speakers who confidently manipulate linguistic resources to perform (Bauman & Briggs, 1990) Singlish are sociolinguistically distinct from those who speak what might be categorized as ungrammatical English because they lack the ability to do otherwise.

In 2010, the Speak Good Singlish Movement (SGSM), a response to the government-initiated SGEM, was formed, with this rationale:

> We not against Speak Good English Movement in Singapore hor. But we feel people should get it right with speaking Singlish and not just English. We are damn tired of people confusing Singlish with broken English. We are damn tired of people kay-kay speak Singlish but really

speak bad English. We are damn tired of people picturing Singlish speakers as obiang chow Ah Bengs and Ah Lians. You dun wanna learn the subtle rules of this natural evolving language, then dun anyhow say it is simple, shallow, and useless please! Singlish is full of culture, of nuances and wordplay. It pulls together the swee-ness in the grammar, syntax, and vocabulary of so many languages. Best OK! (www.facebook.com/MySGSM/info)

The SGSM points out that there is a problem with the government's incautious use of the label "Singlish":

We kept hearing all these non-Singlish phrases thrown about by powerful people as examples of both bad English and Singlish. The gahmen[2] doesn't seem to have a clue to what the difference is, and it really doesn't care. It seems more than happy to throw the baby out with the bathwater. (www.facebook.com/MySGSM/info)

Where the SGSM is concerned, the failure to distinguish between colloquial and ungrammatical English stems from ignorance about and lack of sensitivity to the nuances of language use. This ignorance, according to the SGSM, is attributable to the fact that there are no individuals with language expertise (such as linguists, writers, novelists or poets) in the "gahmen." This leads to a situation where the apparent merits of Singlish (such as strengthening national identity) are being discarded in the course of the government's overenthusiastic but ill-informed attempts to improve the standard of English in Singapore. Thus, the SGSM argues that there is a groundswell of support for Singlish, making any attempt to eradicate it unlikely to be successful:

Anyone who knows enough Singlish has been learning on our page that he or she isn't alone in sensing its importance. If we have lost much of our sense of community through missing historical landmarks and an ever-changing skyline, we have preserved a bit of this in Singlish. Bulldozing Singlish will be this gahmen's greatest challenge yet. (www.facebook.com/MySGSM/info)

And indeed, in 2018, eighteen years after the Singapore government first launched the SGEM, Singlish not only continues to exist, but it might also be described as flourishing. Singlish circulates on YouTube videos, and is used in Singaporean novels, films, and plays. T-shirts, mugs, and various other accessories and merchandise are sold with Singlish words and phrases printed on them.

Data Analysis Activity

The activity for this chapter on LPP, which you'll find on the website accompanying this book, concerns the commodification of Singlish. Language is commodified

---
[2] "Gahmen" is Singlish for "government."

when it is perceived as having an economic value and thus as a resource for socioeconomic competitiveness and mobility. This view of language as a commodity contrasts with other views of language, such as the view of language as heritage. However, even a heritage view of language may become commodified if heritage languages are under pressure to justify why they deserve to be preserved – and if the expected answer is that they, too, can serve as economic resources. In the case of Singlish, the Singapore government has claimed that it is broken English, that it penalizes those who speak it, and that it has no social or economic value. Nevertheless, as the activity will help to make clear, there is evidence that Singlish is becoming increasingly commodified.

Going Further

LPP is clearly not just about language. Students interested in LPP need to be able to forge connections between the study of language and other disciplines such as economics, sociology, and political science, among others. There are not many courses in other disciplines that have an explicit language focus (though the sociology of language is an exception) so it is really up to students to establish insightful and innovative connections themselves, with the guidance of interested academic mentors.

For example, LPP covers a wide range of issues that go beyond Singlish. One key phenomenon that is of major interest to LPP concerns migration. Looking at a society from a national perspective, one might ask whether patterns of inward and outward migration require a rethinking of that society's LPP. As the society becomes more diverse, for example, would new languages need to be officially recognized? Conversely, as speakers shift away from their heritage language, should policies and resources be allocated to help in the preservation of these (potentially) endangered languages? One way to start getting a handle on this issue might be to visit various local neighborhoods, some of which might be showing signs of great diversity and change while others might be become enclaves for specific groups of migrants.

Another phenomenon is that of aging. What are the implications of the prospect of an increasingly elderly society (a prospect that many countries have to deal with) for LPP? We often think of LPP in relation to different named languages, as mentioned above. But what about font size (for weaker vision) or higher volumes for public announcements (for weaker hearing), and even how communication/interaction is effected via social media when many elderly people might not be comfortable with digital technologies? Here, LPP has to be approached from a multidisciplinary perspective, intersecting with disciplines such as urban studies, health, and communication.

Discussion Questions

1. How does one evaluate the success or failure of any particular language policy? What kinds of criteria might you consider relevant?
2. Does it make sense to think of a family as having a language policy? For example, some parents make decisions about what kinds of language practices are acceptable in the household. Even if no conscious decisions are being made, families do obviously use language to communicate amongst themselves. Is this a form of LPP?
3. What do you understand by the phrase "politically correct speech"? Is this an example of LPP?
4. When someone says that "If you are an American, you should speak only English" or "If you are really Chinese, you should speak Mandarin," are there language ideologies at work behind these statements? If so, explain what these specific ideologies might be.

FURTHER READING

Foundational Readings

Ricento, T. (2006) (Ed.). *An introduction to language policy: Theory and method.* Oxford: Wiley.

Spolsky, B. (2009). *Language management.* Cambridge: Cambridge University Press.

Tollefson, J. (1991). *Planning language, Planning inequality.* London: Longman.

Recent Publications

Hult, F., & Johnson, D. C. (2015). *Research methods in language policy and planning: A practical guide.* Oxford: Wiley.

Park, J. (2009). *The local construction of a global language.* Berlin: Mouton.

Wee, L. (2016). Are there zombies in language policy? In N. Coupland (Ed.), *Sociolinguistics: Theoretical debates* (pp. 331–348). Cambridge: Cambridge University Press.

REFERENCES

Bauman, R., & Briggs, C. L. (1990). Poetics and performance as critical perspectives on language and social life. *Annual Review of Anthropology, 19,* 69–88.

Belfast Mela. (n.d.) Welcome page. Retrieved from www.belfastmela.org.uk/

Blommaert, J. (1996). Language planning as a discourse on language and society. *Language Problems and Language Planning, 20*(3), 199–222.

Das Gupta, J., & Ferguson, C. A. (1977). Problems of language planning. In J. Rubin, B. H. Jernudd, J. Das Gupta, J. A. Fishman & C. A. Ferguson (Eds.), *Language planning processes* (pp. 3–8). The Hague: Mouton.

Goh, C. (2009). Perspective on spoken grammar. *ELT Journal, 63*(4), 303–312.

Gupta, A. F. (2010). Singapore Standard English revisited. In L. Lim, A. Pakir, & L. Wee (Eds.), *English in Singapore: Modernity and management* (pp. 57–90). Hong Kong: Hong Kong University Press.

Haugen, E. (1966). *Language conflict and language planning: The case of Modern Norwegian.* Cambridge, MA: Harvard University Press.

Hogan-Brun, G. (2012). Editorial: Language planning in urban spaces. *Current Issues in Language Planning, 13*(3), 145–147.

Khan, N. (2007). Inter-cultural arts policy – challenge paper. Retrieved from www .interculturaldialogue.eu/web/files/64/en/CP-Khan-03.doc

Lo Bianco, J. (2004). Language planning as applied linguistics. In A. Davies & C. Elder (Eds.), *Handbook of applied linguistics* (pp. 738–762). Oxford: Blackwell.

Maryns, K. (2005). Monolingual language ideologies and code choice in the Belgian asylum procedure. *Language & Communication, 25*(3), 299–314.

Maryns, K., & Blommaert, J. (2006). Stylistic and thematic shifting as a narrative resource: Assessing asylum seekers' repertoires. *Multilingua – Journal of Cross-Cultural and Interlanguage Communication, 20*(1), 61–84.

McDermott, P. (2012). Cohesion, sharing and integration? Migrant languages and cultural spaces in Northern Ireland's urban environment. *Current Issues in Language Planning, 13*(3), 187–205.

Otsuji, E., & Pennycook, A. (2010). Metrolingualism: Fixity, fluidity and language in flux. *International Journal of Multilingualism, 7*(3), 240–254.

Park, J., & Wee, L. (2013). Linguistic baptism and the disintegration of ELF. *Applied Linguistics Review, 4*(2), 339–359.

Spolsky, B. (2009). *Language management.* Cambridge: Cambridge University Press.

Stroud, C. (2001). African mother-tongue programmes and the politics of language: Linguistic citizenship versus linguistic human rights. *Journal of Multilingual and Multicultural Development, 22*, 339–355.

Wee, L. (2011). *Language without Rights.* Oxford: Oxford University Press.

(2018). *The Singlish controversy: Language, culture and identity in a globalizing world.* Cambridge: Cambridge University Press.

SECTION 3:
Language Varieties and Variation

12 | Language Varieties and Education

JEFFREY REASER

Applied linguistics in educational contexts is most commonly associated with programs related to language learning (i.e., ESL, EFL, etc.). However, linguistic information derived from studying intra-language variation is equally important in educational contexts. In this chapter, I focus primarily on dialect variation in educational contexts. I do this for a few reasons. First, while everyone understands that linguistic information is crucial to teaching foreign or additional languages, few recognize its importance to teaching in native language contexts. In US schools, vernacular-dialect-speaking children are expected, without instruction or resources, to conform to school language standards: there are no "second dialect" classes. Second, many challenges related to dialect variation in the classroom parallel those of additional language learning. For example, students may experience difficulty with inconsistent aspects of English grammar, such as the various conjugations of *be* or when cultural expectations about language vary, such as the appropriateness of silence or expectations about recounting narratives. The consistency of these challenges across vernacular and non-native speakers motivated the educational linguistics term **"Standardized English Learners"** (SELs), which includes all students who arrive to school speaking a linguistic variety other than that which forms the basis of instruction and assessment (Wilkerson, Miciak, Alexander, Reyes, Brown, & Giani, 2011). Third, listeners respond differently to vernacular and non-native speakers. While listeners may judge non-native speakers negatively, they attribute differences to linguistic circumstances. However, listeners tend to make judgments about personal attributes – intelligence, character, etc. – of dialect speakers. None of this is to diminish the challenges English language learners face in educational contexts. Instead, by focusing on dialect speakers, I hope to illuminate the ways in which knowledge from applied linguistics can ameliorate the experiences of all SELs.

Overview of Key Concepts and Issues in the Role of Language Varieties in Education

When considering the scope of applying linguistics to education contexts, it is helpful to consider three linguistic dimensions: **modality of communication** (i.e., speaking, reading, writing, and listening); **level of language** (i.e., the systems of pronunciation, morphology, syntax, semantics, pragmatics, and discourse routines); and native versus non-native speakers. The intersections of these categories demarcate substantial research opportunities. Just starting to list the possibilities, one could investigate how native speakers learn to read; how non-native speakers learn to read in a second language; how different first languages affect learning to read and write (and speak and listen) in another language; what sounds, grammatical, or syntactic structures of a language cause difficulty for those learning it as an additional language; and so on. To put it generally, applied linguistics in educational contexts seeks to examine effects of variation in all levels of language across all language modalities both within a language (dialects, registers, etc.) and between and among different languages. It does this via methodologies derived from educational research, linguistics, sociolinguistics, sociology, psychology, and ethnography. It then seeks to transform that knowledge into pedagogy.

In educational contexts, perhaps the most compelling applications of linguistic information inform teaching traditional literacy skills (i.e., reading and writing). While linguistic information also informs the teaching of speaking, first language grammar, and additional languages, these pursuits are less foundational to classroom-based and standardized assessments, making traditional literacy skills essential to traditional measures of academic success. Reading and writing skills are also critical across disciplines. In the remainder of this section, I highlight some of the rich research about how linguistic information can benefit the teaching of reading and writing before going on to discuss the role of Critical Language Pedagogy in dialect awareness efforts.

Reading

Applied linguistics can make predictable the reading **miscues** of vernacular-speaking children. For example, the sentence "Ruth's brother missed a game, and the coach doesn't like it" may be read by an **African American English** (AAE) speaker as "Ruf brovuh miss' a game, and da coach don' like it" (example from Reaser, Adger, Wolfram, & Christian, 2017, p. 205). Applying knowledge of the dialect makes predictable the phonetic substitutions for the sounds made by the spelling <th>: at the start of words, voiced <th> is produced as [d]; in other positions, voiced <th> becomes [v], and voiceless <th> becomes [f]. Consonant cluster reduction explains the absent –ed ending on "missed" (pronounced homophonously with "mist"). The absence of the "'s" follows a common grammatical pattern of AAE where speakers indicate possession solely by word adjacency ("My dad car is blue") while Standard English relies on both adjacency and a grammatical marker ("My dad's car is blue"). In both dialects, the first noun is always understood to be the owner of the second noun, so the Standard English "'s" is grammatically redundant. Finally, the substitution of "don'" for "doesn't" reflects a phonetic influence (absence of [t]) and a grammatical influence (use of "do" for "does"). In this example, the critical insight is that the child is not making reading errors; she is, instead, reading the passage fluently in her native dialect. The Penn Reading Initiative (www.ling.upenn.edu/pri/) is one program developed by applied linguists that leverages the predictable nature of reading miscues for vernacular-speaking students as a means of teaching them **codeshifting** (shifting between dialects) strategies.

To linguistically unaware teachers, and on standardized assessments, dialect differences may be diagnosed as reading deficiencies. Sometimes linguistic bias is obvious, such as a decoding test that requires students to distinguish "pin" from "pen," two words commonly said the same in the Southeastern United States. Frequently, however, the bias is subtle, such as a reading comprehension test that relies on cultural background for success. One such test documented by Meier (1973) relied on the presupposition that police officers are always trustworthy and act in helpful ways, an assumption not shared by all cultural groups.

In the United States, the correlation between family socioeconomic status and children's literacy is strong. Overall, children from poorer families perform worse on reading assessments than children from wealthier families, and the gap widens over the children's years of schooling (Murnane, Sawhill, & Snow, 2012). Given that speakers of vernacular dialects tend to come from lower socioeconomic backgrounds, it is reasonable to assume that collectively these students will trail on measures of literacy achievement. Data from the so-called "Nation's Report Card" confirm this assumption: Latinx and African American students in fourth and eighth grade lag behind their white peers (National Center for Educational Statistics, n.d.). Using linguistic knowledge, researchers have investigated this gap from a variety of different perspectives.

One early line of inquiry was the linguistic interference hypothesis, which assumed the mismatch between the dialect and the written language caused reading difficulty. However, causal links between dialect and reading achievement have remained elusive. Thus, more recent applied linguistics work has examined not the interface between written and spoken language, but the interface between teacher and student. Since no teacher intentionally mis-teaches students, much of this work seeks to uncover institutional inequity and teachers' unconscious biases. For example, teachers have been found to interrupt or correct SELs more than non-vernacular-speaking students, call on them less, and hold lower expectations for their success (Terry, 2012). Other work has found that even when vernacular-speaking students read fluently in the vernacular (as in the example above), they are assigned to low-achieving reading groups and exposed to less engaging reading materials, which slows their progression.

There are numerous studies documenting how traditional reading instruction affects different groups. I briefly note three studies of different cultural groups.

Purcell-Gates (1995) documented how differences in Appalachian students' literacy experiences and schools' expectations of those experiences differed and how approved curricula did not meet the needs of these readers. Phillips (1993) found that a common pedagogy that relied on learning through public mistakes resulted in children on the Warm Springs Indian Reservation becoming reluctant to read aloud and resistant to reading in general. Flipping the script, Reynolds, Taylor, Steffensen, Shirey, and Anderson (1982) found that when asked to read a passage that drew on black culture, African American elementary students demonstrated greater comprehension than their white peers. The struggle of some of the white students prompted a young African American student to exclaim, "What's the matter? Can't they read?"

Writing

Though less work has examined dialect variation and writing than dialect variation and reading, many of the results are parallel in nature; namely, schools tend not to be linguistically informed in their teaching of writing to students with different backgrounds. For example, studies have found that students from different linguistic backgrounds organize narratives differently, reflecting differences in community discourse routines. In one classic study, working-class African American children produced narratives with several related episodes, which their teacher deemed disjointed. These children were given little feedback about improving compared to white children who employed a narrative structure expected by their white teacher (Michaels, 1981).

Studies have found varying degrees of vernacular grammatical influence in student writing. In general, anytime a grammatical difference exists between a dialect and standardized English, that difference may be manifested in student writing. For example, it may be expected that an AAE speaker may lack the –s on third person singular verbs ("He live_ with me") or that a Latinx English-speaking student may use multiple negation ("He didn't know nothing"). Additionally, SELs may face predictable struggles with inconsistent grammatical patterns in English, like *do*-support questions: compare the difference between questions formed via verb inversion ("It is finished" becomes "Is it finished?") versus those that require *do* ("You like waffles" becomes "Do you like waffles?"). However, eliminating such influence can be tricky; longitudinal data from a study that followed a group of African American students for sixteen years found that there was not a smooth reduction in dialect influence over time. Instead, dialect-based grammatical features reappeared in student writing whenever they began to use more elaborate syntactic structures (Kohn, Wolfram, Farrington, Van Hofwegen, & Renn, forthcoming). Similar findings exist for non-dialect-based writing features, like punctuation or sentence style, highlighting a conundrum for teachers: the process of learning to write better often coincides with an increase in writing errors.

Pronunciation influences are less straightforward. While some pronunciations do get encoded in students' writing, such as the consonant cluster reduction that happens at the end of words like *mist* ("mis'") or *missed* ("miss"), other pronunciation differences are unlikely to appear in the writing of SELs. While many SELs alter the sounds represented by the <th> letter sequence (commonly as [d], [f], and [v], as described above), children quickly learn to spell these words correctly even though they may never use the standardized English pronunciations.

Extending from these studies of language and dialect influence in student writing, applied linguistics research on teaching writing has recently advanced **code-meshing** approaches. While codeswitching pedagogy has traditionally suggested different language varieties (languages or dialects) should be confined to separate uses (e.g., school vs. home), code-meshing encourages students to intentionally mix different language varieties. Such pedagogy shifts the focus from correctness to appropriateness and rhetorical effect and represents one recent application of linguistic knowledge to producing more culturally affirming pedagogy. A different culturally affirming pedagogy was employed in a study of more than 200 students who spoke Appalachian English, a stigmatized US dialect. The results were transformative: students in the program improved their formal writing assessment scores by 72 percent; over the same time period, students taught via traditional approaches improved by only 9 percent (Clark, 2013, p. 121). Other research has found that permitting vernacular-speaking or ELL students to write without fear of negative evaluation leads to improvements in critical thinking, engagement in school, and thoughtful questions. Recent research has led to linguistically informed pedagogies for helping students to structure narratives, edit their work, and proofread. Finally, other work has attempted to apply linguistic knowledge to inform teachers' assessment of student writing, leveraging information about dialect patterning and tailoring instruction to the unique needs of individual learners. Applied educational linguistics is currently transforming the teaching of writing to SELs, yet this remains an important area of active research.

Dialect Awareness and Critical Language Pedagogy

Dialect awareness programs are an important component for challenging linguistic discrimination; however, knowledge and tolerance are not enough to unseat the entrenched and often insidious linguistic biases that are perpetuated via standard language ideology (Lippi-Green, 2012). Applied linguists working in educational contexts have increasingly advanced pedagogies informed by critical theory and critical discourse analysis, most recently **Critical Language Pedagogy** (CLP). "Critical approaches" aim to make visible the otherwise invisible institutional mechanisms that perpetuate inequality, and the goal of CLP is to equip teachers with skills to apply language knowledge in ways that encourage students to interrogate the hidden power dynamics and societal institutions – including schools – that perpetuate linguistic discrimination. Among the tenets of this approach is the notion that language use is never neutral, and thus, as students learn about language use, they are able to more effectively navigate the world and, in doing so, challenge existing power structures.

The largest study of CLP to-date is Godley and Reaser (2018), which examines the discussions of more than three hundred pre-service teachers at eleven universities as they learned about and grappled with issues of language, power, identity, and culture. The results suggest that pre-service teachers were able to advance from awareness of linguistic facts and general "tolerance" of all dialects to being able to describe ways in which linguistic diversity would be celebrated in their classrooms and how they would use SELs' language varieties as assets, including creating opportunities for writing and speaking in the vernacular, discussing issues of implicit and explicit language bias, and being vigilant to ensure students' voices are treated fairly. This evolution can be seen in one participant's reflection on the CLP curriculum:

> The idea that simply saying you support linguistic diversity isn't enough to counteract the sense of confusion and possibly resentment non-standard speakers feel in classrooms was an important lesson for me. I've always been what I would consider fairly educated about vernacular diversity, and I thought just saying so in my classroom would fix most of my problems – this curriculum taught me that that's not the case, and I must be mindful in finding specific, structured ways for students' dialects to be celebrated in the same way [American Standard English] is. (Godley & Reaser, 2018, p. 160)

These teachers developed knowledge and skills that transformed their notions of literacy education, language and power, language and identity, and systematic linguistic bias. They also were able to offer specific classroom plans for teaching about issues of language and discrimination by responding to and evaluating classroom-based scenarios related to writing, reading, grading, responding orally to students, and leading discussions. The full CLP curriculum and an analysis of students' engagement is found in Godley and Reaser (2018).

The recent direction of applied linguistics in educational contexts is profoundly important, vast in application, and exciting. Paired with new and existing know-ledge of teaching reading and writing, information from the field is currently transforming education programs and classroom practice. And while CLP emerges out of dialect variation in US educational contexts, the approaches and ideas are applicable to teaching language in other contexts, including teaching English to non-native speakers and to dialect variation in other places. Language standards are one of the least critically examined cultural institutions in educational contexts. Almost always, language standards are assumed to be standard for some good reason. Linguistics has demonstrated that this is not the case. And applying that knowledge in educational contexts can transform all types of language learning and use. Entwined with critical pedagogies, it can transform societies.

My Work in Language Varieties and Education

Personal Reflection

My path into applied linguistics was not straightforward. Though I was initially introduced to linguistics via a history of the English language course required of my teacher education program, it was not until I started student teaching that I realized how important linguistics was for teachers: I felt woefully unprepared to meet the literacy needs of my diverse students. I pursued graduate studies in sociolinguistics in hopes of learning more about how and why language varies.

My sociolinguistics coursework and fieldwork taught me the language analysis skills I had hoped to acquire in graduate school, but it did not provide me with answers about what to do about the linguistic discrimination I witnessed in the public schools. I resolved to use my dissertation work to merge my newfound sociolinguistic information with my commitment to social justice educational practices. My mentor, sociolinguistics and applied linguistics pioneer, Dr. Walt Wolfram, had enacted many applied linguistics projects serving communities in which he worked, including an annual trip to teach about the local dialect in the school of one research community, Ocracoke, NC. Having previously participated in this trip, and having helped expand the curriculum, I set out to create a substantial curriculum that explored and celebrated the linguistic diversity of North Carolina. This curriculum had to be accessible to teachers who, like me as a student teacher, lacked linguistic knowledge. The end result was *Voices of North Carolina: Language and Life from the Atlantic to the Appalachians* (henceforth, *VoNC*) (originally Reaser & Wolfram, 2005, revised as Reaser & Wolfram, 2007). This project has spurred much of my applied linguistics work, so I describe it in some detail here, along with the results of a pilot study testing the effectiveness of the curriculum. This curriculum is also the source of the online activities that accompany this chapter.

My Work in Applying Linguistic Knowledge in Educational Settings

As attractive as public schools may be for researchers who wish to share their findings with a large audience, working in educational settings requires balancing competing factors, including time, researchers' goals, mandated curricular goals, assessment, cost, and classroom resources. If our curriculum were to be successful, we knew it would have to fit within existing educational structures. While English Language Arts seems like a natural setting to learn about language, state-mandated testing and curricula made this option unfeasible. Essentially, English teachers had no time or mandate to teach about language variation. We found a more welcoming invitation in social studies, which – in North Carolina – was not subject to standardized testing and had a less prescribed curriculum. Our goals for teaching about language diversity in North Carolina fit perfectly with North Carolina's Standard

Table 12.1 North Carolina SCS objectives addressed in *VoNC* curriculum

NC eighth-grade SCS objective	Met in curriculum by:
1.01 Assess the impact of geography on the settlement and developing economy of the Carolina colony.	The curriculum examines how isolation caused by ocean, swamps, and mountains shaped dialects. Further, geography explains the Great Wagon Road, which has had a lasting impact on North Carolina dialects.
3.04 Describe the development of the institution of slavery in the State and nation, and assess its impact on the economic, social, and political conditions.	Slavery had an effect on the language of many African Americans, which continues to impact the economic, social, and political status of African Americans.
3.05 Compare and contrast different perspectives among North Carolinians on the national policy of Removal and Resettlement of American Indian populations.	The historical contexts of the Lumbee and Cherokee are contrasted, including the early integration and loss of native tongue for the Lumbee and the forced removal and resettlement of the Cherokee.
8.01 Describe the changing demographics in North Carolina and analyze their significance for North Carolina's society and economy.	The Latinx community is one of the fastest growing – and most stigmatized – populations in North Carolina. The linguistic and social effects are examined and misinformation is countered.

Course of Study (SCS) for eighth grade, in which students learn about the history and culture of the state. Since language is intertwined with history and culture, we were able to use linguistic information to meet SCS objectives. Table 12.1 notes just a few of these connections.

With the constellation of possible SCS connections in mind, we defined our key linguistic objectives, which included gaining knowledge of the systematic patterning of all language varieties; understanding links among language, culture, and history; and appreciation for the role language plays in individual and group identity. We were further guided by audio/visual resources available to us, most of which came from our work producing language-based documentaries for television. We sketched a two-week curriculum that offered reasonable coverage of the state's linguistic diversity while touching on about two-thirds of the SCS strands. The specific topics covered by the curriculum were, in order, language attitudes and prejudice, linguistic definitions, levels of language, **style shifting** (i.e., changing the formality of your speech for certain occasions or audiences) and community variation, exemplar dialect patterns, Outer Banks English, Appalachian English, Cherokee (an indigenous language spoken in western North Carolina), Lumbee English (a distinct dialect of English spoken by Lumbee Indians in eastern North

Carolina), AAE, language change in cities, Spanish, and Latinx English. For the pilot study on effectiveness, we bookended the unit with a pre-/post-curriculum survey.

The teachers' lack of knowledge about dialects was overcome via strategic design choices. Our goal was that even upon the first teaching, the teacher, not the text, would be the authority in the classroom. We achieved this by creating very different products for teachers and students. Instead of a "textbook," we created for students a forty-three-page workbook with note-taking sheets, activities, and brief bits of background information. The teachers' manual, meanwhile, was nearly three times larger, at 117 pages. In addition to reproducing the student workbook, it contained daily overviews, extensive background information, answer keys with explanations, teaching tips, additional readings, optional scripted lessons, and pages that could be used as projections. We were also careful to limit the technical vocabulary and to define terms carefully.

The curriculum was distributed with two DVDs containing two interactive maps, twenty-three audio clips, and thirteen video vignettes. In later versions of the curriculum, these materials were made available for free download or streaming (https://linguistics.chass.ncsu.edu/thinkanddo/vonc.php). The rationale for using these audio/visual materials was twofold. First, hearing authentic speakers brings dialects to life in ways that reading cannot; they act as virtual mini-field trips. The media allowed for a more immersive experience and, ultimately, a clearer under-standing of the dialects. Second, some of the videos contained interviews with expert linguists and historians. In these cases, the media served as virtual guest speakers in the classroom. These clips were used strategically to introduce linguistic information or make historical connections which the linguistically untrained teacher may have been unable to make.

The curriculum employed a variety of pedagogies. We incorporated discovery learning, inductive reasoning, deductive reasoning, discussion, and other approaches. A few activities from the curriculum are included on the website accompanying this book. The majority of the activities draw on authentic linguistic data of varying sorts. Students listen to and organize speakers along a standard-vernacular continuum, analyze dialect variations by level of language, decode using the Cherokee Syllabary, and use deductive reasoning to complete cloze-style sentences with dialect vocabulary. Through these controlled language analysis activities, students discover fundamental linguistic facts, including the systematicity of all dialect patterns, that everyone speaks a dialect, and that dialects are intertwined with history and culture. Furthermore, students learn basic techniques for analyzing language data, and they are asked to apply these skills to authentic, idealized, and literary dialects.

How effective was this applied linguistics project? To answer this question, we studied how 129 students, in five classes, taught by three teachers, responded to the curriculum. While a full account can be found in Reaser (2006), the results were overwhelmingly positive. Results of a pre-/post-curriculum survey found students became more knowledgeable and tolerant about dialect variation. The biggest knowledge gains included things like everyone speaks a dialect, dialects have patterns, and many people with a Latinx accent do not actually speak any Spanish. Students also shifted attitudes about dialect speakers. On the pre-curriculum survey, every respondent associated dialects with either laziness or a lack of intelligence (or both). Following the curriculum, students strongly rejected these associations. Quantitatively, the curriculum achieved its goals. And while there were some differences among the effectiveness of the three teachers, all classes responded in similar ways, suggesting that the curriculum was well able to be taught by linguistically untrained teachers.

We also gathered open responses to a couple of prompts. Students overwhelmingly found this type of applied linguistics work important, with over 90 percent agreeing that students everywhere should learn about dialects. Responses to other open-ended prompts illustrate the range of students' responses: they expressed amazement that dialects are patterned. They wrote passionately about the importance of dialects as markers of history, culture, and identity. They were upset that they had never learned about dialects previously. They were upset that dialects are used in discriminatory ways. A few responses include:

- "I learned that I use language stereotypes every time I speak to someone and that I need to be more aware of that."
- "I was surprised at how much racism exists against people with certain dialects."
- "I learned that a dialect doesn't tell anyone if the person is smart or dumb or anything along those lines."
- "I learned that dialects aren't sloppy versions of Standard English. They follow specific patterns that are logical."
- "I never thought of dialects as a part of culture. Seeing all those video clips made me realize how language is a part of culture."
- "There are tons of stereotypes, which are almost always wrong. People should be more informed about dialects, so they would know that dialects represent people's culture and past."

Teachers also responded positively to the program. In a chapter composed by two teachers who used the curriculum in their classes, Ms. Fields-Carey wrote in part,

I have found the study of language variations to be a wonderful way to address differences between people, and this aspect of [this curriculum] has been the most valuable part to me and my students ... Discussing bias in relation to language is a non-threatening way to begin thinking and talking about biases in general.

Through the study of dialects and language differences, my views of what it means to truly teach about the "art of language" has broadened significantly. I now realize that to understand language is not only to know how to speak and write "standard English" correctly, but also to value the right tapestry of language in all its forms. (Fields-Carey & Sweat, 2010, p. 272)

Ms. Fields-Carey further noted that the curriculum "has proven to be empowering for my minority students. For many of them, this is the first time they have been told in a school setting that their dialect is not 'broken'" (Fields-Carey & Sweat, 2010, pp. 273–274). Finally, one of the teachers later reported that on her annual year-end student survey, over 90 percent of her students named the dialect unit as the most important and/or most enjoyable experience from their year. While these reactions are gratifying, they are not entirely unusual. Other applied linguistics programs have received similar reviews from both students and teachers (e.g., Charity Hudley & Mallinson, 2014; Hudgens Henderson, 2016; Sweetland, 2006; Wheeler & Swords, 2006).

By all indications, educators and students are eager for more quality applied linguistics materials that can be used to meet educational goals. To this end, we – and others – have continued to expand the resources available through tradebooks, textbooks, curricula, audio/visual materials, websites, webinars, and other products. Despite this progress, clearly much work remains before applied linguistics information is integrated organically throughout the public school curriculum.

Data Analysis Activity

The website accompanying this book contains sets of data that can be used to discover the rules governing three dialect patterns: grammatical *a*-prefixing in Appalachian English (as in "He was a-huntin'"), *r*-dropping in New England English (as in "Pa'k the ca'" for "Park the car"), and a special grammatical use of uninflected *be* in AAE (as in "The students be talkin' in class" meaning "The students talk in class often"). Collectively, these exercises demonstrate both the systematic nature of language variation and how this linguistic knowledge may be taught in educational contexts. The patterns demonstrate a few different pedagogical approaches, but because they are not being taught in a classroom context, they had to be adapted for individual students. These adaptations are described on the website accompanying this book. Work through the exercises on the companion website to see if you're smarter than an eighth grader!

Going Further

If you're interested in getting involved in work with language varieties in education, a strong background in linguistic analysis is crucial. Taking foundational coursework in phonetics, phonology, syntax, and pragmatics will provide you with skills that are needed to recognize various aspects of dialect variation. A course in sociolinguistics would also be very important for anyone who is interested in this area. Developing a high degree of familiarity with the educational contexts in which these kinds of programs are to be implemented, whether through a degree in education or through other work in the school system, is also necessary for tailoring dialect awareness programs to local curricular goals.

Discussion Questions

1. How would you define "effective language users"? What do you perceive as the most important linguistic knowledge for empowering students to be effective language users?
2. What do you think students who are learning English as an additional language should know about dialect variation in the United States?
3. What are some concrete ways that teachers can recognize students' diverse language varieties as assets in their classrooms? How can they use these assets effectively?

FURTHER READING

Foundational Readings

Alim, H. S. (2005). Critical language awareness in the United States: Revisiting issues and revising pedagogies in a resegregated society. *Educational Researcher, 34*(7), 24–31.

Lippi-Green, R. (2012). *English with an accent: Language, ideology, and discrimination in the United States* (2nd edn). New York: Routledge.

Reaser, J., Adger, C. T., Wolfram, W., & Christian, D. (2017). *Dialects at school: Educating linguistically diverse students*. New York: Routledge.

Recent Publications

Godley, A. J., & Reaser, J. (2018). *Critical language pedagogy: Interrogating language, dialects, and power in teacher education*. New York: Peter Lang.

Paris, D., & Alim, H. S. (Eds.). (2017). *Culturally sustaining pedagogies: Teaching and learning for justice in a changing world*. New York: Teachers College Press.

Young, V. A., Barrett, R., Young-Rivera, Y., & Lovejoy, K. B. (2013). *Other people's English: Code-meshing, code-switching, and African American literacy*. New York: Teachers College Press.

REFERENCES

Charity Hudley, A. H., & Mallinson, C. (2014). *We do language: English variation in the secondary English classroom.* New York: Teachers College Press.

Clark, A. D. (2013). Voices in the Appalachian classroom. In A. D. Clark & N. M. Hayward (Eds.), *Talking Appalachian: Voices, identity, and community* (pp. 110–124). Lexington, KY: University of Kentucky Press.

Fields-Carey, L., & Sweat, S. (2010). Using the *Voices of North Carolina* curriculum. In K. Denham & A. Lobeck (Eds.), *Linguistics at school: Language awareness in primary and secondary education* (pp. 272–276). Cambridge: Cambridge University Press.

Godley, A. J., & Reaser, J. (2018). *Critical language pedagogy: Interrogating language, dialects, and power in teacher education.* New York: Peter Lang.

Hudgens Henderson, M. (2016). *Sociolinguistics for kids: A curriculum for bilingual students* (unpublished doctoral dissertation). University of New Mexico.

Kohn, M., Wolfram, W., Farrington, C., Van Hofwegen, J., & Renn, J. (forthcoming). African American language: Development from infancy to adulthood. Cambridge: Cambridge University Press.

Lippi-Green, R. (2012). *English with an accent: Language, ideology, and discrimination in the United States* (2nd edn). New York: Routledge.

Meier, D. (1973). *Reading failure and the tests (Occasional Paper).* New York: Workshop for Open Education.

Michaels, S. (1981). "Sharing time": Children's narrative styles and differential access to literacy. *Language in Society, 10*(3), 423–442.

Murnane, R., Sawhill, I., & Snow, C. (2012). Literacy challenges for the twenty-first century: Introducing the issue. *The Future of Children, 22*(2), 3–15.

National Center for Educational Statistics. (n.d.). *Reading assessment.* Retrieved from https://nces.ed.gov/nationsreportcard/reading/

Philips, S. U. (1993). *The invisible culture: Communication in classroom and community on the Warm Springs Indian Reservation* (2nd edn). Prospect Heights, IL: Waveland.

Purcell-Gates, V. (1995). *Other people's words: The cycle of low literacy.* Cambridge, MA: Harvard University Press.

Reaser, J. (2006). *The effect of dialect awareness on adolescent knowledge and attitudes* (unpublished doctoral dissertation). Duke University.

Reaser, J., Adger, C. T., Wolfram, W., & Christian, D. (2017). *Dialects at school: Educating linguistically diverse students.* New York: Routledge.

Reaser, J., & Wolfram, W. (2007). *Voices of North Carolina: From the Atlantic to Appalachia.* Raleigh, NC: Language and Life Project at NC State. Retrieved from https://linguistics.chass.ncsu.edu/thinkanddo/vonc.php

Reynolds, R. E., Taylor, M., Steffensen, M. S., Shirey, L., & Anderson, R. C. (1982). Cultural schemata and reading comprehension. *Reading Research Quarterly, 17*, 357–366.

Sweetland, J. (2006). *Teaching writing in the African American classroom: A sociolinguistic approach* (unpublished doctoral dissertation). Stanford University.

Terry, N. P. (2012). Examining relationships among dialect variation and emergent literacy skills. *Communication Disorders Quarterly, 33*(2), 67–77.

Wheeler, R. S., & Swords, R. (2006). *Code-switching: Teaching Standard English in urban classrooms*. Urbana, IL: National Council of Teachers.

Wilkerson, C., Miciak, J., Alexander, C., Reyes, P., Brown, J., & Giani, M. (2011). *Recommended educational practices for Standard English learners*. Austin, TX: Education Research Center, University of Texas at Austin.

13 | Applications of Applied Linguistics to Augmentative and Alternative Communication Device Users in the Workplace

LUCY PICKERING

© Bruno Vincent / Staff / Getty Images

The voice I use is a very old hardware speech synthesizer made in 1986.
I keep it because I have not heard a voice I like better and because
I have identified with it.

Stephen Hawking

Overview of Key Concepts and Issues in Augmentative and Alternative Communication

Augmentative and Alternative Communication (AAC) is an umbrella term used to describe a range of strategies and technologies designed for people with complex communication needs as the result of a developmental disorder such as cerebral palsy or an acquired or degenerative neurological condition such as traumatic brain injury or amyotrophic lateral sclerosis (ALS). All of these conditions can cause **dysarthria** or difficult or unclear articulation of speech in people who have no mental impairment. (Mental impairment and loss of ability to comprehend language may also occur with some of these conditions, but these issues are not addressed in this chapter.) Perhaps the most recognizable AAC user worldwide is the physicist and cosmologist Dr. Stephen Hawking (1942–2018) who is shown above and had a slow-progressing form of ALS or motor neurone disease.

An AAC system is an "integrated group of components, including [any] symbols, aids, strategies and techniques used by individuals to enhance communication" (ASHA, 1991, p. 10). A range of systems are currently available and span low-tech systems that function without electronic components (e.g., picture boards) to

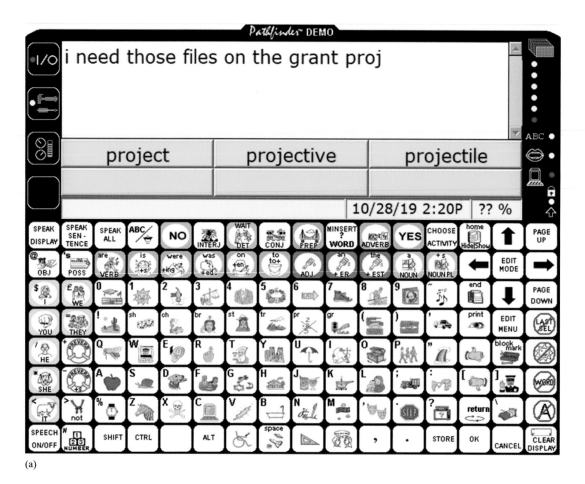

(a)

Figure 13.1 Screenshots of (a) the AAC device "Pathfinder" (© copyright 2019 PRC-Saltillo. All rights reserved.) and (b) the App "Speech Assistant AAC."

high-tech speech generating devices (also called Voice Output Communication Aids or VOCAs) that use computer technology. Increasingly, there is also a use of mobile devices such as smart phones. Access strategies or interfaces with the devices depend on the level of the motor skills of the user and a number are now available including head and eye tracking technology, laser pointers, and swipe or touch interfaces. For example, head-pointing interfaces use optical sensors that track head movement using a small, reflective dot placed on the user's glasses or forehead, while switch interfaces can be activated using any other body part such as the hand, knee, or foot. Two touch screen examples are shown in Figure 13.1. The first is a computerized symbol board and the second is an app available for the iPhone.

Despite this apparent wealth of resources for AAC users, there is an ongoing frustration with VOCAs due to the time it takes users to program spontaneous utterances in a real-time conversational environment. A common misperception is that these devices enable conversations that resemble natural speech in terms of

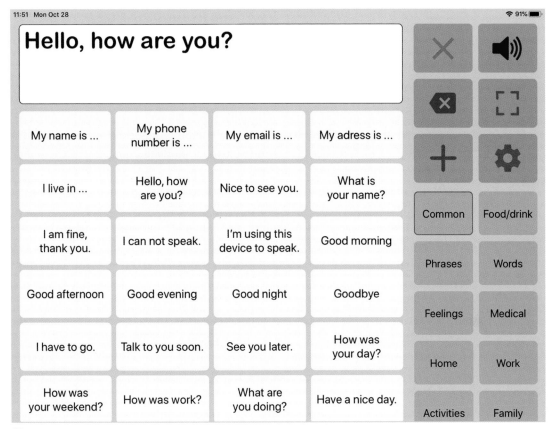

(b)

Figure 13.1 (*cont.*)

speed and fluency; however, this only occurs when users are working with pre-programmed utterances. If users wish to generate spontaneous new utterances (also called SNUG – spontaneous novel utterance generation), devices are quite limited in terms of quickly accessing context-specific language. In fact, one of the most commonly cited challenges with AAC is a limitation on the words and utterances that are available for easy and quick access (Wisenburn & Higginbotham, 2008). Devices typically allow users to express only 65 words per minute, one-third of the average normal conversational rate of 180 words per minute (Dominowska, 2002). Higginbotham and Wilkins (1999) note that these time delays often exclude augmented speakers from inhabiting the same communication "time stream" as their non-AAC user co-participants; users must choose whether to "come in late" or let the opportunity pass. These constraints create an imbalance between AAC and non-AAC users. AAC users have lower initiation rates and fewer conversational turns; users may forget what they were trying to say, and listeners may stop attending (Higginbotham & Caves, 2002; Hoag, Bedrosian, McCoy, & Johnson, 2004). An AAC user describes below how this can frustrate daily interactions:

> Even now with speech on my communicator there are times when my responses aren't
> quick enough and people will go on to the next question or topic while I'm still answering
> the first one or look to people around me to answer for me . . . And this is with people who
> know how frustrating this has to be for me. (Odom & Upthegrove, 1997, p. 259)

One of the reasons for this obstacle with regard to spontaneous utterances is the way in which AAC devices are traditionally programmed using natural language processing (NLP) systems. NLP techniques use computer algorithms to assign probabilities to words or sentences based on statistical language models. As Higginbotham, Lesher, Moulton, and Roark (2012) explain: "word prediction and word completion models are often developed by collecting large text corpora (often exceeding 10 million words) and then making predictions based on patterns observed in those collections" (p. 15). Vocabulary and language patterns are then typically divided into core vocabularies that are assumed to be common among all users and thus highly generic, and fringe vocabularies that contain unique content words that may have a low commonality outside certain basic contexts (Balandin & Iacono, 1998). In other words, as all contextual factors have effectively been eradicated from the language input, it is more difficult to tailor the devices to particular users and their specific needs. Core vocabularies that are more easily accessible typically do not meet the needs of users in the workplace as they require an expanded vocabulary and use words that they do not use in any other context (Creech, 1993). It has been increasingly acknowledged that it is imperative to move beyond this basic programming addressing primarily the expression of generic "needs and wants" of users to systems that allow a focus on domain or genre-specific prediction in order to support AAC users' participation in "socially valued roles" such as workers or parents (Bryen, 2008).

This development requires a sophisticated understanding of linguistic and sociolinguistic patterns used in a given context and within the AAC literature there has been a call to conduct more **social validation studies**, that is, studies that focus on identifying core language patterns by investigating language users' experience in the specific context of interest (Bryen, 2008; Graves, 2000). Thus far, there have only been a few studies examining the workplace. Balandin and Iacono (1998) asked professionals involved in the field of AAC (speech pathologists, teachers, and rehabilitation counselors) to predict what sort of topics and vocabulary might occur in meal-break conversations at work and could be usefully programmed into VOCAs. Overall, approximately two-thirds of the predictions were correct, but approximately one-third of suggested topics did not appear. Graves (2000) also asked non-AAC-using employees to document conversational topics. Sixteen workers in residential homes kept a diary in which they noted topics of conversations and found that areas of interests, leisure activities and food and drink featured most frequently.

Several other studies have targeted AAC users specifically using both surveys and focus groups to ascertain perceived needs and current gaps for AAC users in employment (Light, Stoltz & McNaughton, 1996; McNaughton, Light & Arnold,

2001; Odom & Upthegrove, 1997). Technological difficulties faced by AAC users in the workplace was a frequent topic of discussion, and these included the limited speed of SNUG communication which many felt negatively impacted their communicative effectiveness. One user stated: "Of course, the speed is not like normal speech. So, often a moment passes before one can type a comment. And I find it necessary to edit my comments, and therefore my thoughts are sometimes oversimplified" (McNaughton et al., 2001: 187).

Under any measure, these experiences are understudied, and a clear understanding of the needs of AAC users and their non-AAC interlocutors in the workplace has yet to be fully developed. It is possible that this has been neglected in the field of AAC because it is primarily a linguistic issue rather than a technological one. AAC developers have focused primarily on message formulation and retrieval options and access technologies. Thus, Tetzchner and Basil (2011) note that there is a lack of discussion of "real conversational usage" of people with aided communication:

> Many professionals working with augmentative and alternative communication are more interested in technology and intervention practices than in communication processes; the forms and functions of the utterances produced may not be a real focus for them.
> (Tetzchner & Basil, 2011, p. 148)

Pullin, Treviranus, Patel, and Higginbotham (2017) additionally note that as a field, AAC research may need to consider new research tools as ways of "engaging in accessible and contextual participatory research" (p. 146). This is the locus at which AAC research and applied linguistics research meet, and in the project described below, we leveraged a contextualized and participatory applied linguistics research design to answer the question: What are the specific language needs of AAC users in order to participate in **workplace interactions** as identified through the collection of face-to-face interactions between both AAC and non-AAC users? And the intention was to provide a comprehensive assessment of the typical discourse patterns of both AAC users and comparable non-AAC users in the workplace.

My Work with AAC

Personal Reflection

In the year that I started middle school in the UK, my mother was diagnosed with Multiple Sclerosis (MS), and was confined to a wheelchair. At that time, there wasn't the kind of wide acceptance of accommodations for disabilities that exist now, and I recall many moments of frustration and resentment for my mother and the rest of our family as we tried to negotiate our new status and keep life as normal as possible. So, in 2009, when I was asked to join a project designed to improve the daily experience of AAC users in the workplace, I jumped at the chance.

I collaborated with Carrie Bruce, a research scientist at the Center for Assistive Technology and Environmental Access at the Georgia Institute of Technology, and we received a grant from Georgia State University. The goal of the collaborative project was to develop a workplace-specific corpus focused on the needs of AAC users that could be used to conduct the kinds of social validation studies described above and address some current gaps in our understanding of their linguistic experiences in the workplace.

My Work with the Augmentative and Alternative Communication and Non-Augmentative and Alternative Communication Workplace Corpus

Creating the Corpus   A **corpus** is a principled collection of either written or spoken natural texts. Friginal and Hardy (2014) provide several examples of how and why this approach might be used including, from linguistics, the case of lexicography. A lexicographer who is compiling a dictionary may create a corpus of naturally occurring language to establish the frequency of particular words and the contexts in which they typically appear. In such a case, the electronic corpus that is created will run to many millions of words at which point it becomes impossible to search the data manually. Thus, corpora are also designed to be "machine readable," that is, the data are marked up or annotated in order for software programs to be able to "read" different characteristics of the texts. Typically, these are lexico-syntactic features or **part-of-speech (POS) tags** that tag each word as a noun, verb, adjective, and so on, but corpora can be tagged for any features that are of interest. For example, the Hong Kong Corpus of Spoken English-Prosodic is tagged for intonational features such as falling and rising tones (Cheng, Greaves & Warren, 2005). Specialized corpora can also be created and used to investigate specific questions.

Our specialized corpus targeted AAC device users who were employed outside the home (Pickering et al., 2019). Following the recommendations of AAC researchers (Beukelman & Mirenda, 1992; Higginbotham, 1995; Higginbotham & Bedrosian, 1995), we also collected data from non-AAC users in comparative work contexts. This provided performance data from non-AAC users to which AAC users could be compared and also provided a real-life measure of vocabulary and language use. The corpus comprises over 200 hours of spoken interaction (approximately 1 million words) collected in seven different workplace locations. Four AAC users and four non-AAC users in parallel professional contexts wore a voice-activated digital audio recorder for one week (i.e., five consecutive working days) and recorded their workplace interactions with over 100 interlocutors in total. Details regarding the eight primary participants are given in Table 13.1, which is organized by paired AAC and non-AAC participants.

The eight participants had complete control over the recording process. They started and stopped the recording at the beginning and end of each workday, throughout the day, or when requested to do so by an interlocutor which, of course, resulted in the wide range of recording times among participants shown in

Table 13.1 Information on participants and data collected in each workplace

Participant	AAC Status	Gender	Job / Workplace	Time using device	Type of device	Approximate amount of use in total interaction in workplace	Number of words	Recording time hh: mm:ss
Len	AAC	Male	Administrative Assistant	4 years	DynaWrite	20%	78,797	28:56:10
Alex	Non-AAC	Male	Administrative Assistant				175,272	29:30:41
Ron	AAC	Male	Parks & Recreation Department Manager	4 years	Pathfinder II	80%	9,233	11:26:33
Tony	Non-AAC	Male	Parks & Recreation Department Manager				162,761	44:32:35
Saul	AAC	Male	Director of Information Technology	15 months	Vmax	99%	186,853	24:09:56
Katie	Non-AAC	Female	Information Technology Specialist				101,643	34:34:15
Sarah	AAC	Female	Grant Administrator	8 years	EZ Keys	20%	106,995	12:10:25
Paula	Non-AAC	Female	Grant Administrator				247,888	35:43:00
Total							1,069,442	221:03:25

Table 13.1. Overall, the data set comprised a wide variety of typical kinds of workplace interactions including meetings, informal office talk (including small talk, which is discussed in the data analysis activity), workplace telephone talk, conferences calls, and presentations.

The data were transcribed following an enhanced orthographic transcription scheme based on the T2K-SWAL (TOEFL 2000 Spoken and Written Academic Language) corpus (Biber, 2006) and adapted from Friginal (2008, 2009). Transcriptions include additional interaction-based elements such as non-verbal information (e.g., ambient noise or laughter), length of pauses, number of filled pauses and overlapping speech. All personal identifiers were stripped (e.g., names, proper nouns, addresses, phone numbers) and replaced with generic proper nouns.

The ANAWC is completely tagged for part-of-speech (POS) and other semantic categories using the Biber Tagger (Biber, 1988, 1995, 2006). POS-tags follow every word or punctuation mark in the text output. This tagger combines computerized dictionaries with the identification of word sequences as instances of a linguistic feature (e.g., noun + WH pronoun and not preceded by the verb "tell" or "say" = "relative clause"). There are over 150 POS-tagged categories in the tagged version of the ANAWC, and two sub-corpora were created – one comprising all the data from the four primary AAC users and one with the data from their non-AAC user counterparts. An example of text input from AAC-user Saul and the resulting tagged output is shown in the appendix at the end of this chapter.

Sample Findings from the ANAWC Our initial research has focused on identifying language patterns that distinguish AAC device users' language from that of non-AAC users in the workplace and specifically overall differences in the grammatical and vocabulary features of the AAC users' and non-AAC users' sub-corpora. This is achieved through a method called **multidimensional analysis** in which patterns of co-occurring features are laid out along functional dimensions (see Friginal & Hardy, 2014 for a detailed discussion of this method). Friginal, Pearson, Di Ferrante, Pickering, and Bruce (2013) investigated three dimensions: 1) involved versus informational production – the difference between spoken and written texts; 2) narrative versus non-narrative features – use of linguistic features to tell stories about past events and experiences; and 3) explicit vs. situation-dependent features – use of time and place markers that reflect the physical context of the discourse.

The AAC and non-AAC users patterned in opposite ways across all three of these dimensions. AAC users' discourse was primarily informational. In comparison to non-AAC user discourse, it lacked personal pronouns, private verbs such as *I think*, *I wonder* and typical spoken discourse markers such as *you know, I mean*. There was instead a high concentration of nouns and noun phrases reflecting the often-curtailed responses of the AAC user. An example is given below in which AAC-user

Ron uses only the nouns 'city' and 'address' to communicate with one of his co-workers:

Text excerpt 1: AAC user Ron

AAC-Ron: City

Co-worker: He wants me to do the epic route power out tomorrow morning

AAC-Ron: And

Co-worker: They've got a big swim meet he wants me to get up at three and check if it's snowing go in at four coz the rest of the crew comes in at six on Saturday so I'm gonna get a jump on it

AAC-Ron: And

Co-worker: No just street address will be fine

AAC-Ron: Address

Co-worker: But it's a good thing you asked. I'm listening where is this going in? On the side? On the bottom? You got these upside down sir

AAC-Ron: Right address

(Friginal et al., 2013: 288–289)

These findings support the "trade-off" that AAC users report they often have to make when faced with communicating in real time. It simply is not possible to generate the typical interactional features of conversation and stay relevant in the time stream of the conversation. AAC users' discourse also lacked narrative features in comparison to their non-AAC counterparts. This too is a result of contending with the time delay in creating utterances, which precludes AAC users from spontaneously elaborating on the narrative contributions of others. Where these narrative texts did appear in the AAC user data, they were frequently part of pre-programmed speech such as in the example below from Sarah who was giving a presentation on disability etiquette to a large audience:

Text excerpt 2: AAC user Sarah

AAC-Sarah: [0:06][preprogramed] I would like to introduce Marissa Sanderson my assistant who will interpret for me periodically throughout this presentation [0:02] please feel free to stop me if you have a question or a comment [+] I am here to talk to you about people first language and disability etiquette [0:03] Mark Twain said the difference between the right word and the almost right word is the difference between lightning and the lightning bug [0:02] how many of you have heard the word handicapped? [0:04] the origin of the word handicapped refers to a person with a disability begging with a cap in his hand this is how the majority of society used to view people with disabilities

Similarly, AAC users' texts demonstrated fewer situation-dependent in terms of time or place adverbs such as those shown in the example below from non-AAC-user Paula:

Text excerpt 3: Non-AAC User Paula

Non-AAC: Some paper **right there** no in the uhm **above that**

Co-worker: This one?

Non-AAC: Yeah yeah like **right now** . . you'd you'd be transcribing

Co-worker: Got ya [unclear] ok

Non-AAC: Yeahmmm-hm definitely but as far as just like may be taking some notes **right now** . . or something about you know the type of. . . tasks that she's doing **tomorrow**

Non-AAC: I'll come **in a little earlier** and **this morning** there was an ambulance coming **this way** lights flashing and car turned right there and she froze

(Friginal et al., 2013: 293–294. Excerpts used with permission of Sage Publishing.)

In sum, unlike the typical workplace discourse found in the non-AAC texts, which was interactive and involved, linguistic patterns found in the AAC texts for the most part resembled those found in written corpora, further confirming the limitations of the AAC devices in real-time interaction and offering previously unreported insight into language use in the workplace.

Data Analysis Activity

Interpersonal dynamics and the ability to form positive relationships are considered to be critical "soft skills" that are needed in the workplace (McNaughton & Bryen, 2002). They are built, in part, by the kinds of non-task-related talk that co-workers engage in throughout their workday including what we might call *small talk* or *chitchat* and *joshing* or *banter*. In the activity on the website accompanying this book, you will examine some of the small talk samples that appear in the ANAWC. There is a lot of small talk in all the workplace data we collected, and one of the projects we undertook was to identify what topics were most commonly discussed and how listeners responded to them to help us understand what different kinds of vocabulary are needed. You will find all the materials you need on the website accompanying this book.

Going Further

For work in this area, personal and academic background is important. Personally, I found that "grass-roots" work in the local community, such as volunteering with different organizations to promote the visibility of people with disabilities, educated me well in the kinds of day-to-day experiences that occur both inside and outside the workplace. You can pursue volunteer opportunities in your own community.

Academically, linguistics classes will teach you about the nature of language and communication. General Linguistics and Introduction to Linguistics classes provide a solid understanding of subsystems of language that we have talked about here such as grammar and vocabulary. Classes in Sociolinguistics are useful for this area of work because they discuss contexts of language use such as the workplace discourse.

This chapter has focused specifically on the linguistic experiences of adult AAC users in the workplace but of course, there are many other important issues in the field of AAC that linguistic analysis can be applied to. Two areas are addressed in fields closely related to applied linguistics. First, there is a growing literature on the use of AAC with children with complex communication needs. In April 2018, the CDC issued a report estimating a continued increase in diagnoses of autism disorders for children,[1] and many of these will be assessed for AAC use. This will be done by speech pathologists who have usually studied in departments specializing in Speech Communication Disorders or by special education teachers from departments of education. These programs often have cross-over courses with Linguistics or English departments as their concerns overlap in many areas.

The second area is speech science. While there have been huge strides forward in text-to-speech systems and speech synthesis, it is still not possible to mirror a natural tone of voice with the ability to produce all the inflections that come with it. As one AAC user explains, "I want to be able to sound sensitive or arrogant, assertive or humble, angry or happy, sarcastic or sincere, matter of fact or suggestive and sexy" (Portpuff, 2006, p. 6, as cited in Pullin & Hennig, 2015, p. 170). Classes that investigate these issues can be found in Computational Linguistics programs and also in departments of Human Systems Engineering and Computer Engineering.

Discussion Questions

1. The following YouTube clip shows VOCA-user comedian Lee Ridley, who performed as "Lost Voice Guy" on *Britain's Got Talent* in 2018. www.youtube.com/watch?v=xsqInns6LXQ.

   Watch the clip and then discuss the questions below:
   a. Can you identify the SNUG utterance Lee programs in the clip as opposed to the preprogrammed utterances?

---

[1] www.autismspeaks.org/science/science-news/cdc-increases-estimate-autism%E2%80%99s-prevalence-15-percent-1-59-children

   b. How is it identifiable?

   c. How has Lee prepared for this possibility and how does he prepare the audience for the change in "time stream"?

2. Consider this data sample, which is an extended extract of text extract 2 shown above. Halfway through the extract, Sarah shifts from preprogrammed language to vocalizations (indicated by VOC in the transcripts). These are then interpreted by Marissa who is Sarah's aid. It is not uncommon for AAC-users to use a mix of their own remaining speech ability (i.e., what remains of their oral motor functioning) and their device if they feel they are still partially intelligible to those around them. Three of the four AAC device users in our corpus leveraged this familiarization on a regular basis to attempt to vocalize part or all of their message if they felt that they could make their meaning understood. Discuss why you think Sarah shifted to vocalizing her thoughts.

AAC-Sarah:	[0:06] I would like to introduce Marissa Sanderson my assistant who will interpret for me periodically throughout this presentation [0:02] please feel free to stop me if you have a question or a comment [+] I am here to talk to you about people first language and disability etiquette [0:03] Mark Twain said the difference between the right word and the almost right word is the difference between lightning and the lightning bug [0:02] how many of you have heard the word handicapped? [0:04] the origin of the word handicapped refers to a person with a disability begging with a cap in his hand this is how the majority of society used to view people with disabilities
AAC-Sarah:	also people with disabilities are not heroes or inspirations [voc]
Marissa:	that's one of my pet peeves
AAC-Sarah:	[voc]
Marissa:	I don't want to be anybody's hero I don't want to be an inspiration
AAC-Sarah:	[voc]
Marissa:	I am a person

3. One unanticipated finding from the ANAWC was the amount of non-task-related talk or small talk that occurred in the data. This was particularly salient as it is precisely the kind of fast-paced spontaneous talk that AAC-users cannot participate in. Reflect on your own work environment (if possible, note down what conversational topics occur while you are at work). How much of your work conversation would you estimate is non-task related and what functions does this non-task-related conversation serve?

FURTHER READING

Foundational Readings

Beukelman, D., & Ansel, B. (1995). Research priorities in Augmentative and Alternative Communication. *Augmentative and Alternative Communication, 11*(2), 131–134.

Hourcade, J., Pilotte, T., West, E., & Parette, P. (2004). A history of augmentative and alternative communication for individuals with severe and profound disabilities. *Focus on Autism and Other Developmental Disabilities, 19*(4), 235–244.

McNaughton, D., Light, J., & Arnold, K. (2002). "Getting your wheel in the door": Successful full-time employment experiences of individuals with cerebral palsy who use augmentative and alternative communication. *Augmentative and Alternative Communication, 18*, 59–76.

Recent Publications

Boenisch, J., & Soto, G. (2015). The oral core vocabulary of typically developing English-speaking school-aged children: Implications for AAC practice. *Augmentative and Alternative Communication, 31*(1), 77–84.

Light, J., & McNaughton, D. (2012). The changing face of augmentative and alternative communication: Past, present and future challenges. *Augmentative and Alternative Communication, 28*(4), 197–204.

Pickering, L., Friginal, E., & Staples, S. (Eds.). (2016). *Talking at work*. London: Palgrave Macmillan.

REFERENCES

American Speech-Language-Hearing Association (ASHA). (1991). Supplement 5, 9–12.

Balandin, S., & Iacono, T. (1998). A few well-chosen words. *Augmentative and Alternative Communication, 14*(3), 147–161.

Beukelman, D., & Mirenda, P. (1992). *Augmentative and Alternative Communication: Management of severe communication disorders in children and adults.* New York: Paul Brookes.

Biber, D. (1988). *Variation across speech and writing.* Cambridge: Cambridge University Press.

(1995). *Dimensions of register variation: A cross-linguistic comparison.* Cambridge: Cambridge University Press.

(2006). *University language: A corpus-based study of spoken and written registers.* Amsterdam: John Benjamins.

Bryen, D. N. (2008). Vocabulary to support socially-valued adult roles. *Augmentative and Alternative Communication, 24*(4), 294–301.

Cheng, W., Greaves, C., & Warren, M. (2005). The creation of a prosodically transcribed intercultural corpus: The Hong Kong Corpus of Spoken English (prosodic). *ICAME Journal, 29*, 47–68.

Creech, R. (1993). Productive employment for augmented communicators. In R. V. Conti & C. Jenkins Odorisio (Eds.), *Proceedings of the First Annual Pittsburgh Employment Conference for Augmented Communicators* (pp. 105–108). Pittsburgh, PA: SHOUT Press.

Dominowska, E. (2002). A communication aid with context-aware vocabulary prediction (unpublished master's thesis). Massachusetts Institute of Technology, Cambridge.

Friginal, E. (2008). *The language of outsourced call centers: A corpus-based study of cross-cultural interaction* (unpublished doctoral dissertation). University of Northern Arizona, Flagstaff, Arizona.

(2009). *The language of outsourced call centers: A corpus-based study of cross-cultural interaction.* Amsterdam: John Benjamins.

Friginal, E., & Hardy, J. (2014). *Corpus-based sociolinguistics.* New York: Routledge.

Friginal, E., Pearson, P., Di Ferrante, L., Pickering, L., & Bruce, C. (2013). Linguistic characteristics of AAC discourse in the workplace. *Discourse Studies, 15*(3), 279–298.

Graves, J. (2000). Vocabulary needs in augmentative and alternative communication: A sample of conversational topics between staff providing services to adults with learning difficulties and their service users. *British Journal of Learning Disabilities, 28*(3), 113–119.

Higginbotham, D. J., & Caves, K. (2002). AAC performance and usability issues: The effect of AAC technology on the communicative process. *Assistive Technology, 14*(1), 45–57.

Higginbotham, D. J., Lesher, G. W., Moulton, B. J., & Roark, B. (2012). The application of natural language processing to augmentative and alternative communication. *Assistive Technology, 24*(1), 14–24.

Hoag, L., Bedrosian, J., McCoy, K., & Johnson, D. (2004). Trade-offs between informativeness and speed of message delivery in augmentative and alternative communication. *Journal of Speech, Language, and Hearing Research, 47*(6), 1270–1285.

Higginbotham, D. J. (1995). Use of nondisabled subjects in AAC research: Confessions of a research infidel. *Augmentative and Alternative Communication, 11*(1), 2–5.

Higginbotham, D. J., & Bedrosian, J. (1995). Subject selection in AAC research: Decision points. *Augmentative and Alternative Communication, 11*(1), 11–13.

Higginbotham, D. J., & Wilkins, D. P. (1999). Slipping through the timestream: Social issues of time and timing in augmented interactions. In D. Kovarsky, J. F. Duchan, & M. Maxwell (Eds.), *Constructing (in)competence: Disabling evaluations in clinical and social interaction* (pp. 49–82). Mahwah: Lawrence Erlbaum.

Light, J., Stoltz, B., & McNaughton, D. (1996). Community-based employment: Experiences of adults who use AAC. *Augmentative & Alternative Communication, 12*, 215–229.

McNaughton, D., & Bryen, D. N. (2002). Enhancing participation in employment through AAC technologies. *Assistive Technology, 14*(1), 58–70. https://doi.org/10.1080/10400435.2002.10132055

McNaughton, D., Light, J., & Arnold, K. (2002). "Getting your wheel in the door": Successful full-time employment experiences of individuals with cerebral palsy who use augmentative and alternative communication. *Augmentative and Alternative Communication, 18*, 59–76.

Odom, A., & Upthegrove, M. (1997). Moving toward employment using AAC: Case study. *Augmentative and Alternative Communication, 13*(4), 258–262.

Pickering, L., Di Ferrante, L., Bruce, C., Friginal, E., Pearson, P., Bouchard, & J. (2019). An introduction to the ANAWC. *International Journal of Corpus Linguistics, 24*(2), 229–244.

Pullin, G., & Hennig, S. (2015). 17 ways to say yes: Toward nuanced tone of voice in AAC and speech technology. *Augmentative and Alternative Communication, 31*(2), 170–180.

Pullin, G., Treviranus, J., Patel, R., & Higginbotham, J. (2017). Designing interaction, voice, and inclusion in AAC research. *Augmentative and Alternative Communication, 33*(3), 139–148.

Von Tetzchner, S., & Basil, C. (2011). Terminology and notation in written representations of conversations with augmentative and alternative communication. *Augmentative and Alternative Communication, 27*(3), 141–149.

Wisenburn, B., & Higginbotham, D. J. (2008). An AAC application using speaking partner speech recognition to automatically produce contextually relevant utterances. *Augmentative and Alternative Communication, 24*(2), 100–109.

APPENDIX:

Example of text input and resulting tagged output from AAC-user Saul

Text input

[SAUL]
Right now uh I'm going to call one of our consumers and set up the delivery for Monday but um [+] we have 2 drop off sites in Carolina [+] one being in Columbia and one being in North Charleston [+] we got another call from Spartanburg Spartanburg is close to Greenville [+] and I know Mr. Jim will be back on next week and

Tagged Output

```
Right  ^nn++++
now  ^rn+tm+++
uh  ^uh++++=FILLEDPAUSE
I  ^pp1a+pp1+++
'm  ^vb+bem+aux++
going  ^md"++pmd"++
to  ^md+prd+++
call  ^vb++++
one  ^pn++++
of  ^in++++
our  ^pp$+pp1+++
consumers  ^nns++++
and  ^cc++++
set  ^vbd+++xvbn+
up  ^rb+phrv+++
the  ^ati++++
delivery  ^nn++++
for  ^cs+sub+++
Monday  ^nr++++
but  ^cc++++
um  ^uh++++
```

```
we ^pp1a+pp1+++
have ^vb+hv+aux++
2 ^cd++++=two
drop ^vb++++
off ^rb+phrv+++
sites ^nns++++
in ^in++++
Carolina ^np++++=Carolina
one ^cd++++=one
being ^vbg+beg++xvbg+
in ^in++++
Columbia ^np++++=Columbia
and ^cc++++
one ^cd++++=one
being ^vbg+beg++xvbg+
in ^in++++
North ^nr+pl+++=North
Charleston ^np+++??+=Charleston
we ^pp1a+pp1+++
got ^vbd+++xvbn+
another ^dt++++
call ^nn++++
from ^in++++
Spartanburg ^np+++??+=Spartanburg
Spartanburg ^np+++??+=Spartanburg
is ^vbz+bez+vrb++
close ^in+cmpx+++
to ^in"++++
Greenville ^np+++??+=Greenville
and ^cc++++
I ^pp1a+pp1+++
know ^vb+vprv+++
Mr ^npt++++=Mr.
. ^.+clp+++=EXTRAWORD
Jim ^np++++=Jim
will ^md+prd+++
be ^vb+be+vrb++
back ^rp++++
on ^in++++
next ^rb++++
week ^nn++++
and ^cc++++
```

14 Language Documentation and Revitalization

G. TUCKER CHILDS

Estimates vary, but it is generally accepted that there are 5,000 to 6,500 languages spoken in the world today (1,900 to 2,500 just in Africa). Over half of the world's languages will disappear by 2050, however, meaning that over half of the world's languages are presently endangered (Nettle & Romaine, 2000). By the end of the century it is predicted that over 80 percent of the world's languages will be gone (Krauss, 1992). Clearly if we want to record languages before they die, let alone encourage their survival through a revitalization program, the work is urgent.

Overview of Key Concepts and Issues in Language Documentation

Endangered languages have formed a major preoccupation of North American[1] linguists since the nineteenth century and inspired the rise of American Structuralism, a purportedly user-proof methodology for analyzing Native American languages. The methodology promised to faithfully describe the many endangered Native American languages before they disappeared. The Structuralists' "discovery procedures" have guided much fieldwork since in terms of structural analysis but have been supplemented by language documentarians to include much more than description and structural analysis. In fact, the expected products of a language description – the trinity of grammar, dictionary, and texts – have been much augmented in producing a language's full documentation by videos, pedagogical materials, and the like. Nonetheless, in this early period many solid descriptions emerged (see Childs, Petter, Kaji, Xiaomeng, Chul-Joon, & Hajek (2019) for an overview), in some cases producing the only records of a language now totally gone.

Language Endangerment and Language Vitality

There are numerous criteria for declaring a language to be endangered. Typically it means that the language may have no speakers in the near future, usually in a

---

[1] I use "North America" as a term referring to both Canada and the United States; "America" and "American" refer only to the United States.

generation or two. The reasons for this predicted future state are many but invariably entail children not learning the language. **Language endangerment** can be seen as an early stage of **language shift**, the situation in which a community is beginning to use a language distinct from the one they have historically used. For example, young speakers of indigenous Australian languages were sent to schools and punished for speaking their natal languages, much as in North America with regard to Native American languages and much as in Ireland with regard to Irish. In these cases, people were forced to shift from one language to another. In other cases, the pressures were more subtle and indirect; other shifts were determined by socioeconomic forces.

In the cases discussed thus far, only two languages are involved. One stable outcome is **diglossia**. Diglossia refers to the situation where one language is used for some functions and another language is used for others. In the original formulation of the term (Ferguson, 1959), Haiti, Switzerland, and Egypt were proffered as prime exemplars of the phenomenon. In all of these cases, what were called the two varieties, a "high" and a "low," were historically related; that condition has since been relaxed and diglossia may now refer to two functionally distinct languages used by a single speech community. Usually the outcome is not stable: one language loses functions as another one gains functions. For example, the high variety takes over the more homely functions of the low: the standard will be used in local contexts such as talk between neighbors in daily interactions.

Language shift may not be limited to two languages. In some cases of intense multilingualism, the endangered language may be one of many that gradually loses functions in a multiglossic speech economy. **Multiglossia** is the situation where multiple languages are used for multiple but distinct functions. These situations can be stable but are usually not, just as in diglossia. Languages are differentially accorded prestige. Typically one language loses functions, in what has been termed "leaky" multiglossia, which can eventually lead to the disappearance of one language as part of the linguistic repertoire of community members.

Another outcome of language shift, **language death**, is the possible but not necessary eventual outcome of language shift. It is the situation when a language loses its functions so much that it is not used at all. The term is usually restricted to the case of a language not being spoken anywhere else. In North America, such has been the fate of many indigenous languages, as is described below.

Language vitality, on the other hand, is a measure of how vital the language is to its speakers, basically the opposite of language endangerment. Typical questions that are asked in assessing a language's vitality are: Is it learned by children? Is it used for multiple functions? Is it positively valued by the speech community? All of these are questions that enter into what can be a quantitative evaluation. The original concepts came from the social psychologists and were incorporated into the **Graded Intergenerational Disruption Scale (GIDS)** of Fishman (1991), and later developed by UNESCO and a missionary group, SIL International, into more detailed metrics.

Language Endangerment in Languages of the World

Language endangerment is not limited to North America but is rather a global phenomenon. My own work has concentrated on West Africa. In the countries of Guinea, Liberia, and Sierra Leone, the more widely spoken languages are spreading at the expense of the less widely spoken languages. This is the general pattern in Africa. The massive spread of the Bantu languages (the Bantu Expansion) east to the Indian Ocean and south to the tip of southern Africa occasioned the demise of many non-Bantu languages. Best known is the loss of the Khoisan ("click") languages surviving today only in a few pockets of southern Africa. In the same way many Nilotic languages in East Africa (Democratic Republic of Congo, Ethiopia, Kenya, Sudan, Tanzania, and Uganda) are disappearing. The phenomenon of one language displacing another is known in the literature by the colorful term *glottophagie*, or "language eating" (Calvet, 1974). Such has been the case in every part of the continent, including North Africa, where Arabic has displaced many Berber languages.

Elsewhere in the world language endangerment is just as dire. Typically where language diversity exists, the languages constituting that diversity are endangered. Ninety-six percent of the world's languages are spoken by only 4 percent of the world's population (Crystal, 2000). This includes the languages of Papua New Guinea (900 languages) and the languages of the Native peoples of the Americas. There are many minorities of Africa, Asia, and Oceania speaking several thousand languages that are threatened, as well as small groups of marginalized European peoples such as the Irish, the Frisians, the Provençal, and the Basques.

Historic parallels to the present crisis are not hard to find. For example, around 1000 CE Irish was a militantly expanding language but by 1990 there were fewer than 9,000 speakers transmitting Irish to their children. Several other Celtic languages have disappeared in recent times, and most of the others are in a precarious state. In North America when the Europeans first arrived there were more than 800 indigenous languages. Today only 175 are spoken and most are nearly gone (Woodbury, 2001).

Language Documentation

Language documentation was one response to language endangerment. The initiative came of age with a number of programmatic statements (e.g., Hale et al., 1992; Himmelmann, 1998; Woodbury, 2003) and edited volumes (Austin & Sallabank, 2011; Gippert, Himmelmann, & Mosel, 2006), which presented case studies and guidelines for describing endangered languages. Basic definitions and ideologies were later examined (e.g., Austin & Sallabank, 2014b; Lüpke, 2019). The literature is vast but something of a consensus has been reached that researchers should be involved with the communities they study and should listen to what the community members have to say (see Cameron, Frazer, Harvey, Rampton, & Richardson, 1992).

The first step is to differentiate **language documentation** from **language description**. A classic contrast appears below. Language documentation focuses more on language use, though some believe a good description entails documentation (Chelliah & de Reuse, 2011).

> The aim of language documentation is to provide a comprehensive record of the linguistic practices characteristic of a given speech community. Linguistic practices and traditions are manifest in two ways: (1) the observable linguistic behavior, manifest in everyday interaction between members of the speech community, and (2) the native speakers' metalinguistic knowledge, manifest in their ability to provide interpretations and systematizations for linguistic units and events. This definition of the aim of a language documentation differs fundamentally from the aim of language descriptions: a language description aims at the record of A LANGUAGE, with "language" being understood as a system of abstract elements, constructions, and rules that constitute the invariant underlying structure of the utterances observable in a speech community. (Himmelmann, 1998, p. 166)

Linguists in the past, such as the American Structuralists mentioned above, have focused more on language structure than on language use. The documentation effort, then, differs in kind from description and is much expanded in terms of its scope. Moreover, the study of endangered languages is now more generally directed by representatives from local communities, who determine the eventual products. For example, the communities among whom I have worked in West Africa have more highly favored videos than dictionaries or primers.

One expectation, especially on the part of funders, is that the language documenter produce a sizeable corpus for the community and for future researchers. Thus, part of the task of the language documentarian is preparing language and cultural materials for **archiving**, that is, storing the results of one's work in a transportable, accessible, and searchable format. For cultural reasons of privacy, identity, and independence, not all communities want their data available to all people, so sometimes there will be restrictions on who can have access. Some funders do not allow restricted access. For example, the Arcadia Fund (formerly HRELDP, University of London) requires universal access to all archives, a recently instituted policy.

Archiving

Archiving is a crucial component of language documentation, as stated above. With the rise in technology the products of a project are generally digitized, including written materials, audio and video recordings, transcriptions, and photographs.

Henke and Berez-Kroeker (2016) provide some historical background to the trends in archiving. They see

> four major periods in the history of such archiving. First, a period from before the time of Boas and Sapir until the early 1990s, in which analog materials were collected and deposited into physical repositories that were not easily accessible to many researchers or speaker communities. A second period began in the 1990s, when increased attention to language endangerment and the development of modern documentary linguistics engendered a renewed and redefined focus on archiving and an embrace of digital technology. A third period took shape in the early twenty-first century, where technological advances and efforts to develop standards of practice met with important critiques. Finally, in the current period, conversations have arisen toward participatory models for archiving, which break traditional boundaries to expand the audiences and uses for archives ... involving speaker communities directly in the archival process. (Henke & Berez-Kroeker, 2016, p. 411)

Note the importance of community involvement in the current stage, as is generally now the case with all phases of language documentation. Aside from the technological changes in archiving, paralleling developments in linguistics more generally, the main difference in archiving and in language documentation in general is involving the researched.

The archive with which I am most familiar, the Endangered Language Archive at the University of London (ELAR, www.soas.ac.uk/elar/), now has strict and demanding protocols for the submission of records. These protocols follow the guidelines of the Leipzig Endangered Languages Archive (LELA) of the Max Planck Institute for Evolutionary Anthropology at Leipzig (www.eva.mpg.de/linguistics/past-research-resources/resources/leipzig-endangered-languages-archive-lela.html). Metadata includes all details of a record including details about the documenter(s) and the subjects, where and when the documentation took place, the equipment that was used in producing the record, the genre and topic, and any other information that might be relevant and useful for later searches.

Language Revitalization and Community Involvement

Language revitalization refers to harnessing the products of language documentation to the expanded use of the language, typically in contexts of literacy. The assumption is that with the materials produced by documenters the march toward death can be halted and even reversed. Without the support of the community, however, such efforts are in vain, and few linguists are trained in revitalizing a language. Absent prolonged contact and some expertise, revitalization can be challenging. It also takes some time, usually not a resource at the disposal of an academic.

The calls for revitalization and community involvement are relatively new. While the motivation was justified and the descriptions were solid in nineteenth-century North America, there was little done in the way of revitalization or even in involving the local community in decisions as to how the language should be documented. At a Portland State conference in 2008 honoring Portland native Dell Hymes, a prominent ethnographer of Native American languages, there was a clear separation between the older (exclusively white) and younger researchers as to how the work should be conducted. For example, there was a reluctance on the part of the older researchers to consider archiving their data with the community with whom they worked. Documentary linguistics has taken the lead from the younger researchers in pursuing a course that actively involves the researched (Cameron et al., 1992).

In addition to the obstacles of traditions, not all documenters or even all communities agree that developing literacy is the best use of limited resources, for there are often institutional and ideological barriers and many other needs. For example, when I documented the Mani language that straddled the border between Guinea and Sierra Leone, neither government was interested in supporting the language. Guinea had expended a great deal of energy and resources on the *Alphabétisation* ("literacy") effort during the time of Sékou Touré. Because the program met with little success and much resistance by the educated elite, the country did not continue training in indigenous languages. French became the only language taught in the schools. In Sierra Leone, the situation was similar for there was some initial sentiment for developing the national languages but the interest soon waned. Unfortunately the resources – for example, support for writing primers and training instructors – went to the more widely spoken languages (Krio, Mende, Temne, and Limba), not to the endangered ones (Mani, Kim, Bom, and Sherbro).

On the ideological side of those in power, there is similar resistance. The educated and powerful often have adopted elitist attitudes toward indigenous languages, replicating those of their former colonial masters. The mistaken claim is that colonial languages provide both access to the international community and a neutral language for a country characterized by tribal rivalries. Furthermore, the belief is that there is no value to the indigenous languages. No consideration is given to the speakers themselves and the value they put on their language.

For some researchers and some communities, revitalization and literacy are central goals of language documentation (Nathan & Fang, 2013), but because it is of such an intensely political nature not all efforts are assured of success (Walsh, 2005). Great debates often take place over which dialect will be chosen as the standard or which writing system should be used – for example, a Western one or a special one designed just for the language (e.g., Sebba, 2012). Time is often the limiting factor. For example, an African success story with regard to literacy in Togo is described in Reeder (2017), but this enterprise crucially involved long and intimate contact. It took twenty-five years for the (successful) Rama development program in Nicaragua to be instituted and accepted (Grinevald & Pivot, 2013). Few researchers are able to make such a commitment.

My Work in Language Documentation

Personal Reflection

My original interest in applied linguistics arose during the African independence movements of the late 1950s through the 1960s and on. As an undergraduate I was fascinated by the claims of the Black Power movement for a glorious African past, about which I knew nothing. I wanted to know more. I took some courses in college but still felt ill-informed. After graduating I joined the Peace Corps to see what Africa was all about. My Peace Corps site was at the intersection of the borders of Guinea, Sierra Leone, and Liberia. While I was firmly ensconced in the local Kisi culture, I was overwhelmed by the multilingualism of the area and how tolerant everyone was of the varying competencies in the many languages.

I served as a Peace Corps volunteer in Liberia (1970–1972) and was forced to learn the local language Kisi since no one spoke a language I knew. Even the resident pidgin, Liberian English, which I picked up fairly quickly after arrival, was known only by school children and those who had traveled to the country's metropolis, Monrovia. Kisi was the everyday language of everything, except at the marketplace and in the shops, where other languages and Liberian English were spoken.[2]

During my tour of duty, such questions arose as, *Why were some languages more valued than others? Why was the local language so denigrated by non-Kisi? Why did outsiders not learn Kisi?* All of these questions remained unanswered and stayed on a slow simmer until I stumbled on the wonder of linguistics, where I felt I finally had a mission. Georgetown University had an applied linguistics track and I studied under people like Roger Shuy and Ralph Fasold, early champions of linguistic rights, and the department had a close relationship with the Center for Applied Linguistics, where people such as G. Richard Tucker and Walt Wolfram presided.

Building on my Peace Corps experience, I wanted to help the new nations of Africa. I naively thought that with my training in linguistics I could contribute to the dialogue on language policy in Africa. For the newly independent states, I thought I could help them answer such questions as, What language should be the national language? What language should be used in the schools? What languages should be supported? What sort of support was needed? And so on. Such

---

[2] Interested readers are referred to Childs (2018) for some field anecdotes of my own and to the volume in which it appears (Sarvasy & Forker, 2018) for the field experiences of some of the world's leading fieldworkers.

beliefs were based on something of a colonial mentality that knew little of sociolinguistic issues on the ground.

Despite its applied orientation I left Georgetown after a year for UC Berkeley, returning to California where I had earned my undergraduate degree at Stanford. At Berkeley I worked at the African Studies Center (joint with Stanford), helping PhD students to learn African languages, and interacted with scholars such as Jim Matisoff, Leanne Hinton, and Johanna Nichols, all pioneers in the documentation of endangered languages, as well as with the Africanists Jim Gibbs, Will Leben, and Joe Greenberg at Stanford. It was an inspiring time.

My Work in Language Documentation

As mentioned in the preceding section, I have been fascinated with language contact, multilingualism, and the dynamism of interacting languages and identities for many years. For the past twenty years I have worked on the dying languages of Guinea, Sierra Leone, and Liberia, which all suffered from an outbreak of Ebola (2013–2015), which forestalled my research plans for a few years. Ebola is just one of a series of disasters following on the ravages of various extractive industries, a succession of civil wars, and less than competent governance, to say nothing of the historical forces of slavery, colonialism, and jihads.

My projects have ranged from studying the relatively vital language Kisi, once spoken over a relatively wide area of Guinea, Sierra Leone, and Liberia to less vital ones. These include the dying language Sherbro (2015–2018), the nearly dead language Mani (Guinea and Sierra Leone, 2004–2006 and 2011–2013), and the virtually dead languages Kim and Bom, spoken by only a few speakers in coastal Sierra Leone (2006–2010). All of the languages belong to Bolom, a subgroup within Mel, a language family of Niger-Congo, the largest language phylum in the world. Niger-Congo includes languages spoken over must of sub-Saharan Africa down to southern Africa (including the many Bantu languages mentioned above). I focus below on Sherbro, but the reader is invited to look at related work on Kim, Bom, and Mani (Childs, 2011, forthcoming) and much older work on Kisi (Childs, 1995). Below I outline some of the details of a typical project.

A typical language documentation project, such as those mentioned in the previous paragraph, involves a great deal of planning and preparation, particularly in poor countries such as Liberia, Guinea, and Sierra Leone. The background research is relatively trivial compared to the logistics – for example, setting up a solar power system because there is no electricity (and no gas for a generator!). These countries often lack infrastructure such as roads, particularly in the remote areas to where people speaking peripheralized languages have been pushed. At one research site we traveled entirely by boat and on foot to reach the outlying areas.

Identifying the research site is similarly challenging, as is recruiting qualified staff, both local and non-local. There is also the issue of a research language, a shared language to be used between researcher and researched. Training people who are (computer) illiterate to exploit the many technological resources now available takes time. Time is always a consideration, especially in establishing a relationship of trust, let alone a fully collaborative enterprise. Because the fieldworker has so many masters – for example, the funder, the town chief, one's own belief system – conflicting directives create difficult choices (Childs, 2016).

Once these issues are "settled" (they never are) one can proceed to the actual work of documentation and analysis. My earlier work in the 1980s relied solely on audio recordings and photographs, but now compact and relatively inexpensive video recorders offer both video and high-quality audio typically requiring an external mic. Analytical programs and resources also abound, most of them free, available from the Max Planck Institute (Leipzig, Germany) or SIL International (Dallas, Texas). Much of the analysis can be done in the field, allowing one to better focus the recording and elicitation. The corpus one develops should be many things, not all of which are always feasible given the exigencies of the field context: diverse and representative; as big as it can be; ongoing, distributed, and opportunistic; preservable; ethically collected in collaboration with the community; and migratable to other contexts (a slightly edited version of Woodbury, 2004).

The final step is archiving, and here there are also multiple resources and archives including the Max Planck Institute once again and ELDP at the University of London, where all my work is archived. Most universities also offer archiving possibilities. My own university, Portland State, provides such archiving services. For example, PDXScholar now houses all of my latest work on Sherbro and earlier projects.

The Sherbro language of Sierra Leone, more vital than its closest relatives Bom, Kim, and Mani, can nonetheless be predicted to disappear in a generation or two. As of 2018 there were children who learned Sherbro as their only language but soon shifted to more widely spoken languages and the prestigious creole associated with the young and urban. Temne is dominant in the north, Mende is spreading in the south, and Krio, a former pidgin, is used everywhere, especially in the towns and by the young. None of the non-Sherbro settling in historically Sherbro territory learn any Sherbro beyond rudimentary greetings and a few politeness expressions.

The situation is complex, involving multiple languages and many social factors in addition to those already mentioned. On the island of Bonthe, a historically Sherbro area, these forces play out dramatically in a relatively confined socioecological space. Three outcomes exhibit resilience and indeed adaptability, key concepts in the framework of social ecology. In three different ways in three different places, the Sherbro are responding to encroaching influences. Seeing resiliency in these contexts challenges the prevailing language documentation orthodoxy (Austin &

Sallabank, 2014a) in assigning agency to Sherbro speakers and in refusing to see them as victims (see Duchêne & Heller, 2007). This approach parallels the long-standing beliefs of creolists. In their (and my) view pidgins and creoles are creative adaptations to challenging contexts such as slavery as opposed to the original view as seeing them as debased versions of the colonial variety providing the vocabulary (see Childs, 2006, for an expanded statement of this position). I turn now to the three creative responses of the Sherbro people.

Sherbro Island is not large. The island is 32 miles (51 km) at its longest point and 15 miles (24 km) at its widest; it covers 230 square miles (600 km^2) with a reported population of 28,457 in 2013. The island is, roughly speaking, an isosceles triangle lying on its side with its two long sides extending from the eastern base, which runs roughly parallel to the coast (see Figure 14.1). It is composed of two chiefdoms, Settia and Dema, and a municipality, Bonthe, all three of which represent different responses to language contact.

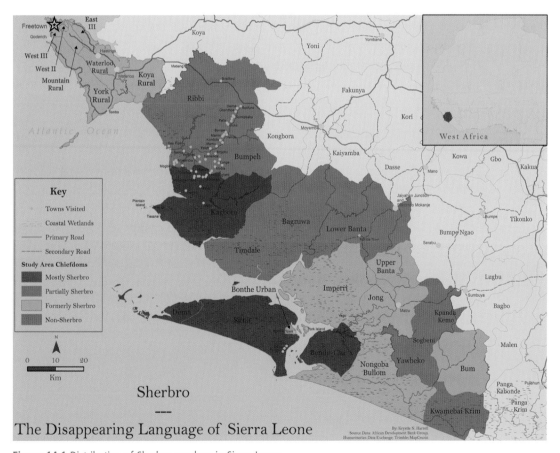

Figure 14.1 Distribution of Sherbro speakers in Sierra Leone

On the eastern edge of the island is the town of Chepo in Dema Chiefdom, where Sherbro has been maintained, primarily because of its isolation (no cellphone coverage!). In the southeastern corner is Yoni, Settia Chiefdom, where the language shift to Mende has taken place. Further north, still on the eastern side, is the Municipality of Bonthe, a once thriving port during the nineteenth century. Few Sherbro speakers can be found in Bonthe, but there has not been a wholesale shift to Mende. The town was originally settled by freed African slaves (as was Freetown) later known as "Krios," and "Krio" is the name of the language they created. Krio is still dominant today as a lingua franca, though most Krios have departed with the collapse of the town's importance. There are significant numbers of both Mende and Temne speakers.

This brief introduction sketches the complexities of language contact and language endangerment.

From my perspective one should not value any one of these outcomes more than another. They are all equally valid responses to a contact situation. In the past there was great value placed on what has been called "the ancestral language or code" (Woodbury, 2005, 2011), a likely non-existent variety that is considered pure and better, especially compared to extant mixed or sullied varieties. The ancestral code is indeed privileged and often serves as the object of documentary efforts. Most modern documentary efforts are more pluralistic and accepting, documenting what people actually speak and valuing multilingualism.

Data Analysis Activities

The website accompanying this book contains two activities relevant to the study of endangered languages. The first activity includes a copy of the final version of "The Swadesh list" (Swadesh, 1971), a set of words created by Morris Swadesh for use in eliciting language samples for language documentation purposes. Swadesh chose the words to represent basic vocabulary, that is, universal, culturally independent words found in all languages. In this activity you will be asked to evaluate the universality of the list he proposed. The second activity examines connections between linguistic and biological diversity. In this activity you will be asked to compare the two and explain why the two are fairly congruent.

Going Further

Becoming involved in language documentation can be difficult for the newcomer. Gaining experience is the greatest challenge. Typically, the route is via involvement with a senior researcher's project or via some previous involvement with a speech community. Most often it occurs as part of a post-graduate degree, though there are cases where an undergraduate has joined an established project.

Another possibility is receiving a starter grant for limited work. Some agencies that provide small grants for junior researchers are: the Endangered Language Fund in New Haven, CT (www.endangeredlanguagefund.org/general-resources.html), and the Foundation for Endangered Languages in Bath (UK) (www.ogmios.org/index.php). In addition, the Endangered Languages Documentation Programme at the University of London supports junior scholars as well as established ones (www.eldp.net/). The Documenting Endangered Languages (DEL) division of the National Science Foundation is another major source for support (www.nsf.gov/funding/pgm_summ.jsp?pims_id=12816).

The best way forward once you've identified an area or a language on which you want to work is to seek advice and support from someone with previous experience. The annual Linguistic Society of America meetings feature sessions on endangered languages and the University of Hawai'i has an annual conference devoted to nothing but endangered languages and language conservation (International Conference on Language Documentation and Conservation (ICLDC; e.g., http://nflrc .hawaii.edu/events/view/89/). You'll meet fellow travelers there who will help out with advice and direction. A final important resource is the Endangered Languages Project (ELP, http://www.endangeredlanguages.com/), an online resource that allows neophytes to plug into a worldwide network of resources and projects.

Discussion Questions

1. What are some causes of a language becoming endangered or dying? For example, has a more numerous group begun moving into the language's historical territory? Has there been a change in political power?
2. How can you tell if a language is dying? What are the structural diagnostics? For example, is the lexicon reduced? Has there been a lot of borrowing into the language? What are the sociocultural criteria? For example, are people ashamed of speaking the language? Do outsiders make fun of them?
3. Should endangered languages be saved? Can they be saved? Sometimes communities want to shift to another language; such is the case with the Mani mentioned above.
4. An endangered language might be spoken in different ways in the different regions where it is used. At the same time, a language documenter may not have the resources to research all of the different varieties. If this is the case, what criteria should language documenters in collaboration with community members use to determine which variety of the language should be documented? What are the consequences of a particular choice for the people who do not speak the chosen variety?

5. In consideration of the reasons why languages become endangered, what are some strategies that might be useful for preserving a dying language? How can one involve the community?

FURTHER READING

Foundational Readings

Austin, P. K. & McGill, S. (Eds.). (2011). *Endangered languages*. Malden, MA: Routledge.

Brenzinger, M. (Ed.). (2007). *Language diversity endangered*. Berlin: Mouton de Gruyter.

Moseley, C. (Ed.). (2007). *Encyclopedia of the world's endangered languages*. London: Routledge.

Recent Publications

Language Documentation and Conservation (the University of Hawai'i). http://nflrc.hawaii
.edu/ldc/

Language Documentation and Description (EL Publishing, School of Oriental and African Studies, University of London). www.elpublishing.org/

Thomason, S. G. (2015). *Endangered languages: An introduction*. Cambridge: Cambridge University Press.

REFERENCES

Austin, P. K., & Sallabank, J. (2014a). Introduction to endangered languages: Beliefs and ideologies in language documentation and revitalisation. In P. K. Austin & J. Sallabank (Eds.), *Endangered languages: beliefs and ideologies in language documentation and revitalisation* (pp. 1–26). Oxford: Oxford University Press/British Academy.

(Eds.). (2011). *The Cambridge handbook of endangered languages*. Cambridge: Cambridge University Press.

(Eds.). (2014b). *Endangered languages: Beliefs and ideologies in language documentation and revitalisation*. Oxford: Oxford University Press/British Academy.

Calvet, L.-J. (1974). *Linguistique et colonialisme: petite traité de glottophagie*. Paris: Payot.

Cameron, D., Fraser, E., Harvey, P., Rampton, M. B. H., & Richardson, K. (1992). *Researching language: Issues of power and method*. London and New York: Routledge.

Chelliah, S. L., & de Reuse, W. J. (2011). *Handbook of descriptive linguistic fieldwork*. Dordrecht, The Netherlands, and New York: Springer.

Childs, G. T. (1995). *A grammar of Kisi: A Southern Atlantic language*. Berlin and New York: Mouton de Gruyter.

(2006). Language creation by necessity, linguistic ramifications of the African Diaspora. In E. K. Agorsah & G. T. Childs (Eds.), *Africa and the African Diaspora: Cultural Adaptation and Resistance* (pp. 99–120). Bloomington, IN: AuthorHouse.

(2011). *A grammar of Mani*. New York and Berlin: de Gruyter.

(2016). Doing what (you think) is right in the field: Problematizing the documentation of endangered languages. In R. Vossen & W. H. G. Haacke (Eds.), *Lone tree: Scholarship in the service of the Koon. Essays in memory of Anthony Traill* (pp. 89–105). Cologne, Germany: Rüdiger Köppe Verlag.

(2018). Forty-plus years before the mast: My experiences as a field linguist. In H. Sarvasy & D. Forker (Eds.), *Word hunters. Field linguists on fieldwork* (pp. 61–78). Amsterdam and Philadelphia: John Benjamins.

(forthcoming). Variations on a theme, the grammar(s) of Bom and Kim, two South Atlantic (Mel) languages. In G. J. Dimmendaal & R. Vossen (Eds.), *The Oxford handbook of African languages*. Oxford: Oxford University Press.

Childs, G. T., Petter, M., Kaji, S., Xiaomeng, S., Chul-Joon, Y., & Hajek, J. (2019). African linguistics in the Americas, Asia, and Australia. In H. E. Wolff (Ed.), *The Cambridge handbook of African linguistics* (pp. 115–136). Cambridge: Cambridge University Press.

Crystal, D. (2000). *Language death*. Cambridge: Cambridge University Press.

Duchêne, A., & Heller, M. S. (Eds.). (2007). *Discourses of endangerment: Ideology and interest in the defence of languages*. New York and London: Continuum.

Ferguson, C. A. (1959). Diglossia. *Word, 15*, 325–340.

Fishman, J. A. (1991). *Reversing language shift: Theoretical and empirical foundations of assistance to threatened languages*. Clevedon: Multilingual Matters.

Gippert, J., Himmelmann, N. P., & Mosel, U. (Eds.). (2006). *Essentials of language documentation*. Berlin and New York: Mouton de Gruyter.

Grinevald, C., & Pivot, B. (2013). On the revitalization of a "treasure language": The Rama Language Project of Nicaragua. In M. C. Jones & S. Ogilvie (Eds.), *Keeping languages alive: Documentation, pedagogy and revitalization* (pp. 181–197). Cambridge: Cambridge University Press.

Hale, K. L., Craig, C., England, N. C., Jeanne, L., Krauss, M. E., Watahomigie, L., & Yamamoto, A. Y. (1992). Endangered languages. *Language, 68*, 1–42.

Henke, R. E., & Berez-Kroeker, A. L. (2016). A brief history of archiving in language documentation, with an annotated bibliography. *Language Documentation & Conservation, 10*, 411–457.

Himmelmann, N. P. (1998). Documentary and descriptive linguistics. *Linguistics, 36*, 161–195.

Krauss, M. E. (1992). The world's languages in crisis. *Language, 68*(1), 4–10.

Lüpke, F. (2019). Language endangerment and language documentation in Africa. In H. E. Wolff (Ed.), *The Cambridge handbook of African linguistics* (pp. 468–490). Cambridge: Cambridge University Press.

Nathan, D., & Fang, M. (2013). Re-imagining documentary linguistics as a revitalization-driven practice. In M. C. Jones & S. Ogilvie (Eds.), *Keeping languages alive: Documentation, pedagogy, and revitalization* (pp. 42–55). Cambridge: Cambridge University Press.

Nettle, D., & Romaine, S. (2000). *Vanishing voices: The extinction of the world's languages*. Oxford and New York: Oxford University Press.

Reeder, J. (2017). *Leadership in literacy: Capacity building and the Ifè program.* Dallas, TX: SIL International Publications.

Sarvasy, H., & Forker, D. (Eds.). (2018). *Word hunters. Field linguists on fieldwork.* Amsterdam: John Benjamins.

Sebba, M. (2012). *Spelling and society: The culture and politics of orthography around the world.* Cambridge: Cambridge University Press.

Swadesh, M. (1971). *The origin and diversification of language.* Chicago: Aldine/Atherton.

Walsh, M. (2005). Will indigenous languages survive? *Annual Review of Anthropology, 34,* 293–315.

Woodbury, A. C. (2001). *Endangered languages.* Austin, TX: University of Texas.

(2003). Defining documentary linguistics. *Language Documentation and Description, 1,* 35–51.

(2004). *What does it mean to document a language?* Paper presented at the AAAS Annual Meeting: Science at the Leading Edge, Seattle.

(2005). Ancestral languages and (imagined) creolization. In P. K. Austin (Ed.), *Language documentation and description, vol. 3* (pp. 252–262). London: School of Oriental and African Studies.

(2011). Language documentation. In P. K. Austin & J. Sallabank (Eds.), *The Cambridge handbook of endangered languages* (pp. 159–186). Cambridge: Cambridge University Press.

15 Stylistics and the Digital Humanities

MICHAELA MAHLBERG AND VIOLA WIEGAND

Overview of Key Concepts and Issues in Stylistics and the Digital Humanities

Once upon a time... If a text starts like this, you will immediately have specific expectations as to how it will continue. While *Once upon a time* is a typical beginning for a fairy tale or children's story, it would not normally work as an opener for a chapter in a textbook. The phrase is an example of how linguistic features are associated with particular texts, and how language creates effects and expectations in the reader. There are many ways in which the choice of words shapes a text. **Stylistics** is the study of linguistic features that make a text distinctive. And **style**, as Wales (2001, p. 371) puts it, is "the set or sum of features that seem to be characteristic: whether of register, genre, or period, etc." Which linguistic features we select in a stylistic analysis depends on what we want to capture. The *Tale of Peter Rabbit* by Beatrix Potter starts: "Once upon a time there were four little Rabbits..." *The Tale of Two Bad Mice* starts in a similar way: "Once upon a time there was a very beautiful doll's-house..." Both are stories for children and begin in a conventional way. Although both texts are by Beatrix Potter, and she begins several of her tales with *once upon a time*, this is not the only characteristic of her style. To describe the style of an author it is important to compare their writing to that of other authors. If you take the beginning of Julia Donaldson's *Room on the Broom*, you will immediately notice a difference: this is a story told in verse. It is not only the formal features that differ between these openings, but also the effects they create. Rhyming patterns and word play have specific effects on the language development of children:

> The witch had a cat
> and a hat that was black,
> And long ginger hair
> in a braid down her back.
> (Julia Donaldson, *Room on the Broom*, 2001)

Instead of "stylistics," the terms "literary stylistics" or "literary linguistics" are also used. They highlight that research in stylistics often focuses on literary texts, as we will do in the present chapter. A stylistic analysis does not have to cover a text as a whole, it might concentrate on a particular extract or even the effects of a specific word or phrase. Stylistic approaches are not limited to literary texts either, as Jones (2014) shows with his work on adverts or Jeffries and Walker (2018) who study newspaper articles. When non-literary texts are being analyzed, stylistics has close ties with discourse analysis and media studies.

The Reader and the Text

Literary stylistics is specifically concerned with the linguistic features that have literary effects, that is, that make the reader perceive a text as a literary text – a work of art. As Leech and Short (2007, p. 11) put it "literary stylistics has, implicitly or explicitly, the goal of explaining the relation between language and artistic function." The artistic function is what creates a response in the reader. Capturing this response, however, is not a straightforward task. In traditional stylistic research, the effects of a text are typically assessed by the analyst who is one example of a reader. More recently, the issue has been tackled through developments in reader response research (Whiteley & Canning, 2017) aiming for a wider empirical basis. **Cognitive stylistics** provides a theoretical framework for the understanding of the reading of literature and the link between the reader and the text. Readers read within specific contexts, and bring prior knowledge to a text to create meaning. An example is the process of **characterization,** that is, the creation of fictional characters. The impression that a reader has of a fictional character is the result of the interaction of cues in the text with existing knowledge about what people are like (Culpeper, 2001; Stockwell, 2009).

Corpus Stylistics – Using Frequencies and Comparisons to Describe Style

As a stylistic analysis focuses on linguistic features, the range of linguistic approaches that stylistics can draw on is almost unlimited. What it is determined by is the text under analysis. If a text seems to have a large number of very long sentences, a grammatical analysis might be a useful starting point. If a conversation between several fictional characters is portrayed, a turn-taking analysis may capture some of the textual effects. Still, as linguistics more widely, stylistics is shaped by trends and developments of new approaches. An important recent linguistic influence on stylistics is **corpus linguistics**. Corpus linguistics is the study of language that is based on data from collections of electronic texts. It uses software to search, display, and quantify linguistic units. Central to corpus linguistic research is a focus on the **frequency** of linguistic phenomena and the comparison of such phenomena within and across individual texts or corpora. Corpus linguistics thus identifies linguistic patterns and accounts for meanings with reference to observable patterns in texts. The noun *time*, for instance, is one of the most frequent nouns in corpora of general English, that is, corpora that contain a wide range of texts. It occurs with different meanings that are distinguished through patterns, such as *the first time, every time, take time*.

Research in stylistics that employs tools and methods from corpus linguistics has come to be known as **corpus stylistics**. Corpus stylistics focuses on the identification of patterns and meanings in literary texts. While corpus linguistics deals with more general patterns and meanings that are found across a range of texts, corpus stylistics can take a more narrow focus, down to accounting for the meaning of a specific word or phrase in a single text extract. Still, for both, comparisons play an important role.

A simple yet powerful example of analyzing meaning via comparison is provided by Louw (1993). He looks at individual words and phrases in two poems by Philip Larkin and compares their meanings in the poems with their use in general language. For this comparison, Louw creates a **concordance** – a table listing the individual uses of a specific word or phrase (as we will illustrate in the section "Our Work on Corpus Stylistics") in a general corpus. This way, Louw (1993, p. 162) is able to show that in Larkin's poem *Days*, the opening line *Days are where we live* foreshadows the meaning of the second stanza, because *days are* is generally "followed by words like *gone*, *over*, and *past*" that are associated with death.

Style in Translated Texts

One area of textual research where the comparative focus becomes particularly obvious is translation studies. Mastropierro (2017) brings together corpus stylistics and translation studies with a detailed case study of Joseph Conrad's *Heart of Darkness* and four of its Italian translations. His approach starts with the corpus stylistic analysis of lexico-semantic patterns in the source text in order to establish a baseline for the translated texts. The word *forest* is one of his examples to show how textual patterns create fictional worlds. *Forest* is a **keyword** in *Heart of Darkness*. This means *forest* occurs statistically more frequently in *Heart of Darkness* than in a reference corpus that contains other works by Joseph Conrad and a reference corpus of texts by other writers (Mastropierro, 2017). Mastropierro (2017, pp. 110–112) argues that the patterns of *forest* are associated with the same semantic fields as the patterns around the related keywords *wilderness* and *jungle*. The three shared semantic fields are "closedness," "darkness," and "immensity." In the concordance in Figure 15.1, closedness is expressed by collocates like *surrounded, fence, edge, closed, limit,* and *border* (see concordance lines 3, 4, 8, 10, 12, 13, 16, and 20). Lines that indicate the field of darkness do not only connote a lack of light, but generally "depict the forest as an altogether inhospitable place" (Mastropierro, 2017, p. 111), as shown by the words *spectrally, primeval, silence, gloomy, shadows,* and *dark-faced* (lines 4, 5, 9, 11, 17, and 18). The final semantic field of immensity is not as widespread across the examples of *forest* as in the patterns of related keywords. Nevertheless, it is present in the collocates *depths* and *deep* (lines 15 and 21).

	Left	Node	Right	Book	In bk.
1	that mysterious life of the wilderness that stirs in the	forest,	in the jungles, in the hearts of wild men. There's	heart	
2	the shoulder-blades. Then the whole population cleared into the	forest,	expecting all kinds of calamities to happen, while, on the	heart	
3	It was on a back water surrounded by scrub and	forest,	with a pretty border of smelly mud on one side	heart	
4	these sticks to bed with them. Beyond the fence the	forest	stood up spectrally in the moonlight, and through that dim	heart	
5	Jove! was in my nostrils, the high stillness of primeval	forest	was before my eyes; there were shiny patches on the	heart	
6	frightful clatter came out of that hulk, and the virgin	forest	on the other bank of the creek sent it back	heart	
7	of an arm for a gesture that took in the	forest,	the creek, the mud, the river--seemed to beckon with	heart	
8	my feet and looked back at the edge of the	forest,	as though I had expected an answer of some sort	heart	
9	were kings. An empty stream, a great silence, an impenetrable	forest.	The air was warm, thick, heavy, sluggish. There was no	heart	
10	reaches opened before us and closed behind, as if the	forest	had stepped leisurely across the water to bar the way	heart	
11	then well on in the afternoon, the face of the	forest	was gloomy, and a broad strip of shadow had already	heart	
12	atever there had been between, had disappeared. Of course the	forest	surrounded all that. The river-bank was clear, and on the	heart	
13	persistently with his whole arm. Examining the edge of the	forest	above and below, I was almost certain I could see	heart	
14	udience, because on a certain occasion, when encamped in the	forest,	they had talked all night, or more probably Kurtz had	heart	
15	rule Kurtz wandered alone, far in the depths of the	forest.	'Very often coming to this station, I had to wait	heart	
16	was looking at the shore, sweeping the limit of the	forest	at each side and at the back of the house	heart	
17	the calm of the evening. The long shadows of the	forest	had slipped downhill while we talked, had gone far beyond	heart	
18	were poured into the clearing by the dark-faced and pensive	forest.	The bushes shook, the grass swayed for a time, and	heart	
19	vanishing without any perceptible movement of retreat, as if the	forest	that had ejected these beings so suddenly had drawn them	heart	
20	he distance, flitting indistinctly against the gloomy border of the	forest,	and near the river two bronze figures, leaning on tall	heart	
21	was keeping guard over the ivory; but deep within the	forest,	red gleams that wavered, that seemed to sink and rise	heart	
22	trees, and the murmur of many voices issued from the	forest.	I had cut him off cleverly; but when actually confronting	heart	
23	convinced, had driven him out to the edge of the	forest,	to the bush, towards the gleam of fires, the throb	heart	

Figure 15.1 Concordance of all twenty-three instances of *forest* in Conrad's *Heart of Darkness* (retrieved with the CLiC web app, http://clic.bham.ac.uk)

Mastropierro's (2017) case study demonstrates how patterns identified in concordance lines point to themes that recur in the description of the fictional world. This analysis of the source text prepares the stage for Mastropierro's (2017) comparison with the Italian translations. He shows that the translations of *forest* have patterns similar to those of the source text due to the existence of an Italian equivalent. Nevertheless, the representation of the "African jungle" differs in the translations, because the additional words *wilderness* and *darkness* referring to it in the source text are translated with a variety of Italian terms. Mastropierro (2017, p. 133) explains that the change in the "cohesive network" of the African jungle in the translations compared to the source text alters the combined effect that they have on the reader.

Digital Humanities

Digital humanities is a much wider field than stylistics. It brings together disciplines from computer science to library and information studies. Digital humanities is not only about texts. It covers a range of digital methods and types of "humanities" data, including music, excavated artifacts, paintings, and so on. It also concerns the preservation and curation of such data and objects. Still, the analysis of texts is of crucial importance and creates links with Big Data Science, since "after numeric input, text has been by far the most tractable data type for computers to manipulate" (Kirschenbaum, 2010, p. 60). Because of the variety of approaches and the terminological diversity that comes with it, it is not always easy to spot similarities across different examples of digital humanities research. So it is helpful to try to understand underlying principles beyond specialist terminology. For example, we have emphasized the centrality of comparison to corpus linguistic research: patterns in one corpus are considered in relation to the norms of a particular genre or the language in general as represented by another corpus (also see Mahlberg & Wiegand, 2018). Comparison is also crucial to stylometry, a field which relates both to stylistics and humanities. It focuses on the distinctive features of the style of a particular author, the linguistic "fingerprint," which makes it possible to determine authorship of texts (e.g., Craig, 2004; Evert et al., 2017).

Our Work in Corpus Stylistics

Personal Reflections

We both came to our current work in corpus stylistics from a background in corpus linguistics. But our individual paths were quite different.

Michaela Mahlberg I made first attempts at corpus stylistics the year I had finished my PhD. My PhD was in corpus linguistics, studying high-frequency nouns, such as *time*, *way*, *place*, *man*, and *woman*. As I was preparing for a job interview, I thought about new research projects I could do, so I had an answer to the standard interview question "What are your research plans for the next five years?" I have always enjoyed Dickens, so I started with *Bleak House*. I put it through WordSmith Tools (Scott, 2016) and tried to systematically identify repeated phrases in the novel. I must admit, it was helpful that my first degree is in Mathematics and English and I had studied Dickens and other nineteenth-century fiction. When I read *Bleak House* for the first time, I was struck by the way in which Dickens used repetition – which clearly had an effect on me as a reader. *Bleak House* was a good novel to start with. It is rather long (about 350K words) and has a relatively large number of clusters that are associated with particular fictional characters, such as *his head against the wall* that describes characteristic behavior of Mr. Jellyby, as in Example (1) (cf. also Mahlberg, 2013). So there was much to say about linguistic patterns and the fictional characters they helped to create.

(1) Poor Mr. Jellyby, who very seldom spoke and almost always sat when he was at home with *his head against the wall,* [...] (*Bleak House*, Charles Dickens, chapter 30)

Not long after my job interview, Martin Wynne organized a workshop on "Corpus approaches to the language of literature" for the Corpus Linguistics 2005 Conference at the University of Birmingham. Martin invited me to think about what I could contribute. So my ideas on corpus linguistics and Dickens got their first public outing.

I also got the job that I had applied for. At the University of Liverpool, I then worked with Michael Hoey, Mike Scott, and Matthew Brook O'Donnell on a project that looked at *The Guardian* newspaper articles to study the relationship between places in which words occur and the meanings and functions they have in these places. For instance, the word *fresh* occurs significantly more frequently in the opening sentence of a news article than in the body of the text. In the opening sentence, *fresh* collocates with words such as *row, controversy,* or *blow* and helps to highlight the newsworthiness of a story. For my research into Dickens, it also seemed like a good idea to consider the positions of phrases in the text. The prominence of *fog* in the opening chapter of *Bleak House* is a prime example of the association of meaning and place. More generally, in fiction, interesting textual places are the speech of characters. Together with Matthew Brook O'Donnell and Catherine Smith I explored this idea, which led to the development of the first prototype of what would become CLiC. CLiC stood initially for "Corpus Linguistics in Cheshire" as we used the Cheshire3 Information Retrieval Engine. In the current CLiC, Cheshire got replaced by a more modern set-up. The acronym now stands for "Corpus Linguistics in Context," highlighting the functionality over the technology.

When I took up a position at the University of Nottingham, I joined the same Department as Peter Stockwell. Peter's research is in stylistics, too, and specifically cognitive poetics. Initially, Peter and I spent a great amount of time talking about why we were not convinced by the other person's approach to stylistics. Eventually, we ended up doing a research project on characterization in Dickens together, which demonstrated how immensely valuable it was to join up our approaches. The funding we won for this work allowed us to develop CLiC further and make it widely accessible for others to use. At present, CLiC runs on a server at the University of Birmingham, where I now work as Professor of Corpus Linguistics. I continue to collaborate with Peter Stockwell, and at Birmingham, Viola joined the CLiC team as a Research Fellow.

Viola Wiegand   My path into corpus stylistics was a little different. I first encountered corpus linguistics in my English linguistics undergraduate degree at Hong Kong Polytechnic University. I was immediately taken by its methodology of collecting texts on a large scale in order to study linguistic features. My BA, MA, and PhD theses all used corpus linguistic approaches to discourse, although the topics are rather different. In my BA thesis, I analyzed the appraisal of Chinese culture in tweets, and in my MA and PhD, I have studied discourses around the notion of surveillance. I began working on the CLiC project while I was still doing my PhD. Although nineteenth-century fiction and present-day surveillance discourses might appear to be rather different, working on both projects showed very clearly how corpus methods can be adapted for analyzing a range of texts, as long as the context of these texts and relevant theoretical concepts for their interpretation are taken into account. The CorporaCoCo package (Hennessey, Wiegand, Mahlberg, Tench & Lentin, 2017) that we developed for the comparison of collocations across corpora is another example of how projects that are rather different can complement one another in meaningful ways. For Dickens the comparison of collocations across speech and narration opens exciting avenues for research, while the comparison of collocations of surveillance over time leads to crucial insights into the development of discourses.

Our Work with the CLiC Web App and Corpora

In our collaborative work, the development of methodological approaches and especially functionalities for the CLiC app has played an important role. This led to a range of analyses of specific patterns in fiction. In Mahlberg and Wiegand (2018), for instance, we draw on the stylistic notions of deviation and norms to demonstrate how the boundaries between linguistic categories – such as direct speech and free indirect speech – are ultimately fuzzy.

The CLiC web app and corpora have become key resources for our research in corpus stylistics and have been adopted widely by other researchers, too. CLiC has been designed to provide a particularly intuitive interface (Figure 15.2). The concordance, clusters, and keywords tabs offer similar functionalities to other corpus tools. The "Counts" tab provides an overview of all books in CLiC and their lengths in words. The "Texts" tab displays the full text, which allows you to read the entire book or simply check the context of particular examples. We will explain the "Subsets" below.

With CLiC, we are specifically interested in exploring the notion of concordance reading. As Tognini-Bonelli (2001) pointed out, concordances are read "vertically," unlike texts, which we read from left to right. Sinclair (2003) emphasized that spotting patterns in concordances requires a systematic approach. Therefore, a specific feature of CLiC is the KWICGrouper. Developed from the initial idea in O'Donnell (2008), this functionality allows users to interactively group concordance lines to support the identification of patterns. KWIC stands for the display format of concordance lines showing the central **Key Word In Context**.

Going back to Mastropierro's (2017) example of concordance lines for *forest* in *Heart of Darkness*, we see how the KWICGrouper helps to highlight patterns. The collocates that Mastropierro identifies as contributing to the semantic fields of

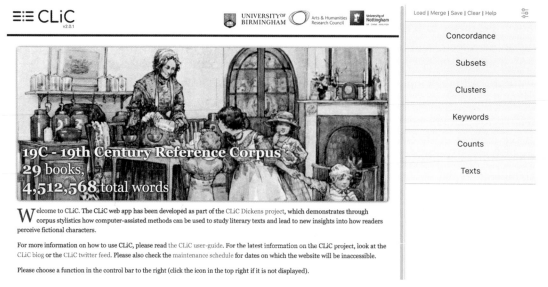

Figure 15.2 The CLiC interface
(http://clic.bham.ac.uk)

closedness, darkness, and immensity (cf. the section on "Style in Translated Texts")
are taken as the basis for this KWICGrouping example. When entering these
collocates into the KWICGrouper, CLiC regroups the concordance lines as shown
in Figure 15.3. The darker lines at the top of the screen contain more matches of the
collocates (in this case two) than the lighter lines (which each contain one match). In
Figure 15.3, we created custom tags to indicate which semantic field the lines belong
to (based on Mastropierro's 2017 analysis). This way of displaying the concordance
highlights Mastropierro's argument that the semantic fields are not created in
isolation, but the patterns interact and create the overall stylistic effect of the forest
in this fictional world. This is particularly obvious in lines 2 to 4, which belong to
the semantic fields of closedness and darkness.

CLiC (Version 2) hosts five literary corpora with a focus on material from the
nineteenth century. It contains over 150 books and more than 16 million words. The
case study in this chapter focuses on the corpus of Dickens's Novels (DNov) and the
19th Century Reference Corpus (19C). All CLiC texts originate from Project Gutenberg (www.gutenberg.org). You can therefore theoretically download texts from
Gutenberg yourself and use your preferred (offline) corpus tool to analyze these
texts. However, the added value of using CLiC is that not only have the corpora
already been cleaned and compiled thematically but also all texts have been
annotated for narration and character speech.

The CLiC corpora are divided into two major subsets: **quotes**, that is, text within
quotation marks, roughly corresponding to character speech, and **non-quotes**,
covering narration. A subcategory of non-quotes are **suspensions**. These are

CLiC
v2.0.1

UNIVERSITY OF BIRMINGHAM   Arts & Humanities Research Council   University of Nottingham UK · CHINA · MALAYSIA

Showing 1 to 23 of 23 entries, Rel. Freq. 597.46 pm, from 1 book, 4 lines / 1 book with 2 KWIC matches, 12 lines / 1 book with 1 KWIC match

db61de3

#	Left	Node	Right	Book	In bk.	closed	dark	immense
1	was on a back water surrounded by scrub and	forest,	with a pretty border of smelly mud on one sid	heart	ǀ	✓		
2	sticks to bed with them. Beyond the fence the	forest	stood up spectrally in the moonlight, and throu	heart	ǀ	✓	✓	
3	empty stream, a great silence, an impenetrable	forest.	The air was warm, thick, heavy, sluggish. Ther	heart	ǀ	✓	✓	
4	g indistinctly against the gloomy border of the	forest,	and near the river two bronze figures, leaning	heart	ǀ	✓	✓	
5	as in my nostrils, the high stillness of primeval	forest	was before my eyes; there were shiny patches	heart	ǀ		✓	
6	my feet and looked back at the edge of the	forest,	as though I had expected an answer of some	heart	ǀ	✓		
7	opened before us and closed behind, as if the	forest	had stepped leisurely across the water to bar	heart	ǀ	✓		
8	then well on in the afternoon, the face of the	forest	was gloomy, and a broad strip of shadow had	heart	ǀ		✓	
9	been between, had disappeared. Of course the	forest	surrounded all that. The river-bank was clear,	heart	ǀ	✓		
10	with his whole arm. Examining the edge of the	forest	above and below, I was almost certain I could	heart	ǀ	✓		
11	Kurtz wandered alone, far in the depths of the	forest.	'Very often coming to this station, I had to wa	heart	ǀ			✓
12	looking at the shore, sweeping the limit of the	forest	at each side and at the back of the house	heart	ǀ	✓		
13	calm of the evening. The long shadows of the	forest	had slipped downhill while we talked, had gon	heart	ǀ		✓	
14	nto the clearing by the dark-faced and pensive	forest.	The bushes shook, the grass swayed for a tim	heart	ǀ		✓	
15	ping guard over the ivory; but deep within the	forest,	red gleams that wavered, that seemed to sink	heart	ǀ			✓
16	nvinced, had driven him out to the edge of the	forest,	to the bush, towards the gleam of fires, the th	heart	ǀ	✓		

Figure 15.3 KWICGrouped lines of *forest* in *Heart of Darkness*, showing all matches with Mastropierro's (2017, pp. 110–112) semantic fields (sixteen out of twenty-three total instances of *forest*)

non-quotes that are surrounded by quotes. Lambert (1981) studied such interruptions of character speech by the narrator or "suspended quotations" specifically in Dickens, and without the technology we have today. The CLiC annotation scheme further distinguishes between short suspensions and long suspensions (with a minimum length of five words for the latter).

In Example (2), the plain text belongs to the non-quote subset, quotes are shown in bold and the long suspension is underlined.

(2) Elizabeth honoured him for such feelings, and thought him handsomer than ever as he expressed them.
  'But what,' said she, after a pause, 'can have been his motive? What can have induced him to behave so cruelly?' (*Pride and Prejudice*, Jane Austen, chapter 16)

The non-quote subset is the largest in both DNov and the 19C, making up a little under two-thirds of the total number of words in both corpora (Table 15.1).

Table 15.1 The composition of the CLiC 2 corpora

Corpus size (in words)[1]	Dickens's Novels (DNov) 15 texts	19th Century Reference Corpus (19C) 29 texts
All text	3,833,544	4,512,568
Quotes	1,377,852	1,647,615
Non-quotes	2,455,666	2,864,944
Short suspensions	25,040	13,561
Long suspensions	83,996	28,698
Text without suspensions	3,724,508	4,470,309

[1] These word counts are taken from the CLiC 2.0.0 "Counts" tab, with the exception of "Text without suspensions," which is the simple difference of the two suspension subsets subtracted from "All text."

Suspensions are only a relatively small section of non-quotes. They are restricted in both location and length and cannot cut across sentence boundaries. Our case study will show that despite their comparatively low proportion in the texts, suspensions fulfill important functions in the texts.

Case Study: Pauses in Character Speech

Suspensions are prime places for information about the context in which speech takes place and the character who speaks or is otherwise involved in the interaction. They also have an important function in describing pauses. Using an early prototype of CLiC, Mahlberg and Smith (2012) show that the word *pause* (in the sense of "silence") occurs significantly more frequently in the suspensions of Dickens's novels than in the rest of the text. Figure 15.4 confirms this distribution for DNov and 19C in CLiC 2. In both corpora, *pause* occurs comparatively more frequently in long suspensions than in the text without suspensions. Since the subsets vary greatly in their word counts (Table 15.1), the comparison in Figure 15.4 is not based on raw frequencies, but **normalized frequencies** per 100,000 words. So in 19C, *pause* is more than twice as frequent as in DNov, because 19C contains fewer suspensions than DNov overall (see Table 15.1). For both corpora, the frequency difference of *pause* between long suspensions and text without suspensions is significant according to a log-likelihood test, $p < 0.0001$ (using the calculator provided by Rayson, n.d.).

Mahlberg and Smith (2012) identify three frequent patterns of *pause* in suspensions: *after a pause*, *after a short pause*, and *after a moment's pause*. The placement of the suspensions in the middle of the speech means that the pause tends to be reported after it occurs in the plot. This reversed sequence is illustrated in Example (3) (Mahlberg & Smith, 2012, p. 63). In the narrative, the "moment's pause" happens before the lofty young man says, "And I suppose." In this example, the suspension

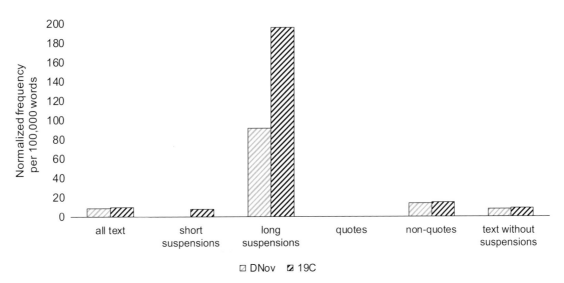

Figure 15.4 Frequency of *pause* across subsets of DNov (Dickens's Novels) and 19C (the 19th Century Reference Corpus) normalized per 100,000 words in CLiC 2.0.0

does not only reverse the plot sequence, but also pauses the speech after a new thought is signaled by "And I suppose."

> (3) 'That's all I say. And I suppose,' added the lofty young man, <u>after a moment's pause,</u>
> 'that visitor will understand me, when I say that's all I say. In short, I suppose [...].'
> (*Little Dorrit*, Charles Dickens, chapter 31)

Table 15.2 gives an overview of the most frequent patterns of *pause* in long suspensions in DNov and 19C, with raw and normalized frequencies. The patterns identified by Mahlberg and Smith (2012) are still at the top. However, concordance lines of *pause* indicate that, in a similar way to Mastropierro's (2017) example of *forest*, *pause* occurs not only in the patterns that are verbatim repeated, but also in more abstract patterns, realized by a variety of lexical forms. An examination with the KWICGrouper (searching for *pause* in the "long suspensions" subset of DNov with the KWICGrouper settings shown in Figure 15.5) further shows that there tend to be two types of *pause* patterns: descriptive and interpretive narratorial patterns. The descriptive type simply states that a pause happens and may specify a descriptive feature by using an adjective like *long* or *short*, as illustrated in Example (4) (suspension underlined again).

> (4) 'Why the truth is,' <u>said John *after a long pause*</u>, 'that the person who'd go quickest, is a
> sort of natural, as one may say, sir; and though quick of foot, [...]' (*Barnaby Rudge*,
> Charles Dickens, chapter 27)

The interpretive type is illustrated in Example (5), including the adjective *disconcerted* that evaluates the pause and its effect on the characters.

Table 15.2 Patterns of *pause* in long suspensions

Pattern	DNov (Dickens's Novels)		19C (19th Century Reference Corpus)	
	Frequency in long suspensions	Normalized frequency (per 100,000 words)	Frequency in long suspensions	Normalized frequency (per 100,000 words)
after a pause	24	0.63	33	0.73
after a short pause	14	0.37	6	0.13
after a moment's pause	13	0.34	3	0.07
after a long pause	6	0.16	1	0.02
after another pause	3	0.08	0	0.00

Note: The normalized frequencies were calculated based on the full size of each corpus. Although a normalization base of 1 million words is more often used for corpora containing over 1 million words, we used the same base as for the normalization in Figure 15.4.

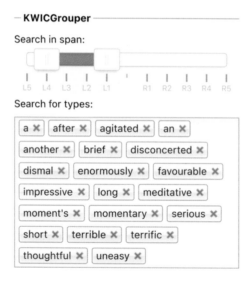

Figure 15.5 The KWICGrouper settings for the search for *pause* in DNov (Dickens's Novels) long suspensions

(5) 'Well, sir,' says the trooper, looking into his hat *after another disconcerted pause*, 'I am sorry not to have given you more satisfaction. If it would be any satisfaction to any one that [...].' (*Bleak House*, Charles Dickens, chapter 27)

Figure 15.6 shows a sample of concordance lines of *pause* after KWICGrouping and tagging the lines for the descriptive and interpretive types. Overall, we

Showing 1 to 50 of 77 entries, <u>Rel. Freq.</u> 916.71 pm, from 14 books, 1 line / 1 book with 4 KWIC matches, 44 lines / 14 books with 3 KWIC matches, 31 lines / 11 books with 2 KWIC matches

db61de3

	Left	Node	Right	Book	In bk.	descr	interp	unclear
1	sir,' added Mr Willet, after an enormously long	pause	during which he fixed his great dull eyes on H₁	BR	I		✓	
2	looking into his hat after another disconcerted	pause,	"I am sorry not to have given you more satisfa	BH	I		✓	
3	n my honour," says Sir Leicester after a terrific	pause	during which he has been heard to snort and f	BH	I		✓	
4	doubt,' returned Mr Carker, after an impressive	pause,	'that wherever Gay is, he is much better where	DS	I		✓	
5	said the gentleman, after another and a dismal	pause,	'why you wouldn't paper a room with represent	HT	I		✓	
6	state of feeling,' said Squeers, after a terrible	pause,	during which he had moistened the palm of his	NN	I		✓	
7	this morning,' he continued, after a thoughtful	pause,	'I was ready to prove a pretty good claim. I	OCS	I		✓	
8	ur, Mortimer,' returned Eugene, after a serious	pause	of a few moments, 'that I don't know.' ¶ 'Don't	OMF	I		✓	
9	"Mr. Carton," she answered, after an agitated	pause,	"the secret is yours, not mine; and I promise t	TTC	I		✓	
10	Doctor Manette, turning to him after an uneasy	pause,	"it is very hard to explain, consistently, the inn	TTC	I		✓	
11	d--if not," adds Sir Leicester after a moment's	pause,	"if not hanged, drawn, and quartered." ¶ Sir Le	BH	I		✓	
12	ere. ¶ 'Why the truth is,' said John after a long	pause,	'that the person who'd go quickest, is a sort o	BR	I		✓	
13	'We'll see, gentlemen,' said John, after a long	pause,	'who's the master of this house, and who isn't	BR	I		✓	
14	is it?' ¶ 'Gentlemen,' said Mr Willet after a long	pause,	'you needn't ask. The likeness of a murdered n	BR	I		✓	
15	oubt,' resumed the secretary, after a moment's	pause,	'that the rioters who have been taken (poor fel	BR	I		✓	
16	' ¶ 'I gather, sir,' said Emma, after a moment's	pause,	'from what you hint at, but fear to tell me	BR	I		✓	
17	what,' he asked very sweetly, after a moment's	pause,	'can I do for you? You may command me freel	BR	I		✓	

Figure 15.6 The KWICGrouped lines of *pause* in DNov (Dickens's Novels) long suspensions (seventeen examples out of seventy-seven total instances)

identified fifty-eight lines that we consider descriptive and fourteen interpretive lines (five are "unclear"). Not all of the interpretive examples are included in Figure 15.6, because some of them contain fewer matches of the pre-modification patterns shown in the KWICGrouper search box of Figure 15.5. An example from an interpretive line with fewer matches is given in Example (6). This example illustrates that not all lines follow the pattern *after a pause*. The *in* instead of *after* further creates a different temporal relation of the suspension to the plot. The KWICGrouper can help with sorting through these nuances. This case study has illustrated how pauses in character speech are an opportunity to make the narrator's presence felt, but also to let the reader experience similar effects of pauses as the fictional characters do (Mahlberg & Smith, 2012, p. 61; Lambert, 1981, p. 67ff.).

(6) 'I took,' says Brewer *in a favourable pause*, 'a cab this morning, and I rattled off to that Sale.' (*Our Mutual Friend*, Charles Dickens, chapter 17)

Data Analysis Activity

The activities on the website accompanying this book will give you the opportunity to explore CLiC for yourself. You will use it to find information on fictional characters, identify clusters that function as building blocks for fictional worlds, and investigate features of fictional speech in particular.

Going Further

If you want to get deeper into corpus stylistics, degrees in language and literature with modules on corpus linguistics and stylistics would be most relevant. As the offer of digital humanities courses is spreading, there is also a range of courses in digital methods more generally. Stylistics and digital humanities offer huge opportunities for interdisciplinary work. Graduate students with a background in a variety of disciplines can find their way into this area with the help of summer schools or a number of freely available online resources. There is plenty of scope for classroom applications, too (e.g., Friginal, 2018), for both native speakers and students of English as a second language. The CLiC Activity Book (Mahlberg, Stockwell & Wiegand, 2017) specifically contains thematic activities written to support secondary school teachers and to allow pupils to explore literature from a new, digitally enabled perspective. Overall, there are many possibilities to develop your own research.

Discussion Questions

1. What opportunities do digital tools offer for analyzing literary texts when the analyses are not possible (or feasible) manually?
2. Can you think of any restrictions that authors face when presenting spoken language in writing? Which features of spoken language are particularly difficult to portray in text? Maybe listen to a conversation on the radio and try to transcribe it.
3. *Practical research activity*: Plan a small research project on characterization. How would you go about finding character information with CLiC? Would

you look for information on a specific character or information about fictional people more generally, across a larger corpus? Which CLiC functionalities would you choose for your searches and why?

4. Can you think of any applications of corpus stylistic (or digital humanities) methods in other fields, like history or cultural studies?

FURTHER READING

Foundational Readings

Leech, G., & Short, M. (2007). *Style in fiction: A linguistic introduction to English fictional prose* (2nd edn). Harlow: Pearson.

Schreibman, S., Siemens, R., & Unsworth, J. (Eds.). (2004). *Companion to digital humanities*. Oxford: Blackwell.

Simpson, P. (2014). *Stylistics: A resource book for students* (2nd edn). London: Routledge.

Recent Publications

Mahlberg, M., Wiegand, V., Stockwell, P., & Hennessey, A. (2019). Speech-bundles in the 19th-century English novel. *Language and Literature, 28*(4), 326–353.

McIntyre, D., & Walker, B. (2019). *Corpus stylistics: Theory and practice*. Edinburgh: Edinburgh University Press.

Underwood, T., Bamman, D., & Lee, S. (2018). The transformation of gender in English-language fiction. *Journal of Cultural Analytics*. Feb. 13, 2018. https://doi.org/10.22148/16.019

REFERENCES

Craig, H. (2004). Stylistic analysis and authorship studies. In S. Schreibman, R. Siemens, & J. Unsworth (Eds.), *A companion to digital humanities* (pp. 273–288). Oxford: Blackwell.

Culpeper, J. (2001). *Language and characterisation: People in plays and other texts*. Harlow: Longman.

Donaldson, J. (2001). *Room on the broom*. New York: Dial Books.

Evert, S., Proisl, T., Jannidis, F., Reger, I., Pielström, S., Schöch, C., & Vitt, T. (2017). Understanding and explaining Delta measures for authorship attribution. *Digital Scholarship in the Humanities, 32*(suppl_2), ii4–ii16. https://doi.org/10.1093/llc/fqx023

Friginal, E. (2018). *Corpus linguistics for English teachers: Tools, online resources, and classroom activities*. London: Routledge.

Hennessey, A., Wiegand, V., Mahlberg, M., Tench, C. R., & Lentin, J. (2017). *CorporaCoCo: Corpora Co-Occurrence Comparison* (Version 1.1–0). Retrieved from https://CRAN.R-project.org/package=CorporaCoCo

Jeffries, L., & Walker, B. (2018). *Keywords in the press: The New Labour years*. London: Bloomsbury.

Jones, R. (2014). Advertising culture. In P. Stockwell & S. Whiteley (Eds.), *The Cambridge handbook of stylistics* (pp. 520–535). Cambridge: Cambridge University Press.

Kirschenbaum, M. G. (2010). What is digital humanities and what's it doing in English departments? *ADE Bulletin, 150*, 55–61.

Lambert, M. (1981). *Dickens and the suspended quotation*. New Haven: Yale University Press.

Leech, G., & Short, M. (2007). *Style in fiction: A linguistic introduction to English fictional prose* (2nd edn). Harlow: Pearson.

Louw, W. E. (1993). Irony in the text or insincerity in the writer? The diagnostic potential of semantic prosodies. In M. Baker, H. Francis, & E. Tognini-Bonelli (Eds.), *Text and technology: In honour of John Sinclair* (pp. 157–174). Amsterdam: John Benjamins.

Mahlberg, M. (2013). *Corpus stylistics and Dickens's fiction*. London: Routledge.

Mahlberg, M., & Smith, C. (2012). Dickens, the suspended quotation and the corpus. *Language and Literature, 21*(1), 51–65.

Mahlberg, M., Stockwell, P., & Wiegand, V. (2017). *CLiC – Corpus Linguistics in Context: An activity book – Version 1*. Retrieved from http://birmingham.ac.uk/clic-activity-book.

Mahlberg, M., & Wiegand, V. (2018). Corpus stylistics, norms and comparisons: Studying speech in *Great Expectations*. In R. Page, B. Busse, & N. Nørgaard (Eds.), *Rethinking language, text and context: Interdisciplinary research in stylistics in honour of Michael Toolan* (pp. 123–143). London: Routledge.

Mastropierro, L. (2017). Corpus stylistics in *Heart of Darkness* and its Italian translations. London: Bloomsbury.

O'Donnell, M. B. (2008). KWICgrouper: Designing a tool for corpus-driven concordance analysis. *International Journal of English Studies* (Special issue: Software-aided Analysis of Language), *8*(1), 107–122.

Rayson, P. (n.d.). Log-likelihood and effect size calculator. Retrieved from http://ucrel.lancs.ac.uk/llwizard.html.

Scott, M. (2016). *WordSmith Tools* (Version 7). Stroud: Lexical Analysis Software.

Sinclair, J. (2003). *Reading concordances: An introduction*. Harlow: Pearson/Longman.

Stockwell, P. (2009). *Texture: A cognitive aesthetics of reading*. Edinburgh: Edinburgh University Press.

Tognini-Bonelli, E. (2001). *Corpus linguistics at work*. Amsterdam: John Benjamins.

Wales, K. (2001). *A dictionary of stylistics* (2nd edn). Harlow: Longman.

Whiteley, S., & Canning, P. (2017). Reader response research in stylistics. *Language and Literature, 26*(2), 71–87.

16 Policy and Planning at a Local Level with English as a Lingua Franca and Teacher Education

TELMA GIMENEZ, MICHELE SALLES EL KADRI, AND

LUCIANA CABRINI SIMÕES CALVO

Overview of Key Concepts in English as a Lingua Franca

The term "lingua franca" has been used to define a contact language that emerges from the need to communicate when speakers do not share a common language. Due to different linguistic backgrounds, interactions taking place in such contexts may develop as pidgins or creoles, that is, a mixture of two or more languages. In other cases, natural languages can serve similar purposes (Mauranen, 2018). Latin, for instance, used to be a lingua franca during the Roman Empire. Actually, the term itself derives from Latin "language of the Franks" (lingua franca) to refer to the language used mainly for commerce in the area around the East Mediterranean Sea. In colonial times, for example, the language of the colonizers (e.g., English in India) was generally imposed as a lingua franca.

Today, any natural language that is widespread and used for vehicular purposes[1] can be considered a lingua franca, and the most notable case is, of course, English. ELF, or **English as a Lingua Franca**, is a broad label that encompasses studies aimed at understanding the transformations in language use in contemporary interactions where English is recognized as the common language by speakers of different languages. It is a field that is also challenging common-sense views of language and communication.

As a new field of study, ELF has already achieved remarkable presence in the specialized literature, with a dedicated journal (*Journal of English as a Lingua Franca*), a series (De Gruyter Developments in English as a Lingua Franca), and a recent handbook of English as a Lingua Franca (Jenkins, Baker, & Dewey, 2018). Innumerous conferences have sessions dedicated to this area, including one that is in its eleventh edition, the International Conference of English as a Lingua Franca. And the field is growing (Jenkins, 2018).

The first studies that addressed ELF date back to the 1990s (e.g., Firth, 1990, 1996), to refer to the contexts where English was used exclusively by and among non-native speakers within a "deficit" approach, that is, the research interest was on

---

[1] A language that is used for communication between people from different linguistic backgrounds.

discovering how communication was successful despite its deviance from "correct" English (Jenkins, 2015, p. 41). Since then, this research area has grown and taken a more positive outlook on the speakers' creative uses of the language. From an initial interest in identifying characteristics of language use among non-native speakers, the area has evolved to acknowledge the complexity of communicative practices in a global world, where people from different linguistic and cultural backgrounds interact through English. Additionally, more recent definitions of ELF do not exclude native speakers from the interactions, despite the difficulty of categorizing native and non-native speakers. Mauranen (2018, p. 8), for example, defines it as "a contact language between speakers or speaker groups when at least one of them uses it as a second language." In fact, how to conceptualize ELF has been one of the key discussions among scholars in this field (see, for instance, Seidlhofer, 2011; Cogo & Dewey, 2012; Mackenzie, 2014; Jenkins, Baker & Dewey, 2018).

One of the authors who first defined ELF as a **contact language** was Jennifer Jenkins, for whom it was "English as it is used as a contact language among speakers from different first languages" (Jenkins, 2009, p. 143). In 2011, another prominent author in this field defined it as "any use of English among speakers of different first languages for whom English is the communicative medium of choice, and often the only option" (Seidlhofer, 2011, p. 7). More recently, Jenkins distinguishes three different phases of ELF research. In phase one, the interest was focused on the phonology and lexico-grammar of ELF communication, with Jenkins's proposition of a Lingua Franca Core. According to Jenkins, it "consisted of the few native English segmental and prosodic items whose absence was found in the empirical data to lead to potential intelligibility problems in intercultural communication" (Jenkins, 2015, p. 53). Corpus-based research is essential to establish the features of this kind of communication and the development of corpora such as the VOICE (Vienna-Oxford International Corpus of English), ELFA Corpus of English as a Lingua Franca in Academic Settings and ACE (Asian Corpus of English) helped establish some regularities, albeit in a constant state of flux. This fluidity is inherent in ephemeral and transient encounters, but ELF can be somewhat less fluid in specific communities such as academics or diplomats, whose interactions can exhibit regular features, or "genres." It was due to the search for these regularities that could eventually be codified and thus characterize a "variety," that some authors interpreted ELF to mean another "variety" of English. However, the variability inherent in interactions among people from different speech communities was acknowledged into the second phase of ELF research.

While the first phase meant an approximation between ELF and **World Englishes** (WE) (and its intention to codify varieties), in the second one there was distancing from the idea of codification. According to Jenkins (2015, p. 55), "ELF, with its fluidity and 'online' negotiation of meaning among interlocutors with varied multilingual repertoires, could not be considered as consisting of bounded varieties, but as English that transcends boundaries, and that is therefore beyond description."

A reconceptualization of ELF is suggested by that author when she proposes to frame English within **multilingualism**. While the first stages of research focused on the notion of English as a language whose variability in ongoing interactions demanded explanations beyond the traditional sociolinguistic concepts, the third phase embraces communication among multilinguals as the social practice to be investigated. For Jenkins (2015, p. 77), "English, while always in the (potential) mix, is now conceived as one among many other languages, one resource among many, available but not necessarily used, with ELF defined not merely by its variability but by its complexity and emergent nature."

As theorizations about ELF seem to get closer to reflections made elsewhere by scholars interested in challenging conventional or monolingual notions of language (such as **translanguaging**[2] or **metrolingualism**[3]), there is recognition that English poses many challenges to researchers interested in understanding how individuals and communities use this language to achieve their communicative purposes in ever more complex, diversified, multilingual contexts.

The difficulty of capturing this new landscape within the realm of the so-called **linguistic globalization** (Blommaert, 2010) cannot be sufficiently underscored. The global spread of English and contemporary waves of (voluntary or forced) migrations have created very complex sociolinguistic realities, in which traditional definitions of what counts as a language or speech community are no longer enough. These ever-expanding possibilities of language use in unforeseeable circumstances have implications for the teaching of English in contexts where it is not a native language and where it is ceasing to be viewed as just an ordinary foreign language to be learned.

Pedagogical implications derived from an ELF perspective were and still are one of the main concerns of practitioners or scholars working from an applied linguistics paradigm. As Seidlhofer (2011, pp. 17–18) reminds us, "in settings where English is conceived as a foreign language ... the focus is very much on where the language comes from, who its native speakers are, and what cultural associations are bound up with it." The teaching is guided by standard language and

---

[2] Translanguaging refers to "using one's idiolect, that is, one's linguistic repertoire, without regard for socially and politically defined language labels or boundaries" (Otheguy, Garcia & Reid, 2015. p. 297). In translingual practices multilingual speakers deploy all of their linguistic resources without distinguishing between different languages.

[3] According to Otsuji and Pennycook (2010, p. 246), "Metrolingualism describes the ways in which people of different and mixed backgrounds use, play with and negotiate identities through language; it does not assume connections between language, culture, ethnicity, nationality or geography, but rather seeks to explore how such relations are produced, resisted, defied or rearranged; its focus is not on language systems but on languages as emergent from contexts of interaction".

"native speakers" norms. As a lingua franca, "speakers will have a command of English that varies along a continuum from minimal to expert," (pp. 17–18) co-constructing norms required by the "interactional exigencies" and not necessarily what "native speakers" would consider "correct." The need for change in the way English is taught was also made by Graddol (2006, p. 19) when he affirmed: "As ever increasing numbers of people learn English around the world, it is not just 'more of the same'. There is a new model. English is no longer being learned as a foreign language, in recognition of the hegemonic power of native English speakers."

However, the convergence in acknowledging the need to rethink the teaching of English as a Foreign Language (EFL) does not mean that English as a Lingua Franca (ELF) is seen as the only way forward. Other conceptualizations of English as a polycentric language, like the WE paradigm, also find acceptance when teachers deliberately challenge the monocentric view of an international standard variety of English, based on native speakers' norms. Matsuda (2017, p. xiii) speaks of the "messiness" of English, that is, "there are different varieties of English spoken in different parts of the world for different purposes that are learned in different ways" and that English language teaching (ELT) needs to bring this heterogeneity into the classroom. This would suggest that different varieties of English, say Indian English, for instance, would be part of the syllabus alongside American English, one of the two predominant varieties in ELT.

Although recognizing that ELF and WE represent quite distinct theoretical approaches and principles, Matsuda (2017, p. xvii) sees it as "more constructive to draw from both (and any other relevant) disciplines to make our teacher education practices as EIL [**English as an International Language**][4]-friendly and informed as possible." In her collection she brought together contributions from teacher preparation programs, entire courses, EIL-informed courses on another ELT topic, independent units on teaching EIL and lessons, activities, and tasks for EIL teacher preparation. From this variety of contexts, ranging from full programs to the occasional addition of a task designed to promote awareness about ELF, we can testify that teacher educators around the world are trying to recontextualize the conceptual developments into practical activities.

Some pedagogical recommendations emerging from the contributions included more exposure to diversity in English (which would include bringing ELF interactions for listening comprehension tasks, for instance), pragmatic strategies to help negotiate linguistic differences (e.g., accommodation or "let-it-pass"),

---

[4] Matsuda (2017, p. xiii) uses the umbrella term "international" to refer to the "function that English performs in international, multilingual contexts, to which each speaker brings a variety of English that they are most familiar with, along with their own cultural frames of reference and employs various strategies to communicate effectively."

promote intercultural awareness (e.g., making the familiar "strange") and critical understanding of the role languages play in society (e.g., the power of the English language in giving access to material and symbolic goods).

One of the approaches that has been successfully developed was designed and implemented by Sifakis and Bayyurt (2018, p. 459). According to them, "ELF-aware teacher learning and development" is "the process of engaging with ELF research and developing one's own understanding of the ways in which it can be integrated into one's classroom context," although recognizing that the ELF conceptual framework is still being constructed.

In their proposal they envisage three phases to raise ELF awareness in class. In phase A (Exposure), the teachers read research literature about ELF, EIL and WE and are invited to consider pros and cons of having one common language for international communication, discussing issues such as the adoption of the so-called Standard English may not guarantee comprehensibility, or how the strengthening of English may weaken people's motivation to learn other languages. At this stage, teachers are invited to examine examples of transcripts from corpus studies (Cogo & Dewey, 2012, for instance). One such example is reproduced below:

S1=Japanese S2= Korean

S1: what is (,) what is your future plan?

S2: ah(.) actually i want to be: translator or interpreter in the future if possible

S1: yes (,) yeah @@@

S2: @@@ah: what about you?

S1: ah i want to be computer programmer ah and also i want to use english with another people

(Cogo & Dewey, 2012, p. 63)

In this example, and in many others of the same dialogue, the omission of the indefinite article is interpreted as accommodation, since "both participants are speakers of languages that do not have an article system."

In phase B, the teachers recontextualize what they read and discussed into their classrooms. At this stage the teachers have to confront their own beliefs about language and English more specifically. It is a demanding phase because of the deeply entrenched views on native speakers, standard language, and error: they have to consider the implications of decentering the native speaker and what "correct" language is. The purpose is not to replace what they have been doing but to integrate an ELF-aware perspective where necessary.

Finally, the third phase is when teachers prepare instructional materials which could include improving the adopted coursebook or designing entirely new materials. Because teaching and learning are so context-dependent it is important to consider course objectives vis-à-vis learners' needs and be sensitive to the goals to be achieved.

Although Sifakis and Bayyurt do not explicitly mention implementation and reflection, it is important to highlight how a teacher development process can benefit from a careful monitoring of the changes in teaching and their effect on students' learning. At this stage, teachers would have to engage in documenting the process and assessing its value in creating safer spaces for students to venture into seeing themselves as successful speakers in ELF settings.

Over the years, as teacher educators, we have tried to bring an ELF perspective into our work and reflect on it. It is about this experience that we comment next.

Our Work with English as a Lingua Franca and Teacher Education in Brazil

Personal Reflections

The three authors of this chapter got involved with applied linguistics at different times. Telma graduated in 1979, after completing a degree in Languages (Portuguese-English) and soon started to teach at the same course, initially, as a teacher of English and later on as a supervisor of student teachers during their practicum in schools. Her interest in English as a global language started in the 1990s, when she came in contact with Alistair Pennycook's (1994) *The Cultural Politics of English as an International Language* as well as other writers who, at the time, were addressing the status of English in a global world (e.g., Crystal, 1997; Graddol & Meinhoff, 1999). Michele and Luciana's journey as teacher educators within the field of applied linguistics interested in the issues of English as a global lingua franca arose while they were taking the MA in Language Studies and had the opportunity to attend Telma's lectures. They found in the ELF perspective several principles they considered needed to be discussed, and the partnership with Telma motivated them to pursue issues they had felt as practitioners and that could be fields of research. The main focus of Michele's and Luciana's PhD research was collaborative teacher education (through communities of practice and coteaching and cogenerative dialogue perspective[5]), and since then we, the three authors, have been discussing, thinking, writing about our attempts to introduce ELF into our contexts, that is, ELT pre-service teacher education.

---

[5] A dialectical practice involving two or more teachers at the elbow of one another (Roth et al., 2004) and whose primary concern is students' learning and whose secondary concern is addressing contradictions and thereby improving learning conditions (Roth & Tobin, 2001). In such meetings named "{coteaching | cogenerative dialogue}", all coteachers debrief a preceding lesson or plan a new lesson as well as provide opportunities for the understanding of the teachers' complex role in the classroom and their ethical responsibility to the students for the effective negotiation of the systems they navigate each day (El Kadri, 2014, p. 35).

Our Work in English as a Lingua Franca

In the last few years, we have taken ELF as a research topic and tried to engage prospective teachers in rethinking what teaching English means nowadays, since our teacher education programs face the challenge of deconstructing historical understandings that associate English solely with native speakers. Because we believe the work of teacher educators is crucial in transforming beliefs and attitudes, we generally emphasize that an ELF perspective in teacher education would join other proposals promoted within applied linguistics which draw on critical frameworks such as **critical pedagogy** and **critical literacy,** focusing on issues of language and power (Gimenez, El Kadri, & Calvo, 2018a). We have argued not only for the need to re-think teacher education programs in light of the discoveries in ELF research, but also for the need to adopt a model that reflects the multicultural and multilingual realities of this language (Calvo, El Kadri, & El Kadri, 2016; Gimenez, El Kadri, & Calvo, 2018a, 2018b, 2018c).

We like to think that our work fits into the efforts of other ELF scholars described in the first section of this chapter as we try to instill a critical perspective to English that is closely associated with studies in this area. Together with other approaches derived from postcolonial perspectives (such as World Englishes), it enables the deconstruction of traditional ways of teaching English (El Kadri, Calvo, & Gimenez, 2017; Gimenez et al., 2018c). We have worked with pre-service teachers and discussed the consequences of having English as a global lingua franca and its implications for ELT in a country like Brazil. In order to do so, we invite future teachers to join us in a dialogue on what teaching and learning this language may mean.

An ELF perspective is relatively recent and controversial (see, for instance, Mackenzie, 2014; O'Regan, 2014). Its reception in applied linguistics in Brazil has addressed conceptual developments (Jordão, 2014; Schmitz, 2017;) and a survey of studies revealed that this is still the major focus of attention. Few investigations concentrated on empirical data or provided practical examples of how to implement ELF in the curriculum (Calvo, El Kadri, & Gimenez, 2013; Bordini & Gimenez, 2014). However, a survey with teacher educators showed that although ELF is acknowledged as an important perspective to be introduced at pre-service levels, traditional language assumptions are not challenged by language courses in those programs, thus resulting in isolated attempts and initiatives by practicum supervisors who had contact with the ELF literature (El Kadri, Calvo, & Gimenez, 2016).

A more recent publication invited teacher educators from other regions of the country to contribute to a collection focusing on their understandings of ELF and how they were incorporating it into their teaching. The chapters reflected on how English can be reframed to have its teaching more sensitive to identity issues (which can include, for instance, accent and intelligibility), to critical awareness of language, and to acceptance of diversity and fluidity inherent in ELF settings. It seems that ELF in teacher education presents itself as an opportunity to deconstruct beliefs or language ideologies on which EFL has been grounded, and that this deconstruction is a first step toward change in teaching and learning (Gimenez et al., 2018a).

In our own work, we have had the opportunity to challenge the beliefs about the notion of normativity that guide mainstream ELT (e.g., that comprehensibility depends on the use of Standard English based on native speakers' norms) both in pre-service and in-service teacher education. Such work operates at the level of awareness of alternatives and to challenge such beliefs, we think it is important to present situations that have and do not have the native speaker as a norm for the teachers to reflect on their impact on English language teaching.

Considering that ELF is understood as a perspective that can inform pedagogical practices, we introduce it in our own teaching as part of the curriculum of courses such as Teaching Methodology or Applied Linguistics at undergraduate levels. With in-service teachers, we have tried to implement activities that can lead them to consider alternative views on the English language[6] and its use in lingua franca interactions (El Kadri et al., 2017; Gimenez et al., 2018c).

In El Kadri et al. (2017), for example, we described our initiative to raise awareness about the new linguistic realities of lingua franca encounters by analyzing a unit dedicated to ELF as part of an online program for pre-service English language teachers. As a retrospective analysis, we highlight ELF aspects that were successfully addressed (e.g., recognition that English is no longer associated only with native speakers; raising awareness about intelligibility and different English accents; among others) and others that need further development, such as articulation of ELF with didactic practices, for example.

In Gimenez et al. (2018c), we described two initiatives at pre-service teacher education level that address the need to consider alternative approaches to "traditional" practices which ignore the changing nature of English as an international language. One of the initiatives was a 30-hour elective course "English as a global lingua franca: epistemological and pedagogical issues," aimed at raising awareness about issues around the uses of "English as a lingua franca" and their pedagogical consequences. The other initiative was carried out during a curricular course and the topic "English as a lingua franca" was implemented in 16 lessons, over 8 days (12 hours). These initiatives show different ways to incorporate ELF in the English **teacher education curriculum** following a reflective model that de-stabilized some of the ideas and principles of English as a foreign language. So, we report on activities that try to challenge the idea that the only English that counts is the one spoken by native speakers. We do so by inviting the future teachers to consider alternative situations where it is spoken

---

[6] See examples of the analysis of the activities proposed in the further reading section.

by successful non-native speakers. Much like the steps suggested by Bayyurt and Sifakis (2013), we ask them to read the literature and pose questions about the implications of what the authors are proposing. The questions aim at challenging their current beliefs and the students are encouraged to plan activities/teaching materials to introduce in their classes.

Most of these activities have to do with oral skills and we emphasize that ELF is not just about different accents, but the use of English that diverges from standard norms (as in the example of a video with Pope Francis[7]) and yet, the communicative purpose is achieved. In all of these cases, we work with participants who already have some level of proficiency in English to be able to understand what the speakers are saying.

Both articles illustrated here (El Kadri et al., 2017; Gimenez et al., 2018c) focused on the analysis of the activities carried out by ourselves that aimed at developing reflection about ELF through different teaching resources (reading texts, watching videos, answering questions, doing activities) and on the students' understandings about ELF when designing lesson plans as part of their assessment. We believe we are at the early stages of acting according to the educational implications of ELF, but we do feel our reflections and experiences are far from ideal, but they are relevant because they signal a movement toward incorporating perspectives that have the potential to challenge the English as Foreign Language (EFL) tradition (El Kadri et al., 2017) and which indicate that there have been attempts to engage with ELF issues in teacher education in our context.

Data Analysis Activity

In order to develop an approach that acknowledges the multiple contexts in which English is used, we suggest a project-based activity in which the students will develop a clearer understanding of ELF by going through the stages of raising awareness about successful communication not depending on correctness according to Standard English. The project described on the website accompanying this book follows Sifakis and Bayyurt's (2013) suggestion that teachers should get familiar with issues related to ELF and connect what they understand about it with their own practical experiences as users and educators so they can engage in a critical reorientation of their beliefs about teaching, integrating ELF in their context of teaching English as a foreign language.

---

[7] Pope Francis speaking in English to young people in South Korea, www.youtube.com/watch?v=BkIJ_W7TzRA.

Going Further

For those who want to become involved in English as a lingua franca or issues in global English teacher education, there are numerous websites with a range of information including pronunciation and ELF corpora that provide examples of educational materials and instructional webinars. These resources can be found on the accompanying website. In addition there is a Facebook group, ELF Ted (English as a Lingua Franca Teacher Education group), led by Prof. Yasmin Bayyurt and Dr. Nicos Sifakis and hosted by Bogazici University in Istanbul. In terms of courses, if your university offers a course on ELF or with an ELF perspective, that would help build your knowledge of the field. In addition, taking courses in language acquisition, multilingualism, World Englishes, and language education can help you gain the background necessary to pursue further work in this area. Living or working in a multilingual setting where English and other languages are used is also very useful for developing a perspective on ELF and its place in language use.

Discussion Questions

1. What are the main challenges of considering ELF in your own context?
2. What are the criticisms of an ELF perspective informing teaching?
3. What are the misconceptions about ELF?
4. How do you feel about the perspective?
5. Which beliefs generally underlie the teaching of English? How might ELF challenge them?

FURTHER READING

Foundational Readings

Jenkins, J., Baker, W., & Dewey, M. (Eds.). (2018). *The Routledge handbook of English as a lingua franca*. London and New York: Routledge.

Matsuda, A. (Ed.). (2016). *Preparing teachers to teach English as an international language*. Bristol: Multilingual Matters.

Seidlhofer, B. (2011). *Understanding English as a lingua franca*. Oxford: Oxford University Press.

Recent Publications

Gimenez, T., El Kadri, M. S., & Calvo, L. C. S. (Eds.). (2018). *English as a lingua franca in teacher education: A Brazilian perspective*. New York: de Gruyter Mouton.

Sifakis, N.C., & Tsantila, N. (2018). *English as a Lingua Franca for EFL Contexts*. Bristol: Multilingual Matters.

Tsantila, N. (2016). *ELF: Pedagogical and interdisciplinary perspectives.* Available from www .researchgate.net/publication/310425612_ELF_Pedagogical_and_Interdisciplinary_ Perspectives

REFERENCES

Bayyurt, Y., & Sifakis, N. (2013). Transforming into an ELF-aware teacher. Paper presented at *Conference on New Frontiers in Teaching and Learning English*, Verona University, Italy, 15 February.

Blommaert, J. (2010). *The sociolinguistics of globalization.* Cambridge: Cambridge University Press.

Bordini, M., & Gimenez, T. (2014). Estudos sobre inglês como língua franca no Brasil (2005–2012): uma metassíntese qualitativa. *Signum: Estudos da Linguagem, 17*(1), 17–43.

Calvo, L. C. S., El Kadri, M. S., & Gimenez, T. (2013). English as a lingua franca: A Brazilian perspective. V International Conference on English as a Lingua Franca- ELF 5, (pp. 1–8). Istambul. ELF 5 Proceedings. Istambul: Bogazici University.

Calvo, L. C. S., El Kadri, M. S., & El Kadri, A. (2016). ELF in teacher education programs: Mapping the proposals presented in ELF 5 and ELF 6. In N. Tsantila, J. Mandalios, & M. Ilko (Eds.), *ELF: Pedagogical and interdisciplinary perspectives* (pp. 268–277). Athens: DEERE – The American College of Greece.

Cogo, A., & Dewey, M. (2012). *Analysing English as a lingua franca – A corpus-driven investigation.* London: Continuum.

Crystal, D. (1997). *English as a global language.* Cambridge: Cambridge University Press.

Firth, A. (1990). 'Lingua franca' negotiation: Towards an interactional approach. *World Englishes, 9*(3), 269–280.

(1996). The discursive accomplishment of normality: On 'lingua franca' English and conversation analysis. *Journal of Pragmatics, 26*, 237–259.

El Kadri, M. S. (2014). *English language teachers changing identities in a teaching practicum: PIBID and {Coteaching | Cogenerative Dialogue} as opportunities for professional learning* (PhD Thesis). Universidade Estadual de Londrina.

El Kadri, M. S., Calvo, L. C. S., & Gimenez, T. (2016). ELF in Brazilian teacher education programs. In N. Tsantila, J. Mandalios, & M. Ilkos (Eds.), *ELF: Pedagogical and interdisciplinary perspectives* (pp. 278–282). Athens: DEERE – The American College of Greece.

(2017). English as a lingua franca in an online teacher education program offered by a state university in Brazil. In A. Matsuda (Ed.), *Preparing teachers to teach English as an international language* (pp. 181–194). Bristol: Multilingual Matters.

Gimenez, T., El Kadri, M. S., & Calvo, L. C. S. (Eds.). (2018a). *English as a lingua franca in teacher education: A Brazilian perspective*. New York: de Gruyter Mouton.

(2018b). ELF in Brazil: Recent developments and future directions. In J. Jenkins, W. Baker, & M. Dewey (Eds.), *The Routledge handbook of English as a lingua franca* (pp. 176–185). London: Routledge.

(2018c). Awareness raising about English as a lingua franca in two Brazilian teacher education programs. In T. Gimenez, M. S. El Kadri, & L. C. S. Calvo (Eds.), *English as a lingua franca in teacher education: A Brazilian perspective* (pp. 209–228). New York: de Gruyter Mouton.

Graddol, D. (2006). *English next*. London: British Council.

Graddol, D., & Meinhof, U. H. (Eds.). (1999). *English in a changing world*. Milton Keynes: AILA.

Jenkins, J. (2009). *World Englishes – a resource book for students* (2nd edn). London: Routledge.

(2015). *Global Englishes – a resource book for students* (3rd edn). Abingdon: Routledge.

(2018). The future of English as a lingua franca? In J. Jenkins, W. Baker, & M. Dewey (Eds.), *The Routledge handbook of English as a lingua franca* (pp. 594–605). London and New York: Routledge.

Jenkins, J., Baker, W., & Dewey, M. (Eds.). (2018). *The Routledge handbook of English as a lingua franca*. London: Routledge.

Jordão, C. (2014). ILA – ILF – ILE – ILG: quem dá conta? *Revista Brasileira de Linguística Aplicada, 14*(1), 13–40. https://doi.org/10.1590/S1984-63982014000100002

Mackenzie, I. (2014). *English as a lingua franca: Theorizing and teaching English*. London: Routledge.

Matsuda, A. (2017) (Ed.). *Preparing teachers to teach English as an international language*. Bristol: Multilingual Matters.

Mauranen, A. (2018) Conceptualising ELF. In J. Jenkins, W. Baker, & M. Dewey (Eds.), *The Routledge handbook of English as a lingua franca* (pp. 7–24). London: Routledge.

O'Regan, J. (2014). English as a lingua franca: An immanent critique. *Applied Linguistics, 35*(5), 533–552.

Otheguy, R., García, O., & Reid, W. (2015). Clarifying translanguaging and deconstructing named languages: A perspective from linguistics. *Applied Linguistics Review, 6*(3), 281–307.

Otsuji, E., & Pennycook, A. (2010). Metrolingualism: Fixity, fluidity and language in flux. *International Journal of Multilingualism, 7*(3), 240–254.

Pennycook, A. (1994). *The cultural politics of English as an international language*. Abingdon: Taylor & Francis.

Roth, W.-M., & Tobin, K. (2001). The implications of coteaching/cogenerative dialogue for teacher evaluation: Learning from multiple perspectives of everyday practice. *Journal of Personnel Evaluation in Education, 15*, 7–29.

Roth, W.-M., Tobin, K., Carambo, C., & Dalland, C. (2004). Coteaching: Creating resources for learning to teach chemistry in urban high schools. *Journal of Science Teaching, 41*(9), 882–904.

Seidlhofer, B. (2011). *Understanding English as a lingua franca*. Oxford: Oxford University Press.

Schmitz, J. R. (2017). English as a lingua franca: Applied linguistics, Marxism, and post-Marxist theory. *Revista Brasileira de Linguística Aplicada, 17*(2), 335–354.

Sifakis, N., & Bayyurt, Y. (2018). ELF-aware teaching, learning and teacher development. In J. Jenkins, W. Baker, & M. Dewey (Eds.), *The Routledge handbook of English as a lingua franca* (pp. 456–467). London and New York: Routledge.

SECTION 4:
Language Cognition and Processing

17 Acquisition of Literacy in a Second Language

KEIKO KODA

As a process of text-meaning construction, **reading** entails retrieving the meaning of a word from its graphic form. To do so, the reader must identify the word based on its phonological and morphological information that are encoded in a sequence of graphic symbols that encodes the word. As such, a reader must constantly connect text information with his/her knowledge – be it linguistic or conceptual – stored in memory. In second language (L2) reading, text meanings are constructed by connecting text information in the L2 with stored knowledge of the learner in the first language (L1). Text-meaning construction in L2 reading involves two languages and is jointly constrained by L2 linguistic knowledge and an assortment of L1 resources available to the learner at a given point in time.

In recent years, **metalinguistic awareness** has attracted considerable attention as a foundational competence supporting word form analysis among reading researchers. Metalinguistic awareness is the ability to think about and manipulate language structure independent from its meaning. Due to its abstract nature, metalinguistic awareness is known to serve as a foundational competence that supports reading acquisition. In an attempt to explore the cross-linguistic interaction in L2 reading, the goals of this chapter are threefold: 1) describing the extent to which L1 metalinguistic awareness is shared across languages; 2) demonstrating the contributions of shared L1 metalinguistic awareness to L2 word reading and learning; and 3) explaining the role of L2 linguistic knowledge in regulating the contributions of L1 metalinguistic contributions in L2 reading development. The chapter first lays the conceptual foundations for examining the unique characteristics of L2 reading, and then describes selected empirical studies that have explored the contributions of L1 metalinguistic awareness to L2 word reading and learning.

Overview of Key Concepts and Constructs in L2 Reading Research

Several concepts are critical for understanding the cross-linguistic interaction between L1 metalinguistic awareness and L2 linguistic knowledge in L2 reading development. This section provides brief descriptions of relevant theories and concepts, including **reading universals,** variation in writing systems, and metalinguistic awareness.

Reading Universals and Language Specificity

According to the universal grammar of reading (Perfetti & Dunlap, 2008), one of the universal properties of reading is its dependency on language in conveying meaning. Inevitably, reading acquisition is constrained by the features of the language in which reading is learned. One such constraint stems from the fact that writing systems do not directly represent meanings because they only encode a word's phonological and morphological information. To gain access to the meaning of the word, a sequence of graphic symbols, such as "cat," must be converted into the sound of each symbol (/k/ /æ/ /t/), and then, into the sound of the word (/kæt/) (e.g., Fowler & Liberman, 1995; Goswami & Bryant, 1992). Learning to read thus entails learning to map spoken sounds onto the graphic symbols that encode them. To be successful, the child must understand that each symbol conveys a spoken sound (the **general mapping principle**), and then learn the specific ways in which the symbols are used to represent spoken words (the **mapping details**).

To grasp the general mapping principle, the child needs to gain several basic insights. S/he must realize, for example, that 1) print differs from other visual objects, such as drawings and posters; 2) that a spoken word can be segmented into smaller sounds, such as syllables and phonemes; and 3) that these sounds systematically correspond to the graphic symbols in the writing system. Because none of these insights is language-specific, once gained in one language, they are readily available in another language, and serve as foundational competencies that support reading acquisition in the language. This, however, is not the case for the mapping details because the relationships between symbols, sounds, and morphemes widely vary across languages. A grasp of the mapping details in a particular language does not of necessity expedite the mapping learning in another language.

In conceptualizing the cross-linguistic interaction in L2 reading, it seems reasonable to assume that facilitation arising from the previously acquired mapping details varies according to the extent to which the sound–symbol–morpheme relationships differ between two languages. The relationship between Russian and Spanish is different from the relationship between Russian and Japanese. It seems logical to postulate that the acquisition of the mapping details in an additional language will be affected by previously acquired L1 mapping skills among learners with similar and dissimilar L1 background. Considering the linguistic dependency of writing systems, it is also plausible to presume that knowledge of L2 sound–symbol–morpheme relationships in the second language governs L2 reading acquisition. Hence, L1 structural insights and emerging L2 knowledge jointly shape the sound–symbol–morpheme mapping skills in L2 reading development.

The clear implication of reading universals is that reading acquisition is constrained by the same set of principles stemming from the universal properties of reading shared across languages. Hence, the foundational skills that are similar across languages are readily available in learning to read in an additional language.

In contrast, language-specific skills emerge through symbol-to-language mapping experience in the target language, and thus reflect the linguistic features unique to the language in which reading is learned. The notions of reading universals and language specificity complementarily provide a basis for conceptualizing the joint constraints imposed by L1 foundational competencies (metalinguistic awareness, in particular) and L2 linguistic knowledge in L2 reading development.

Variation in Writing Systems

As noted above, writing systems do not directly represent meanings. To retrieve the meaning of a word from memory, the reader must analyze its graphic form to identify what the word is through its phonological and morphological information. **Orthographic knowledge** plays a critical role in word meaning retrieval. Orthographic knowledge refers to an understanding of the specific ways in which particular sequences of graphic symbols correspond to phonological and morphological information of words. As such, this knowledge varies widely, but systematically, across languages.

While the basic mapping principle specifies that each symbol represents a phoneme in all alphabetic systems, there is a good deal of variation in their mapping details. As an illustration, Korean and Hebrew are both alphabetic, but the realization of the alphabetic principle markedly differs between the two languages. The Korean hangul consists of twenty-four basic symbols, representing fourteen consonants and ten vowels. Unlike English, the hangul symbols are packaged into square blocks, each representing a distinct syllable. Thus, the hangul system, by design, encodes two phonological levels using distinct graphic units – that is, a phoneme by each symbol and a syllable by each block. Reflecting the dual representations, Korean children develop sensitivity to both syllables and phonemes, and their skills to manipulate phonemes and syllables are equally strong predictors of word reading ability (McBride-Chan, Wagner, Muse, Chow, & Shu, 2005).

Hebrew is a root-derived language and a word's base is a root morpheme. Root morphemes generally consist of three consonants (e.g., *gdl*) that convey abstract semantic information (e.g., "largeness"). Hebrew words are graphically encoded by intertwining root morphemes with word-pattern morphemes. While the root conveys the core meaning of the words formed with it, the word pattern may in some cases carry nothing more than word class information. Because of the prominence of root morphemes, visual identification of the root is central to word meaning retrieval in Hebrew. Reflecting the centrality of the symbol–morpheme–consonant linkages in the root, children learning to read Hebrew are known to develop stronger sensitivity to consonants than vowels (Geva, 2008). Studies conducted with adult readers have also demonstrated that word recognition in Hebrew is affected by word (morpheme) frequency (Frost, Katz, & Bentin, 1987), letter positions in the root (Frost, 2012), and structural salience of the root (Feldman, Frost, & Pnini, 1995). Evidently, the ability to separate the root from the word pattern morpheme is a critical competence in reading development in Hebrew.

The Japanese syllabic script, kana, is known to be one of the most phonologically transparent writing systems. The script consists of 105 symbols encoding 110 syllables (morae). The simple phonological inventory allows the kana script to assign a unique symbol to each of the syllables in spoken Japanese. The near perfect one-to-one symbol–sound correspondences allow Japanese children to acquire kana reading skills quickly with considerable ease. By age 5, more than 60 percent of Japanese children recognize sixty or more (out of seventy-one) basic symbols (Taylor & Taylor, 1995). Ironically, however, the script is not optimal for encoding morphemes because of its phonological transparency. The script cannot discriminate a large number of homophones, such as はし /ha-shi/ corresponding to three different words, including 橋 "bridge," 端 "edge," and 箸 "chopsticks." The use of the kana script is restricted to encoding grammatical morphemes and transcribing onomatopoeia. The morpheme-based script, kanji, is used to encode the majority of content words.

In morphosyllabic Chinese, most characters map directly onto morphemes and their sounds (syllables). In most instances, the sound and meaning of a character are retrieved directly and independently through visual form analysis. The vast majority of Chinese words are bisyllabic and encoded by two characters. Because phonological processing in Chinese words – be it monosyllabic or multisyllabic – entails one-to-one symbol-to-syllable mappings, it is simple and straightforward if the constituent characters of a compound word are familiar to the reader. Morphological processing, however, is more complex and less straightforward because each character in a compound word encodes multiple morphemes. For example, the word for "space" in Chinese consists of two characters 空 (representing three morphemes, including "air," "sky," and "empty") and 間 (representing four morphemes, including "gap," "inter-val," "duration," and "distance"). The ability to select the right morpheme represented by each constituent character in a particular compound word depends on the reader's knowledge of the constituent characters involved and that of the relationship between their meanings (Koda, 2017). Because of the prominence of morphological represen-tation in Chinese characters, sensitivity to the morphological structure of words is shown to be a stronger predictor of initial reading success than is phonological awareness for Chinese readers (Li, Anderson, Nagy, & Zhang, 2002).

The psycholinguistic **grain size** theory (Ziegler & Goswami, 2005, 2006) explains how the consistency with which phonology is represented in orthography affects reading acquisition in different languages. In phonologically transparent systems, such as Italian and Spanish, the symbol-to-sound mappings are efficient at smaller grain sizes (e.g., individual letters). In less consistent orthographies, such as English, the mappings occur at larger grain sizes, such as rime units (e.g., height /h-aɪt/ and sight /s-aɪt/) and syllables. The main claim of the theory is that consistency in symbol–sound correspondences in a particular writing system determines the grain size of the orthographic unit that is optimal for symbol-to-sound mappings in the language. The theory also contends that the child is initially sensitized to larger phonological units, such as words and syllables; and that the initial sensitivity becomes gradually fine-tuned to smaller orthographic units, such as onset and rime distinctions and phonemes, until the child discovers the unit that most reliably represents the corresponding phonological unit.

Metalinguistic Awareness

Over the past three decades, metalinguistic awareness has attracted considerable attention among reading researchers. Bialystok (2001) describes metalinguistic awareness as an explicit understanding of the abstract structure of language. Although it emerges cumulatively through communicative use of language, it is distinct from linguistic knowledge in that it implies an understanding of the structural properties of language that are generalizable across variant surface forms. For example, among English-speaking children, syntactic awareness reflects their realization that the order in which words are presented determines sentence meaning. An abstract notion of this sort contrasts with more specific knowledge of the canonical word order (subject–verb–object) in English sentences. Korean-speaking children's ability to manipulate both syllables and phonemes demonstrates another kind of metalinguistic awareness, namely **dual-level phonological awareness.**

The current consensus is that reading acquisition is fundamentally metalinguistic because it requires the child's understanding of the segmental nature of words and the skills to analyze words into their phonological and morphological constituents (e.g., Fowler & Liberman, 1995; Goswami & Bryant, 1992; Kuo & Anderson, 2008). It has been shown that sensitivity to the phonological structure of spoken words is a powerful predictor of word reading and spelling in the early stages of reading acquisition for alphabetic scripts (e.g., Stahl & Murray, 1994; Stanovich, 2000), and that the ability to analyze words into their morphological constituents empowers the reader to infer the meaning of unfamiliar words (e.g., Carlisle, 1995; Fowler & Liberman, 1995; Tyler & Nagy, 1990). To date, overwhelming evidence makes it plain that sensitivity to the internal structure of words bolsters the symbol-to-language mappings in a number of diverse languages.

Considering the abstract nature of metalinguistic awareness, we can hypothesize that, once developed in one language, metalinguistic awareness will be shared across languages; and that when shared, L1 metalinguistic awareness will enhance the acquisition of symbol-to-language mapping skills in the new language. Over the past three decades, an impressive body of research has addressed the hypothesized benefits of L1 metalinguistic awareness to L2 reading development.

My Work in Second Language Reading

Personal Reflection

When I took my first course on reading in college, I was astonished by the complexity and multiplicity of reading. Until then, I had thought that reading was a single skill along with speaking, listening, and writing; and that it was a receptive skill for uncovering what is presented in a text. Led by curiosity, I read about a half dozen books describing theoretical models of reading. I was surprised once again to learn that all models were built based on research involving native speakers of English; and that their descriptions were not entirely consistent with my experience as a skilled reader of Japanese or English. As a graduate student, I was excited about the prospect of investigating systematic differences in reading acquisition among learners of English as a second language with typologically diverse L1 backgrounds in my dissertation. Since then, I have explored how various linguistic and ortho-graphic properties in the learner's first language affect reading development in a second language.

My Research in the Acquisition of Literacy in a Second Language

This section presents a series of empirical studies I have conducted with my colleagues and graduate students to explore 1) the extent to which L1 metalinguistic awareness is shared between languages; 2) the way in which shared L1 awareness contributes to L2 word reading and learning; and 3) how L2 linguistic knowledge affects the contributions of L1 metalinguistic awareness to L2 reading development. The sections that follow describe distinct ways in which three facets of metalinguis-tic awareness – phonological awareness, orthographic sensitivity, and morpho-logical awareness – are shared across languages.

Phonological Awareness In view of the strong contribution of phonological awareness (PA) to early reading development in a variety of languages, the general consensus is that a portion of PA, an understanding of the segmental nature of spoken words, is a universal competence shared across languages. Since the concept of word segmentation is not specific to any particular language, once gained, it should be readily available in another language. Over the past two decades, L2 reading research has addressed to what extent L1 PA promotes the development of L2 PA and L2 decoding; and how L1 and L2 orthographic distance alters the cross-linguistic contributions of L1 PA to L2 decoding.

To address these questions, Reddy and Koda (2013) investigated how L2-specific symbol-to-sound mapping requirements affected the cross-linguistic relationship between L1 PA and L2 decoding in multilingual students (10–14 years of age; N=52) in a low-income urban community in India. At the time of data collection, they learned to read Kannada and English at an NGO-sponsored school in the community. Kannada is one of the official languages and used as the medium of instruction at the NGO school, but is rarely used for daily communication either at home or in the community. Kannada is a second or later oral language and the first written language for the students. English is also an official language and taught in school as a subject, but it is rarely used in school or in the community. It is a third or later oral language and the second written language. Because the two languages employ distinct writing systems (Kannada using an alphasyllabary and English employing an alphabet), biliteracy development of these students provided a window into the cross-linguistic contribution of PA in L2 reading development. We posed four hypotheses: 1) children would develop both syllable- and phoneme-level PA; 2) the two levels of PA would differently relate to decoding ability in Kannada and English; 3) there would be a close relationship in PA between the two languages; and 4) PA in Kannada would contribute to decoding development in English.

To test the hypotheses, we compared phonemic and syllabic PA in Kannada and English and their relation to decoding in the two languages. Our data showed that 1) syllable-level PA was stronger than phoneme-level awareness in both languages; 2) that the two levels of PA were stronger in Kannada than English; 3) that both syllable and phonemic awareness predicted decoding in Kannada, but phonemic awareness was the sole predictor of English decoding; and 4) that phonemic awareness in Kannada predicted English decoding, but only indirectly, through English phonemic awareness. Collectively, these results provided additional evidence supporting the linguistic constraint on PA development and the resulting variation in the way the two levels of PA are shared between the two languages. As for the cross-linguistic contribution of L1 metalinguistic awareness, the findings suggest that L1 PA and L2 linguistic knowledge jointly promote L2 PA, which in turn, supports L2 decoding development. Hence, the cross-linguistic facilitation from a particular L1 subskill occurs only locally through its corresponding subskill in the target language.

Orthographic Sensitivity   Wang, Koda, and Perfetti (2003) explored the cross-linguistic interaction by comparing the relative impact of L1 orthographic sensitivity on L2 word-meaning retrieval among proficiency matched learners of English as a second language with alphabetic (Korean) and morphosyllabic (Chinese) L1 backgrounds (N=40). As noted earlier, alphabetic systems require intra-syllabic analysis in gaining access to word meanings, whereas in morphosyllabic systems, word meaning retrieval does not entail word/morpheme segmentation as each symbol holistically corresponds to the meaning of the word/morpheme it encodes. The contrast led us to a hypothesis that blocking access to visual and phonological information would induce different reactions among Korean and Chinese ESL learners. In the study, participants were presented with a category description, such as "flower," and then shown a target word and asked to decide whether the word was a member of the category. The task would have been simple if the students had been shown real words as targets. In the experiment, however, the target words were either phonologically (using homophones as targets – e.g., "rows" for "rose") or graphically (using similarly spelled words as targets – e.g., "fees" for "feet") manipulated.

The data revealed that both phonological and graphic manipulations interfered with category judgments of the two groups, but the magnitude of interference stemming from each type of manipulation varied between the groups. Korean learners made more errors with homophonic items (phonological manipulation) while more serious interference occurred with similarly spelled targets (graphic manipulation) among Chinese learners. Although the relative impacts of the two types of manipulation between the two groups were in line with the hypothesized variation, the interaction between L1 background and manipulation type was not statistically significant. The results seem to indicate that 1) the two groups differentially utilize phonological and graphic information in accessing the meaning of L2 words (Korean-speakers relied slightly more on phonological information, Chinese-speakers depended slightly more on graphic information); 2) these differences reflect the variation predicted from the properties specific to their respective L1 writing systems; and 3) proficiency-matched ESL learners are similarly sensitized to L2 orthographic properties because the difference in interference between the two groups was not statistically significant.

The findings seem to imply that L1 orthographic sensitivity has lasting effects on L2 reading development, but at the same time, L2 learners are strongly affected by L2-specific orthographic properties. The non-significant interaction effect between L1 background and L2 manipulation clearly suggests that L2 orthographic properties have a stronger impact, overriding the variance attributable to L1 orthographic experience. In sum, these results seem to indicate that L2 reading development is guided by both L1 and L2 structural insights, sensitivity to L2 structural properties appears to be a dominant force in shaping L2 reading subskills. Thus, the study yielded additional support for a growing body of evidence supporting that L2 reading entails the complex interaction between L1 structural sensitivity and knowledge of L2-specific properties.

Morphological Awareness   In recent years, considerable attention has been given to the role of **morphological awareness** in L2 reading development. An increasing number of studies have examined the contribution of L1 and L2 morphological awareness (MA) to various L2 reading subskills, including decoding (Geva & Wang, 2001; Ramirez, Chen, Geva, & Kiefer, 2010), vocabulary knowledge (Kieffer & Lesaux, 2012), word meaning inference (Zhang & Koda, 2012), and reading comprehension (Koda, Lü, & Zhang, 2013; Zhang, D. & Koda, 2013). Because MA is closely intertwined with vocabulary knowledge and linguistically less independent than PA, it remains unclear what explains the contribution of MA to L2 reading. Are the observed contributions truly indicative of the hypothesized facilitation from transferred structural sensitivity, or do they merely represent a false relationship between the two through third-party variables, such as vocabulary knowledge? To better understand the hypothesized contribution of L1 MA to L2 reading, it was necessary to distinguish morphological awareness (sensitivity to the abstract structure) and vocabulary knowledge (language-specific linguistic knowledge) both conceptually and methodologically.

In an attempt to disentangle the conflation, Ke and Koda (2019) refined the operationalization of MA to focus on its structural properties by minimizing the involvement of a word's semantic information. The refinement enabled us to distinguish MA from vocabulary knowledge a little more clearly than before, which then, allowed us to compare their distinct roles in word reading and learning. We compared the contributions of MA to word-meaning inference both within (L2 MA to L2 word learning) and across (L1 MA to L2 word learning) languages among English-speaking college students (N=50) learning Chinese as a foreign language in the United States. In the study, the participants were presented with a three-character string, and asked to remove the last character from the string, attach it to the end of another character string, and read the new string aloud. The stimuli consisted of two types of strings, including morphologically complex strings each containing a two-character real word followed by a suffix and morphologically simple strings each consisting of three unrelated characters none representing a suffix.

We found that the participants responded faster and more accurately to strings containing suffixes than those without suffixes, and that L2 MA (indexed by performance on the suffix stripping task) significantly contributed to L2 word-meaning inference. However, its contribution was only indirectly through L2 linguistic knowledge. We interpreted the results as indicating that adult L2 learners quickly develop sensitivity to the internal structure of morphologically complex words, as well as the ability to use such sensitivity in learning compound words in the new language. Further analyses revealed that L1 MA predicted L2 MA over and above L2 linguistic knowledge, but not L2 word-meaning inference. These findings corroborate those from our earlier studies, suggesting that metalinguistic awareness is shared between two languages, but the utility of shared L1 awareness is measurably constrained by L2 linguistic knowledge.

To summarize, using finely tuned construct analyses, the three studies described above have enhanced our understanding of the cross-linguistic nature of L2 reading, in general, and the interaction between shared L1 metalinguistic awareness and L2 linguistic knowledge in L2 word reading and learning, in specific. The emerging picture captures the complexities arising from the constraints posed by L2 linguistic knowledge on the learner's access to a variety of resources available in her/his L1.

As shown in the studies above, L2 linguistic knowledge and L1 resources jointly shape L2 reading ability, but their contributions are not as separable and independent as have been assumed. In L2 reading research, L2 linguistic knowledge has been regarded as the single most significant factor for successful comprehension. Considering the centrality of the reader–text interaction in current models of reading, it is vital that we recognize the contribution of L1 resources in L2 reading and an additional role of linguistic knowledge as a medium that grants access to L1 resources.

Moving Forward   To date, research has focused almost exclusively on the cross-linguistic sharing of metalinguistic awareness in word reading and learning. Reading, however, goes beyond word-level processing. To further refine our understanding of the impacts of prior literacy experience, it is critical to incorporate text-level subskills, such as those required for coherence building and inter-sentential inference. Because each of these skills depends on multiple facets of linguistic knowledge, we need to extend the cross-linguistic analysis to identify differences and similarities in the linguistic demands for the acquisition and utilization of a particular text-level subskill between two languages. Such investigations should yield significant additional insights into how L2 reading skills evolve, beyond word reading and learning, which would explain systematic variation in L2 reading development among linguistically diverse learners with varied L1 literacy experiences.

Application Activity

In the activity on the website accompanying this book, you will apply the information in this chapter to the experiences of some real language learners. You will interview a small number of L2 literacy learners and then compare their comments to the concepts and research in this chapter. After hearing your interviewees describe their successes and challenges in L2 literacy, you will be asked to think about how their experiences relate to what you have learned in this chapter about types of writing systems, reading universals, metalinguistic awareness, phonological awareness, and orthographic sensitivity.

Going Further

Second language reading is an interdisciplinary field, including work in psychology, linguistics, and education. Students with an interest in this area should pursue coursework in the foundations of literacy, psycholinguistics, the psychology of reading, discourse analysis, and the teaching of reading. Students with an interest in researching second language reading would benefit from additional courses in experimental design and statistics.

Discussion Questions

1. How might linguistic distance (differences between two languages) affect L2 reading development? What kinds of factors would you need to manipulate to investigate this question?
2. If you are to extend the line of research described in the chapter, which reading subskill would you investigate as a cross-linguistically shareable resource?
3. How could language teachers capitalize on the learner's L1 cognitive, meta-linguistic, and other resources available to adult L2 learners?
4. What could language teachers do to promote L2 metalinguistic awareness?

FURTHER READING

Foundational Readings

Koda, K., & Zehler, A. M. (Eds.). (2008). *Learning to read across languages*. New York: Routledge.

Taylor, I., & Taylor, M. M. (2014). *Writing and literacy in Chinese, Korean and Japanese: Revised edition* (Vol. 14). Philadelphia: John Benjamins.

Recent Publications

Koda, K., & Yamashita, J. (Eds.). (2018). *Reading to learn in a foreign language: An integrated approach to foreign language instruction and assessment*. New York: Routledge.

Verhoeven, L., & Perfetti, C. (Eds.). (2017). *Reading acquisition across languages and writing systems: An international handbook*. Cambridge: Cambridge University Press.

REFERENCES

Bialystock, E. (2001). *Bilingualism in development*. Cambridge: Cambridge University Press.

Carlisle, J. (1995). Morphological awareness and early reading achievement. In L. B. Feldman (Ed.), *Morphological aspects of language processing* (pp. 189–209). Hillsdale, NJ: Erlbaum.

Feldman, L. B., Frost, R., & Pnini, T. (1995). Decomposition of words into their constituent morphemes: Evidence from English and Hebrew. *Journal of Experimental Psychology: Learning, Memory and Cognition, 21*, 1–14.

Fowler, A. E., & Liberman, I. Y. (1995). The role of phonology and orthography in morphological awareness. In L. B. Feldman (Ed.), *Morphological aspects of language processing* (pp. 157–188). Hillsdale, NJ: Erlbaum.

Frost, R. (2012). Towards a universal model of reading. *Behavioral and Brain Sciences, 35*, 263–329.

Frost, R., Katz, L., & Bentin, S. (1987). Strategies for visual word recognition and orthographic depth: A multilingual comparison. *Journal of Experimental Psychology: Human Perception and Performance, 13*, 104–115.

Geva, E. (2008). Facets of metalinguistic awareness related to reading development in Hebrew: Evidence from monolingual and bilingual children. In K. Koda & A. M. Zehler (Eds.), *Learning to read across languages: Cross-linguistic relationships in first and second language literacy development* (pp. 154–187). Mahwah, NJ: Lawrence Erlbaum.

Geva, E., & Wang, M. (2001). The development of basic reading skills in children: A cross-language perspective. *Annual Review of Applied Linguistics, 21*, 182–204.

Goswami, U., & Bryant, P. (1992). Rhyme, analogy, and children's reading. In P. B. Gough, L. C. Ehri, & R. Treiman (Eds.), *Reading acquisition* (pp. 49–63). Mahwah, NJ: Lawrence Erlbaum.

Ke, S., & Koda, K. (2019). Is vocabulary knowledge sufficient for word-meaning inference? An investigation of the role of morphological awareness in adult L2 learners of Chinese. *Applied Linguistics, 40*(3), 456–477.

Kieffer, M. J., & Lesaux, N. K. (2012). Development of morphological awareness and vocabulary knowledge in Spanish-speaking language minority learners: A parallel process latent growth curve model. *Applied Psycholinguistics, 33*, 23–54.

Koda, K. (2017). Reading acquisition in Japanese. In L. Verhoeven & C. Perfetti (Eds.), *Reading acquisition across languages and writing systems: An international handbook* (pp. 57–81). Cambridge: Cambridge University Press.

Koda, K., Lü, C., & Zhang, D. (2014). L1-induced facilitation in biliteracy development in Chinese and English. In X. Chen, Q. Wang & Y. C. Luo (Eds.), *Reading development and difficulties in monolingual and bilingual Chinese children* (pp. 141–169). Dordrecht: Springer.

Kuo, L. J., & Anderson, R. C. (2008). Conceptual and methodological issues in comparing metalinguistic awareness across languages. In K. Koda & A. M. Zehler (Eds.), *Learning to read across languages* (pp. 51–79). Abingdon: Routledge.

Li, W., Anderson, R. C., Nagy, W., & Zhang, H. (2002). Facets of metalinguistic awareness that contribute to Chinese literacy. In W. Li, J. S. Gaffney, & J. L. Packard (Eds.), *Chinese children's reading acquisition: Theoretical and pedagogical issues* (pp. 87–106). Boston: Kluwer Academic.

McBride-Chan, C., Wagner, R. K., Muse, A., Chow, B. W.-Y., & Shu, H. (2005). The role of morphological awareness in children's vocabulary acquisition in English. *Applied Psycholinguistics, 26*, 415–435.

Perfetti, C. A., & Dunlap, S. (2008). Learning to read: General principles and writing system variations. In K. Koda & A. M. Zehler (Eds.), *Learning to read across languages: Cross-linguistic relationships in first and second-language literacy development.* Mahwah, NJ: Lawrence Erlbaum.

Ramirez, G., Chen, X., Geva, E., & Kiefer, H. (2010). Morphological awareness in Spanish-speaking English language learners: Within and cross-language effects on word reading. *Reading and Writing: An Interdisciplinary Journal, 23,* 337–358.

Reddy, P. P., & Koda, K. (2013). Orthographic constraints on phonological awareness in biliteracy development. *Writing Systems Research, 5,* 110–130.

Stahl, S. A., & Murray, B. A. (1994). Defining phonological awareness and its relationship to early reading. *Journal of Educational Psychology, 86,* 221–234.

Stanovich, K. E. (2000). *Progress in understanding reading: Scientific foundations and new frontiers.* New York: Guilford Press.

Taylor, I., & Taylor M. M. (1995). *Writing and literacy in Chinese, Korean, and Japanese.* Philadelphia: John Benjamins.

Tyler, A., & Nagy, W. (1990). Use of derivational morphology during reading. *Cognition, 36,* 17–34.

Wang, M., Koda, K., & Perfetti, C. A. (2003). Alphabetic and non-alphabetic L1 effects in English semantic processing: A comparison of Korean and Chinese English L2 learners. *Cognition, 87,* 129–149.

Zhang, D., & Koda, K. (2012). Contribution of morphological awareness and lexical inferencing ability to L2 vocabulary knowledge and reading comprehension among advanced EFL learners: Testing direct and indirect effects. *Reading and Writing, 25,* 1195–1216.

(2013). Morphological awareness and reading comprehension in a foreign language: A study of young Chinese EFL learners. *System, 41,* 901–931.

Ziegler, J. C., & Goswami, U. (2005). Reading acquisition, developmental dyslexia, and skilled reading across languages: A psycholinguistic grain size theory. *Psychological Bulletin, 131*(1), 3–29.

(2006). Becoming literate in different languages: Similar problems, different solutions. *Developmental Sciences, 9,* 425–436.

18 Distributed Language for Learning in the Wild

JOHN HELLERMANN AND STEVEN L. THORNE

Overview of Key Concepts in Distributed Language

For the average person without training in linguistics, language is usually viewed prescriptively, as something for which there are grammars and dictionaries – for example, rule books that state, definitively, correct forms of the language and how it should be used. What is lost in this standard view is the fact that people use language every day to get things done (order a pizza, ask a favor of someone, apologize, borrow a pencil, greet a friend) without ever consulting the rule books. The anthropological linguist William Hanks (1996) has noted that language has been defined as both an abstract system and an everyday practice; a set of generalizable forms and as temporal action; a cultural fact as well as an individual's utterances. This chapter will focus on the second part of each of these pairs and will introduce theories of, and methods for, observing and analyzing language as it is used in real time. We take language to be the primary symbolic and signifying (semiotic) resource used by humans for meaning-making, one that is adapted to and influenced by the **contexts** in which it is used. Our work is inspired by **ecological** views of cognitive and communicative activity. These views posit that language not only resides in the heads of individuals but is also distributed across and emerges in human interaction with one another and the material world. In particular, our research is informed by **functional theories** of linguistics, such as integrational and **interactional linguistics**, as well as by recent work in cognitive science. Understanding communication and cognition under these theories involves exploring units of analysis that capture coordination between brains, bodies, and the material world.

An Ecological, Interactional, Situated Linguistics

Non-linguists tend to think of language as a static system with rules and singularly correct ways to speak and write. This is, in part, the result of schooling, which teaches students about prescriptive rules for language that are typically based on conventions associated with written language. This characterization of language is also the result of the work of many linguists who have, from the time the discipline was established early in the twentieth century, treated language as, primarily, an abstract system of symbolic representations. In the area of descriptive and structural linguistics, those representations have been analyzed as autonomous working parts of a system of linguistic forms such as phonology or morphology. Within these areas, relatively little attention has been paid to the diverse people and communities using language and the corresponding variability in the use of language across places and social contexts. We consider language to be more accurately described as a flexible and continuously evolving **cultural tool** that is adapted to fit particular contexts by language users. As Vološinov describes it, language as a system of normative forms is a scientific abstraction (1973, p. 98), for it is "solely through the utterance [language use] that language makes contact with communication, is imbued with its vital power, and becomes a reality" (1973, p. 123). In this sense, the presumed "thing" of language is perhaps better described as an action – "**languaging**" (Becker, 1984) – that involves the use of recognizable and recurrent patterns that are "shaped by interactional considerations" (Schegloff, Ochs, & Thompson, 1996, p. 55).

Humans share, to various degrees, physiological attributes, and cultural practices. These common attributes and practices allow language to be shared and produced in a highly collaborative way to perform recognized social activity. Although it may not seem so when producing more monologic talk – for example, making a presentation in front of classmates or speaking in other high-pressure situations – when we use language, we do so collaboratively and creatively within certain constraints. We use language within physical, social, cultural, and environmental contexts and those contexts shape the way we use the resources at hand. Thus, language is a process that is situated in a context that shapes it and at the same time language shapes the situation it is used in. For example, in the situation above, making a presentation in front of classmates, the speech is designed for a particular audience, the presenter responds to questions, and perhaps also relies on visual resources to make points or to remind the speaker of what to say next. Although the speaker may be well prepared, the exact sounds made and words used are adaptations to the time and place the speaker is in. Any experienced presenter will say that the audience plays a large role in how a lecture comes off. Recognizing this is a first step toward understanding language use as an active, collaborative, and situated process. This view of language as a variable process contrasts with the traditional, more common notion of language as a static system.

The notion of language as a permanent, invariable system derives, in large part, from its rendering in written form. Although we acknowledge that written texts are critically important contemporary forms of communication, we remind the reader that written texts are crafted productions (with the exception of, perhaps text messages) with their own structures and grammar. They are characterized by grammatical metaphor (Halliday & Mathiesen, 2004) in which writers use conventionalized language forms in an attempt to reproduce the relevant temporal and spatial context for readers who are temporally and spatially distant. The ubiquity of the technology of writing in literate societies and its visible, material permanence has led to what has been described as a written language bias in linguistics (Linell, 2005). It is also relevant to note that dictates of formal grammatical correctness, typically based on written language conventions, mirror the speech community norms of higher social classes. Attempting to overcome that bias, we are interested in exploring what has been called the primordial site for language and human sociality (Schegloff, 1987), that is, synchronous spoken interaction between people. In this chapter, we discuss this understanding of language as produced for particular situations (**situated**) by cooperating people, a process that has a cultural history but is highly negotiable, emergent, and improvisational.

This primordial site for the study of language features interpersonal interactions and relationships that are the catalyst of language use and development (Vygotsky, 1986). Social interactions are both maintained and produced by contextualized language use. Contextualized language use has been rigorously examined in research from the tradition of **conversation analysis** (Sacks, 1992) and particularly **multimodal conversation analysis** (Goodwin, 2017). This latter line of research has taken advantage of video recording technology (relatively new to the study of language) to show the highly improvisatory nature of language. Researchers using this method examine utterances that are produced in coordination with the context in which they are used, and reciprocally, these utterances also shape that context by the very fact of their being uttered. Even a very different research approach, such as experimental design, shows the mutual influence of text and context despite attempts to control variables so that the phenomenon of interest is not contaminated or influenced by the environment (i.e., Lave, 1993). For example, researchers examining bilingual psycholinguistic processes have found that participants' reaction times are faster when both the context of the experiment (language spoken with the experimenters) and the stimuli were in one language when compared to contexts that used both languages (Boukadi, Davies, & Wilson, 2015). In the natural world, linguistic phenomena are influenced by many physical, social, and interactional phenomena. In this way, language never occurs without a context or history and the research outlined here (as well as our own) seeks to analyze situated language use that is **mediated** by resources such as texts, images, and other people. This approach reconsiders the traditional "bucket" or container metaphor for context (Cole, 1996), – for example, that there is "text" (talk, writing) which is the focus, and everything else around it, the "bucket" ("context"), is for the most part ignored or treated as background in the analysis. In contrast, a distributed, embodied, integrational approach to linguistics treats language ("text") as inseparably and relationally enmeshed with its context of use.

In such a contextualized approach, the starting point for our analyses is the language used for social action that is part of human activity. We investigate **language practices** that may be repeated and are adapted for their context. As the grammar of an individual child's language emerges out of constant exposure to the language(s) around them in the world, the grammar of language (i.e., recurrent patterns of language use) emerges out of society's collaborative and repeated use of communicative repertoires in context (Hopper, 1998).

Learning in the Wild – An Application

The communicative action of languaging, as well as processes of cognition and second language development, are situated in, and in many cases demonstrably interwoven with, material and social contexts. This perspective is informed by approaches that redefine cognition, theoretically and empirically, as situated, embodied, enacted, extended, and **distributed** (e.g., Atkinson, 2010; Bucholtz & Hall, 2016; Clark, 2008; Hellermann, 2018). Distributed and enacted cognition (related terms include extended and social cognition) refer to understanding human actions, such as thinking and communicating, as processes that extend beyond cognitive activity within any single person. The term "distributed" highlights the idea that thinking and doing involve the body and coordination between people as well as with artifacts (i.e., technologies) and environments. From this perspective, neither the brain nor the individual is the exclusive position of cognition; rather, the focus is on understanding the organization of systems of people, situated in material environments, that affect and influence one another in complex and observable ways. When viewed this way, human activity and development are an "ensemble" process that plays out along a brain–body–world continuum (e.g., Spivey, 2007).

The principle of distribution, applied to both cognition and language activity, is not meant to imply symmetry or equal division between individual humans and other people, artifacts, or environments. Instead, the suggestion is that the density of cognitive and communicative activity can shift from brains to bodies and to a range of physical and representational media in the flow of activity (e.g., Cowley, 2009; Thorne, 2016; Thorne & Lantolf, 2007). For example, in our research on spoken interaction on the topic of sustainable technology, we have seen participants discuss bicycle commuting while standing next to bicycle parking racks. During their discussion, they shift their gaze to the racks and then discuss how many bicycles can be parked in bicycle racks available on campus, which suggests that their physical proximity to the bike racks informed the communicative actions that occurred. The notion of distribution suggests an additional consequence, namely that the study of language practice requires units of analysis such as "organism-environment systems" (e.g., Järvilehto, 2009), which describe how change within human agents is accompanied by change to the environment and a reorganization of that organism–environment relation. In the example with the bike rack, while the bike rack itself does not physically change, it becomes a new and more expansive artifact for making meaning. In these ways, distributed, situated, and extended approaches to cognition, communication, and interaction suggest that human action and development emerge from and are enmeshed with specific temporal, social, and material conditions. In the example above, participants talk about specific aspects of bicycle racks while standing next to and shifting their gaze to bicycle racks.

Within **second language acquisition** research, Mondada and Pekarek Doehler (2000, 2004) were among the earliest researchers to develop the position that learning and cognition are processes distributed in, and emergent of, everyday practices of language use. In this view, patterns of language use and understanding are not a priori entities, but rather achievements that are jointly established, maintained, and transformed in ongoing processes of interaction. Mondada and Pekarek Doehler argue for a complementary union between conversation analysis (CA), a method for analyzing talk-in-interaction, and Vygotskian **sociocultural theory**, with its orientation toward the cultural mediation of cognitive functioning and development. They argue for a concept of language competence in which "capacities ... are embedded and expressed in collective action" (2004, p. 515). Further, they contend that the Vygotskian concept of mediation is more than a means for solving problems and creating learning possibilities. Rather, "the process of mediation-in-interaction can be understood as part of the methods by which members construct learning environments, tasks, identities, and contexts" (Mondada & Pekarek Doehler, 2004, p. 515).

In summary: language is a powerful cultural tool for meaning-making that intersects with other semiotic resources in interaction. We focus on language and cognition as situated, shaped by, and shaping the situation in which they are produced. This close entanglement of language, interaction, thinking, and the world necessitates large-scale, intensive, holistic data collection and analytic techniques. In the section below, we discuss exemplar research that will prepare you for the video data analysis activity that concludes this chapter.

Exemplary Research Programs

The work of Charles Goodwin (much of it in collaboration with Marjorie Goodwin) is one of the strongest examples of research on language that focuses on embodied, coordinated, and environmentally mediated aspects of human interaction. Goodwin has investigated human interaction in a wide variety of settings including archeological sites, air traffic control centers, courtrooms, oceanographic ships, and perhaps most notably, in the home with an aphasic language user. In the last of these settings, Goodwin analyzes fine details of language and the context for its use to show how a participant with a limited repertoire of language contributes to complex cooperative social activity. In that research, the participant with aphasia could utter only two words due to a stroke. In his analysis, Goodwin shows that communication can be successfully achieved when mediated by a number of different perceptual and environmental resources. In this case, Goodwin's research shows that a participant who is clinically labeled to be "without language" effectively manages to collaboratively make meaning with others through the use of two words and a range of prosody, gesture, gaze, and objects in the immediate environment (Goodwin et al., 2002).

In a 1995 paper, Goodwin showed the complexity of making meaning on a research ship in which scientists from different disciplines and crew (physical geographers, chemists, biologists, helmsmen, winch operators) needed to coordinate their interaction (lowering a sensor into the desired position near the bottom of the ocean) as their individual research needs can only be met if they talk and work collaboratively. The study shows the complexity of analyzing language and social interaction as it occurs in three-dimensional space using multiple instruments, diagrams, and maps. Focusing on a single actor as is typically done in research is complicated in such a setting because the language use and action of a number of participants must be included in order to understand any one participant's language and social action.

A recent set of applied studies that build on the history of Goodwin's multimodal interaction analysis comes from researchers at the University of Jyväskylä and the University of Tampere in Finland. As with other research from the learning in the wild group, their interest is in how resources from everyday life outside of classrooms can be catalysts for language use and learning (Piirainen-Marsh & Lilja, 2019). Their research involves an intervention that has participants (learners of Finnish in this case) interact with intersecting semiotic fields that result from moving classroom interaction into the local environment and bringing interaction from that environment back into the classroom. The intervention consists of three steps. In step one, the students of Finnish prepare, in the classroom, for a service encounter in a local shop where they interact with expert speakers of Finnish in a real-world context for a particular social action (ordering and buying). In step two, the students conduct the service encounter and video record it. In step three, students bring the video recording of their interaction back to the classroom to view and discuss the language use and social action in their encounter. This intervention provides students with the opportunity to engage in analysis of cooperative and situated social interaction that is purposeful. The video of the interaction then becomes a learning material. These materials for learning are situated and fitted to the particular action and allow students the opportunity to perform the social action in the appropriate context and to actively reflect on that performance through collaborative analysis. In their 2018 paper, Lilja and Piirainen-Marsh show how during these post-recording data analysis sessions, students learn to see embodied interactional routines (rather than just words or grammatical structures) as the objects to focus on for their language learning. When this is recognized, learners can refine their communicative repertoires to have more successful, contextually appropriate foreign language interactions.

Our Work in Distributed Language for Learning in the Wild

Personal Reflections

John Hellermann   My interest in functional/ecological linguistics and learning grew out of my study of music and language. As part of my graduate education in linguistics at the University of Wisconsin-Madison I studied conversation analysis and used those methods to understand how students in a linguistically diverse public high school were socialized into academic discourse registers (Cole & Zuengler, 2008). The method of conversation analysis proved to be appropriate for research grounded in integrational and ecological linguistics because of its focus on the collaborative building of spoken language by two or more participants. I applied this micro-interactional research method to studies of language learning in classrooms. Conversation analysis has not only influenced my conceptualization of language, but also influences the way I work and teach.

Steve Thorne   Beginning with my graduate training at the University of California, Berkeley, I have developed an interdisciplinary research program that investigates technology-mediated educational processes inside and outside of formal education, intercultural communication models of pedagogy, and research that integrates Vygotskian and ecological developmental theories with discourse analytic, usage-based, distributed language, and ethnomethodological approaches to language use and second language development. This research program, in turn, finds its practical application in my commitment to ameliorating educational processes and environments, particularly in the areas of second, foreign, and bilingual language education, technology use in second and foreign language education in universities and schools, and collaborative interventions that involve integrating instructional settings with learning opportunities in the wild.

Our Work in Distributed Language for Learning in the Wild Through Mobile Augmented Reality

In his course on language and technology, Thorne introduced students to the concept of **augmented reality** involving the use of mobile devices to embed and laminate information and queries in specific geophysical locations. Using a free app for the creation of mobile Augmented Reality learning experiences, called ARIS (https://fielddaylab.org/make/aris/), the group designed an augmented reality game for language learning called *ChronoOps* (short for *Chronological Operations*). Augmented reality apps merge virtual images from digital technology with the environment to give users a digitally enhanced experience of place. AR has been used recently in museums, for special events such as the Olympic games, and as a way for furniture sellers to allow consumers to "place" a particular product (sofa, chair) into their home environment. Among AR games, *Pokemon Go* is, perhaps, the most recognizable example. In the *ChronoOps* AR game, players are part of a story line that has them play agents from the future (the year 2070) who have traveled back in time to the present day to document examples of green technology on our university campus that could be instrumental in helping to save the environment for those living in the year 2070. The game is played on an iPhone and uses a GPS map with five numbered locations for players to walk to. Players then access embedded images of the locations they visit and are prompted to orally describe and evaluate the five examples of green technology that make up the game (see Thorne, Hellermann, Jones, & Lester, 2015 for more details). Figure 18.1 shows an image and prompt for the first example of green technology in the game, the practice of bicycle commuting to school and work.

One iPhone is shared among three game players to ensure that cooperative interaction is used to complete the game. This team aspect and the theme of green technology are deliberate design features to engage participants in a pro-social activity and build on our understanding of cognition and language learning being driven by active engagement with the material and social world. Using three video cameras, two of which are mounted on the heads of the game players, we have collected game play data of participants using a number of different languages (English, French, Japanese, Spanish, Hungarian, and German). We have found that the relatively simple game mechanics (i.e., route finding between green technology locations with the goal of submitting video reports to an artificial intelligence in order to save the future of the planet) lead to rich and complex interactional dynamics. Players are asked to find five designated green technology sites and have a GPS map available to them on their phone. However, they are not instructed on which route to take between locations or how to use the map, and cooperatively learn that the zooming in and out on the map will help them see all the locations in context. When players arrive at a location, they are prompted by fairly simple questions about the technology (*What are the advantages and disadvantages of riding a bicycle to campus?*). Players then must collaborate to figure out, and in part construct for themselves, each of these open-ended and underspecified tasks.

Figure 18.1 Image in *ChronoOps* at location 1

Our research has identified numerous systematic interactive and embodied language practices that players use to maintain their physical proximity as a group (Thorne et al., 2015). When a group of three players starts as a team, they hold one another accountable for staying together as a group as they travel across the university campus. When finding their way from one location to the next, players use a number of **mediational tools** including maps (paper, digital GPS, and maps posted on the campus grounds), the city infrastructure (street signs, streets, rail tracks, buildings), and their local knowledge of the university campus as relevant resources in their discussions of best ways to get to next destinations. An often-used mediational tool for interaction is the digital text of the game prompts available on the mobile phone. In our analyses, we noted how the text used in the game was, at various times, read aloud by the phone holder, reread by other members of the group, and we have documented the interactional practices that players use to make the digital text hearable and actionable to the rest of the group, such as how reading the task prompt for a green technology site prepares the group to produce the oral narrative report and to develop strategies for finding next locations (Hellermann, Thorne, & Fodor, 2017).

Once at the location for the report, players brainstorm ideas for the reports in a number of ways including asking passersby for information, using visible environmental features in the area (bicycle racks, public transit hubs, ornamental fountains) and bringing recent news events into their report. When making the report, some groups use cultural knowledge of the genre of news reporting in taking on personae of camera operators and news reporters. We have seen that particular environmental features are repeatedly oriented to and used as a resource for accomplishing tasks in the game while others are noticed by only one group (a solar trash compactor). The broader set of issues we address in our work argues that distributed, situated, and extended approaches to cognition suggest that human action and development are fundamentally interwoven with temporal, social, and material conditions. In this sense, it is not only which various aspects of context are perceptible or potentially relevant, but also what they do or catalyze in terms of interactions with human agents (see Hellermann, Thorne, & Haley, 2019).

Data Analysis Activity

The activity is designed to help you think more about the concepts in the chapter (the distributed, environmentally mediated nature of language) by observing and attempting the first step of a contextualized linguistic analysis: describing what can be seen and deciding on what details to include and not include in a transcription of face-to-face interaction.

Going Further

We recommend that students interested in the research we have described here read work in integrational, systemic functional, ecological, and sociocultural theory to better understand the relationships linking language, culture, and social interaction. Courses in the area of pragmatics (for an understanding of language as social action and indexicality) and spoken discourse analysis (especially multimodal discourse and/or conversation analysis) would be highly relevant. Learning and practicing close transcription of video-recorded interaction incorporating the description of environmental and perceptual stimuli within which the talk and interaction is embedded would also be important.

More broadly, carefully examining the function of language use in contexts of personal interest or societal relevance – for example, in science and mathematics education, legal contexts and courtrooms (i.e., forensic linguistics), news media and advertising – offers applied linguists opportunities to investigate and potentially to engage in prosocial research and interventions that positively transform or enhance aspects of the human condition. Applied linguistics is diverse and includes language-related problem-solving and grappling with educational issues (e.g., L2 pedagogy, assessment, materials development, endangered language revitalization, bilingual education) as well as interfaces with sociological, anthropological, and psychological areas of interest, such as the relations between language and culture, language and power, and language as it relates to perception and cognition (i.e., linguistic relativity). To the degree possible within your educational context, developing interdisciplinary experience in methods, theory, and research cultures is highly recommended for the straightforward reason that many real-world and educationally situated issues are entangled in ways that stretch across disciplinary boundaries. Good preparation, even if not always the most efficient, may include additional coursework, reading, and mentorship from multiple academic departments and/or service learning or internship opportunities.

Discussion Questions

1. Note some questions around language use that you would like to investigate. Then, based on this chapter as well as other readings you have done, formulate a definition of language that you would need as a starting point for your investigation. Having done that, note how one's definition of language affects the kinds of questions a research project can ask.
2. How does a functional/embodied perspective on language and learning allow for new insights into applied linguistics research?
3. In this chapter, we have acknowledged that "language" can be seen as both an abstract and a generalizable system as well as specific actions that occur in particular contexts, places, and times. Describe the advantages and constraints of each of these perspectives and relate them to your analysis of the video data in the Data Analysis activity.
4. If your interest in language use involves how communicative actions are accomplished, how would this affect the units of analysis you would want to use?

FURTHER READING

Foundational Readings

Firth, A., & Wagner, J. (1997). On discourse, communication, and (some) fundamental concepts in SLA research. *Modern Language Journal, 81*(3), 285–300.

Halliday, M. A. K. (1978). *Language as social semiotic: The social interpretation of language and meaning.* London: Edward Arnold.

Hanks, W. F. (1996). *Language and communicative practices.* Boulder, CO: Westview Press.

Recent Publications

Goodwin, C. (2017). *Co-operative action.* Cambridge: Cambridge University Press.

Li Wei (2018). Translanguaging as a practical theory of language. *Applied Linguistics, 39*(1), 9–30.

van Lier, L. (2004). *The ecology and semiotics of language learning.* Boston: Kluwer.

REFERENCES

Atkinson, D. (2010). Extended, embodied cognition and second language acquisition. *Applied Linguistics, 31*(5), 599–622

Becker, A. L. (1984). Toward a post-structuralist view of language learning: A short essay. *Language Learning, 33,* 217–220. https://doi.org/10.1111/j.1467–1770.1984.tb01330.x

Boukadi, M., Davies, R. A., & Wilson, M. A. (2015). Bilingual lexical selection as a dynamic process: Evidence from Arabic-French bilinguals. *Canadian Journal of Experimental Psychology/Revue canadienne de psychologie expérimentale, 69*(4), 297–313.

Bucholtz, M., & Hall, K. (2016). Embodied sociolinguistics. In N. Coupland (Ed.), *Sociolinguistics: Theoretical debates* (pp. 173–197). Cambridge: Cambridge University Press.

Clark, A. (2008). Pressing the flesh: A tension in the study of the embodied, embedded mind? *International Phenomenological Society, 76*(1), 37–59.

Cole, K., & Zuengler, J. (Eds.). (2008). *The research process in classroom discourse analysis: Current perspectives.* Mawah, NJ: Lawrence Erlbaum.

Cole, M. (1996). *Cultural psychology: A once and future discipline.* Cambridge, MA: Belknap Press of Harvard University.

Cowley, S. J. (2009). Distributed language and dynamics. *Pragmatics & Cognition, 17*(3), 495–508.

Goodwin, C. (1995). Seeing in depth. *Social Studies of Science, 25,* 237–274.
    (2017). *Co-operative action.* Cambridge: Cambridge University Press.

Goodwin, C., Goodwin, M. H., & Olsher, D. (2002). Producing sense with nonsense syllables: Turn and sequence in the conversations of a man with severe aphasia. In C. Ford, B. Fox, & S. Thompson (Eds.), *The language of turn and sequence* (pp. 56–80). Oxford: Oxford University Press.

Halliday, M. A. K., & Matthiessen, C. (2004). *An introduction to functional grammar.* London: Hodder.

Hanks, W. F. (1996). *Language and communicative practices.* Boulder, CO: Westview Press.

Hellermann, J. (2018). Languaging as competencing: Considering language learning as enactment. *Classroom Discourse, 9*(1), 40–56.

Hellermann, J., Thorne, S. L., & Fodor, P. (2017). Mobile reading as social and embodied practice. *Classroom Discourse, 8*(2), 99–121. https://doi.org/10.1080/19463014.2017.1328703

Hellermann, J., Thorne, S. L., & Haley, J. (2019). Building socio-environmental infrastructures for learning in the wild. In J. Hellermann, S. Eskildsen, S. Pekarek-Doehler, & A. Piirainen-Marsh (Eds.), *Conversation analytic research on learning-in-action: The complex ecology of second language interaction 'in the wild'.* Cham, Switzerland: Springer.

Hopper, P. J. (1998). Emergent grammar. In M. Tomasello (Ed.), *The new psychology of language: Cognitive and functional approaches* (pp. 155–175). Hillsdale, NJ: Lawrence Erlbaum.

Järvilehto, T. (2009). The theory of the organism-environment system as a basis of experimental work in psychology. *Ecological Psychology, 21*(2), 112–120.

Lave, J. (1993). The practice of learning. In S. Chaiklin & J. Lave (Eds.), *Understanding practice: Perspectives on activity and context* (pp. 3–32). Cambridge: Cambridge University Press.

Lilja, N., & Piirainen-Marsh, A. (2018). Connecting the language classroom and the wild: Reenactments of language use experiences. *Applied Linguistics, 40*(4), 594–623. https://doi.org/10.1093/applin/amx045

Linell, P. (2005). *The written language bias in linguistics: Its nature, origins and transformations.* London: Routledge.

Mondada, L., & Pekarek Doehler, S. (2000). Interaction sociale et cognition située: quels modèles pour la recherche sur l'acquisition des langues ? *Acquisition et Interaction En Langue Étrangère, 12*, 1–18.

(2004). Second language acquisition as situated practice: Task accomplishment in the French second language classroom. *Modern Language Journal, 88*(4), 501–535.

Piirainen-Marsh, A., & Lilja, N. (2019). How wild can it get? Managing language learning tasks in real life service encounters. In J. Hellermann, S. Eskildsen, S. Pekarek Doehler, & A. Piirainen-Marsh (Eds.), *Conversation analytic research on learning-in-action: The complex ecology of second language interaction 'in the wild'* (pp. 161–192). Cham, Switzerland: Springer.

Sacks, H. (1992). *Lectures on conversation.* (G. Jefferson, Ed.). Oxford: Blackwell.

Schegloff, E.A. (1987). Analyzing single episodes of interaction: An exercise in conversation analysis. *Social Psychology Quarterly, 50*(2), 101–114.

Schegloff, E. A., Ochs, E., & Thompson, S. A. (1996). Turn organization: One intersection of grammar and interaction. In E. Ochs, E. A. Schegloff, & S. A. Thompson (Eds.), *Interaction and grammar* (pp. 52–133). Cambridge: Cambridge University Press.

Spivey, M. (2007). *The continuity of mind*. New York: Oxford University Press.

Thorne, S. L. (2016). Cultures-of-use and morphologies of communicative action. *Language Learning & Technology*, *20*(2), 185–191.

Thorne, S. L., Hellermann, J., Jones, A., & Lester, D. (2015). Interactional practices and artifact orientation in mobile augmented reality game play. *PsychNology Journal*, *13*(2–3), 259–286.

Thorne, S. L., & Lantolf, J. (2007). A linguistics of communicative activity. In S. Makoni & A. Pennycook (Eds.), *Disinventing and reconstituting languages* (pp. 170–195). Clevedon: Multilingual Matters.

Vološinov, V. N. (1973). *Marxism and the philosophy of language*. Cambridge, MA: Harvard University Press

Vygotsky, L. (1986). *Thought and language*. Cambridge, MA: MIT Press.

19 | Language, Aging, and Dementia

BOYD H. DAVIS

Overview of Key Concepts and Issues at the Intersection of Language, Aging, and Dementia

There is so much to be learned, so much we don't know about the intersections between language, aging, and **dementia** (the loss of cognitive functioning). The study of language and aging itself is relatively new. In the late 1980s, Kemper and Anagnopoulos called for the study of communicative competence across the life-span, including how older persons disclose "autobiographical reminiscences," interact intergenerationally, and how family members and caregivers talk with disabled older adults (1989, p. 42). If we were to compare two state-of-the-art articles by Heidi Hamilton a little over fifteen years apart (Hamilton, 1999; Hamilton & Hamaguchi, 2015) we would find that they identify key differences in the study of language and aging, such as the rise of interest in their social components. However, the commonalities, the huge areas where we know very little, remain uncharted. In 1999, Hamilton identified three key areas: "the use of language for reflecting and creating identities; and how discourse can reflect the norms, values and practices of society [. . . and] the decline, preservation or improvement of abilities in old age" (cf. Davis & Maclagan, 2016, p. 221). By 2014, studies were blossoming about cognitive aging, social identities, communicative relationships, and what old age might be (Hamilton & Hamaguchi, 2015, p. 706). These studies open the door to new research, new questions, and new applications.

A first question, of course, is where to draw the line that says a person is old or aging. The notion of a specific retirement age, for example, is dissolving. Some people are "old" at 50, others may look but not act or sound old until their eighties. And what do we mean, "act or sound old"? Norms and expectations for being old, acting old, and talking old are changing rapidly. Currently, gerontologists often sort aging populations into young-old, medium-old and old-old: 65–74, 75–84, 85+ (or divided by decades: the 60s, 70s, and 80s); however, aging is highly heterogenic and may depend on social class, race, gender, where you live, who you live with, or your own socialization into what "aging" means. My parents, part of the Greatest Generation (living through the Depression and World War II), thought that aging really didn't start until they were 80 and could no longer chase after their grandchildren; my in-laws thought 62, the typical retirement age for that same age cohort, meant that you sat down and told stories about how things used to be. Norrick (2009, p. 904) comments that many older storytellers contrast "the 'now' me and the 'then' me" with the "'teller' me and the 'character' me." We found this contrast showing up frequently in the storytelling using represented speech from 80-year-olds with early moderate dementia (Davis & Maclagan, 2018b). Indeed, it may have been the socio-pragmatic investigations of **dementia discourse** starting in the mid-1990s that kickstarted the growing number of studies of language and aging, particularly in applied linguistics. Accordingly, the next three sections cover three particularly important aspects of research into language and aging: its interdisciplinarity, the growing use of technology in current studies, and the recognition that pragmatics has importance in understanding the interaction between language and old age.

Academic Fields that Examine Issues of Language, Aging, and Dementia

Multiple fields in linguistics and allied fields such as gerontology and geriatrics, and a range of methodologies offer a wide variety of research opportunities in language, aging, and dementia. There seem to be at least four groups of researchers to consult: 1) linguists who study some aspect of medical or healthcare discourse, perhaps from the perspective of sociolinguistics, cognitive science, or **pragmatics** (language use in context); 2) communications studies specialists who focus on health; 3) clinical linguists; and 4) clinicians themselves (Davis, 2010). Many current studies follow what Mueller and Schrauf (2014, p. 13) outline as the discursivist approach to language and dementia, that is, they use the lens of **discourse** to construct knowledge, because this approach emphasizes:

- social constructionist vs. biomedical approaches to the disease
- preserved abilities vs. irreversible losses
- attention to complex (holistic) cognitive function in meaningful social contexts vs. measurement of splinter skills with artificial tasks
- cognition as co-constructed in dyadic, triadic and group conversation vs. cognition as information processing that takes place within individuals.

Notice that this approach does not block clinical or theoretical approaches to looking at language, aging, and dementia, although it does modify them. An applied linguistics perspective is not exclusively biomedical; instead, as opposed to being purely theoretical, it is empirical or **functional**. It is also, as we suggest above, interdisciplinary. Looking from multiple perspectives at what features of language people retain and how they use them as they age or acquire cognitive impairments gives us greater areas and new questions to investigate about the nature of being a communicating human.

The more we learn about the dementias, the more we discover that they are actually heterogeneous. There are several different types (every **Alzheimer's** organization site lists them on their online websites), and they are not aphasia, although many people with a dementia have some form or degree of aphasia (language impairment). While they progressively impair a person's access to memory which may be deteriorating, they do not block that person's desire to communicate with others. People with dementia continue to want to share parts of themselves, and to be seen as competent and interesting persons with whom a short conversation could be worth a little time. The examples in this discussion will come from research on the language used with and by persons with dementia of the Alzheimer's type, which is the most frequent.

Technology Support

Improved technologies and interdisciplinary collaborations are making it a little easier to locate and identify examples for analysis of discourse by persons who have dementia. Digital **corpora**, searchable collections of electronically archived data, are beginning to be available to researchers through TalkBank (https://dementia.talkbank.org/), the **Carolinas Conversations Collection** (http://carolinaconversations.musc.edu/) and CLARe, Corpora for Language and Aging Research, which combines data and conferences, housed currently at https://wikis.fu-berlin.de/display/clare/HOME. Such sites furnish data for computational and conversational analyses dedicated to developing quicker and more reliable ways to identify dementia in its early stages (see, e.g., Jones et al., 2015; Abdalla, Rudzicz & Hirst, 2018). This data is also being used in efforts to create dialogue for chatbots and interactive social robots. Various sections throughout this discussion lists selected links to internet-hosted video clips, transcripts, and audio; such links often vanish unexpectedly, so one should be prepared to use search engines for additional materials.

Here is an example of computational approaches being used to study language, aging, and dementia. Applied **computational linguistics**, for example, is well described by the explanation at a page in the 2019 website for the Applied Computational Linguistics Discourse Research Lab at University of Potsdam (http://angcl.ling.uni-potsdam.de/):

> On the theoretical side, our work revolves around modeling text structure as a multi-layer phenomenon, with a current focus on coherence relations and their linguistic signals. On the applied side, we work on tasks like genre-sensitive information extraction, sentiment analysis, or argument mining.

Conversation often incorporates question–answer sequences, which can be examined by multiple approaches (including computational) to see if a person's language suggests that something is not right with their aging production. Ever since the **Nun Study** (Kemper, Greiner, Marquis, Prenovost & Mitzner, 2001; Snowdon, 1997), in which autobiographical language samples identified the associations between idea density, grammatical complexity, and dementia, researchers have investigated longitudinal changes in word use and grammatical complexity in authors such as Agatha Christie and Iris Murdoch (Le, Lancashire, Hirst, & Jokel, 2011). What seems ordinary can often be highly useful. A number of studies are beginning to examine how conversation can be used to screen for potential dementia in ordinary visits to a doctor who is not a specialist in neurology; Jones et al. (2015) have found five features that seem applicable and warrant further testing:

> (1) whether the patient is able to answer questions about personal information (for example "how old are you?" or "where do you live?"); (2) whether they can display working memory in interaction; (3) whether they are able to respond to compound questions; (4) time taken to respond to questions; and (5) the level of detail they offer when providing an account of their memory failure experiences. (Jones et al., 2015, p. 3)

What is especially interesting is that, depending on the situation, setting, and participants, the person's responses could be analyzed by specialists in language and social interaction, interpersonal or intercultural pragmatics, discourse or conversation analysis, speech-language pathology, clinical pragmatics, narratology, multilingualism or computational linguistics, and each would find something noteworthy and useful. Again, we see that investigating language, aging, and dementia is interdisciplinary in nature.

Dementia and Pragmatics

We use stories to position ourselves and others as we make sense of our lives and share parts of those lives and those stories with other people. Persons with dementia are not always able to produce a story without some help from a partner. Instead, they can present – with collaboration from a partner – bits and pieces of stories that can lead to others (Davis & Maclagan, 2018a, p. 79). Using pragmatics helps to find those bits and pieces. However, pragmatics in dementia rather quickly becomes complicated. Guendouzi reminds us that in any kind of communicative interaction, "neurotypical" people know – but persons with dementia may not recognize:

1. Where they are.
2. Why they are where they are.
3. Whom they are talking to.
4. Why they are talking to whom they are talking.

(Guendouzi, 2013, p. 43)

Problems with any of these constructs interfere with their ability to make inferences, or handle politeness strategies, or pull up a reasonably "correct" **cognitive schema** to replace a name or an identity in interactions such as this:

R: do you want some more coffee (*looking at Ms. B*) or cookies?

Ms. B: (*looking intently at author*) I know you oh you?

R: yes, I came last week remember?

Ms. C: that's a nice one (*looking at picture*)

R: that's Italy (.) I think.

Ms. A: now (*looks at author*) don't tell me you are from (0.5)

R: England

Ms. A: oh England no I haven't been there and so: what is your name again?

(Guendouzi, 2013, p. 52)

Interestingly, both sociolinguists and clinical linguists focused on speech-language pathology and communications disorders have moved to emphasize the impact of **multilingualism**, particularly on the training needed by formal and informal caregivers on a worldwide basis. In the United States, for example, according to the 2013 Census over 25 percent of migrant residents who are 55 and over are not speakers of English – and 25+ percent of the formal caregivers for care homes are second language speakers. Such percentages take on human faces and human dilemmas in a recent collection on multilingual dementia (Plejert, Lindholm & Schrauf, 2017). This is a worldwide problem. For example, Divita (2014) offers an illustrative set of case studies in a center for Spanish seniors near Paris. De Bot and Makoni (2005) are among several researchers who have called attention to the use by formal caregivers of **elderspeak**, a simplified, high-pitched register often seen as patronizing, with both mono- and multilingual older persons. Nielsen et al. (2011) note that language incompatibilities caused 65 percent of the problems in diagnosing or giving care in thirty-six centers surveyed across fifteen European countries. No matter where you live, aging persons, many with various cognitive impairments such as dementia, are being cared for by those who do not speak their language, know little about their cultural preferences, and may not recognize when they are sad, ill, or lonely.

Applied linguists can develop communicative **interventions** alone or in teams of multidisciplinary professionals. We can help to disperse the stigma of having dementia in the family by helping to reposition and regain the social selves of persons with dementia (Sabat, 2003); we can show how to listen for "small stories" (Georgakopoulou, 2013), those everyday, fragmentary, often overlooked scraps of **narrative** that can give insight to how people learn to handle emerging age identities in ways that support their "doing ageing" (Georgakopoulou & Charalam-bidou, 2011).

My Work with Language, Aging, and Dementia

Personal Reflection

My own work with language and dementia began more than twenty years ago. As an historically trained linguist who typically focused on narrative in sociolinguistic contexts, I had worked with recording, archiving, and interpreting the speech of several different age groups. I was just winding up a collection keyed to conversation and storytelling with multilingual youth (now part of *New South Voices*, https://nsv.uncc.edu/), when doctors found that each of my parents, then in their early eighties, had a different dementia. They could no longer recognize me as anyone other than someone who loved them. I thought that perhaps if I could locate examples of dementia discourse, I could use those to develop ways to communicate with them more effectively. However, it was customary at that time for researchers to destroy or privately archive data after its analysis and published results, which meant that I would need to collect my own. With the help of a nurse practitioner and the director of our university's gerontology program, each of whom introduced me to administrators of memory care residences, I began in 1999 to record naturalistic, spontaneous conversations with an expanding number of residents with dementia, but with one important difference. I wanted the data to be available to other researchers. All their HIPAA-reviewed consents, both by the residents when they were able to go beyond assent to recordings and always by their legal guardians, specified that the recordings and/or transcripts were to be deposited first on secure DVDs and then hosted in a secure digital archive to be housed online and available without any kind of fee to researchers (HIPAA is legislation to protect privacy of medical information: take a look at www.hhs.gov/hipaa/index.html). Once I had recorded consented conversations with several persons with dementia that ranged over two years, I compiled a DVD of audio and transcripts and sent it to thirteen different scholars – who quickly turned into seventeen – in several different fields (phonetics, applied linguistics, gerontology, geriatric nursing, computer science/ virtual reality, corporate informatics, bilingualism, communications disorders, health education and communications studies). They were invited to select conversations as they wished and asked to focus not on what persons with dementia might be unable to do, but on what persons with dementia retain that could be used to enhance communicative interactions. We published our findings in *Alzheimer talk, text and context: Enhancing communication* (Davis, 2005).

My Work with Dementia Discourse

Developing the Carolinas Conversations Collection   Over the next several years, a nursing researcher who was also a sociolinguist, the chair of her college of nursing who was a specialist in dementia training, and I worked to obtain funding to house the growing collection permanently at the Medical University of South Carolina. With the support of the National Library of Medicine of the National Institutes of Health, we were funded in 2008 (G08LM009624) and began training conversation partners in conversation prompts to use with each of two cohorts: two conversations each with seventy-five unimpaired multiethnic older speakers with any of twelve chronic conditions and a longitudinal set of 400 conversations with 125 persons having dementia (Pope & Davis, 2011). Initially, the **Carolinas Conversations Collection**, or *CCC*, held eighty transcripts of persons with dementia (PWD) with thirty-three involved in multiple conversational interviews. Donations made to this cohort are ongoing: from 2008 to 2013, an additional 315 conversations with PWD were collected and partially transcribed and another 120 have been donated since 2014. Currently, the central corpus has 875,739 words, and 692 transcripts with just over 800 hours of transcribed recordings, or 48,000 minutes. The *CCC* is expanding to include several associated corpora: Heather Harris Wright's multifaceted corpus of normally aging persons, 30–90, which is also deposited in *TalkBank*; Sylvie Ratté's Mexican and Ecuadorean Spanish conversations, which are being transcribed, as is Kathy van Ravenstein's collection from low-income older citizens talking about the benefits of exercise for their chronic diseases and their concerns for aging in place.

My Research into Dementia Discourse   My own work draws on sociolinguistics, strongly influenced by my background in historical methodologies, as well as pragmatics; my collaborators are usually, but not always linguists, and are also concerned about positioning persons with dementia in more positive ways. This means our findings are keyed to sociopragmatic as well as cognitive concerns, and are based on naturalistic, spontaneous interaction, which sometimes differs from clinical testing ("just because AD patients performed well on some of our on-line tasks, does not mean they will understand what we say to them in conversation," Kempler, Almor, MacDonald, & Andersen, 1999, p. 244). In addition to maintaining the *CCC*, Charlene Pope and I study caregiver conversations and racial disparities in language of older persons with chronic disease. Jacqueline Guendouzi and I examine pragmatics in dementia (e.g., Davis & Guendouzi, 2013; Guendouzi, Davis & Maclagan, 2015). The research Margaret Maclagan and I have been doing for more than a decade on the pragmatic impact of question–answer interactions has caused us to look more closely at the interaction of discourse markers with pauses and filled pauses and at their use with different formats of narrative and represented speech in formal and informal caregiver interactions, as described below. We want to encourage the development of training that enables caregivers and visitors to change their question-asking habits by moving away from rapid-fire wh-questions that can cause a physical as well as a mental stumble, stop, and fall (Davis, Maclagan, Karakostas, Liang, & Shenk, 2011; Davis, Maclagan, & Shenk, 2014).

Looking More Closely at Constellations of Identities   The term "**constellations**" is taken from De Fina, Schiffrin and Bamberg (2006, p. 2). Here, we are using it to suggest identities forged by connections made among various uses of represented speech within the range of narrative formats offered by speakers with early moderate dementia. "**Represented speech**" is a term for when a speaker uses the speech of another person or persons as part of their own short narrative. For example, "Ms. Tatter" is telling a visitor about when she was a little girl and saw a frog for the first time. She represents what she and her mother said to each other, to show us a scared little girl and a calm, strong mother:

> I ran in the house crying and I said, "that thing just jumped right at me mama." And he said, she said, "Uh, now what did it look like?" And, and I said "I, I can't tell you. It was a thing."
> (Davis and Maclagan, 2018b, p. 2)

Represented speech (RS) is also called constructed dialogue (Tannen, 1986) or reported speech (Cummings, 2016). It typically occurs most frequently in one or more of the narrative formats we identified in a study of thirteen conversations with thirteen different, younger student partners talking with an older white woman with moderate dementia (Davis & Maclagan, 2018a). We argue that persons with early and moderate dementia use all of these formats and that it is incorrect to assume that only stories that a person can tell at length by themselves have value for study and analysis. Instead, we hope to see the development of language interventions which illustrate to unimpaired speakers how to listen for and then help extend the other formats. These are the formats we identified (Davis & Maclagan, 2018b); examples from persons with dementia are in italics, and we have put parentheses around speech from conversation partners:

- narratives which the speakers produce as unsupported monologues that have a beginning, middle, and end
- narratives in which the conversation partner supports the narrator with what are called backchannels (mmm-hmms), repetition, or paraphrases and may even join in with details: *And then after the intermission*. . .(Mmm, you really were enjoying it)
- small stories, which sound like everyday events and are largely ignored, very short stories told "in passing" (Bamberg & Georgakopoulou, 2008): *that day we had the fresh corn for the first time*
- shadow stories "that can stay hidden behind the spoken narrative" unless probed (de Medeiros & Rubinstein, 2015, p. 162): (And why did you hide the doll?)
- narrative chunks, usually either a phrase giving a high point or one offering an evaluation of a longer but untold story, that pops up in talk about something else: *I always did like that movie*
- an occasional chronicle or account, which is largely non-narrative, and which does not contain represented speech: *First you shell the peas and then cook them.*

As people with dementia begin to lose access to working memory and lexicon, well-formed, unsupported monologic stories dissipate. Stories containing represented speech, however, continue to occur and let us infer autobiographical fragments of identities for the teller and biographical elements for the persons who are being told about. These stories are often repeated, becoming rehearsed **performance pieces** as in these two examples from "Lucinda Greystone" roughly five months apart (Davis, 2011, pp. 92, 94; Davis & Maclagan, 2018b, p. 8):

> Her daddy always did tell my daddy, my daddy's name was Hank –"Hank" – and mother's name was Janet, but they called her Jan – he said, "Hank when you took Jan you took my cook, these other girls can't cook nothing." Well then I spoke up and said "Well granddaddy you just come stay with us." He'd come but he didn't stay. [October 2005]
>
> And my granddaddy always did tell me my daddy – my daddy's name was Hank and mother's name was Janet. They called her Jan for sh- short. And he'd say, "Hank, when you took Jan, you took my cook!" Their mother had two or three sisters left at home. "Them other girls can't cook worth nothin'." I said, "Well granddaddy, you'll just had to come eat with us." He says, "Grandma won't let me." [April 2006]

Stories such as these should not always be considered **perseveration**, or uncontrollable repetition, even when they occur in the same conversation. Instead, we have found that small changes in the story signal slightly different "meanings" to be attached. In the first story, we see granddaddy as joking about Jan's cooking as being better than her sisters', and he's ready to come visit. In the second story, granddaddy is represented as making the same joking comment about Jan – but now, his wife (Grandma) won't let him come visit. Tiny differences give us different views of Lucinda, also. She is presenting herself as a character in the story about her grandfather and her father. In the first story, she "speaks up" – almost being sassy as children were not expected to join in adult talk with such gusto. In the second story, she simply represents herself as speaking. Now she is giving an invitation, rather than being an equal character in the story.

Developing Training Materials for Multilingual Caregivers   The training my colleagues and I have developed thus far began with Alzheimer's Association funding for a range of materials for Nurse Aide certification courses at a regional community college in the urban South (Charlotte, North Carolina), and morphed into in-service training workshops for (first- and) second-language caregivers on the job at local memory care residences in the same city. All of the participants needed information about dementia as a condition, the need for conversation during every task-oriented interaction, on-site colloquial uses of language including technical vocabulary, supervisors' ways of giving directions and culture-based expectations for holidays (why red and green in December or orange and black in October?), culturally cued food preferences, and gender-cued restrictions. Instead

You can use conversation to redirect **sun-downing**. Review this scenario:

"Mr. Lee" uses his walker every afternoon to walk back and forth. He seems very confused and even a little frantic. Before you try to redirect his activity, what do you do?

Tell him he has to sit down and be good.
> *This is not a good choice, because it sounds as if you were talking to a child, and he is certainly not a child.*

Ask him where he thinks he is going.
> *Start with something else first. This could be heard as a confrontation.*

Walk beside him and talk about what you both can see.
> *This works well. You can reassure and calm "Mr. Lee" with even a very short conversation. Then you may be able to redirect his activity.*

To keep in mind:
> *Avoid asking Who-What-Where-When-Why questions when someone is walking. Many times, the person who has dementia will stop walking in order to focus on the question, lose their balance, and fall (Davis et al. 2011).*

© Boyd Davis

Figure 19.1 Vignette
(Davis & Maclagan 2018c, p. 217)

of presenting hour-long lectures, we created PowerPoint and video vignettes illustrating a range of issues about space, time, touch, and taboo language and asked participants to share experiences and ask questions. That let us present information from our perspective and learn from theirs. Figure 19.1 illustrates one such vignette.

Data Analysis Activities

On the website accompanying this book, you will find sets of materials: a table of links to websites with transcripts; a table of links to *YouTube* video clips; plus a link to the transcript (and audio) of a full conversation with an aging person (not impaired); and the text of a conversation with an aging person who has dementia. We will ask you to choose a transcript or video, apply a set of discourse-based questions we will furnish, or look at the stories being told, and create a poster or graphic summarizing your findings. We also furnish some photographs for vignettes, ask you to match picture to story, and create a story vignette for one of them.

Going Further

While it's pretty easy to find older people to talk with (try turning around in the check-out line and smiling a hello to start a conversation), you must have permission and their consent to record or study their speech. To gain even more insight into language and aging, become a volunteer with a senior center, a congregate lunch site, or a retirement complex. Like volunteer programs sponsored by hospitals – another good entry point – each will have its own training for volunteers. There is no single program across the country to train you. If you want to look at discourse by persons with dementia, you will need sponsorship, usually through professors in gerontology, psychology, or neurology. But all programs and volunteer opportunities will ask you to do these: spend at least ten hours with one or more people before moving on. Practice active listening. Call people by Mr./Ms./Mrs. and their last name. Don't use "elderspeak" ("Now, honey, wouldn't you like to..."). Don't fire off questions, especially the who–what–where kind. Find at least one thing to compliment. Don't ask if they remember you. Someday you will be old, too.

Discussion Questions

1. What new knowledge will help you combat the stigma associated with dementia?
2. With a partner, trade stories about one of your experiences with older people. What did you talk about with them? What did you learn from each other? What did you and your partner learn from this about language and aging?
3. What stereotypes about aging do you think affect our society as a whole? Do those stereotypes include anything about language? About memory?

FURTHER READING

Foundational Readings

Davis, B. (Ed.). (2005). *Alzheimer talk, text and context*. New York: Palgrave.

Guendouzi, J., & Mueller, N. (2006). *Approaches to discourse in dementia*. New York: Psychology Press.

Hamilton, H. ([1994] 2005). *Conversations with an Alzheimer's patient*. Cambridge: Cambridge University Press.

Recent Publications

Plejert, C., Lindholm, C., & Schrauf, R. (Eds.). (2017). *Multilingual interaction in dementia.* Bristol: Multilingual Matters.

Sabat, S. (2018). *Alzheimer's disease and dementia: What everybody needs to know.* Oxford: Oxford University Press.

Wright, H. (Ed.). (2016). *Cognition, language and aging.* Philadelphia: John Benjamins.

REFERENCES

Abdalla, M, Rudzicz F., & Hirst, G. (2018). Rhetorical structure and Alzheimer's disease. *Aphasiology, 32,* 41–60.

Bamberg, M., & Georgakopoulou, A. (2008). Small stories as a new perspective in narrative and identity analysis. *Text & Talk, 28*(3), 377–396.

Cummings, L. (2016). *Research in clinical pragmatics.* Cham, Switzerland: Springer.

Davis, B. (Ed.). (2005). *Alzheimer talk, text and context: Enhancing communication.* New York: Palgrave.

(2010). Interpersonal issues in health discourse: Caregiver-resident interaction in Alzheimer talk. In M. Locher & S. Graham (Eds.), *Interpersonal Pragmatics* (pp. 381–404). New York and The Hague: Mouton de Gruyter.

Davis, B., Maclagan, M., Karakostas, T., Liang, S., & Shenk, D. (2011). Watching what you say: Walking and talking in dementia. *Topics in Geriatric Rehabilitation, 27,* 268–277.

Davis, B., Maclagan, M., & Shenk, D. (2014). Exploring questions and answers between residents and caregivers. In H. Hamilton & W. Chou (Eds.), *The Routledge handbook of language and health communication.* New York: Routledge.

Davis, B. (2011). Intentional stance, selfhood, and Lucinda Greystone: Twice-told tales from a digital corpus of Alzheimer talk. In P. McPherron & V. Ramanathan (Eds.), *Language, bodies, and health.* New York and The Hague: Mouton de Gruyter.

Davis, B., & Guendouzi, J. (Eds.). (2013). *Pragmatics in dementia discourse.* Newcastle upon Tyne: Cambridge Scholars.

Davis, B., & Maclagan, M. (2016). Sociolinguistics, language, and aging. In H. Wright (Ed.), *Language, cognition and aging* (pp. 221–246). New York: John Benjamins.

(2018a). Narrative and aging: Exploring the range of narrative types in dementia conversation. *European Journal of English Studies, 22,* 76–90.

(2018b). Represented speech in dementia discourse. *Journal of Pragmatics, 130,* 1–15.

(2018c). Challenges and experiences in training international direct care workers. In C. Plejert, C. Lindholm, & R. Schrauf (Eds.), *Multilingual interaction and dementia* (pp. 206–229). Bristol: Multilingual Matters.

De Bot, K., & Makoni, S. (2005). *Language and aging in multilingual contexts.* Bristol: Multilingual Matters.

De Fina, A., Schiffrin, D., & Bamberg, M. (2006). Introduction. In A. De Fina, D. Schiffrin, & M. Bamberg (Eds.), *Discourse and identity* (p. 2). Cambridge: Cambridge University Press.

De Medeiros, K., & Rubinstein, R. (2015). "Shadow stories" in oral interviews: Narrative care through careful listening. *Journal of Aging Studies*, *34*, 162–168.

Divita, D. (2014). Multilingualism and later life: A sociolinguistic perspective on age and aging. *Journal of Aging Studies*, *30*, 94–103.

Georgakopoulou, A. (2013). Small stories and identities analysis as a framework for the study of im/politeness-in-interaction. *Journal of Politeness Research*, *9*, 55–74.

Georgakopoulou, A., & Charalambidou, A. (2011). Doing age and ageing: Language, discourse and social interaction. In K. Aijmer & G. Andersen (Eds.), *Pragmatics of society* (pp. 29–51). Berlin: Mouton de Gruyter.

Guendouzi, J. (2013). "So, what's your name?": Relevance in dementia. In B. Davis & J. Guendouzi (Eds.), *Pragmatics in dementia discourse* (pp. 37–61). Newcastle upon Tyne: Cambridge Scholars Press.

Guendouzi, J., Davis, B., & Maclagan, M. (2015). Expanding expectations for narrative styles in the context of dementia. *Topics in Language Disorders*, *35*, 237–257.

Hamilton, H. (1999). Discourse and aging. In D. Tannen, H. Hamilton, & D. Schiffrin (Eds.), *The handbook of discourse analysis* (pp. 568–589). New York: John Wiley.

Hamilton, H., & Hamaguchi, T. (2015). Discourse and aging. In D. Tannen, H. Hamilton, & D. Schiffrin (Eds.), *The Handbook of discourse analysis* (2nd edn) (pp. 705–727). New York: John Wiley.

Jones, D., Drew, P., Elsey, C., Blackburn, D., Wakefield, S., Harkness, K., & Reuber, M. (2015). Conversational assessment in memory clinic encounters: Interactional profiling for differentiating dementia rom functional memory disorders. *Aging & Mental Health*, *20*, 500–509.

Kemper, S., & Anagnopoulos, C. (1989). Language and aging. *Annual Review of Applied Linguistics*, *10*, 37–50.

Kemper, S., Greiner, L., Marquis, J., Prenovost, K., & Mitzner, T. (2001). Language decline across the life span: Findings from the Nun Study. *Psychology and Aging*, *26*, 227–239.

Kempler, D., Almor, A., MacDonald, M., & Andersen, E. (1999). Working with limited memory: Sentence comprehension in Alzheimer's disease. In S. Kemper & R. Kliegl (Eds.), *Constraints on language: Aging, grammar, and memory* (pp. 227–246). Boston: Kluwer Academic.

Le, X., Lancashire, I., Hirst, G., & Jokel, R. (2011). Longitudinal detection of dementia through lexical and syntactic changes in writing: A case study of three British novelists. *Literary and Linguistic Computing*, *26*, 435–461.

Mueller, N., & Schrauf, R. (2014). Conversation as cognition: Reframing cognition in dementia. In R. Schrauf & N. Mueller (Eds.), *Dialogue and dementia: Cognitive and communicative resources for engagement* (pp. 3–26). New York: Psychology Press.

Nielsen, T., Vogel, A., Riepe, M., de Mendonça, A., Rodriguez, G., Nobili, F., Gade, A., & Waldemar, G. (2011). Assessment of dementia in ethnic minority patients in Europe: A European Alzheimer's disease consortium survey. *International Psychogeriatrics*, *23*, 86–95.

Norrick, N. (2009). The construction of multiple identities in elderly narrators' stories. *Ageing & Society, 29*, 903–927.

Plejert, C., Lindholm, C., & Schrauf, R. (Eds.). (2017). *Multilingual interaction in dementia.* Bristol: Multilingual Matters.

Pope, C., & Davis, B. (2011). Finding a balance: The CCC corpus. *Corpus Linguistics and Linguistic Theory, 7*, 143–161.

Sabat, S. (2003). Malignant positioning and the predicament of people with Alzheimer's disease. In R. Harré & F. Moghaddam (Eds.), *The self and others: Positioning individuals and groups in personal, political, and cultural contexts* (pp. 85–98). New York: Greenwood.

Snowdon, D. (1997). Aging and Alzheimer's disease: Lessons from the Nun Study. *Gerontologist, 37*, 150–156.

Tannen, D. (1986). Introducing constructed dialogue in Greek and American conversational literary narrative. In F. Coulmas (Ed.), *Direct and indirect speech* (pp. 311–332). Berlin: Walter de Gruyter.

SECTION 5:
Language Rights, Power, and Ideology

20 Diversity, Equity, and Language Teacher Education

ROSA DENE DAVID AND KIMBERLEY BROWN

Jimena joins her upper level integrated skills language class that is examining climate change. When she looks at her first assignment, she sees that the instructor has given her a choice of three materials to read or listen to for the task she will complete. She can listen to a podcast, read a blog post, or watch a TED Talk. To demonstrate her learning and indicate her thoughts about the topic, Jimena can choose among three possibilities: she can create an infographic that uses the new information, she can interview a fellow student about this topic, or she can write a reflection that uses the information she has gathered to lay out her current perspective on climate change. Her ability to choose among these possibilities will give her the agency she needs to thrive in her English language classroom.

Overview of Key Concepts and Issues in Diversity, Equity, and Language Teacher Education

What really inspires learning? We know that methods of teaching where students passively listen to a professor's lecture may no longer inspire or engage learners to be active participants in the classroom. Today, educators are learning to move outside of their comfort zones to promote active participation and student-centered learning. However, this approach still isn't enough to engage all learners. A one-size-fits-all pedagogy is unlikely to inspire the full range of students who we may have in our classrooms, whether due to differences in cultures of learning or differences related to learning disabilities.

Now try to imagine a classroom like Jimena's where students have choice in the ways in which they demonstrate learning, and the teachers are committed to promoting creativity, critical thinking skills, and productive communication by any means possible. In this setting, the teacher has to rethink his or her position in the classroom to ensure that all students receive instruction that is not only accessible to all learners, but engages each student and promotes student agency and autonomy both in and outside the classroom. Teaching approaches such as **Culturally Responsive Teaching** (CRT) and **Universal Design for Learning** (UDL) have sought to promote teaching and learning strategies that help all students thrive, especially those who have often been left behind due to differences in engaging with classroom materials. In this chapter, we focus on two such groups: those who have come from different cultural backgrounds than those in mainstream Anglo culture as well as those who are often classified as having learning disabilities. While CRT and UDL differ in their emphasis on the needs of one or the other group, the two approaches are connected by their goal to differentiate classroom instruction to meet the needs of a diverse range of learners.

Universal Design for Learning and Culturally Responsive Teaching are approaches that can co-occur or not. CRT allows all students agency and presence in the classroom. CRT is not merely based on teaching to students' cultural differences, but is rooted in the belief that instruction must be delivered in a manner that is equitable to all learners. Likewise, lessons from Universal Design for Learning do not only benefit learners with disabilities. They can also allow students from different cultural backgrounds as well as other students to step more effectively into their language learning classrooms by allowing for choice and individual agency.

Language teachers' pedagogical choices have a significant impact on the accessibility of their classrooms:

> Faculty play social roles in determining how learners in their classrooms become part of or are excluded from the classroom community and ultimately from learning. When faculty are insufficiently familiar with the needs of particular groups of students and have not received institutional support for acquiring greater familiarity with current best practices or using such practices to restructure their classes, the faculty unknowingly exclude multilingual students and students with learning disabilities from becoming full members of the classroom community. (Brown, David, & Smallman, 2017, p. 83)

CRT and UDL can assist in successful delivery of instruction for all learners, helping teachers ensure that their classrooms are accessible and empowering to all students. Together, these concepts provide the intellectual pushback to neoliberal education to allow teachers to grant greater agency to their learners (Sleeter, 2012), allowing learners to "see [themselves] as responsible for and capable of bringing about educational change" (Villegas and Lucas, 2002, p. 21). Kieran and Anderson (2018) suggest that teachers who are familiar with both concepts can draw upon them equally as strategies to promote classroom equity. Unfortunately, neither of these concepts are well represented in language teacher education beyond the K–12 level.

Cultural Diversity and Culturally Responsive Teaching

The first approach, Culturally Responsive Teaching (CRT), reflects the fact that the home cultures of both teachers and learners, whether in an **English as a Foreign Language** (EFL) context or an **English as a Second Language** (ESL) context, frame preferred ways of engaging in classroom activities. Whether a student is far from home with a teacher who is in their home country or a teacher has left their home country to teach English in another country, classroom expectations are framed by culture. CRT is "a pedagogy that recognizes the importance of including students' cultural references in all aspects of learning" (UDL – Brown University; adapted from Ladson-Billings, 1994). "All aspects of learning" refers to socioemotional, relational, and cognitive dimensions (Hammond, 2015, p. 4).

For Hammond (2015) the most critical dimensions of a culturally responsive framework are awareness of **cultural archetypes**, **learning partnerships**, **information processing**, and **community of learning** development. Awareness of cultural archetypes means that teachers recognize core values of each learner's culture (Smolicz, 1981). Learning partnerships are between the teacher and the learner: they demonstrate to learners that their voices matter. Information processing involves presenting information in a way that learners may be accustomed to culturally as well as providing content that may be linked to students' home cultures. Community of learning development draws on practices articulated by Lave and Wenger (1991) and fosters true links among learners in the classroom. All four dimensions need to be represented in an effective language learning classroom.

Applied linguists who intend to teach need to attend to these dimensions. In the ESL language classroom, we can see what this means by asking the question "What does it mean to be a speaker of English?" A CRT-infused response is that for all learners, assisting them in retaining their sense of self, embracing the value of the community they have come from, and learning that English belongs to them (Kachru, 1988) is paramount. Allowing students to reach their full potential does not mean pushing them into the mold of the dominant culture – a practice reinforced in language classes for immigrants in the twentieth century (cf. Ruiz, 1996). Rather, it means recognizing that one does not have to let go of one's home language: a person can be multilingual and multicultural without behaving identically to members of the dominant culture.

A teacher crafting a language lesson following these principles would include material reflective of their learners, classroom interactions reflective of learner experience and expectations in the classroom, and a classroom dynamic that sees difference as a resource rather than a problem. An instructor could adopt a wide range of strategies to do this. They could, for example, offer students two kinds of final assignment options, allow multiple students to work together on a single paper, or mention areas relevant to students' cultures of origin in class. CRT entails a multidimensional approach that draws on a range of different modes. If a student comes from a highly oral culture, asking them to present an assignment orally instead of in a written paper could represent such an approach.

Learning Disabilities and Universal Design for Learning

The second approach, **Universal Design for Learning (UDL)**, emphasizes the needs of students with learning disabilities. Since the passage of the Americans with Disability Act in 1990, educators in the K–12 system in the United States have been engaged in delivering course material in a manner that meets the needs of particular learners with articulated disabilities. These may range from physical issues to psychological issues. The United Nations Convention on the Rights of Persons with Disabilities (2006) has defined an individual with a **disability** as someone "who may have long-term physical, mental, intellectual, or sensory impairments which in interaction with various barriers may hinder their full and effective participation in society on an equal basis with others" (p. 4). **Learning disabilities** are best understood as hidden disabilities, undetectable by the human eye, that make it difficult for users to process information. In its broadest form, the term "learning disability" describes an individual who may face a wide variety of challenges in regard to one aspect of learning that could affect the acquisition, retention, understanding, organization, or use of verbal and/or non-verbal information (Learning Disabilities Association of Ontario, 2001). Other terms frequently used interchangeably include "learning differences," "learning difficulties," and "learning disorders." For this chapter, we will use the phrase "learning disabilities" for the sake of consistency.

Language learners with a learning disability such as **dyslexia** may experience linguistic issues in areas such as segmenting words into phonological units or keeping verbal material in phonological short-term memory, while others may read at slower speeds, or have issues with articulation, slow speech, or slow word retrieval. Others may have difficulties with spelling and recognizing words and may also rely on a smaller range of vocabulary words. Non-linguistic issues that a language learner may endure could be a smaller span of working memory; difficulty with sustained attention; and difficulties with penmanship, time management, and automatizing new skills.

UDL originally came from the field of architecture as a way to allow individuals with physical disabilities equal access to spaces, but it has since come to represent a series of educational choices designed to provide greater access to all learners, including those with learning disabilities. The Higher Education Act of 2008 describes UDL as follows:

> The term UNIVERSAL DESIGN FOR LEARNING means a scientifically valid framework for guiding educational practice that: (A) provides flexibility in the ways information is presented, in the ways students respond or demonstrate knowledge and skills, and in the ways students are engaged; and (B) reduces barriers in instruction, provides appropriate accommodations, supports, and challenges, and maintains high achievement expectations for all students, including students with disabilities and students who are limited English proficient.
>
> (Higher Education Opportunity Act, 2008)

The central notion of UDL is that all learners benefit from what would once have been an **accommodation** for a single individual. Imagine, for example, a train station with multiple ways to get up and down the train platform: escalator, ramp, elevator, and stairs. Anyone can choose one of these means to get downstairs. A parent might choose to use the ramp or the elevator depending on how tired they are – not only because they have a stroller. Likewise, UDL allows all learners to have a full range of options for their learning.

The notion of flexibility in how information is presented means that learners must have access to what the Center for Applied Special Technology (CAST) terms "**multiple means of representation**" (2011). This dimension relates to teacher obligations: they need to provide access to class content and information in a variety of ways that complement one another. For example, learners would only see a TED talk if the transcription were available simultaneously and could elect to have the transcripts in hand in addition to on screen.

The notion of reducing barriers is captured by the CAST (2011) recommendation to "provide multiple means of action and expression." This aspect is how learners demonstrate mastery of classroom content. For language learners, this could be what is termed a "**negotiated syllabus**" where students have choice in assignments to complete and can recommend new ones themselves. An example in a speaking assignment would allow learners to choose to do a podcast or video, speak to the teacher one-on-one, or complete that task in the classroom with classmates.

The last dimension of UDL is to "provide multiple means of engagement." This involves how student choice and interest are incorporated into instruction. Students can collaborate together and share ideas to create a positive learning environment. For language learners this might involve learning stations where students choose three out of four stations to visit. It might involve students deciding to represent their learning together or creating their own rubric to assess an assignment.

When practitioners in applied linguistics bring UDL principles into their teaching and training, students have options in terms of materials, and piece by piece, scaffolding is provided to all learners to help them complete all assignments. Development of learner agency and autonomy are evident throughout the curriculum presented. Utilizing key aspects of UDL in the language classroom means that information would typically be presented in multiple ways, that learners would often have choices of material to use or assignments to complete, and everyone would benefit from these strategies, not simply individuals with learning disabilities. For example, many course syllabi have "Learning Outcomes" listed. They often begin with phrases such as "Students will be able to…" These statements, while accurate from a teacher's perspective, often mean very little to students and are not engaging. A better choice may be to include "Guiding Questions," framed in a manner that draws students in more. Moreover, guiding questions should be written to benefit the students' overall understanding of the learning objectives and should not be written solely from the teacher's perception or for the teacher's grading schema.

Combining Universal Design for Learning, Culturally Responsive Teaching, and Teacher Training

Applied linguistics is a field that uses language to mediate social problems (Davies, 2007), and the principles of Culturally Responsive Teaching and Universal Design for Learning bring this mediation into the classroom. As Sierra Piedrahita urges us:

> [L]anguage teachers should learn to incorporate more appropriate teaching practices into their teaching repertoire to be able to educate the kind of critical and active citizens our society demands. Although this is also the job of teacher education programs, professional development programs need to include the knowledge, skills, and dispositions related to social justice that may allow teachers to challenge the injustices and inequalities present on a daily basis in different spheres of society. If teaching is a political act, then a social justice perspective can contribute to the kind of preparation teachers require to move to more equal and just teaching practices, which, at the same time, will set an example for students to follow inside and outside their schools.
>
> (Sierra Piedrahita, 2016, p. 203)

Inclusive education has become a buzzword in the K–12 world, yet teachers are often ill-equipped to implement differentiated learning strategies in their classrooms due to lack of training, time constraints, lack of support, fixed curricula, and classroom materials (Haas and Esparza Brown, 2019). Moreover, in the realm of foreign language teaching, educators everywhere struggle to support students with difficulties acquiring an additional language and sometimes question whether a student in their classroom is having issues learning the target language or if these issues may be signs that the student may have a learning disability that has gone undetected in their first language. Being able to distinguish between language learning features and signs of a potential disability should be a part of general teacher education programs and more importantly at the forefront of policy makers' minds, yet the research in this area is underexplored and questions go unanswered.

Teachers who have not been introduced to key concepts in general education will not have a comprehensive understanding of inclusive education practices, even though they will be expected to be able to teach up to forty-five students in one classroom from a variety of socioeconomic, cultural, and academic backgrounds. When thinking solely about the number of students in a class who may face challenges due to a diagnosed or undiagnosed learning disability, it is estimated that anywhere from 10 to 15 percent of any given student population will experience some variation of difficulty (Kormos & Smith, 2012; Root, 1994). It is key that educators have some kind of understanding of how learning disabilities can generally affect a student's overall ability to demonstrate understanding in both their first language and their additional language. When teachers are introduced to teaching

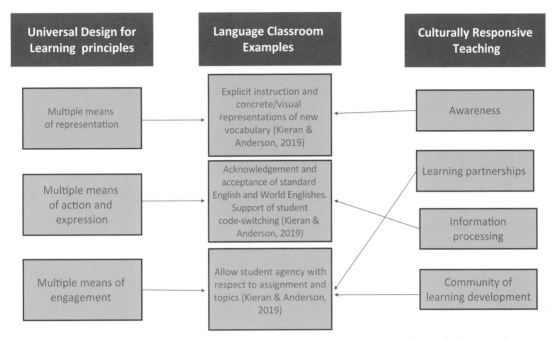

Figure 20.1 Synergy between Universal Design for Learning and Culturally Responsive Teaching in the language classroom

strategies that promote UDL and differentiated instruction for the ELT classroom, their overall teaching practice improves as well, as these strategies can be incorporated into any classroom and will promote the success of all students in any learning environment, not simply the success of those who are perceived to be struggling. Figure 20.1 illustrates how UDL and CRT can be used in complementary ways to achieve these goals in the language classroom.

Bringing Learning Disabilities to the Forefront

One key supporter in the development of teacher training programs with a focus on students with learning disabilities in Latin America has been Gonzalo Fortun, who is an English Language Programs Specialist for the US Embassy in La Paz, Bolivia. Fortun has supported numerous projects within the region to ensure that English language educators in Bolivia have sufficient information and strategies to serve these underrepresented populations, noting that

> an educator's mission is no longer to try to fix the student, but to fix the environment. Teacher education and training needs to be a continuous process so that teachers make their students' learning environment as welcoming and friendly as possible for students to develop themselves as autonomous learners. (Gonzalo Fortun, personal communication, May 28, 2019)

The work of Maiko Hata to ensure that students with disabilities are represented within the TESOL International Association is also monumental as she assembled a team of like-minded individuals to create a TESOL interest section called Supporting Students with Disabilities (SSDIS). This new interest section was approved in November 2018 and had its position within the TESOL International Association at the international TESOL Conference held in Atlanta, Georgia in March 2019. When asked why she chose to devote her time to creating the TESOL interest section, Hata replied:

> Even though people with disabilities are considered to be the largest minority group in the world, this segment has not been receiving almost any attention in the field of TESOL. When I started researching how I can support my adult-aged international students with disabilities, I was unable to find too much that was relevant – it was all about K-12 or English-speaking adult students with documented disabilities. Creating a platform for collaboration made sense, as this would enable all of us to learn what helps, across contexts. (Maiko Hata, personal communication, May 22, 2019)

Our Work in Language, Disability, and Teacher Education

Personal Reflections

Rosie David   As a little girl, I struggled to learn how to read. My memories of primary school include stumbling over words as I tried to read out loud in class and then tracing the illustrations of cartoons on the opposing page with my index finger. My mother understood I was struggling to learn to read despite her best efforts to support me. In March 1990, I was diagnosed with intermittent central suppression, eye movement deficiency, accommodative insufficiency, hyperopia (farsightedness), and convergence insufficiency. This terminology meant absolutely nothing to anyone besides my optometrist, who then used the word "dyslexia" to describe my learning differences. Dyslexia then defined me not only as a student, but also as a child. I spent the equivalent of over two years of my life in vision therapy, both as a child and as an adult. There was a period of time where I inherently believed that I had overcome my battle with dyslexia, but I have learned that:

> To define dyslexia in terms of reading test performance is rather like defining measles as an increase in body temperature. Raised temperature, however, is merely a sign of the infection, not the illness itself. Decreasing the temperature is usually a good thing, but it does not cure the illness. All the knowledge accumulated in dyslexia research indicates that dyslexia is not a disease which comes with school and goes away with adulthood. It is not a temporary childhood affliction; it is a life-long burden. (Frith, 1999, p. 209)

Learning how to self-advocate as a student became a key component of my success. Thus, being able to articulate how I learned and what kinds of accommodations would help me not only succeed, but thrive became ingrained into my own teaching practices as an EFL instructor. I have focused my research agenda on supporting students with learning disabilities and have sought to do so by exploring multisensory and multimodal teaching techniques, inclusive education, and universal design. My disability no longer hinders me. It is a gift.

Kimberley Brown In spite of teaching undergraduate and graduate students in two disciplines (applied linguistics and international studies), many of whom had articulated accommodation agreements with the campus Disability Resource Center, I had never heard of Universal Design before 2014. A complaint was filed against me by a student suggesting discrimination based on an undisclosed disability and filed with the campus office of Global Inclusion and Diversity. In the process of resolving the complaint by compliance with a campus recommendation, I began researching learning disabilities and psychological differences. I struggled to find links between university-level instruction, English language teaching pedagogy, and materials design. I also had enough students with learning disabilities who were being harmed or underserved to become really frustrated with my institution. I began to work collaboratively with Rosie, my co-author, on a series of academic publications and presentations highlighting the importance of this work. I was introduced to a colleague at the University of Oregon, Maiko Hata, who was key in establishing the Supporting Students with Disabilities Interest Section (SSDIS) within TESOL. I was appointed as scholar-in-residence for Culturally Appropriate Teaching in the Office of Academic Innovation at my university for the calendar years 2017–2018 and 2018–2019. Both my research and pedagogical practices now are inextricably linked to the areas discussed above. I advise MA students and design classroom practices to reinforce the role of these philosophical concepts to bring greater equity to the lives of both pre-service teachers and their learners.

Rosie David's Work in Language, Disability, and Teacher Education

In Latin America, English language teacher-training initiatives are on the rise due to the aim to strengthen bilingualism in the region. In Mexico, I served as an English Language Fellow for the Department of State's English Language Program for two years. English as a foreign language (EFL) has been a part of the Ministry of Education curriculum at the secondary level since 1954 (Secretaría de Educación Pública, 2010); however, the desire to offer English to students in primary school is a relatively new concept and has created a need for a larger number of bilingual teachers who are trained not only to teach general education, but also English as a second language (ESL). Many teachers working in the public sector lack formal training in general education and do not have a background in education; thus, they have not been introduced to key concepts in ESL education, let alone Culturally Responsive Teaching and Universal Design for Learning. In many cases, teachers working in the public school system will deliver English classes in Spanish, as they often do not feel prepared to teach an additional language. English is treated as a filler course for teachers who may not have enough teaching hours or speak "some" level of the English language. One of the major challenges that the Ministry of Education faces is creating teacher-training opportunities that support a comprehensive understanding of educational practices and emphasize the importance of English language teaching methodology.

With the increase in bilingual education programs in Latin America, many teachers are seeing that their students often struggle with the phonological patterns of English (which is not spelled phonetically, as Spanish is) and feel ill-equipped to support their students in the language acquisition process. In order to support in-service teachers in Mexico, I implemented a series of teacher training workshops on a wide range of topics and opted to present at a local conference on how to support students with potential disabilities. The number of participants outnumbered the number of chairs. After finishing this workshop, I was continually approached by different educators or schools asking for help, as they too struggled to support the growing number of English language learners (ELLs) with undocumented learning disabilities. As an educator, supporting students with learning disabilities had already become a vocal part of my career, though I did not expect it to grow from a passion into a response to an increasing need that had to be addressed.

My work has taken me all over Latin America. I was invited on two different occasions to support public school teachers in Baja California Sur, Mexico in order to ensure that they had some point of reference to ensure that they were meeting the needs of their students. Additionally, I was invited to provide different teacher-training workshops in Durango, Guadalajara, Queretaro, and Merida. I also participated as an invited speaker at numerous conferences in Mexico, Bolivia, and Honduras. Among the areas covered were theoretical dimensions of learning disabilities, the relationship of government policy to classroom practices, practically scaffolded assignments for teachers to infuse these principles into their teaching, and final projects to meet specific needs of teachers and learners in their own classrooms. This work has continued to grow and has also reached teachers in Colombia and Peru. Today I serve as associate editor of the *Latin American Journal of Content and Language Integrated Learning* and in 2020 we will release a special issue about supporting students with disabilities. This work is valued and has a place in the international dialogue taking place among educators seeking solutions that help them support all of their learners who seek to acquire additional languages.

Data Analysis Activity

In this exercise, you will examine two course syllabi, which are available on the website accompanying this book. One of these two syllabi was designed with a specific focus on integrating principles of Universal Design for Learning and Culturally Responsive Teaching, while the other represents a more typical syllabus. In this activity, you will compare the two syllabi to see how UDL and CRT principles affect the design of course materials by comparing elements that are present in one syllabus and absent in the other.

Going Further

The need to support students with learning disabilities in the English language classroom is growing rapidly, as the international educational community tries to address issues of inclusion across academic levels. While the role of culture in language teaching has long been recognized in the fields of applied linguistics and TESOL, there has been relatively little research done to support English language learners with learning disabilities. However, it is also undeniable that there is a growing interest in this area of study. There is a plethora of resources for individuals who are interested in further exploring learning disabilities, though these materials are generally rooted in general education or in psychology. Good sources of information could be your school's Disability Resource Center or Center for Teaching and Learning, as they often provide support, additional training, and resources for students and faculty alike. Concrete activities and courses you should consider if you wish to strengthen your expertise in these areas include: contacting the Center for Teaching and Learning on your campus, reviewing your library website for special guides, checking for a course offering Universal Design in your School of Education, checking online for MOOC offerings in this area, checking about doing an independent study in this area with a faculty member, and becoming a student member of TESOL and joining the Supporting Students with Disabilities Interest Section (SSDIS).

Discussion Questions

1. Think of an assignment you have completed for a class that did not go well. Are there instructions or adaptations to the assignment that would have enabled you to succeed? Name one or two of them.

2. Think of an academic setting you were in that did not support students whose first language is not English in the same way as other students were supported. What aspects of CRT or UDL could remedy this? Name one aspect from each of these.

3. Critical applied linguistics is concerned with social justice and inequality. How can your growing familiarity with CRT and UDL play a role in remediating these problems in your program of study and in a rapidly globalizing world?

FURTHER READING

Foundational Readings

McCardle, P., Mele-McCarthy, J., Cutting, L., & Leos, K. (Guest Eds.). (2005). Learning disabilities in English language learners: Research issues and future directions (special series). *Learning Disabilities Research and Practice, 20*, 1–78.

Rao, K., & Torres, C. (2017). Supporting academic and affective learning processes for English language learners with Universal Design for Learning. *TESOL Quarterly, 51*(2), 460–472.

Vavrus, M. (2008). Culturally responsive teaching. In T.C. Good (Ed.), *21st Century education: A reference handbook* (vol. 2) (pp. 49–57). Thousand Oaks, CA: Sage.

Recent Publications

Baumgardner, D., Bay, M., Lopez-Reyna, N., Snowden, P., & Maiorano, M. (2015). Culturally responsive practice for teacher educators: Eight recommendations. *Multiple Voices for Ethnically Diverse Exceptional Learners, 15*(1), 44–58.

Edyburn, D. (2010). Would you recognize Universal Design for Learning if you saw it? Ten propositions for new directions for the second decade of UDL. *Learning Disability Quarterly, 33*(Winter), 33–41.

Haas, E., & Esparza Brown, J. (2019). *Supporting English learners in the classroom: Best practices for distinguishing language acquisition from learning disabilities.* New York: Teachers' College.

REFERENCES

Brown, K., David, R., & Smallman, S. (2017). Adopting the principles of Universal Design for Learning (UDL) into international and global studies' programs and curriculum. *Journal of International and Global Studies, 9*(1), 77–92.

CAST (2011). Universal Design for learning guidelines version 2.0. Wakefield, MA: Author. Retrieved from http://udlguidelines.cast.org/

Davies, A. (2007). *An introduction to applied linguistics: From practice to theory* (2nd edn). Edinburgh: Edinburgh University Press.

Frith, U. (1999). Paradoxes in the definition of dyslexia. *Dyslexia, 5*, 192–214.

Haas, E., & Esparza Brown, J. (2019). *Supporting English learners in the classroom: Best practices for distinguishing language acquisition from learning disabilities.* New York: Teachers' College Press.

Hammond, Z. (2015). *Culturally responsive teaching and the brain: Promoting authentic engagement and rigor among culturally and linguistically diverse students.* Thousand Oaks, CA: Corwin.

Higher Education Opportunity Act. (2008). Retrieved from www.udlcenter.org/glossaries/glossary_eng#higher_education_opportunity_act_2008

Kachru, B. (1988). What is a World Englishes perspective? *ERIC/CLL News Bulletin, 12*(1), 1, 3, 4, 8.

Kieran, L., & Anderson, C. (2019). Connecting universal design for learning with culturally responsive teaching. *Education and Urban Society, 51*(9), 1202–1216. https://doi.org/10.1177/0013124518785012

Kormos, J., & Smith, A. M. (2012). *Teaching languages to students with specific learning differences.* Toronto: Multilingual Matters.

Ladson-Billings, G. (1994). *The dreamkeepers.* San Francisco: Jossey-Bass.

Lave, J., & Wenger, E. (1991). *Situated learning: Legitimate peripheral participation.* Cambridge: Cambridge University Press.

Learning Disabilities Association of Ontario. (2001). Learning disabilities: A new definition. Retrieved from www.ldao.ca/documents/Definition_and_Suporting%20Document_2001.pdf

Root, C. (1994). A guide to learning disabilities for the ESL classroom practitioner. *TESJ-EJ, 1*(1). Retrieved from http://www.tesl-ej.org/ej01/a.4.html

Ruiz, R. (1996). English officialization and transethnification in the USA. Paper presented at the annual meeting of the American Anthropological Association, San Francisco, November.

Secretaria de Educación Pública (SEP). (2010). *Programa Nacional de Inglés en Educación Básica: Informe de resultados de la etapa piloto.* México, DF: SEP.

Sierra Piedrahita, A. M. (2016). Contributions of a social justice language teacher education perspective to professional development programs in Colombia. *Profile: Issues in Teachers' Professional Development, 18*(1), 203–217. https://doi.org/10.15446/profile.v18n1.47807

Sleeter, C. (2012). Confronting the marginalization of culturally responsive teaching. *Urban Education, 47*(3), 562–584.

Smolicz, J. (1981). Core values and cultural identity. *Ethnic and Racial Studies, 4*(1), 75–90. https://doi.org/10.1080/01419870.1981.9993325.

The United Nations Convention on the Rights of Persons with Disabilities. (2006). Retrieved from www.un.org/disabilities/documents/convention/convoptprot-e.pdf

Villegas, A. M., & Lucas, T. (2002). Preparing culturally responsive teachers: Rethinking the curriculum. *Journal of Teacher Education, 53*(1), 20–32.

Activist Applied Linguistics

JANET COWAL AND GENEVIEVE LEUNG

> Be the change.
>
> Never think that a small group of people can't change the world.
>
> If you think you're too small to make a difference, you haven't spent a night with a mosquito!

Perhaps you are passionate about applied linguistics and about making the world a more equitable place for all. The goal of this chapter is to provide you with a starting point for considering how you might combine work in applied linguistics with social justice efforts. We outline some of the ways applied linguists contribute to social change while addressing these questions:

- How does Activist Applied Linguistics contribute to social justice work?
- How might applied linguists do something tangible to make a positive difference in the world?

Overview of Key Concepts and Issues in Activist Applied Linguistics

What is Activist Applied Linguistics? We define **Activist Applied Linguistics (AAL)** as doing applied linguistics together with communities in order to make positive social change. In addition to studying social justice issues involving language, activist applied linguists partner with community members to define problems, co-create solutions, and carry out meaningful action toward equity in society. AAL does not occur in a vacuum; it grows and unfolds in specific contexts with common goals and intentional power sharing among applied linguists and communities. AAL is grounded in applied linguistics theory and provides a lens on social equity that focuses on language and its relationships with power. It questions and considers roles that language, its use, users, contexts, language ideologies, and language policies have in creating, perpetuating, or disrupting disparities in society. It applies this lens to take informed action along with others. For these reasons AAL's contributions to activism are both significant and unique.

AAL requires **community engagement**, that is, collaboration with community partners, while applying interdisciplinary concepts from fields such as critical applied linguistics, critical discourse analysis, sociolinguistics, language policy

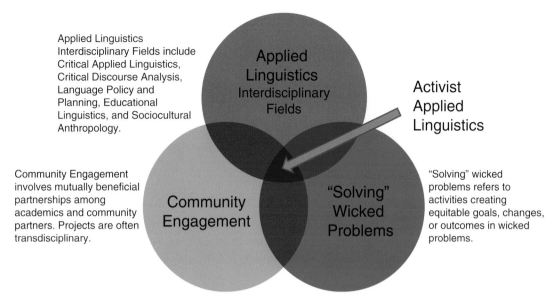

Applied Linguistics Interdisciplinary Fields include Critical Applied Linguistics, Critical Discourse Analysis, Language Policy and Planning, Educational Linguistics, and Sociocultural Anthropology.

Community Engagement involves mutually beneficial partnerships among academics and community partners. Projects are often transdisciplinary.

"Solving" wicked problems refers to activities creating equitable goals, changes, or outcomes in wicked problems.

Figure 21.1 AAL at the intersection of applied linguistics, community engagement, and "solving" wicked problems

and planning, educational linguistics, and sociocultural anthropology in order to address "wicked problems." AAL occurs at the intersection of applied linguistics, community engagement, and "solving" wicked problems (Figure 21.1). Let's look at these components of AAL more closely.

"Solving" Wicked Problems

Wicked problems is a term social scientists use for quandaries in society that are extremely complex, not well understood, and "relentless" (Cooper, 2017). We put "solving" in quotes because by definition wicked problems are unsolvable. However, this doesn't mean we can't take action to try to address them. Examples of wicked problems include poverty, immigration, education, climate change, environment and resources management, and globalization. Wicked problems are multifaceted, multilayered, and intertwined with other wicked problems. Because of their nature, wicked problems involve issues of social equity.

The ways in which people think and talk about these kinds of issues, often referred to as **narratives,** depend on **frames.** Frames refer to the positions and perspectives individuals use to interpret and evaluate narratives. Narratives regarding the causes and solutions of wicked problems vary depending on different people's frames. Since language is fundamentally entrenched and embedded in all facets of society and shapes these narratives and frames, wicked problem issues are also inherently language issues.

One of the ways in which AAL contributes to addressing wicked problems is by providing linguistic views outside of the problem, that is, **meta-perspectives,** of the language surrounding wicked problems. Narratives that aren't noticeable or questioned because they just seem natural, inevitable, or like common sense are referred to as **unmarked**. By taking a meta-perspective, AAL identifies an unmarked narrative as one within a particular frame. This makes room for other viewpoints and possibilities. Thus, AAL contributes to efforts in tackling wicked problems through examining how language frames the ways societies define and approach solutions to wicked problems.

For example, one wicked problem involves people living outside in public spaces. Is this situation described as "homelessness," "house-less-ness," or "people experiencing homelessness"? Each term arises from a particular frame with its own priorities and assumptions about causes, such as a lack of law enforcement, affordable housing, or good paying jobs. Unpacking assumptions in the language used is an important step in understanding issues from different stakeholders' perspectives. In this case, typical stakeholders may include residents, businesses, government agencies, and non-profit organizations. In addition, AAL asks who is or isn't included in the discussion in the first place, and proactively seeks to empower and amplify voices that may be missing, muted, or marginalized. Thus, AAL would intentionally seek to include others in policy creation and implementation such as people who live outside and people who may be marginalized due to language or literacy barriers.

Toft (2014) describes one effort to address this wicked problem that illustrates the kinds of work that activist applied linguists engage in. Drawing on critical discourse analysis, corpus linguistics, and ethnographic methods, Toft engaged in an advocacy and research project together with individuals experiencing homelessness in Seattle. The core of this work was built around Toft's direct involvement with the local homeless organizing community over the course of nine months. Throughout this time period, Toft worked side by side with community organizers in demonstrations, meetings, and public hearings in addition to engaging in both informal conversations and more formal interviews with members of the community. Toft used materials collected through his involvement with the community to understand the narratives and frames that they used to represent themselves and how these narratives and frames contrasted with the ways in which the mainstream media represented them. This project was not limited to research, however. At the request of a local advocacy group, an interdisciplinary team of graduate students and faculty in linguistics, rhetoric, and communication studies at Toft's institution analyzed discourses surrounding homelessness in media and government publications and prepared a report, press release, and press conference to bring the public's attention to problematic representations in these documents (Bawarshi et al., 2008). This effort to enact real change related to a wicked problem is precisely the kind of work that activist applied linguists engage in.

Applying Interdisciplinary Concepts

This section offers several examples of AAL work addressing wicked problems in order to highlight AAL's interdisciplinary nature in applied linguistics.

In studying the wicked problem of systemic inequity in educational settings and incorporating theories of **critical applied linguistics** (Kubota, 2004), Kelleen Toohey's work focuses on sociocultural and sociopolitical aspects of language learning. Her studies of children learning English as an additional language highlight the complexities of language and the co-construction of identity. Her collaborations with K–12 teachers give insights into how university researchers might ethically and respectfully engage and partner with other educators.

Addressing wicked problems situated at the intersections of language, the US court system, and public policy, John Baugh's linguistic variation work on style shifting in African American communities has concrete links to interdisciplinary policy implications in education, law, and medicine. Examining forms of **linguistic discrimination** through dialect variation for minoritized speakers for whom standard English is not native (SENN), Baugh (2009) looks at how linguistic behaviors can be seen as economic commodities with direct impact on one's economic prospects. Using longitudinal research and examining language across the lifespan, Baugh's findings point to linguistic discrimination and the need to look at the intersections of race/ethnicity, social class, and language use and choice. This work has been carried forward by language researchers partnering with legal aid organizations examining court reporter accuracy and African American English (Jones, Kalbfeld, Hancock, & Clark, 2019).

In focusing on wicked problems relating to indigenous language rights, Tove Skutnabb-Kangas's work as a language rights activist and researcher is prolific. She takes on language diversity from an ecological point of view, where the most diverse systems are the ones that are able to survive the best. She also draws on a **linguistic human rights** perspective, which follows guidelines from the United Nations. Critiquing any form of subtractive education through the medium of a dominant language as a form of linguistic genocide (**linguicide**), Skutnabb-Kangas has worked closely with many language reclamation programs in reversing language shift, including that of Aanaar Saami in Finland.

Another example of interdisciplinary work examining wicked problems relating to communities reclaiming their language and culture can be found in Wesley Leonard's projects with the Miami Tribe. Leonard's (2017) work looks at community members' reclamation of the *myaamia* language and how speakers and people of the community can exert agency in supporting their survival, sovereignty, and empowerment. As a tribal member, language program leader, and researcher, Leonard looks at how identity is "authentically" constructed, contested, and reinforced. Using the lens of linguistic anthropology and language socialization, Leonard pushes back against terms like "extinct languages" (using "dormant" or "sleeping" instead) and examines how language identities are entwined with intersecting identities like race and gender.

Engaging in the World Through Collaborating with Communities as Partners

AAL is expressed in many forms, from local to global contexts, in small individual acts to large-scale policy creation and implementation. In all cases, AAL requires community engagement, that is, applied linguist and community relationships and collaborations based on mutual trust and power-sharing. This means that AAL respects and values different kinds of knowledges, published in peer-reviewed journals or not, and that applied linguists doing AAL need to be aware of their own assumptions and positionalities, and how these intertwine in various communities and contexts. A PhD is not necessarily required to do AAL; undergraduate students, graduate students, and alumni of applied linguistics studies, as well as university professors, engage in AAL. What is key is that applied linguists be present, available, and connected with other people, working *together with*, as opposed to *on* or *for*, communities, often times as a member, and using applied linguistics to contribute to co-created community resolutions to wicked problems.

Activist applied linguists may or may not publish about the results of their work or the processes that made that work happen. You can find many excellent examples of AAL online, at community events, and in multimodal works which exist outside of academe and academic publications. Here we provide several examples to inspire you to think about ways *you* might participate in AAL. These examples arise from particular contexts, but wicked problems are everywhere. We encourage you to reflect on your situations and resources, and keeping in mind that no one does AAL working alone, consider how you can make positive change in your own contexts.

In order to address immigration, a wicked problem that frequently includes economic hardships for English language learners (ELLs), Heidi Dryden, an ESOL instructor, created a website with resources for ELLs and volunteer teachers as part of her MA TESOL degree (www.portlandesl.com/). The website is managed by volunteers and lists information regarding free or low-cost English classes along with Google maps of their locations. It also provides resources such as listings of non-profit organizations that welcome ELL volunteers along with the vocabulary used at particular sites so that ELLs can get involved in different communities. As an ESOL instructor at a community college, Dryden creates opportunities for her students to learn English while working for positive change. For example, students in an upper-level writing course drafted statements about their challenges as immigrants and testified at a regular meeting of the Multnomah County Board of Commissioners. Another class ran a mobile clothing closet with their school district's resource fair (H. Dryden, personal communication, July 24, 2018).

In 2016, seeking to get involved in human rights efforts, Daniel Ginsberg, applied linguist and anthropologist, volunteered as a mentor to asylum seekers through a non-profit, non-partisan refugee support and advocacy organization with offices in

New York City and the Washington, DC area. After getting to know him and discovering his background in linguistics, discourse analysis, anthropology, and education, the organization asked him to contribute to their mission by designing and participating in workshops for training other volunteer mentors. In these workshops, Ginsberg presents on intercultural communication while attorneys and social workers share insights from their areas of expertise as well (D. Ginsberg, personal communication, June 22, 2018). Ginsberg's work illustrates key aspects of AAL: using knowledge and skills in applied linguistics and interdisciplinary fields in collaboration with a community partner to act on a wicked problem.

Perhaps a less-known approach in which AAL empowers muted or marginalized voices is by creating or facilitating spaces for people to tell their stories publicly through art. For example, as part of her research collaboration with the Smithsonian Center for Folklife and Cultural Heritage, sociolinguist Amelia Tseng used her background in multilingualism, identity, and education to create and run a "language open mic" event in which people could share stories about their experiences with language during the annual Smithsonian Folklife Festival. In addition, Tseng assisted in a community-driven photo and oral history exhibit, "La Esquina," by acting as a discourse consultant for the project on a panel at Latinx Studies 2018 in which community members were featured participants (A. Tseng, personal communication, July 23, 2018).

An additional example of combining AAL and art is $PEAK OUT, a public participatory project initiated by artist Diane Jacobs in which individuals' handwritten messages about stopping injustice are laser cut into actual currency (Figure 21.2). Applied linguistics students are contributing to this project through generating social media, laser cutting bills, and collaborating with communities in events where participants can create their own messages (Figure 21.3).

Another way community partners can engage in AAL is by examining linguistic and cultural complexities within their communities through **linguistic landscape** projects (refer to Leung & Wu, 2012 for an example in Philadelphia Chinatown). In this case, community members take photos of the language they see in their everyday realities: storefronts, street signs, menus, billboards, posters, and more. They can organize their photos by themes, content, and patterns they notice. In doing this, community member-researchers can take stock of the language use (and inequities) occurring in their own public spheres and decide what kind of local-level actions might need to be taken.

While AAL projects are often time and place sensitive and require intense coordination with community members, it is possible to participate in AAL work that is more flexible. For example, applied linguistics students at Portland State are working with attorneys from the Oregon State Bar (OSB) to make the design and language on the OSB website more accessible to non-attorneys as well as to people with low English literacy or for whom English is an additional language. Projects

Figure 21.2 $PEAK OUT detail. Engagement art piece by Diane Jacobs, photograph by Matt Blum.

Figure 21.3 Mylar panel of bills displayed during a $PEAK OUT community event. Engagement art piece by Diane Jacobs, photograph copyright Julia Ide.

like these are more easily separated into smaller doable chunks that individuals can work on independently. Over time and through community coordination, impactful positive change is possible.

Our Work in Activist Applied Linguistics

Personal Reflections

Janet Cowal   In college I played guitar in a band and became fascinated with transformational generative grammar because of how it relates to composing music and improvising with other musicians; this resulted in my majoring in linguistics. Since then, I have been employed doing work in applied linguistics including perceptual testing of synthetic speech for video games, formal verification of computer network systems, computational linguistics involving name retrieval in large databases, teaching English as an additional language in China, and teaching as a faculty member of Portland State's Department of Applied Linguistics. Doing applied linguistics is extremely stimulating, satisfying, and fun.

When I became a parent, social issues involving language such as education and language policy, and environmental, cultural, and linguistic sustainability became particularly important to me. As a parent, applied linguist, and 4th generation Asian American, I feel strongly compelled to contribute to efforts addressing systemic inequities and creating inclusive environments for current and future generations, especially for those who are not from dominant cultures.

In addition to applied linguistics, I am energized by visual and performing arts; collaborating with others in projects involving art and language gives me great joy. The goal to combine my knowledge, skills, passions, and lived experience in tangible, meaningful work toward positive change in the world is what has drawn me into Activist Applied Linguistics.

Genevieve Leung   I grew up in San Francisco Chinatown with Cantonese as my first language. My family also spoke a variety of Cantonese called Hoisan-wa (台山話), spoken in the United States by the earliest Chinese immigrants who came to work as laborers. In Northern California, there are many Cantonese speakers, so I was rather shocked in college and graduate school to find that for many people, "Chinese" meant only Mandarin. I was disheartened by how little people knew about Cantonese, our speakers, and our immigration histories. Studying sociolinguistics and learning about minoritized languages and marginalized communities armed me with the vocabulary to discuss language, power, and ideologies circulating about language across diasporas and one-nation-one-language ideologies. Yet I felt like Cantonese and "Chineses" were being pushed out of the conversation when scholars were talking about "Chinese," or if in the off-chance they *were* mentioned, they were always mentioned in light of being "less than" or "not as important as" the rise of Mandarin and mainland China. I felt a sense of indignation rising inside me, with a desire to make my community's voices heard and amplified in an arena that seemed increasingly less attuned to the diverse languages that encompass "Chinese." I also reflected on how (more Standard, wealthier Hong Kong) Cantonese speakers were denigrating Hoisan-wa speakers (whose ancestors were mostly uneducated, blue collar workers) for their "non-standard"-sounding Cantonese. These experiences helped me think about how language, power, class, and ideologies all interact and infuse into how people view language learning and teaching, particularly in the decisions that schools, teachers, and parents make in determining which language should be taught in school and/or maintained in the home. My lived experiences and training in educational linguistics helped set up the work and research that I am doing today, which is focused around education and language and cultural maintenance.

Our Projects in Activist Applied Linguistics

In our work, we connect with people who recognize challenges or assets in their communities related to language. Frequently, in addressing wicked problems, partners want to amplify voices that may be marginalized or underrepresented in their own communities or in larger communities. After establishing relationships and trust with community partners, we co-create and co-implement projects to address wicked problems while leveraging our assets and resources.

Janet Cowal   In response to inequities in public education arising from inadequate funding and negative additional language ideologies, I initiated a sustainable partnership between my department at Portland State and a socioeconomically diverse multilingual elementary school that my children attended. At the time, half of the children at the school spoke a language other than English at home (predominantly Spanish, Cantonese, and Vietnamese). The school climate sought to embrace these home languages as assets rather than "an ESL problem." A collaboration between the school and my department made total sense.

The partnership began through: 1) my department inviting the principal to speak at a faculty meeting to introduce us to the school, its language programs, and its culturally, linguistically, and socioeconomically diverse community; and 2) a working session held on-site at the school where our departmental faculty and school teachers sat down together to brainstorm how we could support each other in our missions. We shared our particular contexts' goals, needs, assets, and resources, and explored how they might complement the other's. Aware of some teachers' skepticism of academics and wanting to promote a collegial, respectful atmosphere, I used grant money to provide a spread of refreshments from restaurants owned by school families. This was a visible demonstration of support for school families and appreciation for faculty making the trip off-campus and for teachers giving their time after a long school day.

One of the school's goals was to increase student success and family participation. A challenge then was to figure out how to increase the participation of families from non-dominant languages and cultures. Our department's goal was to provide our students with authentic contexts for experiential learning. A partnership is born! Our goals were co-created into objectives: 1) create an inclusive learning environment that embraces an orientation of language as resource (Ruiz, 1984); 2) seek ways to empower families of non-dominant languages, cultures, and knowledges (Skutnabb-Kangas, 2000); and 3) nurture positive linguistic and social identities in multilingual children (Toohey, 2000).

The partnership was sustained over a decade through relationships among school community members (teachers, families, staff, administrators) and our faculty and students. Teachers opened their classrooms to applied linguistics students who observed and applied theory on-site. Elementary school students benefited with focused attention from "cool" adults who knew something about language. Teachers gave guest lectures in our classes, providing real-life stories of multilingual classrooms. Our faculty incorporated assignments in courses so that students could meaningfully engage with the elementary school community. For example, our students created curriculum and taught ESOL classes for parents that, out of the parents' request, focused on language needed to help their children be successful in school. Another course project involved students collaborating with families to create materials linking language, culture, and environment for use in the school garden.

To realize our goals we co-constructed and co-implemented projects including: 1) a multicultural garden providing an environment for hands-on-learning that values non-dominant languages and knowledges through integrating these into the school curriculum without othering; 2) a CD of original songs created by 3rd–5th grade children in Vietnamese, Mandarin, and Spanish; 3) a community-created mural for the garden classroom that includes nature sayings contributed and painted by members of the school community in their family languages; and 4) the Community and Language Enhancement through Arts Resources (CLEAR) project.

The CLEAR project brought together stakeholders with different concerns, particularly parents who cared about art, language learning, or the environment. University students and faculty engaged with artist Diane Jacobs, elementary school students, families, and teachers to practice using second and heritage languages while doing art. Our goals were to make language learning fun, create a school context that empowered Cantonese-, Mandarin-, Spanish-, and Vietnamese-speaking community members, and integrate children's backgrounds into school curriculum without tokenizing or othering. The children created accordion-style

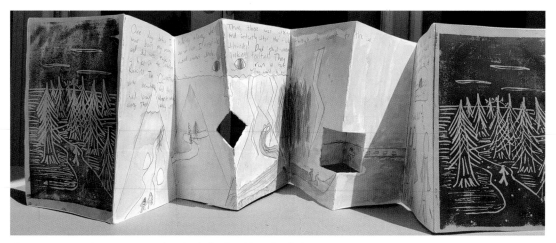

Figure 21.4 Sample pop-up accordion book (back side) with relief print covers.
Photograph by Janet Cowal.

Figure 21.5 Sample pop-up accordion book (front side).
Photograph by Janet Cowal.

pop-up books with relief print covers using styrofoam. The content of the book involved stories from an intergenerational interview (Figure 21.4), original multilingual poetry, and nature (Figure 21.5.)

During class students learned and used phrases such as "please pass the paints" or "I need help" in their target languages. Target language speakers who may not have participated in school activities before volunteered in classes. Students from the department's community activism, second language acquisition, and language assessment courses assisted as participant observers. The project culminated in a well-received exhibition of books and prints (Figure 21.6) and attendees

Figure 21.6 CLEAR relief print book covers on display.
Photograph by Janet Cowal.

included many families speaking non-dominant languages who hadn't previously been inside the school (for additional information on these projects, see www.ActivistAppliedLinguistics.org).

Genevieve Leung   The work I do in San Francisco looks at a dual Cantonese-English language immersion school that made the explicit choice to reflect the minority language speakers of its surrounding community and to teach Cantonese as the target language instead of Mandarin, what many would label an arguably more "economically solvent" Chinese language. The work this school does is remarkable as it teaches a combination of Cantonese to heritage language speakers, recently arrived English language learners (ELLs), as well as to foreign language learners, while at the same time fostering in all their students a sense of community and engagement through Cantonese and Chinese culture.

As a Cantonese heritage language speaker myself, this work in addressing the inequality of representation of "Chinese" is very near and dear to me. Having talked with classroom teachers and parents about their specific needs and concerns, I was asked, as a researcher looking at language acquisition, to discuss the value and benefits of a sustained commitment to Cantonese-English bilingual education (as opposed to English only or switching over to learning Mandarin). The first year I went to the school's PTA meeting, I gave the talk to mostly Anglo, English-speaking parents who had enrolled their children for the sake of additive bilingualism. For these families, any foreign language, Cantonese or not, would have sufficed in "checking the box" of language learning. The following year, the English Language Learner PTA group asked if I could give the same talk but in

Cantonese since the ELL parents were interested in the topic but felt they could not fully access the content in English. While my spoken Cantonese is good enough to interact seamlessly in the United States and in Hong Kong, I had never given a professional/academic talk in Cantonese before, never having been exposed to this genre as a heritage speaker. For weeks I practiced and prepared my slides to fit the needs of my audience, who, unlike the Anglo parents, chose to send their children to this school for the sake of language maintenance, much like how my own immigrant parents sent me, also an English language learner, to a dual language immersion program when I was a child. In the end, it was one of the most rewarding and humbling experiences I have ever encountered because it was a way to provide the material I have been studying and researching on for so long in a linguistically accessible manner to my audience.

Another request the school and parents had was for more Cantonese speakers to serve as tutors and provide additional exposure to Cantonese. To meet this need, I recruited Cantonese-speaking Chinese American students from my university to assist at this school. Many of these students had mentioned to me in passing that they were disappointed that only Mandarin was offered at our university and that they could not take classes to strengthen their own heritage language. The experience of volunteering as Cantonese classroom aides was especially meaningful to my university students, who saw themselves as children in this dual language immersion school learning to read and speak Cantonese, along with doing math in Cantonese! The elementary school students saw adults other than their teachers and parents speaking and learning in Cantonese and enjoying the subject matter.

Were it not for sustained relationships with the school, teachers, and parent groups, I would not have known the wishes of these various stakeholders. Being open to the vulnerable situation of feeling linguistically peripheral and having to work extra hard to develop that register of language to reach my audience made the experience of giving the talk entirely humbling. Being able to reach into my own professional life and draw on the sum of my students' language and cultural repertoires allowed me to reflect on my relationship as a scholar and member of my linguistic community.

Application Activities

We offer two activities related to AAL on the website accompanying this book. The first is an example of the kind of research you might do to inform a plan of action for a project in AAL. The second deals with the practical logistics of doing AAL. In addition, this second activity provides a starting point for your own project in AAL.

Going Further

The world needs activist applied linguists! What are you passionate about? Engage in your own community or get to know and join a community that resonates with you. If you don't have connections, begin by participating in community activities and volunteering. Be a learner. Find out who is there, what they do, and why. Be aware of your positionality and build relationships. Because we were members of and engaged in our communities, we had significant insights that contributed to making our projects meaningful and impactful. Embrace imperfection in yourself and in your community. Social transformation is hard and complicated, occurring in many, many small steps. When wicked problems feel too overwhelming, focus on your circle of influence, that is, what you can do. You can contribute to the journey using knowledge about language, its use and power, and working alongside others!

Discussion Questions

1. Throughout this chapter we have purposefully used the term *equity* rather than *equality*. People engaged in social justice work frequently make a distinction between these terms. If you search online for images using the phrase, "Equality versus Equity" you'll probably find a meme that looks something like Figure 21.7, which is based on a widely adapted meme originally created by Craig Froehle (Froehle, 2016).
Kuttner (2016) critiques this meme and offers something that looks more like Figure 21.8.

Figure 21.7 Traditional Equality versus Equity meme.
Image by Anne Storrs based on Froehle (2016).

Figure 21.8 Revised Equality versus Equity meme.
Image by Anne Storrs based on Kuttner (2016).

What assumptions about power, resources, individuals, and society are conveyed through these different images?

2. What does community engagement mean? Fill in the blank with different prepositions. Are there differences in meaning for you? If so, what are they and what are their implications?

- I am doing research _____ this community. (on, in, for, with, together with)
- I am working _____ this community. (on, in, for, with, together with)

Why do you think the definition of AAL uses *together with*?

3. Imagine that you are involved in a collaborative AAL project with an elementary school like the CLEAR project described in this chapter. While collaborating with elementary school staff to create materials for experiential language and science learning in the school's multicultural food garden, you hear rumors that some parents from a non-dominant culture do not want their children, especially girls, outside digging in the dirt. You don't know why; you've heard some think their children learn better sitting in classrooms doing worksheets. How might you creatively address this situation? Reflect on your own positionalities and assumptions as you consider options.

FURTHER READING

Foundational Readings

Eades, D. (2010). *Sociolinguistics and the legal process.* Bristol: Multilingual Matters.

Harbert, W., McConnell-Ginet, S., Miller, A., & Whitman, J. (Eds.). (2008). *Language and poverty.* Bristol: Multilingual Matters.

Kubota, R., & Lin, A. (2009). *Race, culture, and identities in second language education: Exploring critically engaged practice.* New York: Routledge.

Recent Publications

Cooc, N., & Leung, G. (2017). Who are "Chinese" speakers in the United States? Examining differences in socioeconomic outcomes and language identities. *AAPI Nexus, 15*(1/2), 137–164.

Haeffner, M., & Cowal, J. (2019). A case study of OregonWaterStories.com: Exploring agency with water justice, activist applied linguistics, and a community partner. *Case Studies in the Environment, 2019,* 1–9. https://doi.org/10.1525/cse.2018.001685

Jones, T., Kalbfeld, J. R., Hancock, R., & Clark, R. (2019). Testifying while black: An experimental study of court reporter accuracy in transcription of African American English. *Language, 95*(2), e216–e252. https://doi.org/10.1353/lan.2019.0042

REFERENCES

Baugh, J. (2009). Econolinguistics in the USA. In W. Harbert, S. McConnell-Ginet, A. Miller, & J. Whitman (Eds.), *Language and poverty* (pp. 67–77). Bristol: Multilingual Matters.

Bawarshi, A., Dillon, G., Kelly, M., Rai, C., Silberstein, S., Styagll, G., . . . Thomas, B. (2008). *Media analysis of homeless encampment "sweeps."* Seattle: University of Washington. Retrieved from https://faculty.washington.edu/stygall/homelessmediacoveragegroup/

Cooper, K. (2017). "Wicked" problems: What are they, and why are they of interest to NNSI researchers? Retrieved from https://nnsi.northwestern.edu/social-impact/nnsi-blogs/wicked-problems-what-are-they-and-why-are-they-of-interest-to-nnsi-researchers/

Froehle, C. (2016). The evolution of an accidental meme. Retrieved from https://medium.com/@CRA1G/the-evolution-of-an-accidental-meme-ddc4e139e0e4

Jones, T., Kalbfeld, J. R., Hancock, R., & Clark, R. (2019). Testifying while black: An experimental study of court reporter accuracy in transcription of African American English. *Language, 95*(2), e216–e252. https://doi.org/10.1353/lan.2019.0042

Kubota, R. (2004). Critical multiculturalism and second language education. In B. Norton & K. Toohey (Eds.), *Critical pedagogies and language learning* (pp. 30–52). New York: Cambridge University Press.

Kuttner, P. (October 29, 2016). The problem with that equity vs. equality graphic you're using. Retrieved from http://culturalorganizing.org/the-problem-with-that-equity-vs-equality-graphic

Leonard, W. Y. (2017). Producing language reclamation by decolonising "language." In W. Y. Leonard & H. De Korne (Eds.), *Language documentation and description, vol. 14* (pp. 15–36). London: EL Publishing.

Leung, G., & Wu, M.-H. (2012). Linguistic landscape and heritage language education. *Written Language and Literacy, 15*(1), 114–140.

Ruiz, R. (1984). Orientations in language planning. *NABE Journal, 8*, 15–34.

Skutnabb-Kangas, T. (2000). *Linguistic genocide in education – Or worldwide diversity and human rights?* Mahwah, NJ: Lawrence Erlbaum.

Toft, A. (2014). Contesting the deviant other: Discursive strategies for the production of homeless subjectivities. *Discourse & Society, 25*(6), 783–809. https://doi.org/10.1177/0957926514536839

Toohey, K. (2000). *Learning English at school: Identity, social relations, and classroom practice.* Clevedon: Multilingual Matters.

22 Language, the Law, and Forensic Linguistics

KEITH WALTERS

Overview of Key Concepts and Issues in Language and the Law

The law touches your life in ways you've likely never considered. If you are reading this chapter in the United States, you probably received a syllabus on the first day of class containing information about topics like accommodations for students with disabilities, absences on non-Christian holy days, academic dishonesty, and not disrupting the learning environment for classmates. Statements about these topics are shaped by federal laws and institutional regulations.

Should your professor accuse you of plagiarism or you accuse your professor of not accommodating your religious holidays, odds are that the Dean of Students' office will immediately ask for a copy of the syllabus, which will suddenly be treated as a contract. Indeed, your parents, along with their attorney, may visit the Dean of Students' office to discuss your case; it certainly has happened at institutions where I have taught. In short, the situations became ones involving the interpretation of the language of the policy statement, other relevant documents like the institution's code of student conduct, and perhaps even federal statutes.

Such situations remind us of the **performative nature of legal language**; its existence literally changes reality, setting up categories of what is permissible and sanctionable. At the same time, language, even carefully crafted language, is slippery and open to interpretation. Further, as the example of the syllabus illustrates, any use of language – whether spoken, written, or electronic – can become implicated in legal proceedings as potential evidence.

It should come as no surprise, then, that linguists are increasingly asked to apply their knowledge to a growing range of law-related topics. Among these are the interpretation of language in legal or quasi-legal documents. These could be an insurance policy, a statute, or a syllabus. Linguists are also often asked to assess the value of potential linguistic evidence, which might be a purported suicide note, the draft of an essay that is, according to the instructor, plagiarized, or a text message that could be evidence of efforts to cheat during an exam or threaten a former romantic partner. Later in this chapter, I discuss my involvement in three cases dealing with what are termed **"speak English only in the workplace" rules**, that is, regulations mandating the use of English or some other language under certain circumstances in the workplace and the many kinds of documents relevant in those cases.

Some Key Areas of Research in the Field

A number of linguists have conducted research on various aspects of the legal process. Their training and experience have led them to examine how language functions in specific legal contexts. These researchers have examined questions like the following:

- How might we characterize the register and functions of the language of legal proceedings inside and outside the courtroom (Finegan, 2010; Solan, 2016; Stygall, 2012)?
- Is there evidence that police interrogation techniques have elicited false confessions (Rock, 2010)?
- How do the ways of using language particular to legal contexts like investigations or the courtroom limit access to the legal process for individuals unfamiliar with them, especially those from indigenous or aboriginal groups (Eades, 2016), those for whom English is not a first language in the United States (Berk-Seligson, 2016), or those who are vulnerable in other ways (Zappavigna, Dwyer, & Martin, 2016)?
- Does the manner of courtroom questioning enable those claiming to be the victims of crimes the opportunity to "tell their side" of what happened (Heffner, 2010)? For example, do those who claim to have been raped get to narrate their experience fairly and thoroughly (Ehrlich, 2010)?
- What challenges arise when interpreters, even trained ones, are used in legal proceedings (Berk-Seligson, 2017)?
- Do a judge's instructions to a jury potentially shape the outcome of a case (Dumas, 2015; Tiersma, 2001)?
- What roles might linguists play in the determination of national origin on the basis of the language(s) a refugee or asylum seeker speaks or does not speak (Patrick, 2016)?

Linguists have also applied their knowledge to these and other questions by being part of multidisciplinary teams helping train law enforcement officials, working to improve the comprehensibility of jury instructions, or issuing a white paper on best practices in the communication of legal rights to individuals whose first language is not spoken English, a project also discussed below. Some of these efforts are directly or indirectly part of the larger **Plain English Movement** or **Plain Language Movement** (Adler, 2012), which seeks to reduce the impenetrability of language used in the law and legal processes.

The Meanings of "Forensic Linguistics"

If you look into research in this area, you'll soon encounter the term *forensic linguistics*, which can have a range of meanings. On the European continent, the term sometimes refers to that branch of **English for Specific Purposes (ESP)** focusing on the teaching of English to law students who need to understand the basics of Anglophone legal systems as well as special ways English is used in legal contexts. These systems are based on English common law and precedents, or earlier court rulings. In contrast, continental legal systems, like most of the world's legal systems, are based on civil law, which focuses on the interpretation of a legal code, or set of laws. Increasingly, however, the term is used in much the same way as it is in natively Anglophone countries.

In countries where English is a dominant language, if not *the* dominant language, the term *forensic* generally refers to the use of scientific methods or tools to investigate crimes. Hence, the term *forensic linguistics* can be applied to situations in which someone uses the methods and tools of linguistic analysis in legal investigations, particularly those of a criminal nature.

Categories of Legal Cases

Linguists whose primary legal work is in the domain of criminal law often speak of being forensic linguists. **Criminal cases** are those involving an action considered harmful to society; they are brought by governments often in the name of "The People" of a particular state or "The Crown" in Commonwealth countries. The linguistic aspects of such cases often hinge on authorship or speaker identification. Examples here would include seeking to determine who might have written the ransom note involved in a kidnapping or the anonymous letter of confession in the case of an apparent suicide that was, in fact, a murder, or who might have left a voice message threatening violence against someone. While some forensic linguists are quick to speak of using linguistics to "solve crimes," others are more cautious, pointing out that, with rarest exception, all that existing methods of linguistic analysis are capable of doing is shrinking the pool of likely perpetrators. Rather than "proving" who committed a crime, linguistic methods can sometimes provide a profile of the individual who likely committed the crime, thereby ruling out many who probably did not.

A second category of cases in which linguists are sometimes involved is **civil cases**, which involve disputes between individuals and/or organizations. These cases may deal with author identification – for example, who posted the series of negative reviews of a particular therapist on RateYourTherapist.com that led to a serious loss of income for her? Most, however, focus on issues related to defamation or trademarks. Celebrities, for example, frequently sue tabloid newspapers, the popular magazines you see at grocery-store checkout counters, and, increasingly, online "news" sources for defamation, and at least in the United States and Europe, only

McDonald's can use the Mc^{TM} and Mac^{TM} prefixes thanks to a series of civil law suits by the burger chain that involved linguists as expert witnesses (Butters, 2010).

A final category of cases involves **administrative law**, especially disputes about the exercise of public power; in short, did government officials overstep the law? A 2017 Supreme Court Case in which linguists served as experts was *Matal v. Tam* (2017), in which the Asian American band The Slants sued the US Patent and Trademark Office after it refused to let them trademark the band's name, contending that it was an ethnic slur. The band, of course, argued something quite different: its members had very consciously chosen the name to call attention to and mock the slur and racist language more broadly, thereby robbing it of its power. Although legal scholars understandably see the case as being an important one in ongoing debates about the limits of free speech, the arguments made included those based on linguistic analysis of the term and its use in various contexts.

How Linguists Assist in the Legal Process

You may be wondering how linguists become involved in this work. Many who conduct research in this area have often found some aspect of language and the law to be a fertile field for research questions; others have served as expert witnesses and become interested in particular language-related legal issues. As I explain in the second half of the chapter, a linguist generally serves as an expert by invitation: we can't just go barging into courtrooms or law offices across the country. While there are a few companies founded by linguists that specialize in forensic linguistics, aside from those employed in the field of intelligence, most linguists who do this work serve as private consultants, and many do not call themselves forensic linguists. Rather, they see themselves as linguists who are assisting the courts by providing information that might not otherwise be available but that might prove useful in determining the outcome of a case – the criteria for justifying the need for an expert witness.

In these regards, linguists may play a range of roles. They may simply offer advice to attorneys about whether or not an expert with training in linguistics might be helpful in a specific case. For example, a local law firm asked me to help them determine what role, if any, a linguist might play in a given case and provided me with several hundred pages of documents related to the case to read. As I read, it became clear that there were many language-related issues that were relevant to the case, but the ones that would help their client were far less useful than the potentially explosive ones that would work against their client. I discouraged them from retaining a linguist to assist them as an expert, pointing out why I would decline to work on such a case. They did not retain a linguist, nor, luckily for them, did the opposing side. Hence, there were no linguists involved in the proceedings. By the way, once I had spoken to attorneys for one side about the case, I was prevented by law from contacting the other side or being retained by them even if they had contacted me – a matter of ethics.

Issues of ethics, confidentiality, and even intellectual property also work against those who serve as expert witnesses from publishing research about their work. While there is a growing body of published research on language and the law, including forensic linguistics more narrowly defined, many linguists who serve either are not interested in discussing or are unable for any number of reasons to discuss the details of cases they work on. Some of these issues are treated in the Linguistic Society of America's "Code of Ethics for Linguists in Forensic Linguistics Consulting" (Lingustic Society of America, 2011).

When linguists are retained as experts, they generally write reports, which may become part of the official record of the case. As explained further below, these reports contain their opinions along with support as well as evidence of the expert's credentials and a great deal of customary language, noting that the expert was not coached and that their payment does not depend on the contents of the report or the outcome of the case. In short, the duty of the expert is to serve the Court, not to act as a hired gun. Experts are to serve the **triers of fact**, either a jury or judge, depending on the case, rather than to argue for who is guilty or innocent. "Triers of fact" is a **term of art**, a word or expression having a specific meaning within a particular field. In a jury trial, the jury acts as the triers of fact, determining whether an event actually occurred, while the judge determines matters related to the law, for example, which laws are applicable and whether certain evidence can be included in the hearing. In cases where there is no jury, the judge determines questions of fact and of law.

Additionally, an expert may provide other linguistically informed information to the attorneys, for example, helping them formulate questions to be asked of the other side at various stages in the case. Shuy (2006) offered basic advice for linguists on acting as expert witnesses; he has also published a number of books about cases he has been involved in (most recently, 2017).

Qualifying as an Expert Witness and the Nature of What Counts as Linguistic Evidence

To qualify as an expert witness in the United States, one must be capable of passing what is termed a **Daubert challenge** after *Daubert v. Merrell Dow Pharmaceuticals* (1993) and earlier rulings. These precedential cases, among others, set the legal standards for the admissibility of expert testimony in terms of the qualifications of the expert and the methods of analysis used. While the second half of the chapter details some of the criteria for qualifications, it is worth noting that US courts are becoming increasingly stringent in terms of the admissibility of findings based on particular methodologies, a situation that has led to considerable debate among those who focus on issues of author identification, in particular.

The techniques traditionally used in author identification grew out of literary stylistics, the study of the style of literary texts. While such methods are now generally supplemented by the use of certain tools from corpus linguistics, they are increasingly considered to be highly impressionistic and, hence, unscientific by some courts. That is, in the eyes of these courts, the evidence these techniques produce fails to meet the criteria for admissibility. In contrast, researchers such as Carole Chaski (2012) are working to develop and have patented computational forensic tools that meet the standards of rigor increasingly required by courts. For example, one of the tools Chaski has developed can be used to examine short texts – ransom or purported suicide notes – in cases where there is only a limited number of examples of other texts by an author. The tools have been statistically validated and yield results with a high degree of reliability. Her findings have been admitted by various courts.

My Work with Language and the Law

Personal Reflection

Like many things in my life, my introduction to these issues occurred by chance. Sitting in my office at UT-Austin in 2000, I received a call from an attorney with the **Equal Employment Opportunity Commission (EEOC)** office in San Antonio, Texas; the EEOC is the federal agency tasked with enforcement of the **Civil Rights Act of 1964**, which has since been amended. She began by asking a series of questions: Had I done research and published on issues related to bi- or multilingualism? Had I taught graduate seminars on these topics? Had I supervised dissertations on these topics?

I did not realize it at the time, but she was vetting my qualifications in light of the Daubert criteria for serving as an expert witness, mentioned above. When I answered affirmatively to these questions, she asked if I might be willing to assist the EEOC in a case involving a group of Spanish-speaking housekeepers at a nearby private university who claimed they were being discriminated against in the workplace. Some were US born; others were immigrants from Mexico. All spoke Spanish, and most understood and spoke English, though to varying degrees. Some preferred speaking English to Spanish while others had trouble answering simple questions in English like "How long have you lived here?" Crucially, the university had what is termed a "speak English only in the workplace rule."

Over the next few months, I learned a great deal about these rules, the EEOC's understanding of them, and some of the major prior court rulings, or precedents, on this topic. I read the documents relating to the case that were made available to me. These documents included:

1. The actual complaint, that is, the documents filed to initiate the suit.
2. Subsequent legal documents filed in the case.

3. **Depositions**, that is, testimony taken under oath in an attorney's office, of both the plaintiffs bringing the case and various other employees of the university, which was the defendant.

I also conducted tape-recorded individual interviews with the plaintiffs to assess their abilities in English, something my background in English language teaching had prepared me to do. Additionally, I engaged the help of my partner – now husband – a natively bilingual Mexican American immigration attorney from the Rio Grande Valley, to conduct tape-recorded interviews with them in small groups, asking questions about where and when they used Spanish and English. Our goal was to elicit recorded evidence that they naturally engaged in **codeswitching**. As a sociolinguist, I was well aware that the best way to maximize the likelihood of gathering codeswitched data was to use an interviewer who was like those being interviewed in as many ways as possible: a native codeswitcher who was also Mexican American, who spoke the same varieties of English and Spanish, was familiar with the specific codeswitching practices of the local community, and would likely be perceived as an in-group member in crucial ways. Similarly, I assumed that small group interviews would help minimize the effects of being recorded.

Although the EEOC attorneys with whom I worked never explicitly stated the fact, they were clearly interested in how well the various plaintiffs spoke English and whether or not they regularly engaged in codeswitching. As I later came to appreciate, lest expert witnesses become biased, they are given information about only the parts of the case relevant to their opinion. Further, they are not privy to the attorney's **legal theory**, that is, the specific legal arguments to be used should the case go to trial. Only in the most general sense are expert witnesses members of "the legal team," and they should not construe themselves as such.

As I read the prior relevant rulings on these rules, I quickly became aware that two unresolved legal issues were how to deal with individuals who are able to do a job but not able to do so speaking English fluently and how to deal with the practice of codeswitching in the workplace. In fact, these issues remain unresolved today in many regards because the Supreme Court has never been presented with a case about speak English only rules; hence, there is no "**bright line**," as attorneys say, distinguishing what is legal from what is illegal. Such bright lines, of course, give rise to later litigation as cases involving new sets of facts not considered by the original ruling are filed.

As I also came to appreciate, ironically, these rules' very existence often works to the advantage of employees. In the United States, the bar to demonstrate that a workplace environment is "hostile" is extremely high. However, if there is a speak English only rule that does not meet the EEOC criteria of being clear and consistently enforced, plaintiffs may well be able to have their day in court. This fact reminds us of the materiality, or concrete nature, of linguistic behavior: it can be examined and analyzed in great detail in ways that lay people and many attorneys initially do not appreciate, and such analyses may serve the courts.

My Work Writing an Expert Report and Being Deposed

The attorneys with whom I worked also graciously walked me through the process of writing an expert report without coaching me about what to say. In that report, I presented basic information about the nature of bi- or multilingualism, including codeswitching; in short, I sought to explain what it means to be bi- or multilingual to an audience that would likely be overwhelmingly monolingual. Additionally, the report contained detailed information about my assessments of the various plaintiffs' abilities to speak English and their codeswitching practices during the bilingual interviews.

In such reports, experts present one or more short claims, which are termed "opinions." Each opinion is followed by often pages of supporting data, reasoning, and bibliographic citations both to academic research and to documents from the case, particularly depositions or internal documents like employee handbooks or emails. As an attorney once told a colleague being deposed in a case, "The *e* in *email* stands for 'evidence'."

The attorneys also helped me prepare for my own deposition, which lasted several hours. During the deposition, the attorneys for the defendants asked probing questions about my background and my report. The transcript of my deposition became part of the record of the case. It is worth pointing out that the "official record" of a case consists of all the documents involved, and these must be in English. In situations where an interpreter is involved in a deposition or courtroom testimony, the English-language version of what was said as rendered by the interpreter becomes the only relevant record of what was said.

My report, along with many other documents, was filed with the Court by a court-specified deadline, and within a few days, the university, through its attorneys, informed the EEOC that it was ready to settle the case. In fact, most US court cases are settled out of court. Although that fact often leaves certain legal questions unresolved, the motivations for the defendant to do so are several, including their desire to avoid what may be protracted legal battles as well as what could very well be negative publicity as details about the workplace come out during trial testimony. Such settlements also generally avoid the defendant's having to admit any actual wrongdoing. They may further stipulate that the documents in the case are sealed, that is, not available to the public. The result in this case was a settlement of over two million dollars to the plaintiffs, the largest settlement to date involving speak English only rules.

When the EEOC settles a discrimination case, it always publishes a press release stating the amount and terms of the settlement, which generally include the employer's agreeing to institute new policies and to be monitored by the EEOC for a specified number of years. The press release likewise includes sufficient information about the details of the case to permit attorneys and human resources (HR) offices around the country to track the evolving understanding of the EEOC and the courts with respect to issues of discrimination. When employment discrimination cases are filed or settled, they and their possible implications quickly become discussed on websites for HR professionals since a key HR task is helping employers avoid litigation. Thus, such **out-of-court settlements** often have an impact far beyond the cases themselves, a fact that helps us understand the complexity of how legal rulings and even out-of-court settlements directly and indirectly influence society.

Here, I feel it is important to make several observations about this case and about serving as an expert witness. As I noted, my report was only one of many documents filed with the court by the filing deadline. While I hope my report was helpful in bringing about a settlement, while the attorneys I worked with reported they were very happy with the report, and while I was quite pleased with the outcome of the case, I cannot and should not take credit for the result.

Attorneys like to quote William Gaddis, who wrote, "Justice? . . . You get justice in the next world. In this one you have the law." Linguists, as expert witnesses, are not attorneys, nor are we triers of fact. Those who serve as experts can certainly choose the cases we agree to work on, but we do great harm and misunderstand our role in the legal process if we see ourselves as social justice warriors. In the ten or so cases I've worked with, I have been quite humbled to be able to demonstrate the ways in which research in the field of linguistics helps make sense of the lived experience of various parties involved in cases, particularly those who are in some way marginalized by society. At the same time, my task and goal have been to provide accurate information to the Court that would probably not otherwise be available.

As part of helping me understand the task of an expert witness, the attorneys with whom I initially worked shared an expert report that, as they said, was "worthless." In it, the linguist had offered almost exclusively arguments based on sympathy for the plaintiffs, who belonged to a minority group in the United States, portraying them as victims and the employer as evil. Not surprisingly, the attorneys did not file this report with the Court. What the courts understandably demand is evidence-based argument on topics specifically relevant to the emerging facts of the case.

I have served as an expert in two other cases involving speak English only rules, one brought independently by employees at a large family-owned manufacturing company and the other brought by a group of employees at a large healthcare organization with the support of the EEOC. Both resulted in out-of-court settlements. These experiences have led to other opportunities, including cases involving issues of libel, author identification, medical malpractice, patent violation, threat via text message, and the assessment of the likelihood that the defendant understood his **Miranda Rights** at the time of his arrest. Outside the United States, these rights are usually referred to as "**the Caution.**"

The Broad Range of Issues Where Linguists Can Offer Helpful Information

These experiences have helped me appreciate the broad range of issues where specific knowledge of linguistics and the ability to apply that knowledge can be useful to the legal system. Here I offer two concrete examples. In one of the cases involving speak English only rules, depositions from the employees reported repeated instances in which they were speaking English to an employee from their home country but were accused by US-born employees of violating the speak English only rule. Their retort to the US-born employees was often that the plaintiffs were speaking English but had a "strong accent."

Examination of information from the case, however, made clear that these employees were speaking what Kachru (1992) would term an "**Outer Circle**" **variety of English**, that is, an indigenized variety of the language widely used in their country of origin. This variety of English contained borrowings from the speakers' first language, including terms of respectful address, which were sanctioned in the workplace as violating the speak English only rule. Its phonological system was very much influenced by the languages of their home country. More importantly, these employees' English was heard as "not English but some other language" by fellow employees.

The EEOC attorneys for the case were delighted and impressed when I offered an account of what was going on in these situations, supporting my claims with testimony from depositions and reference to a large body of research on this particular variety of indigenized English, including a dictionary. Courts are quite fond of dictionaries – even Urban Dictionary – according them a status most linguists do not. The attorneys were completely unaware of research on English as spoken in the plaintiffs' home country. In fact, it became apparent that an unresolved legal issue with regard to these rules is how workplaces should accommodate indigenized varieties of English that monolingual speakers of American English may perceive as "not English."

A second example involves the work of the **Communication of Rights Working Group on Guidelines for Communicating Rights to Non-Native Speakers of English in Australia, England and Wales, and the USA** (Communication of Rights Group, 2015), of which I was privileged to be a part. This group of linguists, interpreters, attorneys, and legal scholars worked to come up with a set of "best practice" recommendations for communicating the Miranda Rights or their equivalent in various Anglophone countries, whose legal systems are similar in crucial ways, as noted above. The group's report has found the approval of several professional associations in the fields of law, law enforcement, and linguistics. The hope is that the guidelines will come to influence practice among law enforcement officials; the guidelines have already been cited in some legal cases.

Data Analysis Activity

Linguists working on issues of language and the law, particularly those working in forensic linguistics, spend much of their time analyzing data and writing up their analyses in the form of expert reports that must conform to the genre expectations of legal writing. In this activity, you will analyze data related to the speak English only in the workplace rules discussed above.

Going Further

Someone interested in issues of language and the law would surely want to become familiar with a range of methods of discourse analysis. Training in sociolinguistics, linguistic anthropology, and pragmatics, particularly those aspects of these fields that focus on meaning negotiated in context and issues of language and power, would likewise prove invaluable. Because of the breadth of language-related issues implicated in legal cases, training in the subfields of acoustic phonetics, dialectology, psycholinguistics, syntax, or corpus linguistics would be necessary to work on certain issues. Ultimately, one needs strong basic linguistic analysis skills – the ability to locate, interpret, and explain patterns in all sorts of data sets – and to do so in terms that can be understood by non-linguists.

Interestingly, most linguists whose focus is forensic linguistics or who frequently serve as expert witnesses are not trained as attorneys, although there are a few notable exceptions. In fact, there is general agreement that a linguist does not need such training. However, one must be willing to learn about the categories set up by the law because those categories, rather than the ones familiar to linguists, are the relevant ones for legal work. For example, Chapter 9 by Alissa Hartig illustrates the categories related to the meaning of "from the person" that legal decisions hinge on. Serving as an expert witness almost always requires a terminal degree in the field, thus, a PhD. However, there are positions available for linguistically trained investigators and analysts working with law enforcement, intelligence agencies, and private investigative agencies. Many of these jobs require very high levels of training in computer science. There are graduate programs in the United States and Britain focusing specifically on forensic linguistics.

Discussion Questions

1. Why is the field of language and the law such an expansive one? Can you provide possible cases in which linguists with very different sorts of training – for example, a corpus linguist versus a phonetician, a dialectologist versus an expert on language testing – might have knowledge that would be useful to the courts?
2. What sorts of topics have linguists who have conducted research on aspects of the legal process investigated? Can you give examples of other aspects of the legal process that might merit careful investigation?
3. Which sorts of technologies do you imagine might have applications for linguists interested in issues of language and the law in terms of research or practice?
4. What forces are leading forensic linguists who work on author identification to seek to develop new, more rigorous methods? Why would such methods be necessary, given the role courts play in society? Given the novel affordances of various technologies that continue to be developed?
5. In what sorts of cases or contexts might *Urban Dictionary* (www .urbandictionary.com) be a useful resource? Consider here the sorts of lexical fields that tend to be included in that dictionary as well as the demographics of the dictionary's users and creators as they compare with those of traditional dictionaries.

FURTHER READING

Foundational Readings

International Journal of Speech, Language and the Law (One of the premier journals for work in language and law)

Linguistic Society of America. (2011). *Code of ethics for linguists in forensic linguistics consulting.* Retrieved from www.linguisticsociety.org/sites/default/files/code-of-forensic-consulting.pdf

Shuy, R. W. (2006). *Linguistics in the courtroom: A practical guide.* New York: Oxford University Press.

Recent Publications

Coulthard, M., & Johnson, A. (Eds.). (2010). *The Routledge handbook of forensic linguistics.* London and New York: Routledge.

Ehrlich, S., Eades, D., & Ainsworth, J. (Eds.). (2016). *Discursive construction of consent in the legal process.* Oxford: Oxford University Press.

Tiersma, P., & Solan, L. (Eds.). (2012). *The Oxford handbook of language and law*. Oxford: Oxford University Press.

REFERENCES

Adler, M. (2012). The plain language movement. In P. Tiersma & L. Solan (Eds.), *The Oxford handbook of language and law* (pp. 67–83). Oxford: Oxford University Press.

Berk-Seligson, S. (2016). Totality of circumstances and translating the Miranda warnings. In S. Ehrlich, D. Eades, & J. Ainsworth (Eds.), *Discursive constructions of consent in the legal process* (pp. 241–263). Oxford: Oxford University Press.

(2017) *The bilingual courtroom: Court interpreters in the legal process* (2nd edn). Chicago: University of Chicago Press.

Butters, R., (2010). Trademarks: Language that one owns. In M. Coulthard & A. Johnson (Eds.), *The Routledge handbook of forensic linguistics* (pp. 351–364). London and New York: Routledge.

Chaski, C. (2012). Author identification in the forensic setting. In P. Tiersma & L. Solan (Eds.), *The Oxford handbook of language and law* (pp. 489–503). Oxford: Oxford University Press.

Communication of Rights Group. (2015). Guidelines for communicating rights to non-native speakers of English in Australia, England and Wales, and the USA. Retrieved from www.une.edu.au/__data/assets/pdf_file/0006/114873/Communication-of-rights.pdf

Daubert v. Merrell Dow Pharmaceuticals, Inc. (1993). 509 U.S. 579, 589.

Dumas, B. K. (2015). Navigating the rocky road. In L. Solan, J. Ainsworth, & R. Shuy (Eds.), *Speaking of language and the law: Conversations on the work of Peter Tiersma* (pp. 285–288). Oxford: Oxford University Press.

Eades, D. (2016). Erasing context in the courtroom: Construal of consent. In. S. Ehrlich, D. Eades, & J. Ainsworth (Eds.), *Discursive constructions of consent in the legal process* (pp. 71–91). Oxford: Oxford University Press.

Ehrlich, S. (2010). The discourse of rape trials. In M. Coulthard & A. Johnson (Eds.), *The Routledge handbook of forensic linguistics* (pp. 265–280). London and New York: Routledge.

Finegan, E. (2010). Corpus linguistic approaches to "legal language": Adverbial expression of attitude and emphasis in Supreme Court decisions. In M. Coulthard & A. Johnson (Eds.), *The Routledge handbook of forensic linguistics* (pp. 65–77). London and New York: Routledge.

Heffer, C. (2010). Constructing crime stories in court. In M. Coulthard & A. Johnson (Eds.), *The Routledge handbook of forensic linguistics* (pp. 199–217). London and New York: Routledge.

Kachru, B. (1992). *The other tongue: English across cultures* (2nd edn.). Urbana and Chicago: University of Illinois Press.

Linguistic Society of America. (2011). Code of ethics for linguists in forensic linguistics consulting. Retrieved from www.linguisticsociety.org/sites/default/files/code-of-forensic-consulting.pdf

Matal v. Tam (2017). 582 U.S. _____. [Case not yet published]

Patrick, P. L. (2016). What is the role of expertise in Language Analysis for Determination of Origin (LADO)? A rejoinder to Cambier-Langeveld. *International Journal of Speech Language and the Law*, *23*(1), 133–139.

Rock, F. (2010). Collecting oral evidence: The police, the public, and the written word. In M. Coulthard & A. Johnson (Eds.), *The Routledge handbook of forensic linguistics* (pp. 126–138). London and New York: Routledge.

Shuy, P. (2006). *Linguistics in the courtroom: A practical guide.* New York: Oxford University Press.

(2017). *Deceptive ambiguity by police and prosecutors.* New York: Oxford University Press.

Solan, L. (2016). Transparent and opaque consent in contract formation. In S. Ehrlich, D. Eades, & J. Ainsworth (Eds.), *Discursive construction of consent in the legal process* (pp. 118–139). Oxford: Oxford University Press.

Stygall, G. (2012). Discourse in the US courtroom. In P. Tiersma & L. Solan (Eds.), *The Oxford handbook of language and law* (pp. 369–380). Oxford: Oxford University Press.

Tiersma, P. (2001). Navigating the rocky road to legal reform: Improving the language of jury instructions. *Brooklyn Law Review*, *66*(4), 1081–1119.

Zappavigna, M., Dwyer, P., & Martin, J. R. (2016). Consent and compliance in youth justice conferences. In S. Ehrlich, D. Eades, & J. Ainsworth (Eds.), *Discursive construction of consent in the legal process* (pp. 186–212). Oxford: Oxford University Press.

23 | Ideology in Media Discourse

WINNIE CHENG AND PHOENIX LAM

Overview of Key Concepts and Issues in Ideology in Media Discourse

This chapter about ideology in media discourse begins with a discussion of the role of critical discourse analysis, combined with corpus linguistics, in exposing the perceptions and representations of groups or regions covertly expressed in different types of media discourse. By means of the review of relevant research studies on ideology and media discourse, it will also discuss issues of what this knowledge can help us to understand, and how research studies integrating critical discourse analysis and corpus linguistics could be used to address, problems in society.

Media discourse refers to "interactions that take place through a broadcast platform, whether spoken or written, in which the discourse is oriented to a non-present reader, listener or viewer" (O'Keeffe, 2012, p. 441). The term "**ideology**" is defined by *Merriam-Webster Dictionary* as "a systematic body of concepts especially about human life or culture," (n.d.b) and *Cambridge Dictionary* as "a set of beliefs or principles, especially one on which a political system, party, or organization is based" (n.d.a). Ideology is hence social in nature, and one of the means through which ideology can be revealed is discourse.

In research studies of ideology in media discourse, the use of a combined methodology of corpus linguistics and **critical discourse analysis (CDA)** has proved to be very useful (see, for example, Cheng & Ho, 2014; Cheng & Lam, 2010, 2013).

CDA is a special approach to the study of verbal (text and talk) as well as non-verbal (pictures, film, music, gestures, etc.) forms of discourse that are oriented toward social-political problems or issues, such as racism, sexism, discrimination, and colonialism. It focuses on how discourse is used by social group members to express and resist power, dominance, and inequality, with discourse doing ideological work. An example is Norman Fairclough's (1989, 1992) approach of textually oriented discourse analysis which has been widely used in research on ideology in media discourse. His approach views "language as discourse and as social practice" (Fairclough, 2001, p. 21), highlighting "the significance of language in the production, maintenance, and change of social relations of power" (p. 1).

Despite the value of CDA in addressing social events and promoting social change, CDA has its methodological drawback. A main criticism against CDA is its highly subjective nature. While Fairclough (2003) argues that "there is no such thing as an 'objective' analysis" (pp. 14–15), the fact that CDA research studies are often based on a small number of arbitrarily selected texts as research data implies that analysis of data is only selective and that multiple readings or interpretations are possible (Flowerdew, 2008; Gabrielatos & Baker, 2008). Another criticism of CDA, especially of earlier research studies, is that its methodology is not sufficiently systematic and rigorous (Rogers, 2004) but tends to rely on anecdotal evidence and purely intuitive-based interpretations, and hence negatively impacting the reliability of the conclusions (McCabe, O'Donnell & Whittaker, 2009).

The methodological issues described above can be, and have been effectively, resolved by combining CDA with **corpus linguistics**. A corpus is a collection of pieces of language text in electronic form (Sinclair, 2005) which can be examined by using different computer programs. Corpus linguistic research studies analyze the textual evidence with the aim of finding "probabilities, trends, patterns, co-occurrences of elements, features or groupings of features" (Teubert & Krishnamurthy, 2007, p. 6). Basic corpus linguistic research methods include the study of wordlists, keywords, collocates, concordances, and semantic categories. One common starting point of investigation for corpus linguists is a frequency wordlist, which simply lists out all the words which occur in a corpus in the order of ascending or descending frequency. Patterns may also be observed through the comparison of keywords, that is, words which are significantly more frequently occurring in one corpus when compared with another corpus. To study the association between words, corpus linguists examine **collocates**, that is, words which habitually co-occur in the vicinity of another word. The existence of collocates gives rise to the phenomenon of collocation. The **concordance** of a word in a corpus shows every contextual occurrence of the word in the corpus. It can be analyzed for the study of word co-occurrences, as well as semantic meaning (semantic preferences) and functional or attitudinal meanings (semantic prosodies) (Louw, 1993; Sinclair, 1996). Specifically, semantic preference refers to the pattern of semantically related words with which a word tends to co-occur. An example is the tendency of the word *rising* to co-occur with words related to the semantic categories of work and money such as *incomes* and *prices* in the British National Corpus (BNC) (Baker, Hardie, & McEnery, 2006). Similarly, semantic or discourse prosody refers to the notion that a word may co-occur with a set of words revealing similar attitudinal value which may or may not belong to the same semantic category. An example is the word *happen*, which has been found to co-occur with words denoting unpleasant things or situations such as *disaster* and *drug poisoning* in the BNC (Baker, Hardie, & McEnery, 2006).

Previous research studies of ideology and media discourse have shown that a combination of CDA and corpus linguistics presents a more systematic and rigorous methodology to obtain trends, patterns, and co-occurrences of various linguistic features from corpora of media discourse, from which relevant cultural, social, political, or economic ideologies and positions can be revealed. Studies have been conducted in a range of professional, public, media, and experimental contexts. Examples include reasoning skills employed in promising and unpromising conditions in conflict resolution (Campolo, 2005); lightweight chat in large, distributed, ad-hoc groups (Birnholtz, Finholt, Horn, & Bae, 2005); and the use of gesture and speech to represent size information of pictures from a children's story book (Holler & Stevens, 2007). In conflict news research, Baden and Tenenboim-Weinblatt (2017) investigate media influences in violent conflict, with findings showing the tendency of the media "to cover conflict in an event-oriented, violent-focused, and ethnocentric manner, both during routine periods and . . . during major escalation" (p. 22). In a more recent study, Tourangeau (2018) examines power, discourse, and news discourse related to Canada's GM alfalfa protests. The study finds that when covering the Canadian farmers, and activists' protests about GM alfalfa's "potentially adverse impacts to markets, the environment, and society" (p. 117), news outlets tend to cover "economic and market impacts" but not "broader social, political, and environmental issues" (p. 117). Tourangeau (2018) provided two reasons for the finding, namely news values and media culture privileging "newsworthy" topics.

Ideology and media discourse research has also focused on the study of metaphors. Metaphor is considered a means of activating shared assumptions and cultivating intimacy as it can create "a sense of community" (Goatly, 1997, p. 160). In metaphor studies in media discourse, corpus linguistic methods have been increasingly used (Skorczynska Sznajder, 2010; Soler, 2008). As noted by Baker (2006), the corpus can both "uncover the possible metaphors surrounding a word or concept" and show "how that metaphor works in a range of other cases, enabling researchers to gain a greater understanding of its meaning" (p. 172). In Burnes's (2011) study, a number of metaphors are identified in the news reports of Barack Obama's election which construed a positive image, namely ENTERTAINMENT ("the greatest reality show" in history), DREAM ("dreams melt away" to the reality of next year), and STORY ("triumph" of the American story). At the same time, Burnes (2011) finds that the parliamentary election of Pakistan's president Mr. Musharraf was negatively described, showing interpersonal aggression, with such metaphors as PHYSICAL COMBAT and DISASTER ("debacle" and "routed").

Cheng and Ho (2014) report on a corpus-based critical discourse analytical study which compares the use of collocations, semantic preferences, semantic prosodies, and metaphors in the English-language news reports and Hong Kong government press releases concerning the introduction of the school subject Moral and National Education in Hong Kong in 2012. The analysis of word co-occurrences with the phrase "national education" in the two media corpora shows that journalists use various FIGHT metaphors to describe the attitudes and actions of protesters and the responses of the government. However, their findings show that the government press releases are much more literal, showing a neutral to positive tone and implying that while the planned introduction of the subject Moral and National Education was shelved, the subject will be re-introduced in the future.

In another study of metaphors integrating corpus linguistics and CDA, Kitis, Milani, and Levon (2018) examine the construction of the black middle class in contemporary South Africa in a corpus of twenty mainstream Anglophone South African newspaper titles from 2008 to 2014. An analysis of the collocates of "black middle class," "black diamonds," "clever blacks," and "coconuts" shows "predominantly negative images of wealthy Black people" (p. 167). Integrating corpus linguistics and cognitive approaches to a critical discourse analysis, Wong (2017) analyzes press reports on aggression of social actors in the 2014 Occupy Central political protest in Hong Kong. The language texts examined are English-language newspaper articles published in *China Daily* and *South China Morning Post (SCMP)*. Wong (2017) compares the ten most frequent collocates of "police" and found that *China Daily* portrays police as vulnerable yet professional in their handling of the protesters, whereas in *SCMP* police officers are presented negatively as aggressors. The same social event and social actor group are therefore shaped in very different ways by the two newspapers.

Another relevant study compares discursive constructions of scientific (un)certainty about the health risks of China's air pollution (2011–2014) in Chinese and Anglo-American English-language newspapers (Liu & Zhang, 2018). The study finds that the Anglo-American English-language newspapers highlight "the certainty about health risks through such discursive strategies as prediction, nomination, and the rhetoric of quantification" (p. 1), whereas the Chinese newspaper highlights "the uncertainty about health risks" through "particularizing the Chinese context, complicating the causes of health problems, and arguing for more scientific tests" (p. 1). These findings point to some interesting differences in ideology in media discourse between the East and the West (more on its definition later), an area that our own work also focuses on and that we will illustrate in more detail in the remainder of the chapter.

Our Work in CDA and Corpus Linguistics, Analyzing Ideologies in Media

Personal Reflections

As corpus linguists and discourse analysts, we both have a keen interest in integrating the concepts and methods in both strands into our research in different professional and educational settings. Discourse analysis, in particular CDA, has a long tradition of studying media discourse, and corpus linguistic tools are especially suited to the revelation of language patterns in a large number of media texts. Our research on ideology in media discourse in Hong Kong began with "Media discourses in Hong Kong: Change in representation of human rights" (Cheng & Lam, 2010), followed by "Western perceptions of Hong Kong ten years on: A corpus-driven critical discourse study" (Cheng & Lam, 2013). Born and educated in Hong Kong, we have both been interested in human rights issues not only because they often attract much attention in international news, but also because in Hong Kong, a major political change was introduced in 1997 which involved the transfer of sovereignty from the United Kingdom to the People's Republic of China. After 155 years of British rule, Hong Kong was returned to China on July 1, 1997. Since 1982 when negotiations began between both countries over the future of Hong Kong, speculations had been rife regarding what impact this political transition would bring to the territory, especially the concern whether the rights and personal freedoms enjoyed by Hong Kong people in the past would be maintained after the transition.

In 2007, as the Hong Kong Special Administrative Region entered the second decade of its establishment, we thought it was timely to review how human rights issues had been and were being addressed and reported in the local media discourse. The aforementioned 2010 study, therefore, aimed to determine whether there had been any changes in the way human rights issues were represented in local media discourse before and after the handover, specifically what the changes were, and what might have accounted for the changes.

In our 2010 study, we examined the change in the representation of human rights issues in a corpus of more than 5,000 newspaper articles. The newspaper articles were collected from a leading English newspaper in Hong Kong, *South China Morning Post*, in two periods before and after the change of sovereignty in 1997. The analytical framework adopted was Sinclair's (1996) model of the five categories of co-selection of the lexical item, which is used to examine the extended units of meaning of the lexical item. The five categories are collocation, colligation, semantic preference, semantic prosody, and the (invariable) core. The analysis of instances of the phrase "human rights" in the newspaper corpus as a lexical item shows that the newspaper in question has changed its representation of human rights issues, particularly in China and Hong Kong, over the decade. The finding reflects an ideological shift in the newspaper's stance in response to the current situations in both local and world politics, and that human rights concerns are not merely a nationalistic, but also a culturally dynamic, phenomenon.

In our 2013 study, we investigated the Western perceptions of and relations with Hong Kong a decade after the reversion of the sovereignty from Britain to China in 1997. The study was not only driven by the researchers', as Hong Kong citizens, personal experiences of the transfer of sovereignty but also motivated by a literature review which showed that the West had an overwhelmingly negative view on the future of Hong Kong around the time of the handover.

Specifically, Western discourses in 1997 were particularly concerned about whether Hong Kong would enjoy autonomy as promised and guaranteed by "one country, two systems" and the Basic Law; whether the democracy and rule of law could be preserved; and whether Hong Kong people would be able to enjoy individual liberties (Lee, Pan, Chan, & So, 2001; Pan, 2002). Most of these studies perceived the handover as a decolonization of Hong Kong from Britain to China (Shi-xu & Kienpointner, 2001; Shi-xu, Kienpointner, & Servae, 2005) and the reversion of Hong Kong from capitalism to communism.

Ten years on in 2007, observations, however, had shown a noticeable change in the perceptions of the West. Examples of Western media discourses which affirmed the achievements of Hong Kong after 1997 had emerged. They generally expressed positive views toward Hong Kong during the first ten years under Chinese sovereignty. These initial observations had triggered our interest in finding out the West's understanding, opinions and positions regarding Hong Kong in 2007, compared with those in the period around 1997.

Similar to the methodology adopted in our 2010 study, the 2013 study integrated the theories and methods of corpus linguistics and critical discourse analysis. Specifically, by using corpus linguistic software programs, the study examined a range of Western media discourse of Hong Kong concerning the handover. The purpose of the study is to yield insights into the New Hong Kong in the eyes of the West, which in turn contributes to a re-examination of the relations and power balance between the West and China.

Our Work with Ideology in Media Discourse

To give a concrete example of the analysis of ideologies in media discourse through a combination of CDA and corpus techniques, we now discuss in greater detail our corpus-driven critical discourse study conducted in 2013 which investigated the diachronic change, if any, in the Western perceptions of Hong Kong. In this study, we focused on the portrayal and representation of our home city, Hong Kong, in media texts produced in two three-year periods: the time around the change of sovereignty of Hong Kong (1996–1998) and ten years after (2006–2008). We compared, diachronically, the perceptions of the city as found in Western media sources with those found in Chinese media sources, as Hong Kong has often been characterized as a place where "East meets West" owing to historical reasons. Our study was "corpus-driven" (Tognini-Bonelli, 2001, p. 11) in the sense that we let the frequency patterns observed in the corpus, rather than any existing frameworks and models, guide our analysis. Our aim was to ascertain, through the analysis of frequency patterns in the corpus, whether there were any changes in the West's understanding, opinions and positions regarding Hong Kong over a momentous ten-year period, and to account for the changes by critically examining the socio-political context.

We were fully aware that any study involving comparison between such broad categories as "Chinese" perceptions and "Western" perceptions should guard against over-generalization, and the definition of such categories inevitably entails some subjective judgment. For the purpose of our study, we used "the West" to refer to the Americas, Europe, and Australasia, as an umbrella term commonly employed in the contemporary political and cultural context. In this connection, we collected data representing these geographical locations from a number of representative databases including EBSCOhost and ProQuest to ensure that the coverage of major news sources was as comprehensive as possible for achieving the objective of the study. Using "Hong Kong" and "handover" as search items, we retrieved editorials, feature stories, news articles, and interviews in English containing both search items in the databases. Accordingly, two corpora, namely the Western Media Corpus (WMC) and the Chinese Media Corpus (CMC), were compiled from these media texts. The WMC contained texts from the key regional and national newspapers and magazines as well as from global news agencies and networks in the English-speaking world, mostly in the Anglo-American context. The CMC comprised texts from the top news sources in the Greater China region, that is, Mainland China, Hong Kong and Taiwan. Each corpus was divided into two sub-corpora based on the time period of the texts. In total, approximately 2,500 media texts, amounting to more than 1.5 million words, were collected and analyzed.

One of the unique features of our study lies in the novel methodological approach that we employed by incorporating the two corpus analytic tools *ConcGram 1.0* (Greaves, 2009) and *Wmatrix* (Rayson, 2001) in our qualitative and quantitative analyses. *ConcGram 1.0*, a software program that requires no prior input from users, automatically identifies all of the word association patterns, technically known as "concgrams," that exist in a corpus. Put simply, it discovers and produces as its output all the sets of words which co-occur regardless of constituency variation (e.g., AB and A*B), positional variation (e.g., AB and BA), and both (Cheng, Greaves, & Warren, 2006; Cheng, Greaves, Sinclair, & Warren, 2009). For example, the two-word concgram "play/role" includes such examples as "play a minor role," "role play," and "role it plays." *Wmatrix*, accessible via an online interface, can automatically annotate a corpus semantically by assigning every item in the corpus a meaning label, technically known as a "tag," out of twenty-one major discourse fields that expand into 232 category labels. For example, the term "boozing" is semantically tagged under the discourse field "food and farming," while the term "amused" is semantically tagged under the discourse field "emotion."

Using *Wmatrix* and *ConcGram 1.0*, we conducted our analysis in three key stages to search for frequencies and patterns in the subcorpora of WMC and CMC. First, *ConcGram 1.0* uncovered the most frequent two-word concgrams across the four subcorpora. Second, *Wmatrix* identified the most frequent semantic categories in the four subcorpora, and compared such categories to see which ones were particularly dominant in one subcorpus when compared with the other three. Finally, based on the key semantic categories identified in the second stage, we focused on a concgram containing the proper noun "Hong Kong" and the most frequent co-occurring word in the key semantic categories, that is, "political." We examined in detail its concordance, that is, a list of all of the occurrences of that concgram within the linguistic context in which they occur, to further understand the underlying ideological assumptions and values of the linguistic manifestation associated with "Hong Kong" and "political." Figure 23.1 shows a sample concordance of the concgram "political/Hong Kong."

Based on our analysis and comparison of the patterns of concgrams and semantic categories in the four subcorpora, we found that the Western perceptions of Hong Kong had changed over the ten-year period studied. At the time of the handover of Hong Kong (1996–1998), views presented in the Western media on the city were

```
1    the Basic Law  to increase China's control over political reform in Hong Kong. It ruled that the chief
2    the Basic Law  to increase China's control over political reform in Hong Kong. It ruled that the chief
3    young  talent. In response to questions about political liberties in Hong Kong under Chinese
4          report aggressively on environmental and political issues,  both in Hong Kong and on the mainland.
5    club in the good old British tradition - not political in any sense''.    HONG KONG OVERVIEW - HONG KONG
6          to introduce more accountability into the  political system." At times in Hong Kong's recent history
7    in protest. It was the  beginning of a period of political turmoil that forced the Hong Kong government to
8    to create the conditions for the  emergence of a political class is the Achilles heel of Hong Kong's system.
9          down the streets, muzzling  any whisper of political dissent," says the AP.  Today, Hong Kong is a
10   years, from where I sat as Chief Secretary, the political  transition went extremely well. Hong Kong wasn't
11   WU: There seems to be a lot of discontent on the political front. In the 1960s and '70s,  when Hong Kong
12   reality  becomes political reality." And the political reality, according to Lee, is "All the Hong Kong
13          of Commerce, An Min, that Hong Kong political forces are  wrong ""to think that they are
14   go ahead  unhindered every year in Hong Kong. Political and news websites are not blocked by  censors.
15   go ahead  unhindered every year in Hong Kong. Political and news websites are not blocked by  censors.
16   worries that China would restrict Hong Kong's political and religious  freedoms.  When the celebration
17          ago.  The frozen nature of Hong Kong's political system is just one, striking, instance of how
18   years on China has managed  to make Hong Kong's political demands seem an almost parochial concern.
19          contest  marks a major event in Hong Kong's political development. Such an event would  carry risks for
20          censor themselves. Predicting Hong Kong's political future is difficult because Beijing has yet to
21          unfulfilled promises  regarding Hong Kong's political integrity. Her re-entry into politics as a
22   China? WU: Nothing has moved much on Hong Kong's political front apart from the nearly  daily demonstrations
23   a study on press  practices in Hong Kong by the Political and Economic Risk Consultancy (PERC) that found
24          revolution.  Hong Kong's was a unique political system: undemocratic but free. China was, and
25   of  government, that Hong Kong's was a unique political system: undemocratic but free.  China was, and
26   the social strata of Hong Kong and the  balanced political participation of all social circles and the
27          In that period Hong Kong has  endured mixed political and economic fortunes, the key message being that
28   election show that Hong Kong people prefer more political  competition," says Ma Ngok, a professor of
29          In that period Hong Kong has  endured mixed political and economic fortunes, the key message being that
30   At times in Hong Kong's recent history its political  system has been a matter of global  interest: at
31   the chairman of Hong Kong's largest  pro-Beijing political party, recently questioned whether the events of
32          guarantee Hong Kong's prosperity and render political reforms irrelevant.  These complacent
33          with Hong Kong. Here, as in Hong Kong,  political development. Such an event would  carry risks for
34   of a Hong Kong company with  strong Chinese political connections. The same concerns almost lost the
35   that Hong Kong is "an economic city" not  a "political city". Why then is politics taking centre stage
36          Hong Kong's freedom to push ahead with political reform and a third NPCSC interpretation in 2005
37   of Hong Kong itself, which is not so much  a political entity as a corporation -- a subsidiary of China.
38          Hong Kong could serve as a laboratory for political change on  the mainland, as it earlier served as
39          Hong Kong, Chan is less concerned with the political climate  of Hong Kong's handover as a main factor
40   2047 Hong Kong would keep its own economic and  political system and enjoy autonomy in everything except
```

Figure 23.1 Sample concordance of the concgram "political/Hong Kong" in the Western Media Corpus (WMC) in 2006–2008

mixed, with negative opinions mostly on political issues but positive or neutral opinions on business or economic matters. We saw examples such as "political disputes ahead of the handover" and "freedom to make money in Hong Kong." The central message of such media texts thus seemed to be that Hong Kong remained a thriving business center despite the political disharmony and uncertainty brought about by the change of sovereignty. Ten years later (2006–2008), unfavorable views on political issues in the city were even more dominant in the Western media texts. We saw examples of the concgram "political/Hong Kong" with the semantic preferences of the influence of mainland China on the city's political reform (see Lines 1–3 on Figure 23.1) and of the dismal or uncertain political outlook of the city (see Lines 7, 9, 11 on Figure 23.1).

Compared with the Western media, Chinese media were generally more positive to the political scene of Hong Kong and China's influence in both time periods, and the use of quoting in the report of views was more common through the use of reporting verbs and quotation marks. In particular, the voices of political parties, legislators and journalists from the city were included. In both the Chinese and the Western media, however, the number of unfavorable views increased over time, with a steady rise in the quoting of local individuals. To a casual reader, this gradual diachronic growth in the inclusion of local opinions might not be obvious, but it revealed a greater sense of political awareness and level of involvement in the community and a more mature political environment in Hong Kong (Chan & Chan, 2007). It also hinted at the growing polarization, politicalization, and dissatisfaction of the Hong Kong society, which had been known in the past to be politically apathetic (Degolyer & Scott, 1996). As such, these language patterns brought to light by CDA and corpus methods have to a certain extent unraveled and foreseen the social unrest across the city and the subsequent civil disobedience movement which in a few years' time was about to come.

Data Analysis Activity

We hope the brief summary of our study above has given you some ideas on how CDA and corpus methods can be fruitfully combined to study ideologies in media discourse. In the activity on the website accompanying this book, we have prepared some questions which will guide you through some aspects of the analysis in our study. In particular, the activity will give you some hands-on experience in analyzing patterns of concgrams, comparing key semantic categories, and examining concordance lines so that you will be more familiar with these concepts. We hope this activity will stimulate your interest in conducting similar research yourself.

Going Further

If you would like to know more about corpus linguistics, discourse analysis, and CDA, a good place to start is to study the further readings listed below and the references at the end of the chapter. You may also consider taking relevant courses in corpus linguistics and discourse analysis at your university to be acquainted with the key concepts. These courses will also provide a good general background for actual data analysis. To become practically involved in analyzing media discourse in a CDA framework and to obtain some practical hands-on experience, you may try to select a small number of media texts which interest you and study the texts from a critical perspective, applying notions and techniques discussed in this chapter. Online resources which allow a corpus analysis of a large number of media texts are also available, including from Brigham Young University and The Hong Kong Polytechnic University. Many universities have organized corpus-assisted critical discourse analysis workshops or related training in the area and videos of such events are sometimes available for public access online. These will help you to get a sense of how such studies may be conducted.

Discussion Questions

1. Based on what you have read in this chapter, what are some key issues which researchers focus on when analyzing ideologies in media discourse? Which issue interests you most? What other issues do you think might be addressed?
2. What might be some easily attainable sources of data for studies which analyze ideologies in media discourse?
3. How do you think the Internet has changed the nature of media discourse?
4. Have you experienced any social, political, or cultural event which might be conducive to a critical discourse analysis of ideology?
5. Can you describe a study that you would like to conduct to analyze ideologies in media discourse? What kind(s) of ideologies would that involve? What kind(s) of media texts would be suitable for conducting such a study?

FURTHER READING

Foundational Readings

Fairclough, N. L. (1992). *Discourse and social change.* Cambridge: Polity Press.

Kress, G., & Hodge, R. (1979). *Language as ideology* (1st edn). London: Routledge.

Sinclair, J. McH. (1991). *Corpus, concordance, collocation: Describing English language.* Oxford: Oxford University Press.

Recent Publications

Knoblock, N. (2017). Xenophobic trumpeters: A corpus-assisted discourse study of Donald Trump's Facebook conversations. *Journal of Language Aggression and Conflict, 5*(2), 295–332.

Liu, M., & Zhang, Y. (2018). Discursive construction of scientific (un)certainty about the health risks of China's air pollution: A corpus-assisted discourse study. *Language & Communication, 60*, 1–10.

McEnery, T., McGlashan, M., & Love, R. (2015). Press and social media reaction to ideologically inspired murder: the case of Lee Rigby. *Discourse & Communication, 9*(2), 1–23.

REFERENCES

Baden, C., & Tenenboim-Weinblatt, K. (2017). The search for common ground in conflict news research: Comparing the coverage of six current conflicts in domestic and international media over time. *Media, War & Conflict, 11*(1), 22–45.

Baker, P. (2006). *Using corpora in discourse analysis.* London: Continuum.

Baker, P., Hardie, A., & McEnery, T. (2006). *A glossary of corpus linguistics.* Edinburgh: Edinburgh University Press.

Birnholtz, J. P., Finholt, T. A., Horn, D. B., & Bae, S. J. B. (2005). Grounding needs: Achieving common gound via lightweight chat in large, distributed, ad-hoc groups. In *Proceedings of the SIGCHI Conference on Human Factors in Computing Systems* (pp. 21–30). ACM: New York.

Burnes, S. (2011). Metaphors in press reports of elections: Obama walked on water, but Musharraf was beaten by a knockout. *Journal of Pragmatics, 43*, 2160–2175.

Campolo, C. (2005). Treacherous ascents: On seeking common ground for conflict resolution. *Informal Logic, 25*(1), 37–50.

Chan, E., & Chan, J. (2007). The first ten years of the HKSAR: Civil society comes of age. *The Asia Pacific Journal of Public Administration, 29*(1), 77–99.

Cheng, W., Greaves, C., Sinclair, J. McH, & Warren, M. (2009). Uncovering the extent of the phraseological tendency: Towards a systematic analysis of concgrams. *Applied Linguistics, 30*(2), 236–252.

Cheng, W., Greaves, C., & Warren, M. (2006). From n-gram to skipgram to concgram. *International Journal of Corpus Linguistics, 11*(4), 411–433.

Cheng, W., & Ho, J. (2014). Brainwashing or nurturing positive values: Competing voices in Hong Kong's national education debate. *Journal of Pragmatics, 74*, 1–14.

Cheng, W., & Lam, P. (2010). Media discourses in Hong Kong: Change in representation of human rights. *Text & Talk – An Interdisciplinary Journal of Language, Discourse & Communication Studies, 30*(5), 507–527.

(2013). Western perceptions of Hong Kong ten years on: A corpus-driven critical discourse study. *Applied Linguistics*, *34*(2), 173–190.

Degolyer, M. E., & Scott, J. L. (1996). The myth of political apathy in Hong Kong. *The Annals of the American Academy of Political and Social Science*, *547*, 68–78.

Fairclough, N. L. (1989). *Language and power*. Harlow: Longman.

(1992). *Discourse and social change*. Cambridge: Polity Press.

(2001). *Language and power* (2nd edn). London: Longman.

(2003). *Analyzing discourse: Textual analysis for social research*. London: Routledge.

Flowerdew, J. (2008). Critical discourse analysis and strategies of resistance. In J. Rodney, V. Bhatia, & J. Flowerdew (Eds.), *Advances in discourse studies* (pp. 195–210). London: Routledge.

Gabrielatos, C., & Baker, P. (2008). Fleeing, sneaking, flooding: A corpus analysis of discursive constructions of refugees and asylum seekers in the UK Press 1996–2005. *Journal of English Linguistics*, *36*(1), 5–38.

Goatly, A. (1997). *The language of metaphors*. London: Routledge.

Greaves, C. (2009). *ConcGram 1.0: A phraseological search engine*. Amsterdam: John Benjamins.

Holler, J., & Stevens, R. (2007). The effect of common ground on how speakers use gesture and speech to represent size information. *Journal of Language and Social Psychology*, *26*(4), 4–27.

Ideology. (n.d.a) In *Cambridge Dictionary*. Retrieved from https://dictionary.cambridge.org/dictionary/english/ideology

(n.d.b) In *Merriam-Webster Dictionary*. Retrieved from www.merriam-webster.com/dictionary/ideology

Kitis, E. D., Milani, T. M., & Levon, E. (2018). "Black diamonds," "clever blacks," and other metaphors: Constructing the black middle class in contemporary South African print media. *Discourse & Communication*, *12*(2), 149–170.

Lee, C., Pan, Z., Chan, J. M., & So, C. Y. K. (2001). Through the eyes of U.S. media: Banging the democracy drum in Hong Kong. *Journal of Communication*, *51*(2), 345–365.

Liu, M., & Zhang, Y. (2018). Discursive construction of scientific (un)certainty about the health risks of China's air pollution: A corpus-assisted discourse study. *Language & Communication*, *60*, 1–10.

Louw, B. (1993). Irony in the text or insincerity in the writer? The diagnostic potential of semantic prosodies. In M. Baker, G. Francis, & E. Tognini-Bonelli (Eds.), *Text and technology* (pp. 157–176). Amsterdam: Benjamins.

McCabe, A., O'Donnell, M., & Whittaker, R. (Eds.) (2009). *Advances in language and education*. London: Continuum.

O'Keeffe, A. (2012). Media and discourse analysis. In J. Gee & M. Handford (Eds.), *The Routledge handbook of discourse analysis* (pp. 441–454). London: Routledge.

Pan, X. P. (2002). Consensus behind disputes: A critical discourse analysis of the media coverage of the right-of-abode issue in postcolonial Hong Kong. *Media, Culture and Society*, *24*(1), 49–68.

Rayson, P. (2001). Wmatrix: A web-based corpus processing environment. Computing Department, Lancaster University, UK.

Rogers, R. (2004). *An introduction to critical discourse analysis in education*. Mahwah, NJ: Lawrence Erlbaum.

Shi-xu, & Kienpointner, M. (2001). Culture as arguable: A discourse analytical approach to the international mass communication, *Pragmatics*, *11*(3), 285–307.

Shi-xu, Kienpointner, M., & Servae, J. (Eds.). (2005). *Read the cultural other: Forms of otherness in the discourses of Hong Kong's decolonisation*. Berlin and New York: Mouton de Gruyter.

Sinclair, J. McH. (1996). The search for units of meaning, *Textus*, *9*(1), 75–106.
   (2005). Corpus and text – Basic principles. In M. Wynne (Ed.), *Developing linguistic corpora: A guide to good practice* (pp. 1–16). Oxford: Oxbow Books. Retrieved from http://ota.ox.ac.uk/documents/creating/dlc/

Skorczynska Sznajder, H. (2010). A corpus-based evaluation of metaphors in a business English textbook. *English for Specific Purposes*, *29*, 30–42.

Soler, H. H. (2008). Metaphor corpus in business press headlines. *IBÉRICA*, *15*, 51–70.

Teubert, W., & Krishnamurthy, R. (Eds.). (2007). *Corpus linguistics: Critical concepts in linguistics. Volumes 1–6*. London: Routledge.

Tognini-Bonelli, E. (2001). *Corpus linguistics at work*. Amsterdam and Philadelphia: John Benjamins.

Tourangeau, W. (2018). Power, discourse, and news media: Examining Canada's GM alfalfa protests. *Geoforum*, *91*, 117–126.

Wong, M. L.-Y. (2017). Analyzing aggression of social actors in political protests: Combining corpus and cognitive approaches to discourse analysis. *Journal of Aggression, Conflict and Peace Research*, *9*(3), 178–194.

Literacy, Digital Literacy, Language Education, and Equity

KATHY HARRIS AND GLORIA JACOBS

Overview of Key Concepts and Issues in Literacy, Digital Literacy, Language Education and Equity

What's the first thing you reach for in the morning? Is it your smartphone? Do you keep it next to your bed and use it as your alarm clock? Do you glance at it numerous times during the day in response to texts, emails, or other notifications? What about your computer? Do you have a laptop that travels with you to class and the library or do you have a desktop computer you work on when you're at home? What are other kinds of things that you do on your smartphone or other mobile device, on your laptop or desktop computer? What would your life be like if you couldn't use those devices or even access the internet? How would your life change? Your ability to use digital technology to accomplish daily tasks and solve daily problems is called **digital literacy**. But it's not something you have or don't have. What makes a person digitally literate changes constantly because digital devices, software, and apps are always changing and what you do with them changes as well. But why does digital literacy matter? Research into digital literacy tries to answer key questions such as why using digital technologies is important, who benefits from using digital tools, and how they benefit.

Digital literacy researchers come from many disciplines such as applied linguistics, education, informatics, communications, and media studies. Our work in digital literacy is based on four related scholarly traditions. The first is emancipatory literacy, developed by Freire (1970), a Brazilian adult educator. An international group of scholars, called the New London Group (1996), also provide an important framework for our work. We also think about everyday literacies as described by Knobel (1999) and about people's changing relationship to knowledge and information (Lankshear & Knobel, 2007). The final conceptual piece that grounds our work is the research of Jenkins (2006), formerly of the MIT Media Lab, who developed the idea of participatory culture.

These four ideas are explained in more detail in the following paragraphs. We believe it is important to understand these underlying concepts because it helps us to have a nuanced understanding of how and why digital literacy is an essential aspect of life in the twenty-first century. Furthermore, by asking what is the nature of digital literacy we are able to develop new ways of thinking and expand digital literacy to include digital problem-solving (Castek, Jacobs, Gibbon, Frank, Honisett, & Anderson, 2018).

Freire (1970) argued that reading and writing should go beyond the printed word to include understanding power structures and gaining the skills and knowledge needed to make changes in one's world. Building on the idea that what people do outside of formal educational settings matters, Knobel (1999) argued that the way people use literacy in their daily life reveals the knowledge and skills that people have. Similarly, the New London Group (1996) argued for what they called a pedagogy of **multiliteracies**. Specifically, a multiliteracies approach recognizes the knowledge people bring to a learning environment, including linguistic diversity as a resource. Importantly, a multiliteracies approach includes **multimodal forms of expression**, which involves the use of images, video, audio, gesture and touch, along with traditional written text to support learning. Learning to use these multimodal forms of expression, they suggested, could allow individuals greater participation in their world.

Following changes in website technology that allowed for user interactivity, Jenkins (2006) identified the emergence of a **participatory culture**. According to Jenkins, participatory culture allows people to join and engage in a community by providing support for the production and sharing of creations. One example of this that has been demonstrated to support language learning (Black, 2006) is the fanfiction community. In fanfiction, people write stories based on characters from a much loved piece of fiction, post these in an online forum (such as fanfiction.net), and receive feedback from members of that community. They then further develop their writing and also provide feedback to those who post their own attempts. Belonging to a community provides mentorship and a sense of connection, and it also helps people learn a set of skills that are different from those learned through the use of paper and ink technologies.

Lankshear and Knobel (2007) argued that participatory culture also gave rise to a new "ethos" or shift in how people relate to knowledge and information. According to Lankshear and Knobel, this new ethos means that people are no longer simply recipients of officially sanctioned information and instead become participants, collaborators, and share expertise when creating knowledge. Knowledge, they claim, is less "expert-dominated" (p. 9) and the rules and norms around knowledge production and consumption are more fluid.

What this means, however, is that making sense of and using all the information now available requires a new set of skills and practices, and these practices need to be taught across a variety of settings (Castek et al., 2018) and at all levels, including all levels of L2 classrooms (Harris, 2015). By practices, scholars mean the things that people do with language and technology in their everyday life. For example, a practice might be looking up health information online and getting that information from a combination of videos, illustrations, and written words supported by audio narration – using multiliteracies. As such, a multiliteracies approach should be integrated into the L2 classroom for more authentic and relevant learning (Lotherington & Jenson, 2011). Castek et al. (2018) point to the emergence of **digital problem-solving** as a set of practices adults now must engage in, and further suggest that learning these practices can be accomplished in informal settings such as libraries as well as formal adult education settings. In the next sections of this chapter, we define digital literacy and discuss issues of digital inclusion, which are the structural and societal barriers to engagement in the digital world and to participatory culture. The chapter also contains a section on digital literacy acquisition, which discusses some approaches to addressing the barrier of digital skills and knowledge.

Definition of Digital Literacies

The four frames discussed above build on a definition of digital literacies as a new set of skills and practices that impact daily life, in which people are participants who create knowledge and share expertise. In this view, digital literacies can be broken into four component parts: basic digital skills, the ability to create and communicate information in digital contexts, the ability to find and evaluate information, and the ability to solve problems in digital contexts.

Basic digital literacy includes the skills and practices needed to operate devices and programs. This includes everything from using an input device such as a keypad, touchscreen, oral commands, or a keyboard and mouse, to creating, editing, and saving documents and spreadsheets, attaching a document to an email, getting directions using a mapping application, and so on. It also includes general knowledge about how things work, like where program settings might be located and what options are likely to be available there. The expectation that digital environments continually change is part of basic digital literacy; a website or application might look and operate differently the next time it is visited, new functionality may have been added while familiar functionalities may have changed or gone away.

Basic digital skills are used to communicate across time and space, mirroring print literacy. Voice-over internet, video communication, and text-based messaging applications as well as email have enabled migrants to stay in touch with family, and colleagues to work closely together while on different continents. Everyday digital literacies are required for parents to communicate with their children's teachers, job seekers to find and apply for jobs, and for patients to find health information online. These tasks require basic digital skills as well as the language and practices appropriate for each.

In addition to communication across time and space, digital literacies include new ways to have a voice in the world inside and outside of officially sanctioned sources. Video and text-based blogs provide the opportunity for anyone to share any information or opinion. People share their skills with video, resulting in online videos as a key way to learn skills that were once the purview of instruction manuals and courses. In the classroom, students create videos in project or theme-based learning, which find an authentic audience on the internet. Social media is a relatively new form of virtual communication and has had significant impacts on the daily life of many. Beliefs about which kinds of information are private and which are public is an example of a practice related to social media use.

The internet has become a vital source of information, and the ability to find and evaluate information online is one of the essential digital literacies. For example, adults are likely to go to the internet to find information about a symptom or a medicine that has been prescribed. The ability to search for information is part of the skill required, as is the ability to read in the language of the webpage, and to know what part of the webpage is information versus advertising or other material that is not related to the search. In addition, since anyone can put anything online for any reason, the ability to evaluate the source, relevance, and quality of the information is key. This language-intensive activity is especially challenging for English language learners and English-speaking adults who do not have strong reading skills.

Part of the challenge for many adults is that working online may require them to not only work in an unfamiliar language or register, they also have to figure out how to navigate the technology. As Rosen and Vanek (2017) suggest, even though technology presents new ways of solving problems, technology itself may present a problem that needs solving. For example, a user might struggle to figure out how to log in to a local wireless network when the cellular signal is weak or the user has reached their data limit, and they need to find the address and get directions to their doctor's appointment. This illustrates that digital problem-solving is complex and involves the "nimble use of skills, strategies, and mindsets required to navigate online in everyday contexts, including the library, and use novel resources, tools, and interfaces in efficient and flexible ways to accomplish personal and professional goals" (Castek et al., 2018, p. 2). Flexibility and the willingness to explore and experiment are central qualities of digital problem-solvers. Castek et al. (2018) suggested that these mindsets need to be supported wherever adults are learning how to use digital tools and be digital problem-solvers.

Definition of digital inclusion and digital equity

Digital literacies necessitate easy access to the internet as well as devices to use it. Together, access, devices, and digital literacies comprise **digital inclusion**. Who has access to each is an equity issue; adults with lower levels of education and income, racial minorities, rural residents, and older adults are less likely to have home broadband (Pew Research, 2018). Broadband is internet access that is always on and faster than dial-up access (Federal Communications Commission, 2014). Lack of access to the internet at home has many implications, including implications for health. For example, there is evidence that the use of a patient portal is related to increased quality of healthcare and clinical outcomes, but patients without broadband at home are less likely to use their patient portal (Perzynski et al., 2017). Income is also related to how people access the internet; households earning $30,000 or less annually are more likely to have access to the internet only through their phones and must use their limited data and small screens to do things like apply for jobs and write their school papers (Anderson, 2018).

Digital literacy acquisition

The work in digital inclusion and equity points to why digital literacy acquisition is important, and there exists a growing body of literature that demonstrates the positive impact of digital literacy acquisition on people's lives (Jacobs, Castek, Pizzolato, Pendell, Withers, & Reder, 2015; Schreurs, Quan-Haas & Martin, 2017), but there remains little research into how individuals actually acquire digital literacy. Of the research that has been conducted into digital literacy acquisition, three main points have emerged as particularly relevant for adult learners. First is the finding that the principles of adult learning should be carried into the digital world (Blackley & Sheffield, 2015). Second is the research that demonstrates the importance of experimentation (Castek et al., 2018; Jenkins, 2006). The final, and perhaps most important finding is that social support, which can consist of teachers, tutors, family members, or peers, is important even when learning technology is used (Jacobs et al., 2015; Schreurs, Quan-Haase & Martin, 2017; Tsai, Shillair, & Cotten, 2017).

Adult learning principles, or andragogy, hold that adult learners bring a set of skills, knowledge, and challenges to the learning experience that educators need to recognize and build on. Blackley and Sheffield (2015) define digital andragogy as "the practice of educators to equip and encourage adult learners to choose and use the affordances of accessible digital technologies to personalise their learning and facilitate their interactions with peers and tutors" (p. 408). Blackley and Sheffield further argued that part of a digital andragogy is the recognition that adults learn something when they need to know it rather than learning to be prepared for something unknown in the future. Although Blackley and Sheffield's work was with college students studying to be teachers, Jacobs et al. (2015), who included unemployed older workers, senior citizens, English language learners, or formerly incarcerated individuals in their study, revealed similar findings – adults need to have a reason to acquire digital literacy before they are willing to invest the time into doing so.

Research into digital literacy acquisition has also shown that the willingness to experiment is an important part of the digital literacy acquisition learning process (Tsai, Shillair, & Cotten, 2017). This experimentation is accompanied by the repetition of new skills and the integration of these skills into everyday life. A key difference between the Tsai et al. study and the Jacobs et al. study was that Tsai et al. investigated how older adults learned in unstructured settings, such as from family, friends, or on their own. Castek et al. investigated the digital literacy acquisition process of a range of adults within the structured environment of an in-person tutor-facilitated online learning platform. Despite the difference of setting and participants, both Tsai et al. and Jacobs et al. came to similar results: getting over the fear of technology and being willing to experiment was a key aspect of acquiring digital literacy skills; however, the ability to try new things best occurs within a supportive social environment.

All three studies found that social support is essential if adults are to successfully take up digital literacy practices. Older adults often turned to family members or friends when they wanted to learn digital skills; however, Schreurs et al. found that these individuals often became frustrated with how family members attempted to tutor them. Jacobs et al. found that many study participants of all ages preferred working with tutors rather than family members because tutors were more patient.

Our Work with Literacy, Digital Literacy, Language Education, and Equity

Personal Reflections

Kathy Harris   My interest in digital literacy acquisition started in the field of second language acquisition and the pedagogical practices that support adults learning English. I was part of the adult ESL Lab school, a research project which video recorded low-level adult ESL classes and used the media for research and professional development (Reder, Harris, & Setzler, 2003). Watching the lab school video, it became clear that the literacy skills needed by adults included digital literacies. Adult learners expressed the need to be able to have the language and digital literacy to write an email to a work supervisor, send a message to a child's teacher, find health information online and be able to read and understand it, and so on. Print literacy alone did not meet their needs. As a result of this, I began to participate in projects to help ESL teachers to integrate digital literacies into their classes as well as various projects looking at digital literacy acquisition in the context of health for adult English learners as well as adults still acquiring basic skills.

Gloria Jacobs   Digital literacy research and equity is personal for me. I began using computers in the 1980s and doing so was transformative because it allowed me to move into a new, higher paying career. Then in the 1990s, while teaching English in a high-poverty school, I saw young people spending large amounts of time reading and writing online even as they told me they hated reading and writing. That led me to research adolescent literacy with a focus on the implications of digital technology for literacy learning and development among adolescents. For this research, I drew on the research traditions of linguistics to understand my data. After a number of years researching adolescent literacy learning and technology, I moved into the field of adult digital literacy acquisition. This too is personal for me because I have family members who do not have easy access to digital technology. I've seen first-hand the struggles this represents, and I've also experienced how resilient and creative these family members are as they figure out how to navigate a digital world without easy access to digital tools. My research and my personal experience has broadened my understanding of how being excluded from the digital world impacts individuals' life opportunities. My research has shown how acquiring digital skills can provide otherwise under-served adults with new ways to be heard and make changes in their world. That work has led to additional work with helping people learn to use their online health portals and learning how library patrons use digital technology to solve problems.

Our work in digital literacy and equity

Our work and that of our research group, the Literacy, Language and Technology Research group, has followed a trajectory that examines the learning experiences of adults who are vulnerable to social exclusion because of low income, limited educational experience, or limited English language skills.

The research trajectory began with Reder's (2012) Longitudinal Study of Adult Learning, which followed 1000 adults who did not complete high school over 8 years just as the internet was becoming important in daily life. A key finding described that many adults work to improve their skills by intermittently participating in formal courses, self-study, or a combination of both. Participating in a combination of formal study and self-study lead to the greatest learning gains. Using the knowledge from the research, a team at Portland State University developed Learner Web, a program that combined an online platform and in-person tutoring to help adults meet their goals, including developing digital literacy skills.

As digital literacies became essential in adult life, it was clear that not all people had equal access to the internet, devices to access it and the skills to use both. This lead to a research project focused on understanding the learning processes underlying digital literacy development among vulnerable adult participants. The research group conducted a three-year study in six adult learning sites across the United States, sites that used Learner Web in a tutor-facilitated model. The study, described in Jacobs et al. (2015), was mixed-methods. Data included both quantitative data collected from the Learner Web system and qualitative data consisting of semi-structured interviews of twenty-eight learners, twenty-nine tutors, and fourteen key stakeholders such as computer lab coordinators. Each group of interviewees were asked the same set of questions, but were encouraged to expand on their answers through the use of follow-up questions. Within the quantitative data, there were a large number of variables, and after a great deal of discussion and with the help of a statistician, we decided to focus on the variables that would help us think about how to measure success through the lens of what was important to learners.

Once the audio recordings of our interviews were transcribed, we analyzed the data using inductive coding, which is like tagging. When coding, words are picked that reflect the content of a section of the transcript. To do this, we would read through each transcript and come up with tags or codes based on what we were reading rather than applying preconceived ideas of what we expected to see. All of the transcripts were placed into a data analysis program that allowed teamwork. Members of the team would read through transcripts, apply the codes, and meet to discuss the codes and come to an agreement as to whether the codes reflected what we were seeing in the transcript, and to develop a shared understanding of what each code meant. As we developed our codes, we also began to see connections and patterns emerge. Over the course of a year, these connections and patterns led us to our central findings.

We found that for individuals who have had little to no exposure to digital technology, basic digital skills can be learned effectively within a supportive environment consisting of a curated online program and the presence of a face-to-face tutor. We also found that individuals who are new to digital literacy experience three key moments as they build the set of initial skills: 1) they see the relevance of the digital world; 2) they lose their fear of technology; and 3) they gain a sense of confidence in their abilities to use digital tools.

One aspect of our study that was of particular interest is the findings around bilingual/multilingual learners, the majority of whom were Spanish speakers (Jacobs et al., 2015). Data analysis showed that language choice for learners is complex. The material in Learner Web was available in both English and Spanish, allowing learners to select which language they wanted to learn in, and they could switch between languages at any time. Although 18 percent of the 12,000 learners used the Spanish version of the materials, we found that some would toggle back and forth between English and Spanish. From our interviews, we learned that they would do this to build digital literacy skills at the same time as their English language skills. Some of our English learners told us they wanted to work in English to improve their English skills, while others wanted to do the program first in Spanish to learn the material and then go back and do the program again in English to practice their English skills. Very few of them, however, switched languages in the middle of a lesson. Our interview data also showed us that because of the challenges of navigating multiple languages, multimedia content was found to be a needed and valuable form of support.

Regardless of the language skills of the learners, our 2015 research indicated that accessing health information online was of particular interest to the study's participants. At the same time, the healthcare industry was increasingly relying on digital tools such as **patient portals** to increase access to health information, promote disease self-management, and shared medical decision-making (Ancker et al., 2011). However, access to the internet, devices, and the skills to use them are not ubiquitous; many patients, especially those in under-served groups, experience significant barriers to using **health information technologies**, including limited internet access and inexperience with digital tools (Sheon, Bolen, Callahan, Shick, & Perzynski, 2017; Teiu et al., 2016).

To try to understand digital literacy acquisition in a healthcare context, our Literacy, Language and Technology Research group formed a partnership with a local health clinic, which serves people with low income, to develop learning materials to help patients learn how to use their patient portal as well as improve their digital literacies. This project, described in part in Hill (2016), involved creating a series of online instructional materials that served as an "on-ramp to health portal use" (p. 36) to foster patients' **digital health literacy**. This included multimedia material in English and Spanish that showed patients how to leave messages and ask questions of their health care provider before or after appointments, look up terms they might not understand, access after-visit summaries, access test results, and request prescription refills.

Work with patients at the clinic revealed that many experienced barriers to using their patient portal, despite encouragement from their doctors. Patients experienced a variety of life circumstances that became challenges to their portal use, including cell phone numbers that changed regularly, limited access to devices and data plans, irregular use of email leading to forgotten passwords, physical disabilities with sight or trembling hands, unstable housing that meant difficulty getting paper mail and unstable internet access while some patients described discomfort using internet at the local library. Some patients elected not to use their patient portal due to concerns about privacy and safety of information. Others were afraid that using the patient portal would replace valued human contact with the clinic staff.

The importance of digital literacy

Digital literacy has become an essential part of everyday life. The research discussed in this chapter demonstrates that digital literacy serves as a means for people to become more fully engaged civically, economically, and socially. However, being able to engage in these ways requires access, devices, and skills, which various groups of people experience as barriers. Research into digital literacy acquisition has shown that learning opportunities can be effective if they meet the needs of adults and language learners. If adults are provided with supportive environments that allow them to learn and practice at their own pace, they are able to move past fear of technology and gain a sense of confidence as they begin to see the relevance of technology for meeting their everyday needs. For educators working with adult learners, understanding the role of digital literacy in modern life can be one way to build relevance into learning interactions.

Data Analysis Activity

Materials on the website accompanying this book introduce you to six scenarios for individuals seeking to use an online health portal. The activity asks you to analyze the challenges that these individuals face, drawing on the content of this chapter and your own life experience. You'll need to imagine yourself in the shoes of each individual as you think about what they might experience in facing the challenges.

Going Further

There are a variety of ways to become involved in literacy, digital literacy, and equity work, including staying informed, volunteering, and taking courses. To stay informed, follow the PEW Research Center on Internet and Technology at www .pewinternet.org/ for research on the current state of internet adoption and access, as well as factors that influence both. Another way to stay informed is to subscribe to the newsletter of the National Digital Inclusion Alliance at www.digitalinclusion .org/, an organization advocating for home broadband access, public broadband access, personal devices and local technology training and support programs. The Open Door Collective at www.opendoorcollective.org/ works on poverty reduction initiatives to take advantage of, expand, or improve adult basic skills services to meet the needs and broaden the economic opportunities of low-income adults. Their white papers provide updates and analyses on issues related to literacy and digital literacy as they relate to poverty reduction.

Working as a digital literacy volunteer at a local library, workforce development center, or English language program is a way to work for equity in literacy and digital literacy. These programs are at the frontline in the effort to help individuals with digital inclusion, or access to affordable internet, devices, and the ability to use both.

Issues related to literacy and digital literacy can be found in many disciplines as well as in interdisciplinary degree programs. To learn more about research and social justice work in these areas, consider related coursework in literacy, adult literacy, health communication, social determinants of health, and community health.

Discussion Questions

1. Think about (or make a list of) your own use of digital technologies throughout the course of one week in your life. For each thing that you do, is it necessary to access the internet, use a device, and have skills to use both? In particular, what knowledge and skills do you use? You might think about your own healthcare as an example.

2. Besides healthcare, what are some other aspects of modern life that are impacted if you don't have digital access or skills? What are the ways that this leads to disproportionate disadvantage?

3. The shift to web 2.0 allows people to be both consumers and producers of content on the internet. What are the things that you do that produce content? It might be information, artistic expression, opinion, communication, and so on. Posting on social media is one example of how people produce content on the internet but there are many others. What are some of the barriers that might prevent people from being content producers on the internet? What are the implications for society when some people are able to be content producers while others are not?

4. These days most websites have multimedia content, which includes text, graphics, video, images, and audio. Do a quick internet search for two informational websites on a health or science topic, or other topic of interest to you. Try to find one site that has a commercial purpose and another site that is vetted by a government or official institution. For each, what percentage of the content is text, graphics, video, images, and audio? What purpose is served with the multimedia content? You might ask yourself who would find the content easy to understand and who would find it difficult to understand.

FURTHER READING

Foundational Readings

Jenkins, H. (2006). Confronting the challenges of participatory culture: Media education for the 21st century. MacArthur Foundation. Retrieved from www.macfound.org/media/article_pdfs/JENKINS_WHITE_PAPER.PDF

Lankshear, C., & Knobel, M. (2007). Sampling "the new" in new literacies. In *A new literacies sampler* (pp. 1–24). New York: Peter Lang.

The New London Group. (1996). A pedagogy of multiliteracies: Designing social futures. *Harvard Educational Review*, 66(1), 60–93.

Recent Publications

Jacobs, G., Castek, J., Pizzolato, D., Pendell, K., Withers, E., & Reder, S. (2015). Executive summary: Tutor-facilitated digital literacy acquisition in hard-to-serve populations, a

research project. Retrieved from https://pdxscholar.library.pdx.edu/digital_literacy_
acquisition_findings/9/

Rosen, D. J., & Vanek, J. B. (2017). Technology for innovation and change in adult basic
skills education. *New Directions for Adult and Continuing Education*, *2017*(155), 51–60.
Retrieved from https://doi.org/10.1002/ace.20240

Tieu, L., Schillinger, D., Sarkar, U., Hoskote, M., Hahn, K. J., Ratanawongsa, N., Ralston, J., &
Lyles, C. R. (2016). Online patient websites for electronic health record access among
vulnerable populations: portals to nowhere? *Journal of the American Medical
Informatics Association*, ocw098. https://doi.org/10.1093/jamia/ocw098

REFERENCES

Ancker, J. S., Barrón, Y., Rockoff, M. L., Hauser, D., Pichardo, M., Szerencsy, A., & Calman, N.
(2011). Use of an electronic patient portal among disadvantaged populations. *Journal of
General Internal Medicine*, *26*(10), 1117–1123. https://doi.org/10.1007/s11606–011–
1749-y

Anderson, M. (2018, March 22). Digital divide persists even as lower-income Americans
make gains in tech adoption. Retrieved from www.pewresearch.org/fact-tank/2017/03/
22/digital-divide-persists-even-as-lower-income-americans-make-gains-in-tech-
adoption/on.

Black, R. (2006). Language, culture, and identity in online fanfiction. *E-Learning and Digital
Media*, *3*(2), 170–184. https://doi.org/10.2304/elea.2006.3.2.170

Blackley, S., & Sheffield, R. (2015). Digital andragogy: A richer blend of initial teacher
education in the 21st century. *Issues in Educational Research*, *25*(4), 397–414.

Castek, J., Jacobs, G., Gibbon, C., Frank, T., Honisett, A., & Anderson, J. (2018). Executive
summary. Advancing digital equity in public libraries: Assessing library patrons'
problem solving in technology rich environments. Retrieved from https://pdxscholar
.library.pdx.edu/digital_equity_findings/1/

Federal Communications Commission (2014). Types of broadband connections. Retrieved
from www.fcc.gov/general/types-broadband-connections

Freire, P. (1970). *Pedagogy of the oppressed*. New York: Herder and Herder.

Harris, K. (2015). *Integrating digital literacy into adult English language instruction: Issue
Brief*. LINCS ESL Pro Issue Brief. Washington, DC: American Institutes for Research.
Retrieved from http://lincs.ed.gov/sites/default/files/ELL_Digital_Literacy_508.pdf

Hill, L. (2016). Digital literacy instruction for ehealth and beyond. *ORTESOL Journal*, *33*,
34–40.

Jacobs, G., Castek, J., Pizzolato, D., Pendell, K., Withers, E., & Reder, S. (2015). Executive
summary: Tutor-facilitated digital literacy acquisition in hard-to-serve populations, a
research project. Retrieved from https://pdxscholar.library.pdx.edu/digital_literacy_
acquisition_findings/9/

Jenkins, H. (2006). *Confronting the challenges of participatory culture: Media education for the 21st Century.* MacArthur Foundation. Retrieved from www.macfound.org/media/article_pdfs/JENKINS_WHITE_PAPER.PDF

Knobel, M. (1999). *Everyday literacies: Students, discourses and social practice.* New York: Peter Lang.

Lankshear, C., & Knobel, M. (2007). Sampling "the new" in new literacies. In M. Knobel & C. Lankshear (Eds.), *A new literacies sampler* (pp. 1–24). New York: Peter Lang.

Lotherington, H., & Jenson, J. (2011). Teaching multimodal and digital literacy in L2 settings: New literacies, new basics, new pedagogies. *Annual Review of Applied Linguistics, 31,* 226–246. https://doi.org/10.1017/S0267190511000110

The New London Group. (1996). A pedagogy of multiliteracies: Designing social futures. *Harvard Educational Review, 66*(1), 60–93.

Perzynski, A. T., Roach, M. J., Shick, S., Callahan, B., Gunzler, D., Cebul, R., Kaelber, D., Huml, A., Thornton, J., & Einstadter, D. (2017). Patient portals and broadband internet inequality. *Journal of the American Medical Informatics Association, 24*(5), 927–932. https://doi.org/10.1093/jamia/ocx020

Pew Research (2018, February 5). Internet/Broadband fact sheet. Retrieved from www.pewinternet.org/fact-sheet/internet-broadband/.

Reder, S. M. (2012). The longitudinal study of adult learning: challenging assumptions. Centre for Literacy (Montréal, Québec). Retrieved from www.deslibris.ca/ID/245707

Reder, S., Harris, K., & Setzler, K. (2003). The multimedia adult ESL learner corpus. *TESOL Quarterly, 37*(3), 546–557.

Rosen, D. J., & Vanek, J. B. (2017). Technology for innovation and change in adult basic skills education. *New Directions for Adult and Continuing Education, 2017*(155), 51–60. https://doi.org/10.1002/ace.20240

Schreurs, K., Quan-Haase, A., & Martin, K. (2017). Problematizing the digital literacy paradox in the context of older adults' ICT use: Aging, media discourse, and self-determination. *Canadian Journal of Communication, 42,* 359–377. https://doi.org/10.22230/cjc2017v42n2a3130

Sheon, A. R., Bolen, S. D., Callahan, B., Shick, S., & Perzynski, A. T. (2017). Addressing disparities in diabetes management through novel approaches to encourage technology adoption and use. *JMIR Diabetes, 2*(2), e16. https://doi.org/10.2196/diabetes.6751

Tieu, L., Schillinger, D., Sarkar, U., Hoskote, M., Hahn, K. J., Ratanawongsa, N., Ralston, J., & Lyles, C. R. (2016). Online patient websites for electronic health record access among vulnerable populations: portals to nowhere? *Journal of the American Medical Informatics Association, 24*(e1), e47–e54. https://doi.org/10.1093/jamia/ocw098

Tsai, H. S., Shillair, R., & Cotten, S. R. (2017). Social support and "playing around": An examination of how older adults acquire digital literacy with tablet computers. *Journal of Applied Gerontology, 36*(1), 29–55. https://doi.org/10.1177/0733464815609440

PART C
Next Steps as an Applied Linguist

25 Reading and Writing Empirical Papers in Applied Linguistics

LYNN SANTELMANN

Having been introduced to a range of work in applied linguistics, and having worked through some activities that asked you to analyze language-related information, you are ready to begin exploring your own interests within the field of applied linguistics. Exploring your own interests requires a solid knowledge base of the research in your chosen area and the ability to communicate knowledge to others. In order to gain this knowledge and learn to communicate with others in the field, you need to learn the discipline-specific reading and writing skills used in applied linguistics. While acquiring these skills may seem daunting at first, understanding why applied linguists write the way they do can help you read research articles more strategically and produce research papers that meet the expectations and needs of readers in applied linguistics. This chapter focuses on the structure of empirical research papers and gives tips for both reading and writing these kinds of papers in the field.

To start, it's useful to make sure you understand two terms central to this chapter. First is the term "empirical." *Empirical* is used to refer to work that is based on observations, investigations, or some other sort of data collection, rather than being based entirely on theory. In applied linguistics, the data might come from an experiment, where conditions are manipulated, but they might also be naturalistic, where data is collected from naturally occurring conditions. In other words, empirical is different from experimental. The second term that is central for this chapter is "primary literature," a general term for any texts that report original research, the most typical of which are research articles in journals. Primary literature stands in contrast to secondary literature, which summarizes and provides commentary on research that has already been published, as is typical in textbooks.

How to Read Primary Literature

Students who are reading primary literature often struggle to make sense of what they are reading. Students who can successfully read textbooks can still be flummoxed by the demands of reading research and professional articles. They find that reading primary literature takes far longer than reading textbooks and often come away feeling as if they have understood only part of what they have read. Many of our students have confessed to giving up in frustration after trying to read assigned research articles. Furthermore, because they find reading these articles so difficult, they wonder how they could ever discuss or evaluate them. Why do many students find research and professional literature so difficult to read and discuss? How can students tackle the challenge of reading research articles? This section will first discuss the reasons students find primary literature challenging, namely, audience, motivation, structure, and text style. Then it will give some tips and strategies for first reading and then evaluating articles in the field.

Why is Reading Primary Literature Difficult?

Audience and Motivation   The first difficulty that primary literature presents to students is **audience**; it is not written for newcomers to the field. The target audience, other scholars in the field, is expected to begin reading with some background knowledge in the field. Thus, research articles often do not define terms or provide background accessible to the novice reader. For example, a recent article on how bilinguals represent words, Wu and Juffs (2019), names four models of bilingual word representation in its first paragraph without any explanation of any of them. A beginner in the field may be no wiser after reading that first paragraph than they were before.

The target audience is also usually more well versed in the motivation or reasoning behind research articles than students are. Students are used to reading textbooks which provide factual information about major concepts and clearly spell out debates or issues. Research articles, on the other hand, usually start with a literature review that is perhaps best seen as persuasive writing intended to demonstrate how an author's work fits in with the context of previous work and to build an argument for the study. Thus, an individual article is a single move in a massively asynchronous discussion among experts in the field. For example, the Wu and Juffs (2019) article starts by reminding other scholars of the major theories and issues in the area of bilingual word representation by referring to them by name. Someone versed in this area needs only to be reminded of the Revised Hierarchical Model or the Bilingual Interactive model to be up to speed in the conversation. If all the models were fully explained, the article would require a lengthy introduction which would make it harder to see the purpose of the paper. Introducing topics through references to previous work orients experienced readers and helps them home in on the important new information presented in the study. For students, reading a research article in a new area is like entering into the middle of the conversation. Having joined the conversation late, it's unrealistic to expect the other participants to stop everything and get you up to speed. Instead, student readers will need to work hard to understand parts of the conversation that came before.

Text and Sentence Structure   Another reason why research articles are difficult for novice readers is the **structure of the text** itself. Both the overall structure of the article and the structure of individual paragraphs and sentences may be difficult for students. In terms of overall structure, many empirical research articles follow the structure of *Introduction*, *Methods*, *Results*, *Discussion* (IMRD) as outlined in Figure 25.1. However, applied linguistics is a field with considerable variation in the structure of research articles. Some work clearly follows the IMRD structure while other work, particularly ethnographies and case studies, may take a more narrative approach with a different structure. Thus, it is crucial to examine articles before reading them to get a sense of the overall structure. Even if articles do not follow the traditional IMRD structure, most articles will have a **general-to-specific-to-general** structure that begins with general issues, moves to the specific issue or study, and then moves back to address general issues in the conclusion. This structure also helps experienced readers find key information quickly. If someone wants to find the purpose or research questions of a study, for example, an experienced reader will turn to the section just before the Methods, as that is the most common place this information is presented.

Along with the **discourse structure** of research articles, students must also become accustomed to a different style of text. Academic writing tends to be more formal than other genres. It rarely contains contractions, it uses subordination more than coordination, and contains more technical, discipline-specific vocabulary. Even though most applied linguistics editors accept the first person pronoun (*I*, *we*), most primary literature never uses the second person pronoun *you*. In addition, primary literature avoids reference to personal mental processes (*I think*, *I believe*), and vague or unspecific terms (*sort of*, *things*).

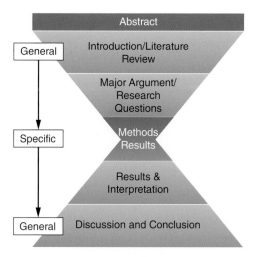

Figure 25.1 Structure of research articles
(adapted from Hill, Soppelsa, & West, 1982)

Sentence and information structure in academic writing is also a challenge to many students. Fang (2004) notes that academic articles contain more content words per sentence than non-academic texts along with technical, discipline-specific vocabulary. Academic writers also use more **extended noun phrases** such as in the following example from Jeffrey Reaser in Chapter 12. Here he produces a twenty-five-word noun phrase beginning with "effects":

> To put it more generally, applied linguistics in educational contexts seeks to examine [effects of variation in all levels of language across all language modalities both within a language (dialects, registers, etc.) and between and among different languages].

This noun phrase contains six prepositional phrases and ten nouns. While this sentence is relatively easy to comprehend, the number of prepositional phrases and density of noun phrases makes it more difficult than spoken language or narrative fiction. Why not just simplify the language, though? One reason is that academic language requires specificity in order to make the ideas clear. If the author had just referred to *variation*, the reader might assume that it meant just pronunciation, rather than the author's intended meaning of variation in syntax, vocabulary, pronunciation in speaking and writing. To make sure that the participants in this asynchronous conversation are discussing the same issues in the same way, these specific, extended noun phrases are essential.

In addition to density, academic texts also have a tendency for abstraction or **nominalization**, turning words that could be expressed by verbs or adjectives into nouns. An example of this can be seen in Chapter 18 where John Hellermann and Steve Thorne write "In this sense, the presumed 'thing' of language is perhaps better described as an action – 'languaging' (Becker, 1984)." In other words, they argue that language should be used as a verb, as in *We are languaging* rather than *We speak a language.* However, later they need to turn *languaging* into a noun to discuss it as a concept: "The communicative action of languaging as well as processes of cognition and second language development, are situated in...". Making this verb into a noun also allows writers to condense information into relatively few words. Finally, nominalizing *languaging* here makes the text flow better, because the sentence then has two coordinated noun phrases with parallel structures: "The communicative action of languaging" and "processes of cognition and second language development." The preponderance of **abstract nouns** in academic writing serves a purpose, but it makes the text more difficult for newcomers to the field.

Strategies for Reading Research Articles

Given the number of reasons that reading research articles is difficult for students (audience, text organization, text structure, abstract vocabulary), what can students do? The following strategies, gleaned from expert readers and findings in cognitive psychology, may help you get through reading the literature.

Recognize the Structure Begin your reading by looking at the structure of the article. Read the abstract, which gives a summary of the major parts of the article, and then look at the main section headings. Does the article use the classic research article structure of Introduction–Methods–Results–Discussion (IMRD), or does it have a different structure? Knowing this will help you locate crucial information. Remember that most articles use the general-to-specific-to-general structure. If you are getting lost in details, go to the introduction or conclusion to get a sense of the big picture to guide you through the details.

Read Actively Read actively, not passively: ask yourself questions about the text and look for answers. Posing questions and seeking answers helps you better understand the text, helps you retain more information, and keeps you from getting overwhelmed with new information. Table 25.1 gives some sample questions to guide you through each section.

Read Selectively, not Sequentially Expert readers read selectively, not sequentially. They do not start with the introduction and plow through without pause to the conclusion. Follow their lead: search out the information you need. Start with the abstract and section headings to give you an overview, continue with the major arguments or reason for the research article (including the research questions, if any), and then the sections that make the most sense for your needs. Do not plunge into careful reading from the first word. Skim first, then read for detail.

Figure 25.2 gives an example of how one expert reader tackled an article. Your takeaway from Figure 25.2 is not that you should follow this path, but that non-sequential reading based on your goals and motivation for reading the article is encouraged. The reader in Figure 25.2 was familiar with the topic, background, and method of the article. She was most interested in the major findings. For this reason, the reader started with the abstract, then went to the research questions (1), skipped to the figures and tables in the results (2), and then went on to the discussion and conclusion (3) to understand the major findings and implications. The second reading of the paper moved from the discussion back to the results (4) to see how the two were related. The reader then looked briefly at the methods (5) to check to see if the authors made any changes to this well-known method, and then moved back to the research questions (6) to see how the methods addressed the research questions. The third pass then went from the research questions to a detailed reading of the discussion (7) to see how the research questions were answered, and then went back to the literature review (8) to relate the discussion to the literature review. The reader finally concluded with re-reading the discussion (9) for the major implications.

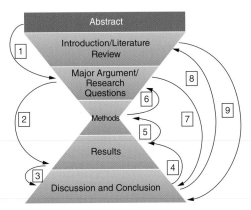

Figure 25.2 Example reading pattern of one expert reader when reading a research article when she was primarily interested in the results

It is important to emphasize that there is not one path through an article. Your path should be determined by your purpose in reading. A reader who is interested in the methods used to address a question may start with the research questions and move directly into a careful reading of the methods, then continue on to see what results those methods produced. Another reader might be most interested in how the researchers got to their research question and begin with a detailed reading of the introduction and literature review, and then move into the methods to see how the authors went about addressing the research question. The path you take will depend on your current knowledge in that particular area and your purpose in reading.

Budget Enough Time   You may have noticed that while reading a paper non-sequentially, the reader's process described in Figure 25.2 also required more than one reading. Reading research articles takes more time than reading general non-fiction or even textbooks. The text is dense, it contains more information, and it must be processed. Novice readers of research often fail to budget enough time and then get frustrated because they cannot understand the text quickly. No one, not even seasoned scholars with years of experience reading research, can understand everything on the first read-through. One difference between experts and novices is that experts have given up the expectation that they will understand everything the first time.

Read   Reading is one of those skills that truly does get better with practice. Read research articles when they are assigned or when you're interested in the topic. Reading research articles will improve your understanding of academic work, even if you find the articles difficult. In addition, reading academic articles will improve your writing because you will gain an implicit understanding of the structure, syntax, and vocabulary of the field.

In addition, read for pleasure outside of academic reading. The best thing for increasing reading speed and improving vocabulary is reading things that are new to you. The good news is that you don't have to read James Joyce's *Ulysses* or Tolstoy's *War and Peace* to get the benefits from reading. For example, I recently read a delightful mystery series set in India by British writer Vasneem Khan. These mysteries, featuring Inspector Chopra and his elephant side-kick, are interesting, funny, and easy to read. They also contain low-frequency words such as *vulpine* and *inscrutable* that will improve your vocabulary as well as numerous words from Indian English such as *tiffin*, *dhoti*, *haveli*, and *kurta*. Adding vocabulary and practicing reading need not be a chore.

Evaluate Articles   Finally, when reading research articles, you may be asked to discuss or critique the article. Many students' first response when being given this task runs something like this "*I'm a beginner in this field. How can I possibly have anything useful to say about something an experienced scholar wrote?!*" Don't panic. Though the task may seem daunting, you can use skills you already have and your growing knowledge of the field to make your evaluation. Evaluation is a crucial skill for any information you want to use, regardless of the source. Because the internet and social media have made information (and disinformation) easy to spread and nearly instantaneous to access, everyone needs to be able to evaluate what they read. This holds true whether you are reading opinion pieces on the internet or rigorously reviewed academic articles.

Evaluating an article does require you to read the article thoroughly, more than once. Concerns or questions you have upon first reading may be resolved after you've taken time to understand an article more thoroughly. As a reader, it's important to try to understand why researchers made certain choices or how they supported certain claims before leveling criticisms. At the same time, a second or third reading may reveal flaws or concerns that you didn't notice in your first read-through. While many newcomers to a field are hesitant to raise any critique, if something isn't clear after careful study, that is a problem with the paper. Sometimes newer scholars bring fresh perspectives to the field that more senior scholars need to hear.

Table 25.1 presents some of the questions to ask when reading a research article. These questions are divided into *information* and *evaluation*. The information questions will help you understand the details of the article and will provide the evidence that you will need to evaluate the article. The evaluation questions will help you create a reasonable, evidence-based assessment of the article.

Table 25.1 Questions to ask for understanding and evaluating research articles

Information Questions	Evaluation Questions
Introduction and Literature Review	*Introduction and Literature Review*
• Where is the article published? Is the journal peer reviewed, meaning that other researchers have reviewed and commented on it before it was published?	• Does the author introduce sufficient background information from previous research so that their target audience can understand the purpose of the article and the reason for the research questions?
• What is the author's purpose in writing the article?	
• What research gap is being addressed or what research tradition is being extended in this article?	• Is the article current or out of date? If it's over a decade old, is it a "classic" or have the findings been superseded by subsequent research?
• Who is the target audience for the article and what would they hope to get out of it?	• Do the references back up the author's claims?
• What is the date of the article?	• Are there references to different authors or does one author/set of authors predominate? If one author predominates, is this because the author is using a particular theory or because few other people have researched this area?
• Who does the author cite for setting up their argument?	
• What are the research questions or what is the statement of purpose?	
• Does the author state which theories they are working with or what frameworks inform their research? What are they?	• Does the author make a clear argument for why this research is important and why the reader should care?
Methods	*Methods*
• Who or what is the author studying?	• Does the article present sufficient detail so that you could replicate the study if you chose to?
• How is the study set up? What did the participants do?	
• How were the data collected? What materials or instruments did the author use? Where can you find them?	• Is the population or are the texts that the author is studying appropriate to the research questions? Is there any bias to who/what is being studied?
• How are the data analyzed?	• Is the analysis that the author uses appropriate for the kind of data they collected?
	• Does the article present enough information about the data analysis that someone could undertake a similar analysis?
Results	*Results*
• What are the major results?	• Does the author present the findings clearly and in an orderly fashion?
• What information is in the tables and figures? Can you interpret those tables or figures?	• Do the authors provide evidence for the claims they make in the results?
	• Are the tables and figures clear? Easy to understand?

Table 25.1 (*cont.*)

Information Questions	Evaluation Questions
	• Are tables/figures missing any major parts (are the axes on charts clearly labeled, for example)? Do the numbers in the table make sense and add up?
	• Are the tables and figures relevant to the topic at hand?
	• Are the interpretations of the results reasonable based on the information presented? Can you think of other reasonable interpretations?
Discussion and Conclusion	*Discussion and Conclusion*
• What are the major claims of the article?	• How does the work contribute to understanding?
• How do the findings address the research question(s) or purpose of the article?	• Is the paper convincing?
• What is the significance of the claims?	• Does the author adequately address or acknowledge any limitations or flaws?
• What limitations does the author note, if any?	• Does the author address other potential interpretations or counter-arguments?
• How do the findings link to the previous research introduced in the introduction?	• Do the results support or other contradict articles and does the paper discuss this?
	• Does the discussion overgeneralize (extending the findings to contexts that were not part of the study or could not be reasonably inferred from the study)?
	• Does the article have a subjective or objective tone? Is that tone appropriate for this type of article?
	• What contributions does the paper make, despite any flaws it might have?

Writing about Data in the Field of Applied Linguistics

This section will focus on one type of **writing** that often is difficult for students starting out in the field: writing research papers using empirical data. Many students find this challenging because they have not had to write papers using data before. In addition, data in the field can vary from quantitative, experimental studies to descriptive, qualitative ethnographic studies. Furthermore, because the field is diverse and interdisciplinary, the structure of published articles can vary both within and across journals (e.g., Yang & Allison, 2004). Despite this variation, we can give some general tips for writing and some generalizations about structures for empirical research articles. This section will first discuss general tips and then move on to generalizations about structures.

General tips for writing

One important skill in becoming proficient at writing in any field is understanding the **discourse structure** of the genre that you are learning. This is one reason why *reading* research articles in the field is so important if you want to write research. Reading in the field helps you develop an implicit understanding of the flow of information, the vocabulary, the tone of the text, and the types of sentence structures used. In addition, an explicit understanding of the genre can be helpful. The next section will discuss key features of empirical papers in applied linguistics to help you develop an explicit understanding of the expectations of the field.

One important aspect of skilled writing is determining your audience so you can write with your audience in mind. If you do not understand your audience, you are likely to provide too little (or too much) information. Many students who are writing for courses assume, quite logically, that their instructor is their audience and thus write with the classroom **context** in mind. However, that assumption often leads students to omit crucial information or to misunderstand the writing task. When students write for a classroom context, they tend to write with the shared, oral context of the course in mind. In a classroom discussion, students don't need to define terms or make shared information obvious. Instructors, however, are reading from a professional context. They are looking for students to explicitly use information covered in class or the readings and to make clear connections between ideas in their writing.

Assuming a shared, discussion-like context in writing can be dangerous, and an analogy might make these dangers clear. When you're in the kitchen getting ready to drain noodles, if you have someone standing next to you, you can say "Get me that thing," waving a hand in the general direction of the object you need. If, however, the person who is helping you isn't in the kitchen, you'd need to say, "Please come get the colander down from the top shelf for me." Writing should always be approached as if your reader is not in the kitchen with you. As a writer, you need to make explicit information that could be assumed in spoken language or due to shared context.

How then, do you determine how much information to give your reader if you don't assume a shared context? A good rule of thumb is to assume that you are writing for an intelligent peer who is not in the metaphorical kitchen with you. You could assume that an intelligent peer understands some of the basics of cooking. Thus, you wouldn't have to explain what noodles are, where the kitchen is, or why a colander is needed. But even an intelligent peer with some information needs more than "Get me that thing" if they don't know the context. Imagining an intelligent peer who shares the basics but not the details of your context will usually help you provide enough context to satisfy instructors and later, if you go on to further education, enough context for thesis advisors or journal editors. Your peers may change over time, but the concept still holds.

How do you know if you've provided enough context? The only way to find out is to get **feedback** from readers and to take the feedback you get seriously. Getting feedback is uncomfortable because it is face-threatening, that is, it raises the possibility that your work is not liked. Writers of all levels of experience can feel defensive when receiving feedback. However, if you can view feedback as an opportunity to make your ideas and your writing stronger, you will become a better writer.

The necessity of feedback raises another important factor in writing: Write multiple drafts. No one produces great drafts the first time around. Teachers, advisors, and journal editors can usually sniff out a first draft after a few paragraphs. Instructors may let a first draft pass (though without a top mark), but thesis advisors and journal editors won't be so kind. The first draft helps the author get the ideas out and think about the topic. As a result, it's what's called *writer-based prose* – written to meet the needs of the writer (Flower, 1993; Flower & Hayes, 1981). But if you stop there, your audience may never understand those ideas. The second (and subsequent) drafts should be undertaken to make the text *reader-based prose* – text that makes sense to a reader (Flower, 1993). Writers achieve reader-friendly text by providing examples, making connections between ideas explicit, providing transitions between paragraphs and sections, and taking out extraneous information. Surface features such as spelling, punctuation, and formatting should be edited only after several drafts with content and organization revisions. While writing multiple drafts is important, it's also important not to agonize over your writing forever. The perfect paper or journal article has never been written, nor will it ever be. There's always room for improvement even after several drafts. At some point in time, you need to submit it with all its imperfections. Even major scholars in the field need to revise their papers after they have submitted them for publication. Sometimes the best paper is indeed a finished paper.

Writing each section of an empirical paper

In addition to using general tips for writing, applying an explicit understanding of the structure of empirical papers will help improve your writing. The IMRD structure of most empirical papers in the field has already been covered in the previous section on how to read in the field. This is the basic structure we recommend for writing empirical papers in the field, although your instructors may guide you in some adaptations of this structure, depending on the approach and methods of your study. IMRD is a well-known structure that can apply to multiple disciplines and it can be easily adjusted to fit the needs of many kinds of papers. Within each section of the research paper, there are usually expected discourse moves and sentence structures. A good general resource for writing empirical research papers is Swales and Feak's (2012) textbook *Academic Writing for Graduate Students*. Although aimed at second language speakers of English entering graduate school, it provides a readable description of academic writing suitable for many students. Another useful resource is Morley's (2018) *Academic Phrasebank*. This website provides typical phrases and sentence frames used in academic writing. These phrases have been drawn from a corpus of academic content, and can be explored either by sections of a research paper (e.g., introduction, describing methods, discussing findings) or by general language functions (e.g., being critical, comparing and contrasting, describing trends). The phrases provide a model for framing your ideas while remaining short and general enough that you cannot be accused of plagiarism.

A considerable number of articles have focused on the structure of empirical research papers after the pioneering work of Swales (1990). As you may recall from Chapter 9, Swales conducted a genre analysis of academic writing. Swales's original study focused mainly on introductions, and introductions remain perhaps the best-studied section of research papers. Work on methods, results, and discussion sections has been added by others, allowing us to present an overview of the rhetorical structure of each of the sections of an empirical research paper (e.g., Amnuai & Wannaruk, 2013; Peacock, 2011; Swales, 1990; Wannaruk & Amnuai, 2016; Yang & Allison, 2003). The structure of each section is discussed briefly below.

While these sections are presented in the order they appear in the final paper, it's important for students to know that papers are rarely written in this order. For example, the introduction is often the last section of a paper to be finalized. Most research begins with a **purpose** and **research questions,** and scholars work both backward and forward from there. Note too that many research projects in applied linguistics are driven by a purpose and research questions and not hypotheses. It is not necessary to have a hypothesis to test to have a purpose for research as you saw from the many examples in Part B of this textbook. Working backward from a purpose requires the researchers to find previous literature to establish the importance of the issue, as well as appropriate methods for investigating it. Working forward leads the researchers to refine their purpose, operationalize their research questions, and think carefully about what exactly they are investigating. Often, exploring previous research or trying to operationalize a question leads to refinement/reworking of the question itself. Refinement of the question will then require additional background or tweaks in the methodology. Even after data are collected, the earlier parts of the paper are often revised. Researchers may have findings that require them to address new issues in the introduction or they may uncover new implications in the discussion that require additional background earlier in the paper. They may realize that they altered the methodology slightly from what they had originally proposed and need to clarify what they did. Writing and revising is an iterative process, and revisions in one section often have cascading effects on other sections. Don't despair when this happens. It's a normal part of the process.

Introduction   **Introductions** are often the most difficult section for students to write because the task seems intimidating: introduce the topic, why it is important, and what's already known about it. The last requirement can sometimes send students diving into the pool of previous research to find everything that's ever been written on the subject. When students try to do this, they quickly drown in previous literature. Alternatively, students are afraid to move on from the introduction because they fear they may have missed a study on the topic. However, introductions do not require an author to report everything that has been previously published about a topic. Instead, the purpose is to build an **argument** as to why the research topic is needed or interesting.

Overall, the introduction should move from general to specific, either making the case for the research to be undertaken or explaining the task the student has been assigned. Swales's (1990) well-known schema for research paper introductions determined that introductions consist of several predictable **discourse moves** that present the context and past literature; show gaps, or the necessity for current research; and describe how the paper will address those gaps. Swales called these moves: **Create a Research Space** (CARS). The major discourse moves of the CARS model, as introduced by Swales and Feak (2012) are:

Move 1: Establishing a research territory
Move 2: Establishing a niche
Move 3: Occupying the niche

The first move introduces the topic and often explains why it is important, interesting, or problematic. The obligatory part of the first move reviews previous work in the research territory. Move 2 can establish the niche by indicating a gap in the literature, raising a question, or extending previous knowledge. Finally, Move 3 outlines the purpose or states the nature of the present research, explaining how it is addressing the niche. Move 3 may also optionally outline a research hypothesis, announce major findings, state the value of the research, or give an overview of the structure. The use of these optional moves depends on the field. Applied linguistics papers rarely announce major findings in the introduction, for example, but often state the value or give an overview.

The language used in these moves is generally in the active voice – for example, *Several studies have investigated* – and in simple present or present perfect tense – for example, *Data from several studies suggest...* or *This paper compares...* (Swales, 1990). These tendencies can be seen in typical phrases from the *Academic Phrasebank* (Morley, 2018) in Table 25.2.

Methods   Student writers should know that **methods sections** in published articles often present less detail than is ideal. Published articles are subject to length restrictions and methods sections are one place where writers rely on their audience

Table 25.2 Discourse moves in introductions in applied linguistics articles with sample phrases.

Move	Sample phrases from Morley (2018), adapted for applied linguistics contexts.
Establishing a territory	Motivation is a major area of interest within the field of second language...
	To date there has been little agreement on how to define bilingualism...
	While Krashen (1985) focuses on input, Swain (1985) is more concerned with output...
	To date, numerous studies have investigated the use of modals in legal writing...
Establishing a niche	Previous studies of college language teaching have not dealt with the impact of ADA accommodations on...
	Few studies have investigated the use of augmentative communication devices outside school settings...
Presenting the present work	This paper explores how second language writers...
	This paper compares the different ways in which language policy affects...
	The specific objective of this study was to demonstrate how language, art, and identity intersect...

to fill in details from a shared background. Thus, commonly used methods or procedures such as survey design or data analysis are frequently reduced to a sentence or two. This reduction often leaves little detail to fully replicate the study. Students, on the other hand, should aim for enough detail in their methods that someone reading the paper should be able to faithfully replicate the study.

According to data from Peacock (2011), methods in language and linguistics articles have two obligatory moves and several optional moves, which are shown in Table 25.3. Obligatory moves are moves that are found in all articles, while optional moves (shown in italics) are used if they fit the needs or the purpose of the study. The obligatory move Subjects/Materials describes the participants in a study or the materials (literature, corpus) used in the analysis. Procedures, as the name suggests, describes in detail how the data were collected. Data Analysis is a very frequent third move and describes how the data were analyzed, including any coding decisions. Context/Location, describing the physical context of the research, is another frequent move in this field. Other, less frequent moves that can be placed before, after, or between these moves are: Overview, Research Questions/Aims, and Limitations.

Methods sections are generally written in the past tense, and this is the section of the paper where the most passive voice is found, e.g., *Qualitative and quantitative*

Table 25.3 Summary of discourse moves in methods sections in applied linguistics articles with sample phrases. Moves in italics are optional; moves in regular type are obligatory.

Move	Sample phrases from Morley (2018), adapted for applied linguistics contexts
Overview	*This study was exploratory and interpretative in nature.*
	Qualitative and quantitative research designs were adopted to provide...
	This paper uses Critical Discourse Analysis (CDA) to investigate...
	A quantitative approach was employed to examine processing speed for...
Research Aims/ Questions/Hypotheses	*This paper discusses how developmental language disorders...*
	Two primary aims of this study were to document how literacy and technology...
Subjects/Materials	Forty-seven students studying English at the university level were recruited for this study.
	Two groups of subjects were interviewed, students who had studied abroad and those who had not...
	Primary inclusion criteria for the participants were exposure to a second language after the age of ten...
	Five students were excluded from the study for failure to follow directions...
Context/Location	*We recruited participants from 15 programs across ... covering urban and rural areas...*
	137 participants from an intermediate level class were recruited...
Research Instruments	*There are a number of instruments available for measuring motivation...*
	Standardized tests (e.g., TOEFL) and self-report are currently the most popular measures for ascertaining language level...
	The design of the questionnaires was based on...
	The questionnaire was designed to measure the following...
Procedure	To measure frequency of language use, a question asking ... was used.
	For questions on attitudes about dialects, a Likert scale was used.
	We gathered data from multiple sources at three points during the term...
	After training, participants were told that...
	The data were recorded on a digital audio recorder and transcribed using a...
Data Analysis	*Statistical analysis was performed using SPSS software (version 20).*
	Themes were identified using grounded theory...
	Transcripts were coded for...

research designs were adopted... or *Forty-seven individuals were recruited...* However, when active voice is used, the use of the first person pronoun (I/we) has become increasingly well accepted in research articles in recent years, especially in social science research – for example, *We interviewed fifteen participants after the lessons...* Further sample sentence frames and phrases for each of these moves are given in Table 25.3.

Results   **Results sections** present the results. In terms of content, results sections sometimes contain just a description of the results and sometimes contain a combination of results and discussion. Quantitative studies tend to separate the two; qualitative studies often include discussion and interpretation along with a presentation of the results. Table 25.4 presents the major moves in results sections according to Yang and Allison (2003), who analyzed results and discussions sections of journal articles in applied linguistics. Reporting Results is the most common and the only obligatory move in these sections. Reporting Results presents the evidence, with appropriate statistical or qualitative examples for support. Often these results are accompanied by a summary device such as a table or figure to illustrate the results. Whenever possible, this summary device should be placed after the description of the important information. Always tell your reader what to look

Table 25.4 Summary of discourse moves in results sections in applied linguistics articles with sample phrases. Moves in italics are optional; moves in regular type are obligatory

Move	Sample phrases from Morley (2018), adapted for applied linguistics contexts
Preparatory Information	*The first set of questions aimed to...*
	The purpose of Experiment 3 was to...
Reporting Results	Strong evidence of the influence of anxiety was found when...
	The difference between the study abroad and stay-at-home groups was/ was not significant.
	The themes identified in these responses are presented in Table 1...
	As shown in Figure 1...
	The differences between language use at home and school are highlighted in Table 4.
	From the chart, it can be seen that by far the greatest demand is for...
	One participant commented: '...'
Commenting on Results	*Surprisingly, only a minority of respondents...*
	The correlation between time spent gaming and language proficiency is interesting because...
Summarizing Results	*In summary, these results show that...*
	Together these results provide important insights into...

for when examining a table or a figure so they know what important information is contained there.

The other three moves in this section are optional. Preparatory Information is sometimes used to set up the structure for Reporting Results. Commenting on Results indicates the significance of the results. This commenting can be accomplished in several ways: interpreting the results, comparing the results with the literature, or accounting for the results. The other two moves provide a transition into or out of the results section. One note on Commenting on Results: comparing the results with the literature is more common in papers that combine Results and Discussion sections. Papers that separate the two sections are more likely to interpret results in the Results section and save the comparison to the literature for the Discussion section. Summarizing the Results is just that: a summary.

Results sections are almost exclusively written in simple past tense, as they are describing a specific study that has ended – for example, *Three themes were identified from the interviews...* Additionally, they tend to use the active voice more than passive voice, though both are found – for example, *Figure 1 demonstrates...* or *Strong evidence was found...* Sample sentence frames and phrases for reporting results, commenting on results, and evaluating results are given in Table 25.4.

Discussion   The **discussion section** is perhaps the second-most difficult section for students to write, often because they are not sure what exactly is supposed to go into this section. Discussion sections move from specific to general and should, after discussing the importance of the results, link up to the themes and ideas raised in the introduction. Furthermore, they are a place where the author is free to give their own opinion, as long as it can be supported by the data.

The major discourse moves in the discussion section overlap to some extent with the results section (Yang & Allison, 2003). These moves are given in Table 25.5, with optional moves in italics. The only obligatory move found in all articles is Commenting on Results. This commentary could include interpreting results, comparing results with the literature, accounting for results (especially with unexpected findings), and evaluating results. The large number of other optional discourse moves shows that discussion sections are rather variable in their structure. These optional discourse moves are: Background Information, which are usually statements related to research questions or aims of the study, or theoretical background; Reporting or Summarizing the Results, which usually sets the stage for the commentary; Evaluating the Study, which includes stating the value and acknowledging the limitations of the study and its methodology; and Deductions from the Research, which usually consists of making recommendations either for pedagogy or for future research.

Discussion sections, like introductions, contain both simple present and simple past, and mostly active sentences – for example, *The current study found...*, *These*

Table 25.5 Summary of discourse moves in the discussion section of applied linguistics articles. Moves in italics are optional; moves in regular type are obligatory.

Move	Sample phrases from Morley (2018) adapted for applied linguistics contexts
Background Information	*As mentioned in the literature review. . .* *The first question in this study sought to determine. . .*
Reporting or Summarizing Results	*The current study found that. . .* *Another important finding was that. . .* *The most prominent finding to emerge from the analysis is that. . .*
Commenting on Results	One unanticipated finding was that interaction declined. . . Contrary to my hypothesis, this study did not find a significant relationship between proficiency and motivation. . . This finding is consistent with that of Smith (2000) who. . . This finding is contrary to previous studies which have suggested that heritage language learners. . . A possible explanation for this might be that socialization affected. . . It is difficult to explain this result, but it might be related to. . .
Evaluating the Study	*The study contributes to our understanding of writing. . .* *The present results are significant in at least two major respects.* *However, these results were not very encouraging for explicit instruction* *A limitation of this study is that only one class was studied. . .* *In spite of its limitations, the study adds to our understanding of. . .*
Deductions from Research	*It can thus be suggested that automated analysis of. . .* *These results provide further support for the hypothesis that. . .* *These findings may help us to reach students who. . .* *There are still many unanswered questions about . . .* *Further research should be undertaken to investigate. . .*

results support previous work. . ., or *One possible explanation for these results is. . .* Further examples of the types of sentences used can be found in Table 25.5. Discussion sections end with a brief conclusion (often a paragraph) that gives the major findings and any take-home messages the authors want to impart.

Going Further

Now that you have some strategies for reading and writing empirical research, we hope that you'll continue to explore your interests in the field. There are a few different places where you can begin your search. If your library subscribes to any academic databases that publish research in applied linguistics, these are the best place to get started. Linguistics and Language Behavior Abstracts (LLBA) is one useful database that will allow you to focus your search on articles that are directly relevant to applied linguistics, and your professor or a librarian at your institution can help you identify other good databases and ways to access them. If you don't have access to databases like this, you can use Google Scholar (www.scholar.google .com) or academic file sharing sites like Research Gate (www.researchgate.net) to search for research articles. While these search methods are less efficient than using a field-specific database, they may still help you to find articles on the topics that you're interested in. If you come across an interesting article that you can't access directly, it's also worthwhile to think about contacting the author. Most authors are happy to share an article that they've authored with you individually if you aren't able to access it through your library or elsewhere online.

The IMRD format that we've provided in this chapter can be adapted to most assignments for which you're required to write about your own data analysis. If you continue taking coursework in applied linguistics, you'll probably also be asked to write other genres as well, such as an annotated bibliography to help you get an overview of existing research in a given area. You will also get more practice writing literature reviews, which typically form part of the introduction section of a research article. A literature review goes a step beyond an annotated bibliography by not just summarizing existing research but instead synthesizing the research in this area in order to make an argument about possible gaps or next steps in the field. No matter what genre you're writing, though, keep in mind the needs of your audience. What information do they need in order to understand the context you're describing? Make sure to get feedback and write multiple drafts to ensure that you're producing reader-based prose.

Discussion Questions

1. Look back at one of the chapters in Part B that you read. Identify a passage (paragraph or series of sentences) about research that you found difficult to comprehend in that chapter.
   a. Examine the sentences for text/sentence structure, extended noun phrases, and vocabulary (especially abstract nouns or nominalizations) to determine what aspect of the text made that passage difficult.
   b. Rewrite the passage in language that is easier to comprehend, keeping in mind the functions of academic writing. What functions of academic writing did you have difficulty maintaining while re-writing the text? Have a peer compare the original passage and your rewrite. Did the meaning change or was there meaning lost in your rewrite?

2. Look back at the list of *Further Readings* in one of the chapters in Part B that you read. Find a journal article listed in one of those chapters and look at the structure of the article.

   a. Examine the article for overall rhetorical structure. What structure does it use? Is this structure explicit (with headings) or implicit (no headings)? Does it use the IMRD structure? A variation on this structure? Or something completely different? How is the structure related to the content?

   b. Choose one section of the article and look for the discourse moves listed in the tables in this chapter. Which of the discourse moves for that section does the paper use? Mark the beginning and end of each move you identify. Does it use all the obligatory moves? How many optional moves can you find? Is there any repetition?

3. In this chapter, we said that students who are writing in applied linguistics "should aim for enough detail in their methods that someone reading the paper would be able to faithfully replicate the study." Take a look at the details below. For each detail below, indicate whether or not you think it would need to be included in a methods section for readers who want to replicate the study. If there are any details below that may be relevant for one type of study but not for another, mention this. Explain the rationale behind each of your responses.

   a. The ages of the participants in the study.

   b. The specific colors that the researcher used to mark different categories while coding the data.

   c. The categories that were included in the coding scheme.

   d. Information about data that was initially collected but excluded from the final analysis.

   e. The fact that the researcher reviewed the data multiple times.

   f. The length of the data samples.

   g. A list of the questions that were included in a survey.

   h. Information about how texts or participants were selected for the study.

REFERENCES

Amnuai, W., & Wannaruk, A. (2013). A move-based analysis of the conclusion sections of research articles published in international and Thai journals. *The Southeast Asian Journal of English Language Studies*, *19*(2), 53–63.

Fang, Z. (2004). Scientific literacy: A systemic functional linguistics perspective. *Science Education*, *89*(2), 335–347.

Flower, L. (1993). *Problem-solving strategies for writing* (4th edn). New York: Harcourt Brace Jovanovich.

Flower, L., & Hayes, J. R. (1981). A cognitive process theory of writing. *College Composition and Communication, 32*(4), 365–387.

Hill, S., Soppelsa, B., & Watt, G. (1982). Teaching ESL students to read and write experimental research papers. *TESOL Quarterly, 16*(3), 333–347. https://doi.org/10.2307/3586633

Morley, J. (2018). The Academic Phrasebank. Retrieved from www.phrasebank.manchester.ac.uk/

Peacock, M. (2011). The structure of the methods section in research articles across eight disciplines. *Asian ESP Journal, 7*(2), 97–124.

Swales, J. M. (1990). *Genre analysis: English in academic and research settings*. Cambridge: Cambridge University Press.

Swales, J. M., & Feak, C. B. (2012). *Academic writing for graduate students: Essential tasks and skills* (3rd edn). Ann Arbor, MI: University of Michigan Press.

Wannaruk, A., & Amnuai, W. (2016). A comparison of rhetorical move structure of applied linguistics research articles published in international and national Thai journals. *RELC Journal, 47*(2), 193–211. https://doi.org/10.1177/0033688215609230

Wu, Z., & Juffs, A. (2019). Revisiting the Revised Hierarchical Model: Evidence for concept mediation in backward translation. *Bilingualism: Language and Cognition, 22*(2), 285–299. https://doi.org/10.1017/S1366728917000748

Yang, R., & Allison, D. (2003). Research articles in applied linguistics: Moving from results to conclusions. *English for Specific Purposes, 22*(4), 365–385.

(2004). Research articles in applied linguistics: Structures from a functional perspective. *English for Specific Purposes, 23*(3), 264–279.

26 | The Path Forward

SUSAN CONRAD, ALISSA J. HARTIG, AND LYNN SANTELMANN

Throughout this book, you've been introduced to a wide range of work in applied linguistics. Now that you've seen some of the diversity of the field, it may be useful to take a step back and consider what you read in Part B in a larger context. When reading individual chapters, it's easy to get caught up in the details of the information presented, and you may begin to wonder how all these different studies can possibly belong to a single field. The following overview of the themes found in the book will highlight the key features that unify this broad range of work as well as some of the core issues that are important in applied linguistics today. To do this, we return to the definition of applied linguistics presented in the first chapter, considering how it connects to key characteristics and themes that have come up throughout the book. We'll take a look back at concrete examples from various chapters that illustrate these ideas.

After looking back, we'll then move on to consider how you can find your own path forward in applied linguistics. We'll talk about steps you can take to further develop your background for work in applied linguistics, both through formal academic coursework and other relevant experience. These recommendations can help you move from learning about the field to becoming an applied linguist yourself.

Major Themes Running Through This Book

Diversity and Unifying Characteristics of Work in Applied Linguistics

The first chapter of this book introduced you to applied linguistics by noting both the diversity of work and the unifying characteristics of this field. We defined applied linguistics this way:

> Applied linguistics is a field that investigates the development and use of language in real-world situations and institutions. It aims to understand how language choices reflect and create contexts, and to address communication-related problems. Applied linguists analyze language in context and examine social and psychological factors related to language use or development.

Having read multiple chapters, you should now have a more concrete sense of the range of topics that applied linguists study and the diversity in how applied linguists approach language-related issues. The sections in Part B covered diverse topic areas – language acquisition; language socialization; language varieties and variation; language cognition and processing; and language rights, power, and ideology – and there was also diversity within each area. For example, within language acquisition, major examples in the chapters addressed the teaching of second language pragmatics for college students interacting with instructors in English; the teaching of Russian heritage language in a community school; language brokering in Arab-American immigrant families; identity development in online and face-to-face language learning; automated systems for assessing lexical and syntactic development in English L2 writing; and the assessment of developmental language disorders in Icelandic-speaking, French-speaking, and multilingual children. These topics require different expertise and experience and they used different methods of data collection and analysis, but they all fit within applied linguistics.

Following directly from the definition above, one of the major unifying characteristics of work in applied linguistics is that it seeks to understand and mitigate language-related problems in the real world. As you read, you probably noticed that some chapters were explicitly focused on helping to improve problematic situations – for example, serving as an expert witness for the Equal Employment Opportunity Commission, helping caregivers communicate more effectively with people with dementia, or increasing access to digital literacy for adults vulnerable to social exclusion. And in activist applied linguistics, you saw how applied linguists can work with an overt agenda for enacting change in the world. Other chapters provided examples of work that makes a less direct but nonetheless important contribution because they make the underpinnings and consequences of language choices explicit. For example, when Lionel Wee problematizes assumptions about named languages being distinct, self-contained systems, he might not enact a direct change in the world, but he can have an impact on how people think about language and the evaluative judgments they make about others' use of language. If you are motivated by the idea of directly contributing to changes, that's great, but even if not, your involvement in applied linguistics can be important for helping other people understand the impacts of language choices. Even by discussing some of the ideas and studies you have read in this book, you can start contributing to an awareness and understanding of the complex issues associated with language in nearly every facet of daily life.

Another distinguishing characteristic of applied linguistics that we highlighted in Chapter 1 was the central role of systematic language analysis. As explained further in Chapter 2, the study of language occurs under many different approaches, so although it is a unifying characteristic, there is also diversity within it. In the chapters of this book, you saw that different approaches can be applied in the same area of work – for example, within the section focused on language socialization, where there is naturally a social orientation, the chapter on literacy education used a specific functional theory of linguistics – systemic functional linguistics – for genre-based literacy education while the chapter on language socialization and culture in study abroad used a more general social approach for studying socialization and honorific use in a study abroad program in South Korea. In the section about varieties of language, the discussion of augmentative and alternative communication (AAC) considered the language needs of AAC users through a structural and functional analysis, while the discussion of English as a Lingua Franca (ELF) applied a critical perspective to ELF in Brazil. Even a chapter related to cognition might emphasize its social nature, as in the discussion of "distributed language" in language learning in the wild. This diversity of approaches is welcome in applied linguistics. Discussion question 2 at the end of this chapter asks you to review chapters you read and think further about the approaches you saw, ways they were combined, and their advantages and disadvantages.

Threads Through the Chapters: Technology, Interdisciplinarity, Multilingualism, and Personal Stories

We also suggested in Chapter 1 that you keep track of four major threads that are interwoven through the chapters of the book, noting how they appeared in different ways. Here are some of the points you may have noticed.

Technology   Technology was infused in chapters in several different ways. It was the direct focus of concern in some, such as Harris and Jacobs's work on access to digital literacy. In others, such as Nike Arnold's analyses of online interactions, it provided a context for study. Technology was also apparent as a methodology in many chapters. Automated assessment of language would not exist without technology, nor would the corpus linguistics techniques described in several chapters. Technology was also noted as having an impact even when it wasn't a methodology; Tucker Childs, for example, mentions that language documentation now almost always produces digital products, even for realia accompanying the language samples. Given the speed of advances in computer software and digital technology, it seems likely that technology will have increasingly important impacts on applied linguistics in the future. Some expertise with computer-assisted aspects of applied linguistics – whether writing code, knowing computer-assisted analysis techniques, understanding teaching with technology, or some as-yet unimagined computer application – is likely to be useful for the next generation of applied linguists.

Interdisciplinarity   Humans are complex creatures, and their use of language doesn't exist separate from other aspects of life, so all fields that teach us something about humans or society have intersections with applied linguistics. Did you notice the variety of different fields that were mentioned in chapters? There was computer science, teacher education, psychology, speech-language pathology, law, history, anthropology, gerontology, political science, and many more. Sometimes applied linguists already had training in one of these specific areas, sometimes they gained background that they needed for their area of work, and often they had collaborators. In addition, sometimes specialist expertise or skills were useful, such as community organizing or policy making.

It takes time to build background knowledge or develop relationships with colleagues in other areas. If you plan to pursue work in applied linguistics, now is a good time to reflect on the areas you found most attractive and consider the other disciplines that can give you useful background for those areas.

Multilingualism   In some countries, such as the United States, it can be easy to forget that multilingualism is typical for much of the world. Many people forget, too, that multilingualism can take many forms, not just the traditional vision of a person who is equally comfortable in any domain in more than one language. You may have noticed that multilingualism arose in this book in many ways. People were using (or learning to use) additional languages and heritage languages. You were probably not surprised that many chapters had examples of people acquiring English (or a specialized variety of English) as an additional language because it was a means to accessing greater power or opportunities in society. However, you might have been surprised that the status of the English native speaker norm was questioned and considered inappropriate in settings where English is used as a lingua franca in the midst of other languages. You may have been introduced to new challenges with multilingualism, too, such as the challenge of accurately identifying developmental language disorders in bilingual children or of training caregivers for people with dementia.

Although English still dominates many professional and educational settings, multilingualism is increasingly visible in applied linguistics, reflecting the world norm. We expect the influence of multilingualism to become even more firmly established in work in applied linguistics in the future, with increasingly more work acknowledging multilingualism as a resource and describing the benefits of multilingualism to help lay people in predominantly monolingual countries understand it better.

For us as editors of this book, a major challenge was trying to cover as many different languages and regions of the world as possible while also covering different topic areas and different methodologies. Unfortunately, many languages and regions of the world were not represented in cited studies or chapter examples. You might want to look up other articles or books about those that interest you (see discussion question 3 at the end of this chapter).

Personal Stories   We asked each of the chapter authors to explain how they got into their area of work because we know that people get started in applied linguistics through many kinds of personal experiences. You will have seen, as we suggested in the introductory chapters, that contexts of experience often shaped the research questions the authors were asking, the way the authors situated their work within the language–context continuum presented in Figure 2.1, and the methods with which they addressed their research questions. We hope you noticed, too, how personal most of the connections to research were. Many authors connected their work to family experiences – with their parents or their children, or their own experiences growing up. Some authors noted that their interest and motivation in a certain area started in a course they had, which connected to phenomena in a personal experience. Some, like Lucien Brown in South Korea, were led into applied linguistics by reflecting on their own language learning experiences. For some, early work in a particular community led them into applied linguistics as a career, as with Tucker Childs's work in West Africa and David Rose's work with Indigenous Australian communities. Others were well into a career in applied linguistics and then had an experience that expanded the directions of their work, as described by Kim Brown's moving into Universal Design for Learning.

Students often think of researchers as working in an impersonal, isolated academic environment. We hope you have seen from the chapters in this book that that image is grossly misleading for applied linguistics. Most applied linguists are motivated to understand and improve conditions and equity in the world not as an abstract idea, but rather as something that has grown out of personal experiences. They pursue work that they find personally meaningful as well as socially relevant.

New threads will emerge in applied linguistics in the future, and new scholars – some of them readers of this book – will be the ones who develop those threads. But of all the threads, we hope that personal as well as social meaningfulness will continue to be a defining characteristic in the field, creating the passion that is characteristic of the applied linguists whose work you read in this book.

Finding Your Own Path in Applied Linguistics   As you saw throughout the book, applied linguists work in a broad range of areas and their paths into applied linguistics came at various stages of their education or career. The diversity of possible entry points into the field are also reflected in the Going Further sections at the end of each chapter in Part B. In that section of each chapter, authors suggested coursework, experiences, and skills that can lead to further work in the field as well as resources that are available for getting involved in specific areas. There were some broad trends across the areas covered in the chapters as well as important specialized preparation that students can undertake if they're interested in a particular subfield.

Coursework Unsurprisingly, coursework in core areas of structural linguistics such as phonetics and syntax were recommended in several chapters. However, approaches to linguistics that emphasize language in use were even more prevalent. Discourse analysis was the course that was most frequently recommended by authors across the chapters in Part B, appearing in over a third of them. Sociolinguistics, corpus linguistics, and pragmatics were also frequently recommended, as were courses in research methods and various areas of language pedagogy. Applied linguistics is a field that values theory, research, and practice, and the courses recommended across Part B reflect these values.

You may have also noticed the interdisciplinary nature of the recommended coursework. Coursework in psychology and education were both frequently mentioned, highlighting the important connections that these disciplines have with applied linguistics. More specialized recommendations for coursework demonstrated how unexpected combinations can lead to innovative work in applied linguistics. These suggestions included, for example, courses in literature, neurology, political science, human systems engineering, and computer science. Whatever your interests are, there's a good chance that you can find a way to connect them to language and contribute to further development of the field.

If you are reading this book for a course in a department of applied linguistics, you probably already have some ideas about how you can move forward with a path in the field. Your degree program will likely require you to take coursework in language analysis and second language acquisition. Depending on your program, you may be able to focus elective courses on specific areas of applied linguistics that are of interest to you, such as language teaching, forensic linguistics, or computational linguistics.

If you're coming to applied linguistics from another field, taking similar kinds of coursework to those required for an applied linguistics degree can be a good start. Many departments of world languages offer courses in translation and interpretation or language teaching. In a college of education, you might find relevant courses related to literacy, theories of learning, and bilingual education. Psychology departments offer human development courses, not only for infants and children, but also for adults and geriatric populations. In an English department, you could look for relevant courses in the digital humanities or in composition and rhetoric, especially those that focus on genre analysis or teaching second language writing.

You may also decide to combine an interest in applied linguistics with work in a different field. For example, many skills and perspectives that you learn in applied linguistics – from phonetics to sociolinguistics – can be applied directly to speech-language pathology.

Furthermore, taking coursework in computer science and learning the basics of a programming language are essential for getting involved with work in corpus or computational linguistics. Work in computational linguistics or natural language processing also requires some fairly advanced knowledge of statistics, and so taking statistics would help you on that path. Statistics courses are also incredibly useful for anyone interested in assessment – and, in fact, for anyone who wants to become more involved with research or understand it more fully.

You might also decide to work primarily in another field but complement that work with an applied linguistics perspective. Fields ranging from anthropology to psychology to communications draw on analytic approaches that are widely used in applied linguistics, and having a strong understanding of language will enhance your analytical abilities. Even fields seemingly distant from applied linguistics such as medicine or dentistry need applied linguists to examine how language is used, investigating how it can affect everything from the doctor–patient relationship to treatment outcomes. Critical perspectives and activist applied linguistics can inform work in politics or public policy. Fields such as social work, teaching, law, medicine, or any setting where there is a power differential between professionals and their clients can also benefit from a critical perspective on language, seeing how language plays a role in power dynamics and the effectiveness of interactions.

Other Experiences   While there's an old joke about how much linguists hate it when you ask them how many languages they speak, the experience of learning at least one other language – especially one that's significantly different from the language or languages that you grew up speaking – is an excellent idea for any applied linguist. If you decide to pursue a path in language teaching, having had the experience of learning another language in a classroom setting will make you much more aware of the challenges that students face as well as some of the typological differences that distinguish languages.

Even if you plan to work exclusively in your first language, having the experience of seeing language from another perspective can lead to insights that would be difficult to achieve as a monolingual. Michael Halliday, for example, developed his theory of systemic functional linguistics (SFL) in part based on his experience of learning Mandarin Chinese. Even though much of his textual analysis focused on texts in English, his experience of learning Chinese allowed him to think differently about categories of meaning in language. Without a contrasting perspective, it's difficult to see your own language clearly. Of course, if you already speak more than one language, you have a distinct advantage for a career in applied linguistics! If you grew up in a bilingual or multilingual setting, you probably have an intuitive sense of how languages differ, and additional coursework in the analysis of one or more of the languages you already know can be very helpful for developing more conscious awareness of these differences.

The authors of the chapters in Part B highlighted a wide range of other concrete experiences that are useful for students with an interest in applied linguistics. Volunteering and finding other ways to get involved in communities were some of the most frequently recommended experiences. This in part reflects the emphasis in applied linguistics on addressing communication-related problems in the real world. Study abroad was another frequent recommendation, as was interviewing language learners or other populations that you're interested in working with. Several authors also suggested working on a research project, whether on your own or as part of a research team led by an established researcher.

Knowledge, Skills, and Dispositions   Several different kinds of knowledge, skills, and dispositions were highlighted across the chapters as well. Many of the authors emphasized the importance of developing skills for analyzing language in use, often in a specific framework such as conversation analysis or Systemic Functional Linguistics, as well as more general analysis-related skills, such as transcription and statistical analysis. The authors also highlighted the importance of being familiar with specific theories that can help explain social and psychological factors related to language use or development.

Being an effective applied linguist isn't just about academic preparation, however. As several authors highlighted, working in applied linguistics often requires strong interpersonal skills and the ability to collaborate with others. It requires curiosity and willingness to learn about areas that may sometimes fall outside of the traditional boundaries of the field. In their personal reflections, authors often highlighted the need to learn about a community or discipline that was unfamiliar to them initially. Making interdisciplinary connections often requires a willingness to step outside of your comfort zone, so it is useful for an aspiring applied linguist to be open to new experiences and tolerant of ambiguity. Being willing to work on your communication skills is important, too. Practicing speaking and writing for a variety of audiences and purposes – and learning from the reactions you get – can help you develop skills to communicate effectively with people of diverse backgrounds.

Resources for Going Further   Several resources can help you move forward in the field. One of the most frequently mentioned resources in Part B was mentors and advisors who can help you pursue your interests and chart your path through the field. Special interest groups organized through professional organizations or informal online communities organized through social networking sites can both be excellent starting places for getting involved in an area that interests you. As several authors recommended, academic or professional conferences can be a great way to learn a lot about a particular area of the field in a short time, as well as a way to make connections with other researchers and practitioners. You can find training in specific areas through webinars, workshops, and even free online courses. If you're more interested in browsing, you can also find websites, newsletters, and academic journals online. As a couple of authors pointed out, some of the best resources for getting involved in applied linguistics might be right on your own campus or in your neighborhood!

Conclusion

Applied linguistics is an exciting, diverse field that can help you understand everyday experiences and problems. If you have a passion for language, applied linguistics will allow you to explore that passion. Once you are able to analyze language and the contexts it occurs in, you will see language issues everywhere you look. Given the breadth and diversity of the field, there are a range of possibilities for how and where to explore your language interests – and you can use your knowledge to address issues in your life, your community, or the world at large. In the words of one of our colleagues: "You can change the world with applied linguistics!"

Discussion Questions

1. The definition of applied linguistics used in this book covers the development and use of language, and social and psychological factors.
   a. For the chapters you read, is it possible to separate the study of language development from the study of language use? Explain why or why not. Are you attracted more to studying the development of language, its use, or both? Why?
   b. Many applied linguists feel drawn more to either social factors or psychological factors although some combined both. List the chapters you read that emphasized social factors, those that emphasized psychological factors, and those that combined the two. Does one or the other appeal more to you? Why?
2. Review all the chapters you read and do the following:
   a. Classify them by their approach to investigating language: structural, functional, cognitive, social, multimodal, translingual, critical, or some combination of these. (You may want to review Chapter 1 as you do this.) Note whether the approach was explicitly named, and tell what characteristics allowed you to identify the approach whether or not it was named.
   b. Pick your two favorite chapters and for each explain:
      i. Where does the example of the author's own work fall on the language-context continuum presented in Figure 2.1?
      ii. What does this perspective highlight that other approaches would likely miss? What didn't this approach allow you to see?
3. What languages and cultures that you are familiar with weren't covered in this book? Use a library database or online scholarly search engine to check for research on those languages and cultures. Provide a brief summary of the work you find – for example, how much is there, do publications appear to be

increasing or decreasing, what topics areas are popular, and what languages are publications in? Are you surprised by what you find? Why or why not?

4. Think about your own personal story related to applied linguistics. What communication-related problems have you experienced that you would most like to study and help to address? Describe what you experienced, how you might study it, and what kinds of applications you would like from such a study.

5. Plot out your path forward in applied linguistics. Even though your interests may change as you learn more, it's useful to think ahead. Sketch out a general plan for a year or more, listing the types of courses you would like to take and experiences you would like to have. Then describe your next steps more concretely – for example, which courses will you take next term, and where will you apply for research or other experience that you want? It may take some investigating to discover all the opportunities available to you.

Index